Prisoners' Rights

D1554988

Prisoners' Rights: Principles and Practice considers prisoners' rights from socio-legal and philosophical perspectives, and assesses the advantages and problems of a rights-based approach to imprisonment. At a time of record levels of imprisonment and projected future expansion of the prison population, this work is timely.

The discussion in this book is not confined to a formal legal analysis, although it does include discussion of the developing jurisprudence on prisoners' rights. It offers a socio-legal rather than a purely black letter approach, and focuses on the experience of imprisonment. It draws on perspectives from a range of disciplines to illuminate how prisoners' rights operate in practice. The text also contributes to debates on imprisonment and citizenship, the treatment of women prisoners and social exclusion.

This book will be of interest to both undergraduate and postgraduate students of penology and criminal justice, as well as professionals working within the penal system.

Susan Easton is Reader at Brunel Law School.

Prisoners' Rights

Principles and practice

Susan Easton

Routledge
Taylor & Francis Group

LONDON AND NEW YORK

First published 2011
by Routledge
2 Park Square, Milton Park, Abingdon, Oxon, OX14 4RN

Simultaneously published in the USA and Canada
by Routledge
711 Third Avenue, New York, NY 10017

*Routledge is an imprint of the Taylor & Francis Group,
an informa business*

© 2011 Susan Easton

The right of Susan Easton to be identified as author of this work has
been asserted by her in accordance with the Copyright, Designs and
Patent Act 1988.

Typeset in Times New Roman by Taylor & Francis Books
Printed and bound in Great Britain by CPI Antony Rowe, Chippenham,
Wiltshire

British Library Cataloguing in Publication Data
A catalogue record for this book is available from the British Library

Library of Congress Cataloguing in Publication Data
A catalog record for this book has been requested

ISBN: 978-1-84392-809-6 (hbk)
ISBN: 978-1-84392-808-9 (pbk)
ISBN: 978-0-203-82968-4 (ebk)

For Byron, Clarence, Cleo, Crosbie and Bosun

Contents

Acknowledgements

Some of the formative ideas in this book developed from previously published articles. This book includes material from these articles although the arguments have been developed in the light of recent changes. I am grateful to the publishers, John Wiley, Taylor & Francis and Sage for permission to use material from the following articles: Susan Easton (2006) 'Electing the electorate: the problem of prisoner disenfranchisement', *Modern Law Review* 69 (3) 443–52, published by John Wiley (http://eu.wiley.com); Susan Easton (2008) 'Constructing citizenship: making room for prisoners' rights', *Journal of Social Welfare and Family Law*, 30: 2, 127–46 published by Taylor & Francis (http://www.informaworld.com) and Susan Easton 'The prisoner's right to vote and civic responsibility', *Probation Journal* (2009) 56(6) 224–37, published by Sage (http://online.sagepub.com).

Some of these ideas were also presented in papers given to the Criminal Justice Research Group at Brunel University and to the Sentencing and Punishment stream at the Socio-Legal Studies Association Annual Conferences in 2007 and 2010. I am grateful to participants for their comments and especially to my colleague, Christine Piper, with whom I have had many stimulating discussions on some of the issues raised in this book. I have also benefited from the positive contributions of students on our sentencing and penology course and from my experience of teaching in prisons. I would also like to thank the anonymous reviewers of the original proposal for their suggestions and the staff at Willan and Routledge for their assistance.

July 2010

Table of cases

Abbreviations

CPT	European Committee for the Prevention of Torture
ECHR	European Convention on Human Rights
EPR	European Prison Rules
HMCIP	Her Majesty's Chief Inspector of Prisons
HMIP	Her Majesty's Inspectorate of Prisons
IMB	Independent Monitoring Board
NOM	National Offender Management Service
PR	Prison Rules
PSO	Prison Service Orders
SMR	Standard Minimum Rules

1 Prisoners' rights

From social death to citizenship

Introduction

This book examines the role of prisoners' rights in moving convicted prisoners from a state of social and civil death towards a recognition of their citizenship grounded in social inclusion.[1] It argues that the notion of citizenship can be reconstructed to include prisoners and that a rights-based approach is crucial in moving the prisoner from the status of a non-person, who is socially dead, towards citizenship. Only such a reconstruction will lead to substantial improvements in the treatment of prisoners and to the raising of standards in prison while alternative methods, including new managerialist strategies, have been less effective in achieving significant improvements.

Reference will be made to the treatment of prisoners in the United States, the United Kingdom and the Netherlands as these states, despite their differing histories, cultures and social contexts, face similar political problems in maintaining integration and stability in the face of social fragmentation. While there are similarities between political processes in both the USA and the UK, we also find a 'time lag', as some of the problems they have experienced of prison expansion and increased punitiveness and prison disorder, occurred here later. The development of the courts' treatment of rights claims will be considered in Chapter 2. The United States is also of interest because it is more extreme than the UK in the level of incarceration and the austerity of its regimes. In the USA there has been a substantial increase in the prison population so that it is eight times higher than in 1970. By December 2008 the prison population exceeded 2.3 million compared to 1.2 million in 1990, but it fell slightly to just over 2.2 million by June 2009 (ICPS 2010). This situation has been described as 'mass imprisonment' and there are also large numbers are on parole and probation. This expansion reflects changes in public attitudes, the importance of crime and punishment as a political issue and an increasingly vociferous media which plays on fears of crime. While the prison population has increased in most western countries since the early 1990s, the increase in the United States has been more dramatic.

The experience of other jurisdictions can also provide insights into the negotiation of prisoners' rights claims. Clearly, there are many other societies whose experience would be of interest but the USA and the Netherlands have been selected as they appear to lie at opposite ends of the spectrum.[2] There are significant differences between the USA and Europe, principally the commitment to the death penalty, rejected in Western Europe decades ago, and greater use of mandatory minimum sentences.

However, the differences between the European and American experiences should not be overstated. In recent years penological debates have tended to focus on what has been described as American 'exceptionalism', exemplified by the fact that the USA retains a commitment to the death penalty and has high levels of incarceration and punitiveness. Certainly this debate raised important issues about political and cultural differences, but perhaps under-plays the similarities between the European and American penologies, the-ories and practices. Whitman (2003), for example, compares the USA unfavourably with France and Germany and attributes this to deep-rooted cultural differences, including the tradition of respect for the dignity of the individual in France and Germany, missing in the USA, which reflects his-torical pressures including the reaction against fascism. Zimring focuses on the tradition of vigilantism missing from Europe, while van Zyl Smit and Snacken see respect for human rights as part of the European cultural heri-tage, so European prison regimes at a formal level recognize prisoners have rights which follow them into prison and any rights infringements will be assessed on the principle of proportionality (Zimring 2003, van Zyl Smit and Snacken 2009).

This focus on American exceptionalism fails to take account of the fact that increased punitiveness and expansion of imprisonment are trends found worldwide in the past twenty years, including Western Europe. Prison expan-sion seems to be a global phenomenon. For example in Australia we find a similar expansion in the population since the 1990s, with an increase in retri-butivism and scepticism regarding the rehabilitation and reform of offenders, increased punitiveness of the public and sentencers, as well as the develop-ment of managerialist approaches and privatization of prisons.[3] In the UK, well over half the population do wish to restore the penalty but motions to do so have repeatedly failed in Parliament, so attitudes between the UK and the USA on capital punishment may not be so far apart. We also find increased punitiveness across Europe. Moreover, in both the USA and the UK fear of crime has persisted despite falling crime rates.

But there is considerable variation within the United States and within Europe on penal policy and practice. In the USA, of course, many states have abolished the death penalty or rarely use it and there is a strong and well-established abolitionist movement. There are also differences between states in levels of imprisonment and in some states the imprisonment rate fell in 2008. There have also been periods when the penalty has been suspended, for example, following the decision in *Furman v Georgia* 405 US 238 (1972). As Garland (2005) notes, even when the death penalty is administered in the USA the aim is to minimize pain by using lethal injections, and to accord the individual as much dignity as possible, for example by carrying out executions in private, compared to states such as Saudi Arabia where beheadings are administered in public or states where the individual is stoned to death, such as Iran and Somalia. Article 104 of the Iranian Penal Code prescribes that when executing for adultery the stones should not be large enough to kill the person by one or two strikes, nor so small that they could not be defined as a stones. So it is clear that the aim is to cause pain and that the death should be slow to maximize the pain and suffering. Furthermore in the USA the use of the death penalty is limited to first degree murder in contrast to states where it may be used for much lesser offences and for acts which many would not see as criminal at all, such as adultery and homosexuality, in Somalia and Iran.

In contrast, the use of the penalty has narrowed considerably in the USA and there have been repeated constitutional challenges to outlaw it under the Eighth Amendment prohibition on cruel and unusual punishment. Its use is now prohibited on those who are under 18 following *Roper v Simmons* 543 US 55 (2005) and on those who are mentally retarded following *Atkins v Virginia* 536 US 304 (2002). It is also conceivable that the Courts could go further in the future and reject the penalty itself.

Moreover, some states have more progressive penal policies than others and there is a long a tradition of prison reform, partly influenced by the Quaker movement and the prisoners' rights movement flourished in the USA in the 1970s. Moreover, as we shall see in Chapter 2, constitutional challenges in the courts have secured many advances in the treatment of prisoners and the Supreme Court has played a key role in the protection of prisoners. There is also a variety of imaginative programmes, for example in Denver, Colorado there is an inmate canine training programme in women's prisons where offenders follow a training programme using rescued and donated dogs and learn skills they can use outside but also benefit from the relationship with the animals inside the facility. So the punitiveness highlighted by commentators is a relatively recent feature rather than an intrinsic feature of American culture.

There is also considerable variation within Europe. While European prison conditions and prison law are seen as a model which respects human rights and human dignity, this does not apply throughout Europe. Eastern European prisons have poor conditions and few resources, Belarus retains the death penalty and the Russian Federation has high incarceration rates, poor conditions in many of its prisons and has been slow in implementing change in response to reports from the Committee for the Prevention of Torture (CPT) although of course within the Federation itself, which covers a large geographical area, there is considerable variation (see Piacentini 2004). Within Turkey the death penalty was only recently relinquished and human rights abuses of detainees as well as poor physical conditions in prison persist. Many of the Article 3 cases on torture and inhuman and degrading treatment in detention heard by the European Court of Human Rights relate to Turkey.

Nonetheless, it is fair to say the commitment to prisoners' rights in Europe is at present stronger than in the USA. The formal protection of prisoners' rights is more developed in Europe and this has had an impact on penal practice in Western Europe. But in the past the protection of rights in the USA exceeded what was available in Europe and the prisoners' rights movement was much stronger there and achieved more in the 1970s. In fact Garland (2005) sees the recent punitiveness in the USA as a reaction against the advances achieved by civil libertarians in the past and against the permissiveness of the 1960s and 1970s. But some governments in Western Europe, notably the Dutch government, have been able to insulate themselves more easily from public pressures and from the media.

Attention will therefore be given to the Netherlands which is usually seen as lying at the opposite end of the spectrum to the United States, as one of the most progressive and humane penal systems in the world and in Western Europe, in terms of physical conditions, regime quality, prisoners' rights and access to visits. This progressive approach has a long history and the Netherlands abolished the death penalty in 1870, nearly a century before the UK. However conditions in the Dutch external territories of Aruba and the Netherlands Antilles have been criticized by the CPT. The Netherlands has been seen as the 'exception' within Europe, avoiding the extremes of US expansion or harsh regimes and has retained this status notwithstanding the pressures of penal expansion.

What is also unusual about the Netherlands is the absence until recently of widespread public punitiveness or moral panics over crime, or a sensationalist tabloid press demanding tougher penalties, which contrasts sharply with the UK, as Pakes has argued (Pakes 2007). The system of proportional representation in the Netherlands to some extent means that political parties may distance themselves from punitive demands from the press or the public. Moreover, the elite of judges and prosecutors have shared the view that prison has limited value in solving the problem of crime and harsh punishment may exacerbate the problem and prevent the reintegration of the offender into society. At the same time, we do find in the Netherlands similar changes to the UK, an increase in punitiveness over the last twenty years and a greater role for new managerialist approaches, increases in crime rates and the expansion of the prison population which has impacted on the quality of the regime. Since the mid-1980s the prison population in the Netherlands has tripled, and compared to other Western European countries, including Germany, it now has a higher incarceration rate. In 2008 it reached 100, exceeding France and Germany. In 2010 the Netherlands incarceration rate fell to 94 compared to 87 for Germany and 96 for France (ICPS 2010). While the Dutch rate is substantially lower than the USA, Dutch judges, politicians and the public are now more punitive and the courts show a greater willingness to impose custodial sentences, longer sentences, as well as preventive sentences and to punish persistent offenders, similar trends to those found in the UK (Piper and Easton 2006/7). Sentences have become longer, the custody rate has increased and there has been an increase in drugs crime which attracts longer sentences, although the proportion of prisoners serving longer sentences is lower than in the UK. However, this has meant an increase in cell sharing and a decline in resources available to prisons. But despite these changes, conditions within Dutch prisons still remain superior to those in other European societies. At the same time, there is still a strong commitment to welfarism in the wider society and a range of community options are available to sentencers and prison numbers are now falling to the extent that cells are being rented to Belgium to use spare capacity and avoid closing prisons. Dutch prisons are usually cited as an example of humane containment as prisoners until recently had their own cells, and the regime is less intrusive. There is a recognition of the damage resulting from imprisonment and more scepticism over the value of prison in reforming, rehabilitating or deterring prisoners and a commitment to normalization, that is, that prison life should approximate as closely as possible to life in the community.

Although all three jurisdictions, the USA, the UK and the Netherlands have their own unique histories and cultures, what is of interest is the fact that they have faced common problems in relation to crime, social change, changing public attitudes, and prison expansion, which has increased pressures on prisons to cut costs as well as public anxieties over dangerousness and a stronger focus on risk management, and increased scepticism over prison's potential for rehabilitation. So it is interesting to see whether these pressures have resulted in similar strategies or whether pressures towards increased punitiveness have been resisted.

The significance of prisoners' rights

Recognition of prisoners' rights is most strongly associated with retributivist theory. The concern with due process rights in the 1970s was associated with the revival of retributivism, for example, von Hirsch's *Doing Justice* (von Hirsch 1976). Moreover the focus on recognition of the autonomy and agency of individuals within retributivism and the concern with equality and proportionality underpin a rights-based approach to imprisonment.

The history of prison reform in England is associated with an approach largely unsympathetic to rights jurisprudence and rights talk, namely utilitarian pragmatism which sees the primary aims of punishment as deterrence, rehabilitation and public protection and places most weight on the interest of the public. Its founder Bentham (1789) had little confidence in the value of entrenched rights as beneficial for the individual or society as a whole, and dismissed rights as mere nonsense (Bentham 1843). Furthermore when rights conflict, choices will be made on the criterion of what is best for the greatest number of people. Moreover, since Bentham wrote, the basic premise of utilitarian penology, the less eligibility principle, has been a major stumbling block to penal reform. But this is not to say that Bentham accepted poor conditions. On the contrary, he argued that we should not impose unnecessary pain, rather the pains of punishment should be linked to a positive outcome, on a rational theory of punishment (Bentham 1789). This also should not imply that a system based on utilitarian principles would inevitably find it difficult to accommodate prisoners' rights as we can find progressive regimes such as Finland where prisoners' rights are respected while the aim of punishment is primarily consequentialist.

However, the utilitarian focus on the principle of less eligibility clearly has implications for the quality of conditions of prison life, as rights may protect prisoners from the full rigour of the less eligibility principle. But while deterrence may be difficult to combine with a rights-based model, a rehabilitative regime can also be predicated on rights and conversely respect for rights can promote rehabilitation by promoting a sense of civic responsibility. Moreover, within an incapacitative regime where the prisoner is detained for public protection reasons, a rights model could still govern treatment within the prison regime. Moreover, some recent defenders of utilitarianism, such as Bagaric have argued that utilitarianism is compatible with respect for rights, and that rights protection may promote utility insofar as it meets with public approval and enhances respect for the penal system (Bagaric 2001). But rights are subsumed within the overarching framework of utilitarianism and once they are weighed in the balance they may be sacrificed instead of trumping competing claims. So as we shall see in the next chapter, the institutional needs of the prison have often defeated rights claims in practice. The rights of the victim have been given prominence in restorative justice, but it has also emphasized the right of the offender to discuss his crimes with the victim. The aim is to reintegrate the offender into society, and like desert theory, restorative justice recognizes the agency of the offender.

These theories when applied to punishment will have implications for the mode of punishment, the quantum of punishment and the nature of the prison regime itself. For desert theorists, separation from the community and loss of liberty should be sufficient to satisfy the retributivist rationale and no further losses should be imposed. Respect must be accorded to the individual on retributivist theory and degrading and stigmatizing punishments are precluded which for some desert theorists may include a prohibition on the death penalty (von Hirsch 1993). On a utilitarian model, the level of security imposed should be no more than is necessary to meet the goal of public protection and regimes should be constructed in ways which allow prisoners to contribute to the community within prison and to the wider society when they return and these social goals usually will take precedence over individual interests and rights.

Although there is considerable debate in jurisprudence on the meaning of rights, and the scope of rights, it is clear that a notion of the individual's autonomy and agency is a precondition of holding rights. Rights protect individuals from the state and protect the weakest individuals in society from the majority by according individuals the right to be treated with equal concern and respect. In the context of imprisonment rights offers a means of assessing prison regimes and have an important role in protecting individuals from harsh and degrading punishments and from populist punitiveness.

Rights are also valuable in giving legitimacy to systems of punishment. As Dostoevsky observed in the *House of the Dead*, the degree of civilization of a society can be judged by the way it treats its prisoners. We have well-established principles for the humane treatment of prisoners of war, whether conscripts or volunteers, under the Geneva Convention, with, for example, access to mail and medical care, even if enforcement of those rights may be problematic in practice. We also recognize the rights of those accused of war crimes. This is clear from the conduct of the tribunals at Nuremberg in the past and currently at The Hague where those accused of crimes against humanity have been accorded due process procedural rights to ensure a fair trial. If they are convicted and given a custodial sentence by the International Criminal Court it is accepted that they should be confined in humane conditions.

The essential feature of rights is precisely that they are available to all, even those who appear to be less 'deserving' than others and therefore rights should not be linked to virtue. Because of their universal nature, rights protect those accused of the most heinous crimes, so it would seem inconsistent and unjustifiable to deny the benefits to those accused or convicted of lesser offences.

Clearly, respect for rights will make a significant contribution to prisoners' sense of justice which may be a precondition of stability in prisons as the Woolf Report on the prison riots of 1990 argued (Woolf and Tumim 1991). It also brings the position of prisoners closer to ordinary citizens. Respect for rights emphasizes the common ground of prisoners and ordinary citizens and imposes obligations on the prison to provide humane and constructive regimes. If rights are not respected then prisoners may resort to other methods to achieve change which raise the risk of disorder. In the UK major changes were achieved in the 1990s through the recommendations of the Woolf Inquiry which was set up in response to a series of riots (Woolf and Tumim 1991). So if respect for rights is more firmly embedded, it would be harder to 'turn back the clock' on prison conditions especially in response to public punitiveness and would ensure stability.

Rights also transcend the boundaries of the public and private sectors engaged in punishment and so they can provide protection for those detained in both public and private sector regimes in the UK and in the USA, where the private sector is heavily involved in the provision of punishment. In the USA constitutional rights apply in private and state contexts while in the UK rights under the European Convention protect the prisoner in both state and privately run prisons.

However, while philosophical approaches to rights are important, the focus in this book will be on practical rather than philosophical or metaphysical issues, as without adequate mechanisms of implementation and enforcement of rights, rights are clearly of little value to prisoners. So we will be considering a range of rights, including the rights to be held in conditions which are not inhuman or degrading, the right to access to medical care and to rehabilitation programmes. These will be discussed in relation to adult prisoners rather than in relation to juvenile offenders or those held in immigration detention, both of which merit detailed discussion but which lie outside the scope of this book. It will be argued that a rights-based approach offers a greater prospect for improvements in the treatment of prisoners and for the raising of standards in prison, for example, in contrast to managerialist approaches. It is also a means of challenging the social exclusion of prisoners while detained within what Goffman would describe as a total institution. This is an institution physically cut off from the outside world, in which all aspects of life, work, leisure activities and sleep are conducted within the institution, everyday life is intensively regulated with coercive sanctions for a wide range of behaviours and these rules are strongly enforced, and the relation between staff and inmates is one of social distance (Goffman 1961). In such an environment small irritations between prisoners or between prisoners and staff can have a cumulative effect so clear and effective procedural rights may defuse tensions. Rights may also be important in protecting against 'informal punishments', such as arbitrary transfer, which in the past was used as a means of punishment.

It will be argued that respect for prisoners' rights would also benefit the wider society as well as prisoners themselves, as rights may have implications for reducing re-offending. Respect for rights may limit the negative impact of imprisonment and by treating prisoners as autonomous individuals capable of making choices and as responsible citizens, better prepare them for release.

A book arguing for prisoners' rights may well raise the response of why prisoners need rights when they already have sufficient protection from abuse within the existing prison regime framework. Here critics might refer to the undisputed fact that English prisons have improved considerably since the early 1990s with clear prison standards, prison league tables which name and shame the worst 'offenders' and arguably encourage improvement, as well as the framework of domestic and European Convention jurisprudence now circumscribing prison management. This question will be addressed by considering the current problems with prison conditions. A rights-based approach may be better able than the reliance on targets and performance reviews of new managerialism to achieve improved treatment of prisoners and raise standards in prison.

Rights also offer a means of challenging the social exclusion and the invisibility of prisoners. The recognition of prisoners' rights, including civil and social rights, affirms prisoners re-inclusion into society and recognizes them as having equal status and value rather than as second-class citizens. Defining the prisoner as the possessor of individual rights, rather than as a member of a class defined in terms of risk, may also offer one way of countering the invisibility of the individual within new penologies which focus primarily on risk assessment. While prisoners' rights are not a panacea for all the problems of the modern prison, they can make a substantial impact on prison conditions.

The political process in the UK is now in some respects more favourable to the recognition of prisoners' rights. International rights instruments, including the European Convention on Human Rights, have assumed increasing importance for the protection of prisoners in the UK and the recognition of prisoners' rights has gone much further than the USA, where the focus remains much more strongly on security, control and penal austerity. Prisoners' rights under the Convention have in some respects filled the gaps in public and private law.

The impact of the Human Rights Act 1998 and the expansion of European Convention jurisprudence has benefited prisoners and improved their treatment. Judges are now more willing to find breaches of Article 3, the right not to be subjected to inhuman, cruel or degrading treatment, compared to the past (see Chapter 4). The House of Lords has also given some limited protection under the Act to those held in UK detention facilities in Iraq, in *Al-Skeini and others v Secretary of State for Defence* [2007] UKHL 26.

In the past prisoners in the UK have been neglected by governments who have seen few or no political advantages in improving prisons. On the contrary, concessions to prisoners have been seen as problematic in the light of the perceived punitiveness of the public, compared to the political benefits of increased punitiveness and penal austerity. Moreover given the 'invisibility' of prisoners and their physical separation from society, the public have been less aware of the problems within the prison estate. This separation also means that prisoners are vulnerable as they are both economically and politically weak yet they are living in a relatively high-risk environment with risk of assault and theft and sharing cells and association time with other offenders, who may well be incarcerated for offences of violence.

Taking rights seriously

Of course even if a rights-based approach is accepted in principle, and rights are acknowledged by the courts and by the prison administrators, there may still be problems ensuring that rights are taken seriously in practice. A rights sceptic might argue that even if we have formal rights, they are of limited value given the problems prisoners face in bringing claims as well as problems of enforceability and delays. Recognizing prisoners' rights is one step, but enforcing them is another matter, as prisoners may lack the literacy or skills required to bring a claim, or be serving too short a sentence to make filing a claim worthwhile especially as in some cases it may take years for prisoners to get their 'day in court'. Bringing a claim requires a relatively high level of literacy. Obviously prisoners' skills is an important issue and needs addressing. However, skills provision within prisons is improving and the number of skills awards is a key performance target and is being given priority, although the aim obviously is to improve employment prospects rather than to facilitate litigation. So when prisoners in the USA succeeded with their claims in the 1970s they still faced the problem of non-compliance or lengthy delays on the part of the prison authorities. If enforcement of judgments ultimately rested in the hands of prison officials who were the object of the original claim and who were resistant to change, then enforcement was likely to prove difficult. Bringing litigation is still costly in terms of time and money and demands a high level of skills and support.

Similarly in the past in the UK before the Human Rights Act, it could take considerable time for a prisoner to have his day in the Strasbourg Court. In the case of *Campbell and Fell v UK* (1984) 7 EHRR 165 it took 16 years for the prisoners' case to be heard in Strasbourg. However, the abolition of the European Commission on Human Rights and the enactment of the Human Rights Act 1998 have meant rights claims can be processed more speedily. But the speeding up of prisoners' claims could be improved further and perhaps campaigning groups could take on test cases which affect large numbers of prisoners rather than litigation being conducted on an individual basis.

Rights may be depoliticized or neutralized by poor enforcement, lack of assistance in bringing claims or inadequate remedies. The move towards rights may be resisted by states because of the resource implications and the fear of the floodgates of litigation opening. Also, of course, in practice rights claims may be defeated by the institutional needs of the prison, as we shall see in Chapter 2.

Moreover, in a period of recession where there are numerous demands on public funds, diverting funds to improve prison conditions to satisfy rights claims may not be popular with the public. There was vociferous criticism in the popular press and in some sections of the public in March 2009 of the compensation awarded to prisoners for the degrading conditions in Barlinnie. Yet the public's attitude to prisoners and prisons is ambivalent, stories about prison and offenders are very popular, including those which focus on the prisoners' perspective, so there is clearly considerable public interest but at the same time a strong commitment to penal austerity. Moreover, the sufferings of prisoners have provided the inspiration for many literary works which remain popular in the UK including Dickens' *Little Dorrit*, Hugo's *Les Misérables* and Wilde's *The Ballad of Reading Gaol* but perhaps they only remind the public of past mistreatment rather than current problems.

The problem now is finding room for prisoners' rights within the current political and cultural climate with its emphasis on crime control and risk management, as well as financial pressures on public spending. The recognition of prisoners' rights is heavily dependent on the political climate, and progress can be impeded in a punitive political climate. Despite significant advances in the past there is now concern among the public and politicians that too much latitude has been given to prisoners and that some retrenchment is needed. Efforts to extend and entrench rights have been resisted by successive governments who have much preferred the less onerous and cheaper provisions of earned privileges, which can be used to control prisoners, to maintain order and discipline, whereas rights impose financial costs if they entail a rise in prison standards to meets the courts' demands, or in defending alleged breaches and if rights are universal, clearly the potential class of complainants is broadened. But prisoners have made full use of the Convention since its inception, and especially since the Human Rights Act 1998.

Although the rise of prisoners' rights is usually associated with the 1970s, the quest for prisoners' rights has a longer history and can be traced back to the Bill of Rights of 1689. The key provision of the Bill of Rights is the prohibition on cruel and unusual punishment in the serving of sentences, but it took until the mid-twentieth century for this to be used as a means of guaranteeing prisoners' rights in practice in the United States. Demands for prisoners' rights were voiced in the 1970s and the 1980s and reformers have seen the pursuit of rights protection as the key to improving the prison system.

As we shall see in Chapter 2 the development of prisoners' rights has not been a linear process but there have been both advances and some retrograde steps here and in the USA. Concerns about unnecessary and frivolous claims culminated in the USA with the passing of the Prison Litigation Reform Act, 1995 designed to reduce the number of rights claims. In the UK we do not have a comparable statute limiting claims, but recent cuts in legal aid support for prisoners claims have been introduced with the aim being to deter trivial claims and to cut costs in the light of a substantial increase in claims over recent years.[4] The increase in claims may reflect a number of factors including greater awareness of rights, the increase in prison numbers and the rise in the number of prisoners serving indeterminate sentences. Changes in legal aid funding for prison law, to reduce and fix fees and limit judicial review to public interest cases, were introduced in July 2010 following a consultation by the Legal Services Commission. This may mean that firms will avoid taking on such work, particularly if there are oral hearings or the amount of work cannot be reasonably calculated, or that work may be given to more junior staff.

Terrorism and insecurity

Moreover, in addition to the pressures of prison expansion and popular punitiveness and funding cuts we now have the problem of terrorism impacting on the development of prisoners' rights and becoming a major influence on political life. Terrorism has been a key issue in the Europe and, as in the United States, September 11th marked a watershed and still casts a long shadow over the criminal justice process in Europe as control and surveillance for security purposes competes with demands for more rights for suspects and prisoners.

Terrorism has implications for prisoners' rights at a number of levels. The war on terror has been used to justify emergency powers and the extension of detention. It has added to the public's fear of crime and to uncertainty.[5] In the USA, 9/11 was a turning point in the treatment of those suspected of committing terrorist offences, and, as we shall see, this has meant the debates on prison conditions in the USA have mostly focused on the detention and treatment of foreign national prisoners held in Guantanamo Bay, and campaigns have been conducted to accord these prisoners the same rights in detention as US nationals hold on the mainland.

As terrorist campaigns have extended to Europe, this has affected public attitudes and arguably increased public punitiveness and fear of crime and has impacted on attitudes towards particular groups of prisoners. In the UK, concerns over security from terrorist attack have shaped the public's anxieties over crime but there has been considerable debate on the problem of detention of terrorist prisoners and the use of measures such as control orders and special treatment of those accused of terrorist crimes. The Strasbourg Court, while recognizing the problems for states dealing with terrorist violence, and the concerns following 9/11 and the July 7 bombings in London in 2005, nonetheless emphasized in *A and others v UK* Application No. 3455/05 (19 February 2009) that Article 3 enshrines the most fundamental values of democratic societies so that even in the most difficult circumstances torture and inhuman and degrading treatment are prohibited. While the state's concern over an imminent terrorist attack were understandable, the derogation from Article 5(1) to permit indefinite detention was disproportionate.

In the Netherlands, concerns over terrorism, crime and immigration fused with a concern over Islamic extremism. At the same time all the mainstream parties have moved further to the right. The emergence of political parties which feed on fears of terrorism and extremism and the Islamization of Europe, is a new but significant development. This fear of Islamic terrorism was intensified in the Netherlands because of the murders of politician Pim Fortuyn in 2002 and film director Theo van Gogh in 2004. Fortuyn, who created his own political party Pym Fortuyn List, committed to anti-Islamic policies, was killed by Volkert van der Graaf, who gave as one of his motivations for the killing a desire to protect weaker groups in Dutch society and to protect Muslims from persecution. Mohammed Bouyeri who was convicted of the murder of van Gogh, referred to the fact that van Gogh had made a film *Submission* which had criticized the treatment of Muslim women, and in which pictures of female victims of abuse were overlaid with texts from the Koran. The film, scripted by Ayaan Hirsi Ali, focused on the experience of a woman in a violent marriage who was raped and then punished for adultery.

Both murders influenced public perceptions of crime and immigration. Before his death Fortuyn was gaining support and soon after his death his party obtained 26 seats in parliament, although it subsequently lost them. Fortuyn's legacy has been inherited by Geert Wilders who has attracted increasing electoral support from voters, and this increased further following his exclusion from the UK in 2009. Research by TNS Nipo for the magazine *Vrij Nederland* found that 40 per cent of the Dutch population agreed with many of his concerns over the Islamification of the Netherlands and that if there were an election at that time, he would receive 18 per cent of the vote which in an electoral system based on proportional representation is quite significant.[6] In the June 2010 election Wilder's Freedom Party (PVV)[7] won 24 seats in Parliament, more than double the number in the previous election.

The Netherlands has also become far less tolerant of ethnic minorities, refugees and asylum seekers which is a major shift, given the strong tradition of tolerance in the past. Immigration has also become a much more important political issue among all the major parties. However, the attack on immigration has focused on what is seen as the threat to Dutch tolerance from Islamic values, and particularly liberal values of respect for women and gay rights. This was exemplified by Fortuyn who had highlighted his homosexuality in debates on Islamification before his death. The shift in attitude toward immigration has also occurred at a time of scepticism over rehabilitative policies.

Terrorism has also changed the prison population itself as the number of prisoners imprisoned for terrorist offences in Europe has increased and this has led to fears that some prisoners will use the prison arena to convert recruits to extremism. Within Dutch prisons, there are now special separate wings in prison for offenders convicted of terrorist offences, to prevent them from recruiting other prisoners and terrorist prisoners can be held on indeterminate sentences (see Boone 2007).

In the UK prisoners awaiting trial for terrorist offences are usually held at Belmarsh, although there have been concerns that they will radicalize and recruit other prisoners. In the UK the number of Muslim prisoners increased from 8 per cent of the total prison population in 2003 to just over 12 per cent in 2010. A Report on Whitemoor in 2008 where Muslim prisoners account for 28 per cent of the prison population said that this 'appeared to be leading to anxiety and apprehension on the part of some staff' (HM Prison Service 2008: 5). Concerns have also been expressed by prisoners about intimidation from radical Muslim gangs. Imams at Feltham and Aylesbury Young Offenders Institution Institutions were dismissed for unprofessional behaviour in 2001 for distributing inflammatory material to prisoners in the aftermath of 9/11. Prisoner officers have received training on how to detect potential extremists. However the Prison Inspectorate has been critical of the tendency of officers to assume Muslim prisoners were potential terrorists and warned that this blanket treatment may actually drive some prisoners further towards extremism (HMIP 2010b). While some prisoners have converted to Islam inside prison, they resent the fact that this will be seen as evidence of radicalisation. Moreover in some cases the conversion may be for instrumental reasons (see Chapter 7).

A report for the European Commission argued that the role of prisons in Europe for recruitment for terrorist acts was increasing and urgent attention needed to be given to this issue. The rate of religious conversions in prison is higher than outside and the majority of conversions are to Islam (Neumann and Rogers 2008: 39–44). The problem had been experienced in France, the Netherlands and the UK. The report said that in the short term it might be necessary to hold jihadist prisoners separately although this might be problematic in the longer term. It argued that 'Governments need to pay urgent attention to the situation in European prisons, which are likely to become a major hub for the radicalization and recruitment efforts into Islamist militancy' (Neumann and Rogers 2008: 93–4). Included in its recommendations is more support for prisoners on their release.

Terrorism may also increase tolerance of poor prison conditions as the public may be less willing to fund liberal prison regimes for those who have committed crimes against civilians, especially if the whole community is seen as the potential victim of terrorist crime. While analogies have often been drawn between the Irish paramilitary campaigns in the 1970s and 1980s and Islamic extremist groups operating in the UK now, a key difference is that the majority of sectarian attacks from the 1970s to the 1990s were directed at military or state targets. When civilian targets were occasionally targeted by the provisional IRA this alienated the civilian population and undermined their support at home and abroad. However, in the case of modern Islamic extremist groups civilians appear to be the primary targets.

Prisoners as citizens

The denial of full citizenship rights to prisoners raises a number of key questions, namely how citizenship has come to be constructed in such a way that prisoners are excluded and whether there are alternative broader concepts of citizenship which can include prisoners. The question of how prisoners come to be accorded a status which resembles the 'social death' status of slaves in slavery-based societies and how this has been justified will be considered, with reference to changing concepts of citizenship and their implications for prisoners' rights in the United Kingdom and the United States.

These questions are particularly pertinent now that citizenship currently has such a high profile in the UK as a focus of political and academic interest evident, for example, in discussions of British citizenship or 'Britishness', as a focus of policy, and also in the emphasis on responsibility and voluntary work as an avenue for, and affirmation of, citizenship. Citizenship is now part of the national curriculum and passing an examination in citizenship is a precondition for naturalization as a British citizen.[8] The Government has also emphasized its perception of the relationship between state and citizen as one based on rights and responsibilities.[9] The concept of citizenship has emerged in political discourse as a dynamic status which acts as a focus for rights issues. At the same time, it provides an ideology and repository for notions of responsibility and belonging. These debates over citizenship are a pervasive feature of contemporary political, legal and public debates in European states, including Ireland, for example, where there has been a referendum on citizenship (Harrington 2005, Mullally 2005). The development of multi-cultural states marked by diversities of ethnicity, culture and religion has highlighted the problems of defining citizenship (Rogers and Tillie 2001). Citizenship has also been a focus for debate worldwide in the context of globalization, and given the problems of sustaining a national identity in the context of migration and the development of transnational communities (Joppke 1999, Carens 2000 and Kiviston and Faist 2007). Furthermore, citizenship is a politically based concept constructed through the political ideologies of both communitarians and libertarians.

A notion of citizenship which is reconstructed to encompass prisoners would affirm the importance of universal rights in our culture and also bring social benefits in addressing the problem of social exclusion, an issue which is now politically fashionable and embedded in political discourses. This recon-struction is necessary because citizenship has often been construed in ways unfavourable to the recognition of prisoners' rights: prisoners as a group have been excluded from formal citizenship rights by classical and most modern concepts of citizenship.

The meaning of citizenship

The notion of citizenship is Janus-faced in the sense that it has been inter-twined with equality and universalism, for example, suffrage for all, regardless of class, sex or race, and, at the same time, it has been used as a means of social exclusion, through the defining of boundaries between citizens and non-citizens. There are also conflicts between constructions of citizenship as inclusionary, with an emphasis on universal suffrage and universal rights, as a way of transcending pluralities in society and overcoming distinctions of class, status and ethnicity, and a focus on citizenship as an exclusionary concept, using it to exclude those from outside the state, or from different cultures. The inclusionary concept is epitomized by the Declaration of the Rights of Man and the Citizen, 1789 and in modern thought by Marshall (1950) and Titmuss (1968). But in the past citizenship has been used to demarcate territory, to exclude slaves, migrants and women. Others, such as Bentham[10] see the notion of universal inalienable rights as metaphysical nonsense and instead construe rights as positive rights endowed by the state (Bentham 1843).

The question to consider is whether the construction or discourse of citi-zenship is one which can make room for prisoners' claims and specifically for prisoners' rights. This is problematic in relation to modern concepts of citi-zenship which have rooted the notion of citizenship in terms of the social contract, with an assumption that the person who benefits from the protec-tion and advantages of society is also obliged to obey its rules and, by defi-nition, the prisoner is the outsider, who seeks the benefits without the corresponding burdens. Running through social contract theory is an obligation on the part of the citizen to pay taxes, and to respect others' rights to life and property, in order to benefit from safety and security (Hobbes 1651, Locke 1689 and Rousseau 1762).

So the responsibility of the citizen has been a precondition of the benefits of citizenship. The social contract is still seen as a means of securing and explaining social order in modern secular societies, in imposing obligations on citizens, in return for self-preservation and protection from others.

The concept of citizenship is not clear-cut, but it is terrain which has been fought over by communitarians and libertarians, each seeking to define citizenship in ways which reflect perceptions of the relationship between the state and the citizen, and, because of these political resonances, attempts to limit or extend citizenship have been problematic. Moreover, how citizenship is defined will have implications for groups and individuals on the boundaries. Groups may be excluded from citizenship for a variety of reasons, for example, because of their nationality, or in the past, because of their slave status, or in the case of felons, because they are deemed to forfeit citizenship voluntarily through their misdeeds. Citizenship is enjoying a revival and is now a fashionable concept crucial to debates on social cohesion in modern Europe (Jansen *et al.* 2006). However, it has a long history, its roots are much older extending to antiquity, for example, in the writings of Aristotle and of the Stoic philosophers (Aristotle 1992, Long 2007).

Debates over citizenship have included arguments over who should possess citizenship and clearly this has been a politically charged issue and the link between citizenship and virtue is complex. Running through classical and some modern notions of citizenship is the concept of virtue but how the concept of 'virtue' is constructed is crucial when considering the status of prisoners. In earlier constructions of citizenship, for example, in Aristotle's *Politics* the citizen was defined as a member of the city with rights, duties and obligations. In classical concepts of citizenship, citizenship is seen as promoting virtue, so the purpose of the city as a political entity was to promote a good and ethical life and facilitate a just society. The citizen was independent and virtuous, and virtue was construed as acting for the good of the city rather than for his own interests. Aristotle acknowledged that someone who is not a good man in all aspects of his life could still be a citizen, provided that he could perform the political duties of a citizen conscientiously (Aristotle 1992). His notion of the individual as a *zoon politikon* presupposed an emphasis on social co-operation and realization of political aspirations only through participation and interaction with others in the life of the community.

Since then governments have used the notion of citizenship to embody moral condemnation and moral worthiness, and have denied citizenship to the 'unworthy' as well as the immature and incompetent. So increasingly in recent political discourse, there is an emphasis on the notion that citizenship must be earned, for example, through long service in the form of residency for migrants, or now by passing appropriate tests for citizenship, including knowledge of the host country, or by proving one self worthy of citizenship through allegiance to core values. The Labour Government favoured a system of earned citizenship in which credits would be accrued, for example, by civic and voluntary work, but lost for law-breaking.[11] This notion that citizenship may be earned or lost through misdeeds is also reflected in the fact that convicted prisoners in the UK lose their voting rights while in prison but can regain them on release after they have served their sentence.

As well as disputes over the obligations and duties of citizenship, there have been arguments over which groups should possess citizenship status. For example, in classical Greece, women, slaves and those from other states, were excluded, with women defined simply as the bearers of future (male) citizens. In modern European societies, full citizenship has been denied to prisoners, recipients of welfare, migrants and women. For example, in England, under the 1834 Poor Law Amendment Act once a person claimed poor relief, he lost the civil right to vote, a political exclusion of the poor which persisted until 1918. But while women and the poor have gained the vote, convicted prisoners are still disenfranchised. What these groups share historically is a denigration of their status, a denial of full personhood which allows them to be constructed as less deserving of the full benefits of citizenship. Defined by their 'otherness', itself a historically contingent construct, they have been treated as outsiders by virtue of their country of origin, their impecuniousity or their misdeeds. This is very clearly enunciated, for example, in the UK Government's justification of prisoner disenfranchisement in the case of *Hirst v UK (No. 2)* Application No. 74025/01 (6 October 2005) that 'Convicted prisoners had breached the social contract and so could be regarded as forfeiting the right to take part in the government of the country' (at para 50). Citizenship has been construed by Marshall as creating positive rights to benefits given by the state in order to promote social wellbeing and this approach focuses on social rights rather than the purely individual civil or political rights found in most rights charters for example, the European Convention on Human Rights and the UN Declaration of Human Rights. Without them citizenship rights are hollow (Marshall 1950). This issue has also been stressed in some Marxist critiques of rights (Bloch 1967 and Baynes 2000). Communitarians such as Sandel and Etzioni have emphasized the interdependence of citizens within the social framework (Sandel 1982, Etzioni 1993). In contrast libertarians have conceptualized the citizen as an atomistic individual, constructing citizenship as an exercise of choice and consumer rights (Bellamy and Greenaway 1995).

Including prisoners

Is there room for the prisoner within any of these notions of citizenship? Most concepts of citizenship have excluded prisoners because of the requirement of virtue. Prisoners have received little recognition within classical, social contractarian, or New Right models of citizenship. In contrast, a welfarist model, predicated on a commitment to citizenship and universal social rights, affords a possibility of the inclusion of prisoners (see Marshall 1950, Titmuss 1968). If applied to the prison context, it might also include a right to rehabilitation which would impact on the level of support for rehabilitative programmes and the quality of life within prison.

The concept of citizenship most favourable to the notion of prisoners' rights is one which sees citizenship as an instrument of social inclusion rather than exclusion, and which incorporates social rights. The view most relevant here would be Marshall's notion of citizenship which is premised on equality, as all citizens possess equal rights and duties, and on the inclusion of the weakest groups in society, and a focus on social welfare (Marshall 1950). While most western constructions of citizenship have focused on civil and political rights, including the right to vote and due process rights, Marshall saw social rights, including rights to housing, education and welfare, as key ingredients of citizenship as they facilitated political participation and social inclusion, by engaging weaker or disadvantaged groups in the political process and integrating them into society. But on this construction of citizenship, rights also entailed obligations: for example, the right to education imposed a duty on parents to send their children to school.

This 'welfarist' approach was influential in the political context of the 1950s and 1960s. But in the 1980s and early 1990s, more individualistic models of citizenship became fashionable again. In particular, the notion of citizenship was captured by the New Right and the citizen was redefined as a consumer of services as exemplified by the Citizen's Charter (Cabinet Office 1991). The notion of citizenship in both the UK and the USA was more narrowly defined within the context of a 'nightwatchman' state, rather than a supportive welfarist state.

But it is difficult to configure prisoners within the New Right model of citizenship, for although prisoners who commit economic crimes might seem to fit the model of the self-interested individual revered by economic individualism, they are also excluded by New Right theory for making 'bad choices'. Furthermore, as a 'consumer' of prison services, the prisoner is clearly in a weak position. With no purchasing power and no opportunity to exercise consumer sovereignty by moving his or her consumption elsewhere, the prisoner is effectively excluded from the normal operations of the market.

The managerialist approach, which also became dominant in the 1980s and 1990s and is now well-established in the Prison Service, has also allowed little room for prisoners' rights, although the quality of prisons has been measured and assessed and made more transparent, so the problems with particular prisons are publicly highlighted through league tables and performance reviews. The consumer in this model is still ultimately the taxpayer, rather than the prisoner, and the dynamic of new managerialism is far removed from a notion of prisoners' rights or prisoners as citizens. New managerialism has meant that the emphasis has shifted to a focus on prisons providing Value For Money, and the quest to drive down costs impacts on conditions of detention.

NOMS states in its *Strategic and Business Plans* that one of its core values is to 'treat offenders with decency and respect' (Ministry of Justice 2009a: 3). It also refers to its plan to 'manage prison capacity to meet the required standards on decency and safety and ensure control is maintained' (ibid: 28) but there are no enforceable rights to such treatment, or to ensure that the relevant key performance targets are met. Whether these targets have actually been met and their implications for the quality of prison life will be considered in Chapter 4.

The second challenge to the penal-welfare model, which focused on rehabilitation and treatment, came from a quite different source, the due process movement. The polarization between rights and utilitarianism was also expressed in the attack on the traditional rehabilitationist models in the early 1970s for their failure to give recognition to due process rights when sentencing offenders, and for allowing indeterminate sentencing and punishment, and for legitimating the use of coercive treatment-based approaches (American Friends 1971).

Although the fight for due process enhanced rights to challenge detention and offered a restraint on indeterminate sentencing, this was a double-edged sword, as it also resulted in a weakening of the penal-welfare model which incorporated social rights into its concept of citizenship and ultimately adversely affected prisoners. While it was initially launched from a radical perspective, it created a vacuum in which rival approaches could flourish, including what has been described by Feeley and Simon as the New Penology which focuses on risk management (Feeley and Simon 1992). This approach is less receptive to rights claims or to the inclusion of prisoners within the benefits of full citizenship.

It is therefore ironic that prisoners' assertion of their rights could be seen as instrumental in the dissolution of the penal-welfare model which, in other respects, emphasized the inclusion rather than the otherness of prisoners. Garland sees this spread of due process into the penal system, as part of a wider process in which the legislatures have 'reclaimed the power to punish that they had previously delegated to experts... This undoing of what Foucault called "the Declaration of Carceral Independence" began with the American prisoners' rights litigation and the gradual spread of due process considerations into the prison system' (Garland 2001: 151).

The penal-welfare model was also weakened by 'evidence' of the failure of rehabilitative programmes in preventing reoffending. For example, the response to the article by Martinson in 1974 which reviewed the findings of research studies of a range of programmes and found that with few exceptions these efforts to rehabilitate 'had no appreciable effect on recidivism' was to conclude that 'nothing works' even though Martinson was pointing to the problem of lack of proof of effectiveness (Martinson 1974: 25). The rehabilitative model was therefore attacked from two directions, it was seen as ineffective as 'nothing works', but was also under attack from the due process movement. As Garland (2001) has argued, the challenge to the rehabilitative ideal from those arguing for due process rights, allowed a space in which rival philosophies and policies less sympathetic to prisoners' rights could flourish. Furthermore the growing focus on the victim has proved unhelpful to prisoners' rights movements and coincided with the middle-class withdrawal of support for a welfare model, itself linked to their experience of crime. As he says:

> This sanctification of victims also tends to nullify concern for offenders. The zero sum relationship that is now assumed to hold between the one and the other ensures that any show of compassion for offenders, any invocation of their rights, any effort to humanize their punishments, can easily be represented as an insult to victims and their families.
>
> (Garland 2001: 143)

According to Garland, the withdrawal of support for the penal-welfare model also means that 'less eligibility' is now being given priority, affirming the social as well as penal exclusion of offenders. The criminal history of prisoners is seen as undermining their moral claims. So once again we find the assertion of a notion of citizenship which is equated with virtue.

However, Garland's gloomy prognosis may be over-pessimistic as the demand for rights by prisoners, as we shall see, is not receding despite attempts to limit prisoners' litigation in the USA. Moreover, rights instruments are increasingly being used internationally and within the UK, to do battle with the principle of less eligibility. The domestic courts and the European Court of Human Rights have been obliged to give more weight to prisoners' rights claims, even if this means weakening the less eligibility principle as we shall see in Chapters 3 and 4.

Prisoners as non-citizens

The notion of imprisonment itself as a form of social death entailing exclusion from full citizenship rights has persisted both formally and de facto in the treatment of prisoners despite the abolition of civil death statutes in both the UK and the USA. Prisoners are still being excluded by definitions of them as second-class citizens. Citizenship is being used to define social boundaries, and in the most extreme form of this view, non-citizens may be defined as non-persons who are 'socially dead'. This has been, and to an extent still is, applied to prisoners, just as it was to slaves. Not only is citizenship a dynamic status but so, also, is the complex relationship between citizenship, imprisonment and social death in both jurisdictions.

The legal concept of civil death, with its origins in slavery, has historically been applied to prisoners, so defining them as both outsiders and non-persons. The notion of social death is broader than civil death. Children, for example, may be excluded from civil rights, including the right to vote, because of their immaturity, but this temporary status does not necessarily entail a broader definition of non-personhood and is not based on a perceived lack of moral worth. But in the case of prisoners and slaves, the civil death is expressive of a more fundamental exclusion from society, both physical and symbolic. Indeed, in some American states disenfranchisement is permanent for some offenders depending on the type of offence and their criminal histories. There are obvious similarities between the status of the slave and the prisoner, both may be subjected to status degradation rituals, including branding, tattooing, and special clothing, traditionally used as marks of enslavement but some of which survive today in the modern prison context.

There are parallels between the movement of the slave from social death toward citizenship in the United States in the nineteenth century and the movement of the prisoner towards citizenship in the twentieth-century in the USA and the UK. The movement from 'no rights' to residual rights, to entitlements and positive obligations on the state in dealing with prisoners, has taken over a century and is not yet complete.

In his seminal study of slavery, *Slavery and Social Death*, Patterson defines the slave as a person who is socially dead, de-socialized, depersonalized and uprooted from his milieu and who is seen as a degraded person (Patterson 1982: 38). The slave in slavery-based societies was subjected to rituals to symbolize his enslavement. As Patterson notes, the letters GAL were burnt on the shoulders of galley slaves and TP, *Travaux perpetuels*, was branded on to prisoners sent to the *Bagnes*, the convict prisons which replaced galley slavery in 1748. The *Bagnes* lasted until the mid-nineteenth century and here prison labour was used to create public works. The use of branding on these 'public slaves' was not abolished until 1832.

The symbolic annihilation of personhood was epitomized by the tattooing of camp serial numbers onto prisoners' bodies at Auschwitz to make it easier to identify the dead, and the use of coloured patches to identify subgroups of Jewish, gypsy, gay and 'asocial' prisoners. Even in the first decade of the twenty-first century prisoners may be forced to wear special uniforms and to shave their heads to undergo what Goffman would call a mortification of the self as their former identity is eroded (Goffman 1961). This reduction of personhood can also be seen as part of a process of animalization as Davis argues (Davis 2006). Historically there are also links between war and slavery as prisoners of war have been used as forced labour and effectively enslaved. Furthermore, as Davis argues, in some cases prison labour has been more deadly and more extreme than in the forced labour of slavery, for example, the use of forced labour in Nazi concentration camps, and in the gulag in Stalinist Russia and during the Maoist period in China (Davis 2006: 36).

Slavery and punishment have always been closely intertwined. Imprisonment has been shaped by slavery and the imposition of slavery has been used in the past to punish prisoners of war and offender and their families. Patterson describes how enslavement was used as a punishment for serious offences in most pre-modern societies, including ancient Greece and Rome, Japan and China (Patterson 1982: 126).

Also running through the experience of both slavery and imprisonment is moral condemnation and public denunciation. Both slaves and prisoners are construed as the enemy, the outsider. Patterson distinguishes two modes of representing the social death of slavery, intrusive and extrusive: in the intrusive, the slave was 'ritually incorporated as the enemy on the inside' who could not belong because he was 'the product of a hostile alien culture', while in the extrusive mode, the failure to belong resulted from a failing to meet minimum standards of behaviour, for example, through destitution or criminality. As Patterson says:

> We may summarize the two modes of representing the social death that was slavery by saying that in the intrusive mode the slave was conceived of as someone who did not belong because he was an outsider, while in the extrusive mode the slave became an outsider because he did not (or no longer) belonged. In the former the slave was an external exile, an intruder; in the latter he was an internal exile, one who had been deprived of all claims of community. The one fell because he was the enemy, the other became the enemy because he had fallen.
>
> (Patterson 1982: 39)

The similarities between the slave and the prisoner are more than merely superficial. Just as the prisoner retained a slave status following the abolition of slavery, so the notion of penal servitude persisted in Europe. Patterson charts the use of penal slavery from galley slaves to the use of penal labour, for example, in the construction of public works in Europe, which continued until the mid-nineteenth century (Patterson 1982). Sellin has also shown how the punishment of free persons has been strongly influenced by the forms of punishment meted out to slaves, and the legacy of slavery has inhibited the humane treatment of offenders (Sellin 1976).

When the institution of slavery was formally ended in the United States, by the ratification of the Thirteenth Amendment in 1865, an exception was made for prisoners in the penal system: 'Neither slavery nor involuntary servitude, *except as a punishment for crime* whereof the party shall have been duly convicted, shall exist within the United States, or any place subject to their jurisdiction.' Although the Fourteenth Amendment extended citizenship to all, including former slaves, felons or 'outlaws' were excluded from this advance.

Most states responded to these exceptions by enacting 'civil death' statutes which meant that the prisoner was excluded from civil rights or citizenship: the prisoner could not vote, own property, or exercise parental rights over his children. This was clearly enunciated in *Ruffin v Commonwealth of Virginia Ruffin v Commonwealth of Virginia* (1871) 62 Va (21 Gratt) 790 where the Virginian court stated that the prisoner through his crime loses all rights except those which the law gives him, and he has no more rights than a slave; the prisoner is 'the slave of the state'. The prisoner was legally defined as dead, had no rights and no remedies for prison conditions, no legal standing in relation to property rights, and lost custodial rights over his or her children. Given this civil death or non-personhood, the courts were reluctant to become involved in supervising prison conditions, treatment or discipline and were able to justify their 'hands off' approach, approved in *Ruffin* in 1871, which lasted until 1944, and the case of *Coffin v Reichard* 143 F 2d 443 (6th Cir 1944). The effect of this was to leave prisoners exposed to risks of violence or poor treatment.

Similarly, in the United Kingdom, prisoners in the past lost both civil rights and property rights on conviction. Although the Forfeiture Act 1870 abolished most forms of forfeiture, it retained a voting disqualification for prisoners and in that sense can be seen as a civil death statute and the forerunner of the ban on convicted prisoners' voting preserved in subsequent statutes including the Representation of the People Acts of 1969 and 1983.

Even when civil death statutes were repealed in the USA, the movement from slavery to freedom was obstructed as prisoners retained a de facto second-class position, stemming from their former status as non-persons. This is reflected in the felon disenfranchisement laws which are still valid law in many American states (see Chapter 8). These laws have often been construed as a backlash against the Thirteenth, Fourteenth and Fifteenth Amendments which allowed former slaves to vote. The Thirteenth Amendment ended slavery, the Fourteenth Amendment gave equal rights to freed slaves and the Fifteenth Amendment in 1870 prohibited racial discrimination in voting and gave the vote to African-American men.

However, although many former slaves did vote and were also elected to state legislatures, during the Reconstruction Period (1865–77) intimidation and violence were used to discourage freed slaves from voting. In addition there were lawful measures, which although prima facie neutral in practice, had a disparate impact on African Americans and limited their voting rights, including residency requirements and grandfather clauses which were not struck down until 1915 and a poll tax, which was abolished in 1964, and literacy tests which were eventually outlawed in 1965. Although poor whites were also adversely affected by these requirements, they were re-enfranchised by the early twentieth century; black Americans did not achieve this until 1965 with the enactment of the Voting Rights Act.

As well as these measures to discourage voting, the laws on felon disenfranchisement were adopted between 1865 and 1900 to limit the voting rights of felons. By 1900, 38 states had limits on felons voting. Clearly this was crucial as it also meant that they could not sit on juries or participate in public life or use political processes to protect their interests. So voting limits and felon disenfranchisement need to be seen in the political and social context of segregation. Voting disqualifications were also retained for felons and foreign nationals. Criminal codes were also expanded after the end of slavery to include offences it was thought freed men would commit, such as vagrancy and miscegenation. In addition, after the civil war black males were often incarcerated on flimsy charges. These problems were not confined to the southern states (Wood, Budnitz and Malhotra 2009).

The new practice of convict leasing was also developed which meant that once convicted, prisoners could be leased out to work on the same plantations from which they been freed. Convict labour would be rented out to mining companies and farmers by Governors in the Southern states and the use of chain gangs in prison uniform was comparable to the use of slave labour before the war and freed slaves were also threatened with penal labour as a means of control (Davis 2006: 328). Moreover, because convict labour provided a ready and potentially unlimited supply of labour, there was less incentive for the owners of mines and factories to treat prisoners as well as they needed to do with their own slaves, so in many cases the conditions of prisoners, which have been graphically described by Oshinsky, were worse than slavery (Oshinsky 1997). The existence of this reserve army of labour meant that little effort was made to improve conditions to attract workers, just as the use of forced labour in Nazi Germany meant that these workers experienced the worst imaginable conditions.

The Voting Rights Act 1965 contained provisions which protected voter registration and provided for federal enforcement and of course segregation formally ended in 1954 with *Brown v Board of Education* 347 US 483 (1954) and with the Civil Rights Act in 1964. Resisting voting rights was difficult after the Second World War as 1.2 million African Americans served in that war[12] with massive casualties, just as it was hard to resist demands for full voting rights in the UK after the losses and sacrifices of the First World War. However, the current felon disenfranchisement laws perpetuate the exclusion of black American males because of the disparate impact of the rise in imprisonment on young black males. Thirteen per cent of African-American males have lost their votes which is seven times the national average (The Sentencing Project 2010). In some states the disenfranchisement persists on release from prison, so the transition from offender to ex-offender carries with it the stigmatization of their prior non-citizenship, despite the enactment of Rehabilitation of Offenders statutes designed to prevent this, just as the manumitted slaves' relations with the community and former owners were shaped by their prior status. Recent campaigns in both jurisdictions have focused on the issue of voting rights in symbolizing their exclusion (see Chapter 8).

Social death included both social exclusion and civil death, the loss of fundamental citizenship rights, such as the right to vote, for both slaves and for prisoners. Because prisoners were ascribed this slave status of non-personhood, the courts in the USA were reluctant to interfere with the day to day running of the prison, to step beyond the prison door to scrutinize conditions which in turn left the prisoner exposed to the risk that any abuse or violence would go unchecked. How this situation was changed through the courts is, therefore, of current interest and will be considered in Chapter 2.

Conclusions

As we have seen, prisoners' rights need to be understood within their political and social context. History shows that success in establishing prisoners' rights in the USA and the UK is contingent on the political context, including the political construction of citizenship. This wider political climate may make governments more or less receptive to responding favourably to prisoners' rights claims, and is crucial to understanding the ascendancy and decline of prisoners' rights, as will become clear, for example, when we compare the developments in the 1970s and 1990s in Chapter 2. But the micro-political context may also be relevant when we consider power struggles between competing groups within the criminal justice system, for example prison officers, prison managers, probation officers and other agencies, over the disputed territory of rehabilitation.

It will be argued that prisoners' rights in the UK and the USA are crucial in moving convicted prisoners from a state of social and civil death towards a recognition of their citizenship grounded in social inclusion. The concept of citizenship argued for here is one that includes social rights, including the right to rehabilitation, as well as the established right not to be subjected to inhuman or degrading treatment or punishment under Article 3 of the European Convention on Human Rights and Article 5 of the UN Declaration of Human Rights.

In recent years international human rights instruments have been used in the UK with some success to strengthen and extend the rights of prisoners in relation to a wide range of issues. However, this success has been limited in its impact because in responding to the courts' judgments, governments have perceived prisoners' wrongdoing as justifying rights infringements under the Convention and under domestic law, and in doing so, diminished their citizenship. This is illustrated most clearly in relation to what might be seen as the prime symbol of citizenship, the right to vote. This debate on felon disenfranchisement also highlights the problem of non-personhood here and in the United States, and will be considered in more detail in Chapter 8.

2 The historical development of prisoners' rights

Rights versus discretion

Introduction

This chapter will consider the issue of prisoners' rights from an historical perspective in examining the tension between rights and discretion in the UK, the United States and the Netherlands. In Europe and the United States in the 1960s and 1970s demands for prisoners' rights included demands for minimum wages for prisoners, improved conditions, as well as complaints over the censorship of mail, prisoners' treatment in disciplinary hearings and their lack of due process rights. The impact of these campaigns for prisoners' rights by radical civil rights activists and inmates will be considered as well as subsequent developments and their political and social contexts. This will be followed in Chapter 3 by a discussion of the increasing importance of international human rights jurisprudence.

The tension between rights and discretion, which has shaped the development of prison law in the UK since the 1970s, has been played out in the context of public law. The key cases relating to the treatment of prisoners in public law and their implications will be considered. As we shall see, judicial review has assisted prisoners in challenging administrative decisions and increased their chances of fair and just treatment. The advantage of judicial review was that it potentially covered a wide a range of areas, including segregation and transfer, as well as access to the courts, allocation and a wide range of policy issues. Many of the improvements in prison conditions in this period have resulted from the expansion of public law into the prison arena. This progress has been further consolidated since the Human Rights Act 1998 came into force as the courts have been reviewing the decisions of public bodies for Convention compliance.

At the same time, there is an ambivalence in the courts' response to prisoners' rights claims. Prisoners' rights have often been resisted by the domestic courts who have retained considerable discretion for the prison authority in decision making. The courts in the UK, like the USA, have sought to reconcile meeting prisoners' rights claims with institutional needs, and prisoners have generally been more successful in demanding procedural justice than in challenging the conditions in which they are confined. Moreover, when rights have been recognized they have been defined as narrowly as possible to prevent further inroads into the prison authority's discretion and the primary focus has been on procedural protection in the form of strengthened due process rights.

In the 1970s, prisoners' rights were seen by campaigners as a means of ameliorating the poor conditions of the pre-Woolf era, and also as a way of challenging the treatment of detainees in Northern Ireland, held under emergency legislation, who were detained for extended periods before trial in conditions which, in the view of the European Court of Human Rights in *Ireland v UK* (1978) 2 EHRR 25, amounted to inhuman and degrading treatment. The failure to recognize prisoners' due process rights, for example, was also a key factor in the unrest in British prisons in the 1970s and 1980s. So the Woolf Report concluded that promoting a sense of justice and fairness is essential to achieving stability in prisons (Woolf and Tumim 1991).

The tension between rights and discretion can be traced back to the early 1970s and is reflected in the subsequent evolution of prison law. As the American Friends Service Committee, a Quaker group strongly committed to prisoner reform, and favour of a bill of prisoners' rights, observed in *Struggle for Justice* in 1971 that: 'The movement for prisoners' rights runs directly counter to the growth of unfettered discretionary powers; it calls for shifting power from administrators towards those who are on the receiving end' (American Friends Service Committee, 1971). We find a constant struggle between the assertion of rights claims and the attempts by the prison authorities to place limits on those rights.

The prisoners' rights movement in the UK

While prison reformers in the 1970s and 1980s focused on rights as a means of improving conditions, as we have seen, utilitarianism rather than rights discourse shaped prison reform in the past in the UK. When we compare the United States and the United Kingdom, we find a similar pattern, a greater willingness to acknowledge prisoners' rights in the 1970s, but also judicial resistance and ambivalence, regarding further expansion of prisoners' rights, as well as prison disorder and attempts to reassert prison discipline. However, there were also some important differences, for example, the strong link between the prisoners' rights movement and the civil rights movement in the 1970s in the USA was missing in the UK. Nonetheless, the 1970s and 1980s was also a time of unrest in the UK, for example, with the miners' strikes in 1972, and in 1974 and again in 1984. The 1974 strike resulted in a three-day week to conserve electricity and this strike was blamed for the fall of the Heath government.

There were also prison riots, protests, disorder and disturbances in the 1970s principally in dispersal prisons, including Albany and Parkhurst (King and Elliot 1977), albeit not on the scale of the Attica prison uprising in the USA in 1971, which involved 1300 prisoners and resulted in 40 deaths.

However, by the 1980s, prisons in the UK were relatively calmer. The issue of imprisonment did not attain the political significance it reached in the USA, but the role of the law in preventing political challenges was highlighted by challenges to bail conditions imposed to prevent striking miners from secondary picketing during the miners' strike in 1984. The right to picket was seen as a key weapon in the protection of workers' interests. Within prisons in that period republican and loyalist prisoners saw themselves and were later treated by the state as political prisoners and indeed prisoners imprisoned for qualifying offences were later eligible for early release on licence under the provisions of the Northern Ireland (Sentences) Act 1998, under the terms of the Good Friday Agreement. But while they retained a distinct political identity within prisons, sectarian prisoners were separated and their protests did not mobilize non-sectarian inmates. Disorder and protests in prisons tended to be expressed in most cases individually rather than collectively, and the state responded with increased staff training on how to handle disorder and the development of control and restraint techniques. But the underlying problems and conflicts within prison were not resolved and the more extensive and dramatic prison riots in the UK in 1990 were instrumental in bringing about significant changes in the prison system, insofar as they stimulated the Woolf Inquiry and subsequent Report, which ultimately generated substantial changes in conditions and treatment (Woolf and Tumim 1991).

An embryonic prisoners' rights movement did emerge in the UK in the early 1970s when the group, Preservation of the Rights of Prisoners (PROP), was formed by prisoners and ex-prisoners to preserve, protect and extend prisoners' rights, and to improve prison conditions. PROP contributed to debates on penal policy, formulated a Charter of Rights and published reports on the Hull prison riots in 1978 and on Wormwood Scrubs in 1979. It also organized strikes and demonstrations. But it had less impact than its counterparts in the United States and few of its demands were met. The National Council for Civil Liberties was also involved in providing information to prisoners on aspects of sentencing, appeals, prison disciplinary proceedings, and on who to contact to deal with their grievances, and on their entitlements (Coote and Grant 1972). The organization Radical Alternatives to Prison (RAP) was also set up in 1970. It was active until 1987 and reformed in 2003. However, as its name suggests, its agenda was primarily abolitionist rather than reformist or rights-based. While supporting progressive reforms, it was primarily concerned with campaigning against imprisonment, especially for children, and with fighting prison expansion. The Association of Prisoners has also been set up by an ex-offender, John Hirst, which reports on developments in the treatment of prisoners in its online blog *Prisoners' Voice* and campaigns on issues such as voting rights. The labour movement in the UK has had little contact or cooperation with prisoners as a group and their interests may conflict if prisoners are performing tasks at much lower rates than unionized labour. However, unions may contain individual members with experience of the prison system.

The political climate of the 1970s and 1980s contrasts sharply with the current social and political context of the UK, where there is increased punitiveness and the group who might see themselves as political prisoners, Islamic extremist prisoners, are more isolated from the majority of the civilian population and maintain their distance from other prisoners.

Residual rights

In English law prisoners' rights have been construed 'residually', that is they exist unless specifically or impliedly excluded by the law. As Lord Wilberforce said in *Raymond v Honey* [1983] 1 AC 1 the prisoner 'retains all civil rights which are not taken away expressly or by (necessary) implication' (at 9). While prisoners have the same civil rights as non-prisoners except for those taken away by the fact of imprisonment, they receive no special rights because they are prisoners.

The UK courts have in the past been reluctant to intervene in the day-to-day running of the prison, and prisoners have had to fight hard to establish their rights, and success in the UK was achieved later than in the USA. The case of *Raymond v Honey* can be seen as the equivalent of the earlier case of *Coffin v Reichard* 143 F 2d 443 (6th Cir 1944) as both recognize that rights extend beyond the prison door. But this still leaves plenty of scope for discretion, and 'by necessary implication' means taking account of the administrative requirements of the Prison Service, which has tended to favour the prison authorities rather than the prisoner. Nonetheless, in *Raymond v Honey* which concerned a prisoner who tried to commit his Prison Governor for contempt of court, the House of Lords stressed that prisoners had a basic right of access to the courts, bringing the prisoner and prison life firmly within judicial scrutiny. In the later case of *R v Secretary of State for the Home Department ex parte Leech (No. 2)* [1994] QB 198 the Court of Appeal said that this right could only be limited by necessary implication if there was a pressing need and only by the minimum necessary to meet that need. But this clearly leaves considerable scope for discretion.

The interplay between rights and discretion shapes prisoners' life inside prison. Everyday life within prisons is circumscribed by the Prison Act 1952 and more importantly the Prison Rules made under delegated legislation, under s 47 of the Act. Although some of these Rules are designed to protect prisoners from each other and from their keepers, for example, the use of restraint and control techniques, many of the rules leave plenty of scope for interpretation and discretion, for example, PR 6: 'Order and discipline shall be maintained with firmness, but with no more restriction than is required for safe custody and well ordered community life.' Although the Rules use language such as 'shall be' and refer to 'entitlements', there are problems of enforceability and obtaining a remedy for breaches of the Rules. Although public law has been more successful than private law in protecting prisoners' interests, nonetheless negotiating primary and secondary legislation is difficult for prisoners with limited resources.

The prisoners' experience of prison life will be affected by a range of administrative decisions, on the type of prison to which the prisoner is allocated, conditions within it and arrangements for release. Prisoners do have some statutory rights, for example, to the number of letters and showers, which are clear-cut, but in other areas, such as segregation, transfer, categorization, allocation and discipline, much more discretion is accorded to the prison authority especially in relation to issues of risk assessment. Moreover, it is only relatively recently, since the early 1990s, that decision making on issues which affects prisoners' lives has become more transparent, in giving prisoners the reasons for decisions which affect them. The problem in the past is that the courts in the UK, like those in the USA, have been reluctant to interfere with decisions on issues such as transfer or segregation if they are taken on security or operational grounds.

Before the recent expansion of European Convention jurisprudence, the framework for redress for prisoners with grievances was confined to public law and tort, both of which offered limited success. Most private law claims brought by prisoners have been in negligence. If harmed by another prisoner, a prisoner could sue the Home Office if it is reasonably foreseeable that they would have been assaulted and the prison authorities failed to take the necessary steps to protect them, and of course it may be more profitable to sue the prison rather than an impecunious defendant. But the court will look at the context in which the action takes place and the standards applied will be those appropriate to the prison environment. Actions for false imprisonment have been less successful, although a prisoner did obtain damages when she was detained longer than necessary in the case of *R v Brockhill Prison ex parte Evans (No. 2)* (2001) 2 AC 19.

As the Prison Rules are imposed by statute as delegated legislation, this would seem to raise the possibility of bringing an action in private law for breach of statutory duty and claiming damages for injuries. But in *Becker v Home Office* (1972) 2 QB 407, the court ruled that the prisoner cannot bring an action for breach of statutory duty for non-compliance with the Prison Rules, because of the fears of a floodgates problem, and concerns that opening the doors to complaints would undermine prison discipline. Lord Denning stressed that 'If the courts were to entertain actions by disgruntled prisoners, the governor's life would be made intolerable. The discipline of the prison would be undermined. The Prison Rules are regulatory directions only. Even if they are not observed, they do not give rise to a cause of action' (at 418). But this still left open the avenues of judicial review and limited actions in tort, for example, negligence.

Following *Becker*, the domestic courts in the UK for many years were reluctant to interfere with the day-to-day running of the prison and as we shall see, a similar approach was taken in the USA. In both private and public law cases, the UK courts have taken, and will take account of, the need for the smooth functioning of the prisons in the public interest, the 'operational' reasons for decisions and administrative necessity. The Prison Governor is seen as the person best placed to make judgements regarding safety and security.

While the House of Lords has ruled that the prisoner cannot bring an action solely for the breach of statutory duty in private law for failure to observe the Rules, public law may be used. The exercise of discretion in applying the Rules may be subjected to judicial review as the court made clear in *R v Deputy Governor of Parkhurst Prison, ex parte Hague, Weldon v Home Office* [1992] 1 AC 58. Here a claim for a breach of statutory duty in relation to a segregation decision failed in private law as the Court said that Rule 43 was not intended to confer a right of action on the individual prisoner. But if the statutory language did not suggest a private right and redress was not possible in private law, then the appropriate remedy would be judicial review. So Prison Rules breaches do not give rise to specific rights within private law but can be challenged by other means. So in this sense the line between tort and public law has become blurred as potential tort actions may be raised through judicial review.

The courts have taken the view that the Prison Rules were not intended to create private rights, but were concerned only with the management, treatment and control of prisoners and usually the prisoner will not have suffered a financial loss through the breach. Given this, judicial review may offer a more appropriate and effective remedy. This issue was revisited in relation to detainees held under the Prevention of Terrorism Act in *Cullen v Chief Constable of the Royal Ulster Constabulary* (2003) UKHL 39 which concerned the denial of the right of access to a solicitor. The House of Lords held that where such a fundamental right has been breached, it would be open to the court to award damages even if the applicant has not suffered a financial loss. The Court also said that the *Hague* decision was limited to rules relating to the treatment, control and management of the prison.

Private prisons are subject to the same legal framework as public sector prisons, namely the Prison Act, Prison Rules and Prison Service Orders and Instructions and inspected by the Prison Inspectorate. In private prisons the prisoner could bring a private law claim against the company which is vicariously liable for its employees, but in cases, for example, such as medical negligence, rights claims could also be brought against the state under Article 3.

Judicial review

Because private law has proved to be a relatively weak means of enforcing minimal standards in prisons, much greater use has been made of public law, which has met with greater success. But even here the courts have in the past avoided a 'Prison Inspectorate' role as far as conditions are concerned, but have been happier dealing with procedural justice, for example, with disciplinary regimes and quasi-judicial functions.

The 1980s saw an expansion of judicial review in the UK which enhanced procedural justice within the prison system. This expansion reflected the increasing complexity and diffusion of governmental powers, and a corresponding broadening of the boundaries of public law, and increased concern by the judiciary to exercise control over discretionary powers, a liberalization of the grounds of review and procedural reforms governing applications for review. Prisoners' rights claims were a key element of the expansion of judicial review in this period.

Since the 1970s, prison law has become integrated into public law and has now become overlaid by human rights law. The courts have focused on the issues of irrationality, illegality and abuse of powers across a wide range of areas of prison life, and have made the full range of public law remedies available to aggrieved prisoners, for example to prisoners transferred for disciplinary reasons.[1] When reviewing the exercise of discretion by the Secretary of State, the courts will consider if the minister has acted unreasonably, unfairly or has exceeded his powers. Prior to the Human Rights Act, the test of irrationality would have been the *Wednesbury* test, defined in *Associated Provincial Picture Houses v Wednesbury Corporation* [1948] 1 KB 233, namely that the decision was so irrational that no reasonable authority could have arrived at that decision. However, the primary focus now would be on proportionality, as emphasized in *R v Secretary of State for the Home Department ex parte Daly* [2001] UKHL 26. But the nature of the prison enterprise makes it particularly difficult to challenge the exercise of discretion and the emphasis will be on 'striking a balance' between competing rights and interests.

The notion of a legitimate expectation has been used in public law to protect individuals from the caprices of governments and public bodies, although this is clearly not as strong as a formal right. There is no guarantee that the court will find a legitimate expectation if the law the is not clear-cut, and administrative expediency will be a factor in the courts' decision. It has been used by prisoners most effectively with procedural matters rather than prison conditions, for example, in relation to the use of criteria for decisions on home leave and challenges to the Home Secretary's role in setting the tariff for a mandatory life sentence in *R v Secretary of the State Department ex parte Doody* [1994] 1 AC 531. In that case Lord Mustill said that there is a presumption that administrative powers will be exercised fairly and comply with the principles of natural justice which may mean the opportunity to make representations and disclosure of reasons for any departure from these principles. Where there are matters of discretion, then it is open to the prison authority to change policies and procedures provided that they do so by the proper means. Many improvements in prison conditions have resulted from the expansion of public law into this area. Prisoners have also won procedural rights in relation to decisions on release and the granting and refusal of parole and prisoners serving mandatory life sentences are entitled to know the length of the tariff part of the sentence and the judge's reasons, or they would be unable to challenge a decision (see Chapter 5). Prisoners now also have a right to be given reasons for being categorized or retained in Category A, and being transferred or segregated, as the Court stressed in the cases of *Hague* and *Weldon* in 1992, and in the later case of *R v Secretary of State for the Home Office ex parte Duggan* [1993] 3 All ER 277. The exercise of discretion in making such decisions is reviewable.

The courts will examine the reasons very closely where issues of natural justice arise. But decisions regarding the maintenance of good order and the day-to-day running of the prison will accord more freedom to the Prison Governor, as the person on the spot best able to make decisions on security matters. However, if fundamental liberties are at stake, such as denial of early release or delays in parole decisions, the courts may be more willing to become involved. Challenges have been brought by IPP prisoners, for example, concerning problems of access to offending behaviour courses which they need to complete successfully to provide information to the Board in reaching its decision, for example, in *Secretary of State for Justice v James* [2009] UKHL 6 May 2009. Although these challenges have not succeeded in obtaining release for the prisoners concerned, they have highlighted the problems faced by IPP prisoners.

When rights are claimed whether in private or public law, or under the European Convention, the courts will look at the claims in the context of the needs of the institution for good order and security and in private law, prison conditions are judged against the standard expected of a prison rather than a luxury hotel. The history of judicial review shows that judges, when dealing with prisoners' claims, are more comfortable dealing with procedural matters, with the provision of natural justice rather than substantive justice, or becoming involved in the supervision of prison conditions. But where judicial or quasi-judicial functions are in issue, then the judiciary are more willing to perform a supervisory role.

Given the courts ambivalence about prisoners' rights in the past, acknowledging the broad discretion of the prison authority has been a way of neutralizing rights. However, recently we find a more critical approach reflecting the impact of European Convention jurisprudence. The domestic courts have acknowledged the right of the Prison Service to formulate policies which take account of the smooth running of the prison, and the protection of the public, but have stressed that policies should not be applied in a blanket way without a proper consideration of individual cases. For example, in *R (P) v Secretary of State for the Home Dept* (2002) EHWC 1018 Admin, an infirm elderly prisoner was placed in Category A despite the fact that he was unlikely to be well enough to escape. The Prison Service argued that this was irrelevant because the criterion for Category A was that the prisoner would be highly dangerous to the public, the police or the security of the state if he did escape. The Court said that while the Prison Service was entitled to have a policy to make the escape of dangerous prisoners virtually impossible, it should still consider prisoners' cases on an individual basis. This meant that if a prisoner's escape risk could be managed with lower security, then it would be unlawful to preclude consideration of this. Categorization is clearly a key area of concern to prisoners as it affects the quality of life and access to resources. Subsequent cases have taken a similar approach to *P*. The court criticized the reclassification of a whole group of prisoners from D to C, which meant moving from open to closed prisons, without a full assessment of individual risk in *R (Vary and others) v Secretary of State for the Home Department* [2004] EWHC 2251 (Admin). The routine handcuffing of prisoners on hospital visits without any prior risk assessment first was criticised by the Court in *R (Graham) v Secretary of State for Justice; R (Allen) v Secretary of State for Justice* [2007] EWHC 2910 (Admin). This emphasis on individualized risk assessment also reflects the jurisprudence of the Strasbourg Court which has been very critical of blanket policies applied indiscriminately to whole groups of prisoners.

However, in *R (Palmer) v Secretary of State for the Home Department*, [2004] EWHC 1817 (Admin) a challenge to a recategorization was brought when prisoners were moved to a closed prison following an incident at an open prison when a prisoner escaped and died. Some of the prisoners had five years left to serve. The court said while prisoners can and do have a legitimate expectation that they would remain in open conditions, provided that they observe the rules, the Home Secretary was entitled to adopt a revised policy at any given time and prisoners do not have a legitimate expectation that a revised policy could not be extended to them. A past decision under a previous policy does not prevent a further decision under a new policy. Following this case, a new policy on Category D prisoners was formulated, which stipulates that cases must be decided on individual merits. It also states that prisoners should not be transferred to an open prison if they have more than two years to serve before their release date. If a longer-term prisoner absconded, it would undermine public confidence in the system. The court also said that prisoners should not be given the right to make representations before recategorization decisions were made, as this would be too burdensome for the prison, but the requirements of fairness would be satisfied by the right to appeal a recategorization decision, once the prisoner has been given the reasons for it.

The assertion of prisoners' demands through private or public law may be limited as leave is needed for judicial review and in view of the scope for discretion on the part of the Secretary of State. The Prison Service can justify and defend its stringent policies if it can establish that a particular decision was made because of necessity and issues of security are still given considerable weight. Judicial review has had most impact on procedural justice and specifically on the position of prisoners in disciplinary hearings. In *Leech* v *Deputy Governor of Parkhurst Prison* [1988] AC 533, the Court decided that any prison disciplinary hearing could be reviewed on the grounds of unfairness, procedural defects or irrationality. Although in the past the Courts resisted comparing a disciplinary hearing to a court hearing to limit Article 6

Convention challenges, the protection of Article 6 has now been extended to disciplinary matters as we shall see in Chapter 5. But judicial review has performed an important protective role for prisoners.

The impact of public law is also reflected in the improved fairness of prison decision-making procedures, for example, in the obligation to give reasons to prisoners for decisions which affect them. Procedural fairness underpinned the recommendations of the Woolf Report which led to substantial changes in prison conditions and procedures in the 1990s (Woolf and Tumim 1991). Although the Woolf Report used the language of public law, grounded in fairness and procedural justice, rather than the rhetoric of rights, it did recommend an enforceable code of Minimum Standards and a statutory limit on overcrowding. Its focus on fairness, on treating prisoners with respect and justice advanced procedural rights, and its emphasis on minimal standards also enhanced substantive justice. Some of its proposals were implemented but in a diluted form; for example, the Minimum Standards are not enforceable and there is no statutory limit on overcrowding as Woolf had advocated. Woolf also recommended compacts between the prison and the prisoner, setting out their obligations, which were greater than privileges but not as strong as rights, but the Incentives and Earned Privileges Scheme introduced instead rests on earned privileges which may be withdrawn. But if these demands had been couched in terms of rights, it is questionable whether the government of the day would have accepted them.

Moreover, in the 1990s, alternative means of improving prison regimes such as Key Performance Indicators and Targets of the New Managerialism, were introduced. These provided greater transparency and publicised the limitations of individual prisons, and the quality of the prison regime as a whole. But there is little that the prisoner can do if the targets are not met and no remedies available or compensation for that failure within the framework of managerialism.

In the UK, we find a tension between the assertion of rights claims and the emphasis on the institutional needs of the prison in resisting those claims. So during the 1990s, the focus within prison governance shifted from concessions to legitimate expectations to new managerialism, against the background of an increase in public punitivism. But the managerialist imperative has coexisted alongside another route for prisoners' rights claims which they did not fully exploit until the 1980s and which has expanded since 2000, namely the European Convention. The scope of judicial review as an avenue for pursuing prisoners' rights has been enhanced by the Human Rights Act and the increasing strength of rights culture now compared with the 1980s. Human rights jurisprudence has now become part of public law.

Prisoners' rights litigation in the United States

In the United States the space given to prisoners' rights may be seen as an expression of the conflicts between the judiciary and Congress, between notions of adjudication within the judiciary, particularly between judicial review and judicial supremacy, the tensions between the courts and the Government, as well as between different branches of government, and conflicts between political movements in the wider society. The 'hands off' approach affirmed in *Ruffin v Commonwealth of Virginia* (1871) 62 Va (21 Gratt) 790 persisted until well into the twentieth century in the United States.

The case of *Coffin v Reichard* 143 F 2d 443 (6th Cir 1944) was therefore significant because habeas corpus was extended by the Federal District Court to conditions of confinement and in this sense presaged the later English case of *Raymond v Honey*. The court in *Coffin v Reichard* held that 'A prisoner retains all rights of an ordinary citizen except those expressly or by necessary implication taken from him by law, which rights include the right to personal security against lawful invasion' (at p. 445). While the prison had the right to hold the convicted prisoner, it also had a duty to protect him from assault and injury. The prisoner was entitled to habeas corpus – even if lawfully held in custody – if he was deprived of a right to which he was lawfully entitled in confinement, the deprivation of which made imprisonment more burdensome than the law allows, or curtailed liberty to a greater extent than the law allows. This case created an opportunity for the federal courts to examine life inside state prisons, although they did not actively engage in the supervision of conditions until the mid-1960s.

So in *Stroud v Swope* 187 F 2d 850 (9th Cir 1951), for example, although Stroud succeeded in commuting his death sentence to imprisonment, he was unable to succeed in successive challenges to his confinement and to the conditions in which he was held. Rather, the courts' role was limited to removing from prison those who had been illegally confined. There had to be good cause for a person to be in prison and the burden is on the authority to show this, so prisoners were able to use the English Habeas Corpus Act of 1679 to challenge unlawful detention in prison. However, here the Court said the doctrine of habeas corpus did not affect what happened inside the prison, only the boundaries between the prisoner and the outside despite the approach in *Coffin v Reichard*. The development and extension of the doctrine of habeas corpus also reflected the political struggle between different agencies of government as Duker observes (Duker 1980).

The courts' reluctance to step beyond the prison door from the 1940s to the early 1960s, was based in part on deference to the expertise of the prison authorities in managing the prison, partly on the fear of the floodgates opening to endless litigation if the courts become more involved in supervision, and concerns over maintaining the separation of powers between the legislature, the executive and the judiciary, and most importantly the view that, prisoners were non-persons so less worthy of the courts' attention. The assumption here was still that prisoners did not deserve special protection and that citizenship must be 'earned'. The notion of citizenship still depends on assumption of *proven* worth which prisoners have rebutted through the criminal acts leading to their conviction and therefore cannot claim protection by the courts. This concept of citizenship has enabled and exacerbated the marginalization of prisoners within the political process and in public consciousness and also legitimized the exclusion of prisoners from public purview.

Recognizing prisoners' rights

However, the judicial 'hands off' approach was contested inside and outside the courtroom by prisoners refusing to accept their social death without challenge. In the 1960s and 1970s, prisoners in the United States sought to reassert their claims to citizenship through the development of a prisoners' rights movement as well as by the direct action of rioting and disorder. Their efforts embraced demands for formal due process rights and humane conditions of incarceration. Similarly, in the UK the movement specifically for prisoners' rights flourished in the 1970s, although movements for prison *reform* had been active since the eighteenth century in both societies.

In the 1960s the Warren Court, which lasted from 1953 to 1969, developed its key role as a protector of civil rights in the United States (Graham 1970). It upheld challenges to segregation in the landmark case of *Brown v Board of Education*, 347 US 483 (1954). It also initiated a 'due process revolution' in the criminal justice system exemplified by the key cases of *Mapp v Ohio*, 367 US 643 (1961) and *Miranda v Arizona*, 384 US 436 (1966). But this was possible because of wider political and social factors, including the fact that this was a period of social and political unrest, with strong challenges to US domestic and foreign policy.

In the changing political climate of the 1960s and 1970s, and under the leadership of Chief Justice Warren, the court began to take a more interventionist approach in response to prisoners' assertion of their constitutional and civil rights. If the constitution created and endowed individuals with citizenship rights, and if these survived the transition to prison, then prisoners argued, they should be recognized as citizens notwithstanding their crimes. A number of key cases brought prisoners within the expanding rights discourse. Cases have been brought using s 1983 of the Civil Rights Act 1871 to argue that the individual has been deprived of a right given by the Constitution. *Monroe v Pape* 365 US 167 (1961) revived the use of the 1871 Civil Rights Act and allowed federal litigation against states for the deprivation of civil liberties, giving a basis for prisoners' rights litigation. This case paved the way for prisoners to file cases for damages and injunctions in the federal courts when the states abused their individual rights. Bringing a constitutional case in the federal courts may be preferable as officials are given more immunity in states. Civil rights actions, using s 1983, have been brought in both public and private prisons and more remedies may be available in the latter as there will be fewer immunities for those working in private prisons. *Monroe* was followed three years later by *Cooper v Pate* 378 US 546 (1964) in which the US Supreme Court protected access to religious publications and rejected the hands-off principle extolled in *Ruffin v Commonwealth of Virginia* by recognizing that prisoners retained their constitutional rights during incarceration and that this meant that life inside prison could be subject to scrutiny. By contrast, in *Ruffin*, the prisoner was deemed to lose all rights except those the law gives him and has no more rights than a slave. These cases embraced the notion that the Constitution followed an offender beyond the prison door. The Act was used again in the 1970s to challenge poor prison conditions as it gives more remedies than habeas corpus, and more rights to discovery, as well as the right to bring a class action. Moreover many cases have been settled out of court.

However, the extent of this constitutional protection fluctuated in subsequent years as Bronstein observes (Bronstein 1980). In *Wolff v McDonnell* 418 US 539 (1974) the United States Supreme Court held that 'though his rights may be diminished by the needs and exigencies of the institutional environment a prisoner is not wholly stripped of constitutional protections when he is imprisoned for crime. There is no iron curtain drawn between the Constitution and the prisons of this country' (at 556). Because the Constitution created and protected citizens, prisoners retained some elements of a citizen status despite the fact of imprisonment.

In the years that followed, several key cases in the USA brought prisoners within the emerging rights discourse of the period. Following *Wolff v McDonnell*, the courts in the 1970s showed greater willingness to engage in the scrutiny of prison conditions reflecting the radical cultural and political climate and demands for civil and due process rights. A range of prisoners' rights were acknowledged by the courts, including the due process rights of prisoners to be given notice of charges against them, and reasons for decisions which affect them, and the right to an impartial body in disciplinary matters as well as the right to medical treatment, and access to correspondence. The courts recognized the prisoner as a person/citizen who does not lose all his or her constitutional rights at the point of sentencing. Those rights endure during the period of incarceration, including when facing charges or further punishments under the prison disciplinary system.

Prison conditions in the United States have been challenged through habeas corpus, and bringing constitutional challenges, using litigation at state and federal level, and using the federal Civil Rights Act and through individual and class actions. The courts have looked at the totality of conditions, so even though conditions on their own might not constitute cruel and unusual punishment. their cumulative effect would be sufficient to support a claim. Judgments have often resulted in court orders to meet specific standards by a specific deadline. The Courts have used a hierarchical approach and have been more willing to protect rights when fundamental rights from the Bill of Rights, are at stake, but are more likely to defer to the needs of the prison and to allow infringements where lesser rights are concerned. A significant recent development was the decision by the District Court to order a reduction in prison numbers and improve health care in California's prisons within a fixed period in *Coleman v Schwarzenegger* US District Court, No. Civ. S-90-0520

(4 August 2009). However, the case is going to the US Supreme Court in October 2010.

In the USA, to some extent, the fight for rights was easier than in the UK in the 1970s because rights claims could be framed around issues of constitutionality. For example, the First Amendment was used to claim rights to receive and read political tracts, to challenge the censorship of mail, and to protect freedom of religion for black Muslims. The Eighth Amendment has been used to challenge poor conditions, solitary confinement, and physical and mental abuse. Black Muslims also won rights to freedom of religion and the right to attend religious services, and to have access to the Koran in *Cooper v Pate* 378 US 546 (1964). The due process clause of the Fourteenth Amendment has been used to secure the right to cross-examine witnesses in disciplinary proceedings, the right to counsel where proceedings resulted in loss of substantial rights and due process rights in relation to parole and to challenge excessive surveillance after parole. The equal protection clause of the Fourteenth Amendment has been used by prisoners to bring claims of racial and sexual discrimination. The Fourth Amendment has been used to obtain security from unwarranted search and seizure in relation to the confiscation of property. The value of a constitutional foundation to the development of prisoners' rights has also been highlighted by Lazarus who sees this as very significant in achieving enhanced protection of prisoners' rights in Germany (Lazarus 2004).

The prisoners' rights movement

Resistance to the brutality of prison life in the 1970s united black and white prisoners. The increasing political awareness of prisoners and their refusal to accept their conditions, resulted in part from the imprisonment of black and white civil rights activists in the USA, who mobilized prisoners to protest and campaign for change. It also reflected the political climate outside the penitentiary. Campaigns in the USA focused on issues such as indeterminate sentences rather than poor conditions per se, and on the shifting criteria of parole boards which Mitford has described as a system of double jeopardy in which the prisoner is sentenced twice, first by the court and secondly by the parole board (Mitford 1973). The attack on treatment-based models also reflected demands for due process rights and also scepticism whether treatment was actually provided, but was instead essentially surveillance and observation of prisoners. There were also concerns over the use of prisoners as experimental subjects by drug companies testing new products on prison 'volunteers'.

The American Civil Liberties Union (ACLU) was also heavily involved in prisoners' rights in the 1970s. It set up the National Prison Project in 1972 which remains the only national litigation programme operating for prisoners. It has initiated class actions on a range of issues, for example, for better medical care for prisoners with HIV, TB and cancer, and the protection of prisoners from sexual assaults. It has also challenged overcrowding and unconstitutional prison conditions, and has secured a number of legal victories. In March 2005, it brought an action to defend the due process rights of prisoners on solitary confinement in Ohio Supermax Prison. In March 2010 it filed a complaint against the Idaho Correctional Centre arguing that it allowed a culture of violence to flourish unchecked. The ACLU is particularly concerned with informing the public of the social and financial impact of a penal policy which emphasizes incarceration rather than rehabilitation. The experience of the prisoners' rights movements in the USA has demonstrated the role of rights in improving prisoners' conditions and it has brought prison conditions to the attention of the public.

Prisoners in the USA have also had the advantage of being able to bring class actions. For example, in 1970, a class action, was brought against the prison system in Arkansas in *Holt v Sarver* (1970) 308 F. Supp 363 (E.D.Ark). In this case, the Court found that conditions amounted to cruel and unusual punishment, following which the prison authorities were ordered to improve conditions. Following *Holt v Sarver* and the involvement of the federal judiciary in the review of prison conditions, state correctional systems were more inclined to negotiate settlements rather than to proceed to court (Leeke, 1980). A class action was also brought by female prisoners to demand parity with male prisoners in access to educational and recreational resources in *Glover v Johnson* 478 F. Supp 1075 (1979). In 1980 prisoners brought a class action in *Ruiz v Estelle* (1980) 503 F. Supp 1295 (1980) which established that the management of prisons in Texas resulted in conditions amounting to cruel and unusual punishment and the case led to improved conditions for all prisoners in the state of Texas. These issues will be considered in more detail in Chapters 4 and 7.

Campaigns for prisoners' rights in the 1960s and 1970s developed from the civil rights movement which focused on including Black Americans, women and prisoners, as well as inspiring the gay rights movement. Prison was seen by radical activists and some inmates as a key arena or site of the struggle for the recognition of civil rights, and for full citizenship for marginalized groups, as the number of black and Hispanic prisoners increased. Many of the civil rights activists were themselves incarcerated in the course of their campaigns. The effect of imprisonment had a further radicalizing effect on them, as well as mobilizing and politicizing their fellow prisoners. Some of the key tracts on prison conditions in that period were written by black civil rights activists, including George Jackson, Malcolm X and Angela Davis (Jackson 1971, 1972, Malcolm X 1987 and Davis *et al.* 1971). The impact of black civil rights activists on the prisoners' rights movement of the 1970s is recorded by Mitford (Mitford 1973). Davis has remained actively involved in campaigns for decarceration and the abolition of imprisonment (Davis 2003).

The demand that all groups should be treated with respect and fully included within social and political life underpinned the demands for prisoners' rights in the 1970s and this emphasis on social inclusion is still a key element of demands for prison reform in the USA today.

Prisoners' rights were a key strategy in challenging their social death, reclaiming citizenship status and personhood for prisoners and a means of transcending their social exclusion. Radical lawyers active in the civil rights movement also began working with prisoners as the prison system was seen as particularly repressive of poor and black communities. Moreover, prisoners themselves generated changes in prison conditions through their demands, as the Attica riot in 1971 brought prisoners back into the political arena and to the attention of the public. The selection of black prisoners for punishment, sometimes for relatively trivial crimes, heightened the perception of oppression. George Jackson, for example, spent 12 years, mostly in solitary confinement, for stealing $70.

The period also saw the establishment of the Prisoners' Union set up in San Francisco in the early 1970s to establish' rights for prisoners as citizens and workers including the right to collectively bargain, to restore and protect civil rights, to abolish indeterminate sentences, and to secure the right to unrestricted access to the press and the judicial system. By 1973 it had 3000 members, and published its own magazine, *The Outlaw*. It sought to break down the separation or 'otherness' of prisoners. Strikes by prisoners in the USA did achieve pay increases in some cases and some prisoners' unions are still active. The Missouri Prison Labor Union, for example, which has 500 members, is currently campaigning for a moratorium on the death penalty, as well as seeking to improve prisoners' living conditions.

While the campaigns of the 1970s and early 1980s were not always successful, reflecting the courts' ambivalence towards developing prisoners' rights, there were some significant victories which improved and humanized prison regimes, for both adults and juveniles. The rise of the prisoners' rights movement was not limited to the USA and the UK, but also found in Australia in the 1970s, in a period of unrest, when demands for change came from prisoners themselves. For example, a riot in Bathurst jail in New South Wales was followed by an inquiry into the harsh conditions in prisons. This Royal Commission published its Report in 1978 and the Nagle Report was a turning point in the treatment of prisoners and led to a number of key reforms (Dawes 2002). Australia had experienced prison riots in 1924 and 1974 and the fight for prisoners' rights has a long history. The first civil case brought in New South Wales was by a prisoner, Henry Kable, transported with his wife Susannah Holmes in 1788, following a conviction for burglary, who successfully sued the ship's captain for the loss of his goods on the voyage (Neal 1991). This heralded the beginning of Kable's new life which culminated in his appointment as Australia's first Chief Constable.

The retreat from judicial activism

But by the late 1970s, more weight was given by the courts to the institutional needs of the prison and they retreated from the 'hands on' approach. Like the English courts in that period, the US judiciary, when they did engage in supervision of prison regimes. were more likely to address procedural than substantive issues. During the late 1970s and 1980s, the court's interventionism was fading as the concern for the protection of prisoners' constitutional rights was displaced by the quest for crime control and the war on drugs, reflected in changes in sentencing law and policy. The declining judicial support from the courts for substantive rights for prisoners at that time reflects the more conservative composition and philosophy of the Supreme Court, and the wider political climate which had moved to the Right, reacting against the radicalism of the earlier period. This resulted in a reluctance to endorse an inclusive concept of citizenship which embraced prisoners' rights.

In the United States, the Burger Court, which lasted from 1969 to 1986, had initially seemed sympathetic to prisoners' claims and was responsible for some radical decisions such as *Roe and Wade* 410 US 113 (1973). But by the late 1970s, this was no longer the case and, as Singer notes, we can see a distinct shift in its jurisprudence as the expansion of prisoners' rights was checked by the Supreme Court, allowing more discretion to the prison authorities (Singer 1980). In *Jones v North Carolina Prisoners' Labor Union, Inc.* (1977) 433 US 119 prisoners argued that their constitutional rights were violated by Regulations prohibiting prisoners from soliciting fellow prisoners to join the union, and banning union meetings. But the Supreme Court rejected this claim. It decided that the right of association of members of the prisoners' union, could be limited by prison officials in the exercise of their discretion to prevent disruption, or to comply with the legitimate and pressing objectives of the prison environment. The facts of confinement and the needs of the penal institution impose limits on constitutional rights, including those derived from the First Amendment.

Arguably prisoners' unions presented a more serious challenge as prisoners were organized and often directly challenging the management of the prison. So where there is a serious assertion of rights which challenges fundamental issues of control and management, the courts may be less willing to accede to these demands.

In *Bell v Wolfish* 441 US 520 (1979) the Supreme Court gave more weight to the need for security and order in prisons. Here remand prisoners claimed that restrictions on reading materials, body cavity searches, shakedowns and double bunking amounted to punishment before conviction. But Justice Rehnquist concluded that the conditions of confinement did not infringe upon the detainees' rights and that issues of prison management were matters outside the jurisdiction of the judiciary, provided that these administrative procedures are implemented in the genuine interests of safeguarding institutional security. Restriction of rights had to be reasonably related to penological interests and aims. So where the emphasis is on the control of prisoners, we find less scope for recognizing prisoners as full citizens.

The tide turned decisively in *Hudson and Palmer* 468 US 517 (1984) when the Supreme Court acknowledged that prisons had a duty to provide secure and sanitary conditions for both prisoners and employees, but decided that the loss of many rights may be necessary to accommodate the institutional objectives of the prison. Similarly in *Turner v Safley* 482 US 78 (1987) the Court again deferred to the needs of good order in prison and also moved away from a strict scrutiny test, where the limit on rights must be strictly tailored to a compelling government interest, towards a rational relationship test, so limits on rights are acceptable if they are reasonably related to the pursuit of legitimate political aims. There must be a reasonable or rational relationship between the restriction on the right and the state interest.

The retreat from prisoners' rights and from a construction of prisoners as citizens continued in the 1990s which saw both the revival of chain gangs, re-introduced in 1995 in Alabama, and the loss of education grants, known as Pell grants, for prisoners in 1994 (see Allen and Abril 1997, Page 2004, Chapter 4). In *Wilson v Seiter* 501 US 294 (1991) the court also held that a party claiming that conditions of confinement violate the Eighth Amendment must show a culpable state of mind on the part of prison officials. The 1990s was also marked by increased punitiveness, longer sentences and the introduction of Three Strikes Laws. The Prison Litigation Reform Act 1995 has also made it more difficult for prisoners to bring civil rights actions under s 1983. The Act, passed in 1996, was introduced to reduce the number of complaints and attendant financial costs, in the context of a substantial increase in prisoner petitions between 1987 and 1995, and to weaken federal oversight of state prison conditions. It imposed a requirement that, with very few exceptions, all internal remedies and grievance procedures should be exhausted before bringing an action, whereas before the Act this was a matter for the court's discretion. To deter prisoners from bringing vexatious or trivial claims, the Act also requires prisoners to pay court filing fees, although this may be by instalments. No actions can be brought for mental or emotional injury unless physical injury can also be shown. The statute also introduced a 'three strikes' rule: if an action is struck out because it is deemed frivolous or malicious, then after three such strikes, the prisoner must pay all filing fees in full in advance if he wishes to bring another action unless the complainant is in imminent danger of serious physical injury. When the Act was passed public attention was focused on apparently frivolous complaints such as the prisoner who demanded smooth instead of chunky peanut butter, or the prisoner who complained that a prison officer had not invited him to a pizza party for a departing prison employee.[2] But many of the cases brought by prisoners have concerned much more serious matters such as physical and sexual abuse, and the denial of medical care. But these developments have not dampened the flames of litigation. Although the Act did lead to an initial fall in the number of actions, the number has since fluctuated (Belbot 2004). So there has been an ongoing tension between demands for the extension of rights and resistance to it. However, if there is no room for change within the framework of the internal complaints system or the wider legal system, then prisoners may resort to direct action to change their conditions as they did in the 1970s.

These limits on prisoners rights claims have been enacted during a period of expansion of the prison population. The USA has the highest incarceration rate in the world at 748 per 100,000 of population in mid-2009 (ICPS 2010). There is still concern over the quality of prison conditions and prison is still an unsafe environment for many prisoners with a high incidence of rape (see Chapter 4). But there has been some limited progress in recent years with new legislation aimed to protect prisoners from sexual assault was also enacted in the 2003 Prison Rape Elimination Act and there is more protection for disabled prisoners from the Americans with Disabilities Act 1990 (see Chapter 7).

Although there have been limits imposed on rights claims, the experience of the prisoners' rights movements in USA has shown is the value of rights in improving prisoners' conditions and bringing those conditions to the attention of the public. What has been missing in the USA however is the pressure from international human rights law and standards which, as we shall see in Chapter 3, has been a key factor in the improvement of prison conditions in Europe. Although that role has been taken to some extent by the US Constitution, as we have seen, it has often been neutralized in the context by being balanced against practical utilitarian considerations and outweighed by institutional needs.

Some changes in the composition of the Supreme Court are now taking place and it was hoped that the election of Barack Obama would lead to improvements in the treatment of prisoners and that the political climate would be more favourable to the advancement of prisoners' rights. During the presidential campaign, Obama had been critical of some of the more conservative justices on the court for protecting the strong rather than the weak and singled out the Warren Court for praise but also expressed concerns over a revival of judicial activism. Since his election Justice Souter has retired and Obama has endorsed Sonia Sotomayor, the first Latino judge, whose nomination has now been accepted by Senate and he has also nominated Elena Kagan to replace Justice Stevens.

In 2008, before the presidential election, the Court had recognized the constitutional rights of prisoners held in Guantanamo Bay in *Boumediene v Bush* 553 US 723 (2008). Within days of taking office, Obama closed the CIA detention programme and revoked past orders authorizing the use of torture in the fight against terrorism and moving the trial of those accused of 9/11 bombings to the federal court. However, Obama has supported the subsequent refusal to extend constitutional rights to prisoners held in Bagram air base in Afghanistan. When Obama was first elected, hopes of change were high as for many he epitomized the values of the earlier civil rights period and the fact of his election was itself seen as the fruition of those earlier civil rights struggles. There were expectations of change in administration of justice for those held for terrorist offences and promises were made to close Guantanamo Bay. However, there have been delays in implementing this is due in part to the problem of finding states who will accept these inmates.

Also the focus has been on extending existing prisoners' rights to prisoners held in Guantanamo Bay, rather than improving or extending the rights and conditions of domestic prisoners held in state and federal prisons.

The evolution of prisoners' rights in the Netherlands

In the nineteenth century prisoners in the Netherlands had no formal rights but, like those in the UK and the USA, lost their civil rights by committing their crimes and were at the mercy of prison governors with few opportunities for complaint although there was some oversight of prison conditions through a prison inspection process. By the early twentieth century there was more interest by politicians in the impact of imprisonment and as the century progressed, international standards for imprisonment gradually developed (see Chapter 3). During the post-war period there was much more interest in the impact of imprisonment and judges were more aware of this literature and its findings.

The humanity of the Dutch prison system has been attributed to a number of factors including the tradition of Dutch tolerance, the experience of internment during the German occupation, and more specifically the influence of the so-called Utrecht School, associated with the Institute of Criminology at Utrecht University and originally founded by Willem Pompe in 1934. This School rejected positivistic criminological approaches and favoured rehabilitation rather than punishment and on developing alternatives to custody and was a major influence on the development of Dutch penal policy in the post-war period.

Prisoners themselves became more assertive in the 1950s and a book *Prisoners' Opinions* was published in 1959. A prisoners' rights movement emerged in the late 1960s in the Netherlands and was followed by similar developments in France, Belgium and the UK in the 1970s. Prisoners started to form unions in 1960s and 1970s, to publish their views and campaign for improvements, equal treatment and civil rights. Groups of activists outside prison took up the struggle for those inside. The Coornhert-Liga named after Volkert Coornhert, a sixteenth century Dutch philosopher, reformer and political prisoner, was founded in June 1971 and became a major pressure group for criminal justice reform on a wide range of issues (Butting and Jorg 1983). Its campaigns have included issues such as deaths in custody. The Lawbreakers' Union (Bond voor Wetsovertreders) has also brought legal actions on behalf of prisoners and demands for prisoners' rights to the attention of the public and politicians as Franke notes (Franke 2007). This group is still active today. These campaigns resulted in improvements in prisoners' rights in a number of areas, including rights to visits and leave, and also led to changes in the Penitentiary Principles Act and accompanying regulations which govern prison law. Prisoners also received the right to vote in 1986 which is still being sought by prisoners in the UK and the USA. A handbook on prisoners' rights, the *Bajesbroe*, which provided practical information for prisoners was published in 1982.[3] Minimum Rules for prisons were introduced by the 1993 Penitentiary Principles Act which gave prisoners a new framework of rights and prohibition of any suffering beyond the deprivation of liberty. The Rules were modified by the 1998 Penitentiary Principles Act. Rights discourse has also influenced youth justice systems since the 1970s with enhanced rights in relation to appeals, complaints and disciplinary procedures (uit Beijerse and van Swaaningen 2007). Sentencers have a wide range of options set out in the Penal Code.

The Principles of Prison Administration Act 1953 (Beginselenwet Gevangeniswezen) made social reintegration the key principle governing prison regimes in the Netherlands. Activities should be provided to prepare the individual for his return to society. This principle of reintegration has been retained in the 1999 Penitentiary Principles Act which also emphasizes that the prisoner's liberty should not be limited more than is necessary for the purposes of imprisonment, or to keep good order in the prison (see uit Beijerse and van Swaaningen 2007). The legislation refers to prisoners' rights on a wide range of issues including access to work and activities, procedures for complaints and disciplinary matters, and access to visits and the use of single cell accommodation.

The Netherlands does not seem to have suffered the problems of riots and disorder found in the UK and neither does it have the problem of industrial disputes which the UK encountered in the 1980s. A major comparative study by Downes, *Contrasts in Tolerance*, studied the experience of prisoners in both regimes in the 1980s and included interviews with prisoners who had sampled both regimes, and found that the 'depth' of imprisonment was greater in the UK (Downes 1988), The humanity of the Dutch regime has often been attributed to Dutch traditions of tolerance, themselves rooted in the experience of the Nazi occupation and the fact that many Dutch citizens in the Dutch resistance were incarcerated during the War and so the experience of imprisonment went beyond 'common criminals' to otherwise law-abiding members of society, including the middle class and professionals who were later to take important roles in public life. While this is certainly the case, it is also true that imprisonment of resistance members and partisans occurred throughout occupied Europe but did not necessarily result in progressive penal regimes in the post-war period. However, the fact that over the last 30 years, some political leaders have also been former prisoners, most notably Nelson Mandela and Vaclav Havel, who have served their time alongside ordinary criminals, highlights the issue of imprisonment and the problems of drawing a sharp division between law-abiding citizens and common criminals. Both Mandela and Havel ordered the release of political prisoners when they came into power.

But in the Netherlands there has also been a tradition of tolerance and consensus rooted in the 'pillarization' of Dutch society (Downes 1988, Franke 2007). Within Dutch society there have been four distinct 'pillars' or blocs, Catholics, Protestants, liberals and socialists, but they have always worked cooperatively and who have been tolerant of each other and of differences in society. The Netherlands has also in the past, until relatively recently, welcomed migrants and provided a refuge or safe harbour for those in exile although as we saw in Chapter 1 this has now become strained. Tolerance in the penal context has also reflected the influence of Calvinism, and particularly the view that sinners can redeem their sins and are not beyond hope. The tolerance has also been reflected in the wider society in sexual libertarianism with a tolerance of prostitution and liberal policies on recreational drug use.

Within Dutch penal policy we find a range of theoretical approaches, a combination of desert theory with a strong commitment to proportionality but also a focus on utilitarian objectives of deterrence and rehabilitation and a commitment to indeterminate sentences particularly in the use of psychological punishments. Prosecutors have the power to divert cases from the criminal justice system and to waive prosecutions. The relatively small size of the Netherlands, has also made it easier to facilitate frequent contact between judges and prosecutors and political leaders, Ministers of Justice and policy makers.

All these influences have however become strained in recent years so the positive view Downes and others paint of Dutch society is more appropriate to the past than the present time. The political and social context has also changed with secularization, a decline in tolerance, and increased concern over crime and this has been overlaid by the impact of terrorism and anxieties over immigration as we saw in Chapter 1. When Downes conducted his study there were concerns in some parts of Dutch society that prosecutors had too much discretion to waive prosecutions and that prisons were too indulgent, although the conditions in Vught have subsequently been criticized by the European Committee for the Prevention of Torture (CPT) and the European Court of Human Rights.

There has also been an increase in the detention of aliens, illegal immigrants, asylum seekers, and migrants with expired visas. These are held in detention centres with fewer facilities and no fixed terms, no work or other programmes and problems of contact with outside world (see van Kalmthout 2007). Concerns over immigration have also led to increased deportations. Both immigration policy and penal policy have become more stringent. Ethnic minorities form a larger number of prisoners. The Netherlands has been subject to pressure from other European countries to be tougher on drug crimes. There has been increased public concern over dangerous offenders following a policy decarcerating the mentally ill into the community and some high-profile attacks by mentally ill offenders. These fears were exacerbated by the escape of a violent sex offender who killed his victim. This has mobilized individuals to participate in 'white marches' – silent marches protesting against violence. The White Marches were expressions of public concern and anger over violent crime. They were held first in Belgium in 1996 in the wake of the Marc Dutroux case. Dutroux had murdered, abused and abducted young girls in 1996. These were followed in 1997 by silent marches in the Netherlands following the murder of Joes Kloppenburg and in 1998, 30,000 people marched in Gorinchem following a shooting (see Boutellier 2004).

Conclusions

While Dutch tolerance has been increasingly strained this has not resulted in a contraction of prisoners' rights and rights are still well established within the Dutch prison system. However, in the USA and the UK, the courts have always tried to reconcile prisoners' demands for rights with institutional needs. So while prisoners' claims were advanced by public law in the UK in the 1980s, by the 1990s the focus in the prison service was on the new managerialism rather than the evolution of rights. Nevertheless, this 'rights gap' in English law was filled to some extent by the European Convention and international rights standards as we shall see in Chapter 3. Prisoners had used the European Convention to assert prisoners' rights in the 1980s when one of the most pressing issues for prisoners was a failure to respond to grievances and a refusal to inform prisoners of the reasons for decisions which affected them, but the use of Convention rights to advance prisoners' claims has expanded in recent years. The courts have become more active in imposing liability on public bodies and since the Human Rights Act 1998 are more likely to demand compensation from public bodies for non-compliance, whereas in the past, they have taken the view that if public bodies were liable in damages this would distract them from making decisions in the public interest.[4]

3 The increasing importance of international human rights law and standards

Introduction

International human rights law and standards have become increasingly important within the European context as prison regimes are subjected to more intense scrutiny by the courts. These international law obligations impose duties on states to provide a humane regime. So prison authorities have to justify their policies and procedures against these human rights standards. These human rights instruments include the United Declaration of Human Rights (UNDHR), the International Covenant on Civil and Political Rights (ICCPR), the European Convention on Human Rights (ECHR), the findings of the European Committee on the Prevention of Torture (CPT) and the European Prison Rules (EPR). Prisoners' rights are also international in a broader sense as the reputation of a state on the international stage will be judged in part by its treatment of prisoners and when foreign prisoners are detained, the attention of the international community will be focused more closely on prison standards. Within international human rights law and particularly European Convention jurisprudence, we find a strong foundation for prisoners' rights, although some of these rights may be qualified. However, the prohibition against torture in international human rights law allows for no exceptions or derogations and is a general binding principle, *jus cogens*, which applies to states irrespective of whether they have ratified a particular treaty.

The development of these international standards on detention is a dynamic ongoing process and has contributed to the improved standards of detention within prison and pre-trial at the police station. As more states have joined the Council of Europe, their prison regimes have been brought under the scrutiny of the European Committee for the Prevention of Torture and the European Court of Human Rights. However, the impact of international human rights law may vary according to local and national traditions, the financial resources of states and the national and local awareness of human rights issues. But while some of the human rights treaties have been incorporated into domestic law, not all their provisions are binding on states parties and there may be problems of implementation and enforcement of formal rights. The use of torture by states around the world is widespread as documented by groups such as Amnesty International and Human Rights Watch, despite formal acceptance by those states of the prohibition on torture and the status of the prohibition. As well as the practice of torture, there is also considerable variation worldwide in prison conditions. Some states have very harsh conditions and do not comply with the most basic minimum standards, some states formally accept rights but do not implement them, through lack of political will, insufficient resources or the appropriate organizational infrastructure. There is also the problem that if visits are conducted periodically and at selected institutions, these correctional facilities may be 'upgraded' for the purpose of the visit, but these conditions may not be representative of the state's penal regime.

Within some European states we find the most highly developed system of prisoners' rights, including monitoring and inspection, in the world; the view that prison should be used as a last resort, which should be imposed only in accordance with law and not arbitrarily; and increasingly, the view that the deprivation of liberty is sufficient punishment and the subordination of the principle of less eligibility to the principle of normalization, that is, the principle that prison life should be as close as possible to positive aspects of life outside.

Within European jurisdictions, Convention jurisprudence has played a more important role in recent years and in many respects functions as a Prisoners' Rights Charter, with the result that European Standards are now seen as the most advanced in the field of imprisonment. However, as we shall see, there still remain a number of significant problems. In recent years international human rights instruments have been used in the UK with some success to strengthen and extend the rights of prisoners, for example, in relation to issues such as disciplinary hearings, family life and health care. For UK prisoners, the European Convention on Human Rights which is now incorporated into domestic law following the Human Rights Act 1998, is the most important source of rights. The impact of the Convention in the specific areas of prison conditions, procedural justice and contact with the outside world will be considered in Chapters 4, 5 and 6. The impact of the HRA is wide-ranging insofar as it has firmly grounded a rights-based culture in the domestic courts. In the past, Convention rights sometimes met with a lukewarm reception within the domestic courts, but now legislation will be assessed for compatibility with the Convention, and the Courts have approached this task robustly in many areas of law. So prisoners have succeeded in many cases in bringing claims in the domestic courts which have led to changes in prison practice. Moreover, the establishment of a new Commission for Equality and Human Rights by the Equality Act 2006, which has taken over the work of the former Equality Commissions, the Commission for Racial Equality and the Equal Opportunities Commission, has strengthened the rights culture as it also has a responsibility to promote the protection of human rights and the Equality Act 2010 has increased the scope and requirements for positive action (see Chapter 7). In this climate rights claims have become more common and more effective for prisoners. Within prisons, there is now much greater awareness on the part of prisoners and officers of the rights implications of decisions and policies. All prisoners in England and Wales receive a booklet explaining their rights under the Act and the Convention on entry into prison. All primary and delegated legislation must be Convention compliant.

In the UK, the less eligibility principle which has been an essential element of imprisonment here for centuries, is now being 'brought to heel' by rights claims, tempered by the European Convention on Human Rights and the Human Rights Act and a new culture of rights which has grown up with the Act. Existing rights under the Convention have become more strongly entrenched and acknowledged by the courts. But notwithstanding the advances secured by these campaigns, it is important to be aware of the limitations of the Convention and other international rights instruments. The history of prisoners' rights is paved with failure as well as success. In the 1970s advances were made in areas such as access to correspondence and procedural protections, but until recently, challenges in relation to living conditions were less successful. In the UK there is an expanding body of penal law drawn from international rights standards. The significance of these sources will be considered.

The United Nations Declaration of Human Rights

The United Nations Declaration of Human Rights adopted in 1948 provides protection against abusive treatment in detention before or after conviction. The most relevant provision for prisoners is Article 5 which prohibits the use of torture and cruel, inhuman or degrading treatment and punishment. This is also the source of Article 3 of the European Convention which is also expressed in domestic law on police detention in s 76 of PACE and Article 4 of the European Union Charter of Fundamental Rights (2000/c 364/01) and Article 7 of the International Covenant of Civil and Political Rights. The UNDHR, like the European Convention, was shaped by the experiences of war, and fascism, occupation and internment in European states, although of course it now encompasses a vast range of states, political regimes and prison systems.

The United Nations has been an important source of prison policy and standards worldwide. International prison standards developed in the interwar years. The League of Nations, the forerunner to the UN, and the International Penitentiary Congress in 1925 did try to establish minimum rules before the Second World War. Minimum Rules for prisons were published by the League of Nations in 1929 and accepted in 1934. But of course this does guarantee that states will adopt or implement them. The UN published its Standard Minimum Rules for the Treatment of Prisoners (SMR) in 1955. These Rules were drafted and adopted by the First United Nations Congress on the Prevention of Crime and the Treatment of Offenders, held in Geneva in 1955, and approved by Economic and Social Council Resolutions in 1957 and 1977.[1] These Rules were the model for the European Prison Rules adopted by the Council of Europe, and contain very detailed provisions on a range of areas of prison life, including disciplinary offences, complaints procedures, the treatment of mentally ill prisoners, remand prisoners and segregation. Neither the Standard Minimum Rules nor the European Prison Rules are formally binding on states. But the UN General Assembly has said that these rules should be taken into account when interpreting Article 10 of the International Covenant on Civil and Political Rights and the Standard Minimum Rules have been used to interpret the UN Convention against Torture.

The International Covenant on Civil and Political Rights

The International Covenant on Civil and Political Rights (ICCPR) was adopted in 1966 and came into force in 1976, and has been an important source of prison standards. The key provisions relevant to imprisonment are Article 6, the right to life, which has implications for deaths in custody and specifically the failure to protect prisoners from other prisoners. If a prison authority is aware of a risk to prisoners it should act on that risk. It is also relevant to the control of prisoners particularly in riot or escape situations, so the use of force should be proportionate. Article 7 prohibits the use of torture, cruel, inhuman or degrading treatment or punishment. Article 9 protects the right to personal liberty, so the individual should not be subject to arbitrary or unlawful detention. Article 14 protects the right to a fair trial and Article 17 protects the individual from unlawful or arbitrary interference with his family, privacy, home or correspondence, which clearly has implications for issues such as prisoners' visits and contact with the outside world.

But the most important right for prisoners is Article 10, aimed specifically at detainees, which requires that those deprived of their liberty be treated 'with humanity and with respect for the inherent dignity of the human person', that the penal system should aim at the reformation and rehabilitation of prisoners, that convicted and remand prisoners should be confined and treated separately, and juveniles should be separated from adults and treated according to their juvenile status. It imposes a positive duty on states to treat prisoners appropriately and to prohibit treatment which fails to treat prisoners with respect for their dignity. Article 10 is also significant because it refers to rehabilitation. As with any rights instrument, these key terms are subject to argument and interpretation and have been applied to a wide range of prison regimes.

Article 28 of the ICCPR sets up the UN Human Rights Committee to oversee the implementation of the Covenant. States are obliged to submit Reports to the Committee who can also request reports from states if there are concerns, and individuals can go to the Committee if they have exhausted internal remedies. The Committee reports back to states parties and makes appropriate recommendations. States can also bring complaints against other states to the Committee for breaches of the Covenant.

However, very few prisoner cases have been brought worldwide and none within Europe, as European prisoners are able to use the European Convention on Human Rights to assert their rights claims. Moreover, some states, including the United States, have ratified the Covenant but with reservations. Prisoner cases referred to the Human Rights Committee under the ICCPR include cases relating to the alleged torture of prisoners in Tajikistan see *Sharifova et al v Tajikistan* 1209/2003 (2007, 1231/2003 (2008), 1241/2004 (2008).[2] Cases have also been brought against Turkey and Uruguay.

The Human Rights Committee has developed its jurisprudence interpreting these key Articles, but its decisions on individual complaints and its Reports are not legally binding on states parties. There is also jurisprudence on conditions in prison, including overcrowding and poor sanitation, from cases referred to the Committee.

The UN Convention against Torture

The UN Convention against Torture was adopted by the UN General Assembly in 1984 and came into force in 1987. Its aim is to prevent torture by obliging states to take measures to prevent torture and to punish those who commit torture. It makes torture an extraditable offence and also prohibits the extradition of individuals to states where they may be tortured. It gives states universal jurisdiction to hear allegations of torture where individuals cannot be extradited. Torture is defined in Article 1 of the Convention: as an act by which severe pain or suffering, whether physical or mental, is intentionally inflicted on a person in order to obtain information or to punish him, by a public official or other person acting in an official capacity. The UN Committee against Torture (CAT) was set up in 1988 to supervise and ensure the compliance of states parties with the Convention and it is intended to have a preventative role. It meets regularly, publishes annual reports, conducts visits and makes recommendations to states in the light of its findings. States can bring complaints against other states and individuals can bring complaints to the Committee. States are obliged to provide remedies including damages.

A case was brought under the Convention Against Torture by a prisoner in Australia challenging his extradition to the United States but it did not succeed. In *L.J.R. v Australia* 316/2007 (10 November 2008) the prisoner argued that his extradition would breach Article 3 of the Convention against Torture because in the USA he would be tortured, placed in solitary confinement, sentenced to death and probably be held on death row for a long period. The Committee stated that it was aware of reports of brutality and excessive force in US prisons and sexual violence, although measures to address these have been implemented. But it found no specific evidence relating to his ill-treatment if extradited and concluded that extradition would not breach

Article 3 of the Convention. The Committee had received assurances from the USA that the death penalty would not be sought and could find no evidence he would be subject to torture, if placed in an American prison or would be at particular risk of contracting HIV. The prisoner had also complained that he had been ill-treated in the Australian prison system, but the Committee found no evidence to support this. A case was also brought to the Committee under the Convention concerning the deportation of a Turkish national from the Netherlands in *S.G. v the Netherlands* 135/1999 (12 May 2004) but the Committee ruled that the risk of torture must be foreseeable, real and personal and did not accept that there was such a risk in this case.

The Committee in its Concluding Observations on the Second Report submitted by Turkey, has expressed concern over continuing allegations of the use of torture, the failure to prosecute or punish torturers and the death of prisoners resulting from hunger strikes (CAT 2003). The Third Report from Turkey was submitted in 2010 but the Concluding Observations of the Committee have not yet been published. The Committee in its Concluding Observations on the Second Report of the United States in 2006 expressed concern over the use of secret detention facilities and criticized the view of the USA that the Convention was not applicable at times of armed conflict, and recommended the closure of Guantanamo Bay (CAT 2006: para 22).

Although prisoners in Europe may bring complaints about their treatment under UNCAT or the ICCPR, they are more likely to bring a complaint under the European Convention as this is more likely to result in change in penal practice as well as financial compensation. A new Optional Protocol to the UN Convention against Torture adopted by the General Assembly in 2002 contains provisions for annual international inspection and systems of national monitoring. Although some European states have ratified this Protocol, reviews are already conducted by the European Committee for the Prevention against Torture, so it is unclear whether these visits would occur as part of that review process, or separately, or whether new independent bodies to conduct reviews would be established. Within the European penal context, the European Prison Rules, the Reports of the European Committee for the Prevention of Torture and Inhuman or Degrading Treatment or Punishment and the European Convention on Human Rights already play a key role in guiding and improving prison standards.

The European Prison Rules

The European Prison Rules (EPR) seek to apply international standards on imprisonment to the treatment of prisoners in the penal institutions of the states' parties who have adopted them, rather than referring specifically to rights. The Rules were based originally on the UN Standard Minimum Rules published in 1955 and first adopted by the Committee of Ministers of the Council of Europe in 1973. These European Standard Minimum Rules for prisoners were replaced by the European Prison Rules in 1987 and these new

Rules gave more emphasis to respect for human dignity. They were revised again in January 2006, with new provisions for remand prisoners. The changes in the Rules reflect the jurisprudence of the European Court of Human Rights, as well as the work of the European Committee for the Prevention of Torture (CPT). The Rules overlap with the standards applied and developed by the CPT.

The latest European Prison Rules adopted by the Committee of Ministers of the Council of Europe in 2006 set out basic principles, recommendations and requirements of good practice to govern the treatment of prisoners in states which have adopted them.[3] These Rules apply to public and private prisons within member states. The Rules are not binding but merely 'soft' law so states cannot be compelled to comply. Most European states, including the UK, have adopted them and they have been an important means of assessing conditions in the Netherlands and Germany. As de Jonge notes, while at best they currently exert moral pressure, they do provide a means of assessing prison systems on a wide range of issues and if they were implemented fully, they would have a significant effect on penal practice (de Jonge 2007). They may also be used as part of staff training. However, prisoners can also rely on the 'hard law' of the Convention and its binding decisions and judgments, which sets limits on what are acceptable standards and policies in the context of detention. Prisoners have cited the rules in support of their claims brought under the European Convention although usually the Court will focus primarily on Convention rights rather than the standards in the Rules.

The first six Rules set out the basic principles governing imprisonment. EPR 1 states: 'All persons deprived of their liberty shall be treated with respect for their human rights.' The starting point here is that prisoners do retain their human rights beyond the prison door. EPR 2 states: 'Persons deprived of their liberty retain all rights that are not lawfully taken away by the decision sentencing them or remanding them in custody.' The implication here is that any detention has to be justified and lawful and undertaken by the appropriate body and that prisoners retain all rights that are not taken away by the fact of imprisonment and this is a similar approach to the English courts in *Raymond v Honey* [1983] 1 AC 1. But Rules 3, 4, 5 and 6 go further. EPR 3 states: 'Restrictions placed on persons deprived of their liberty shall be the minimum necessary and proportionate to the legitimate objective for which they are imposed.' Restraints on prisoners should not go beyond what is necessary to achieve security and the purposes of imprisonment. EPR 4 states a key principle namely that 'Prison conditions that infringe prisoners' human rights are not justified by lack of resources.' This is clearly very important and has implications for issues such as overcrowding and access to courses. The inadequacy of resources as a justification has also been challenged by the Strasbourg Court. EPR 5 states the basic principle of normalization: 'Life in prison shall approximate as closely as possible the positive aspects of life in the community.' So apart from the inevitable loss of liberty, then prison life should still be as close as possible to normal life, so this would have implications for issues such as visits, access to newspapers and participation in the political process, including voting rights, as well as access to work and recreation, although this may of course conflict with the less eligibility principle (see Chapters 4 and 8). EPR 6 states: 'All detention shall be managed so as to facilitate the reintegration into free society of persons who have been deprived of their liberty.' This has implications for the provision of courses which address offending behaviour, as well as for provisions of skills and has implications for the right to rehabilitation. These basic provisions clearly have implications for cuts in prison budgets, overcrowding and the broad spectrum of prison conditions which will be discussed in more detail in Chapters 4–7 below). These general rules make clear the principles on which regimes should be organized.

Similarly EPR 102.1 stresses that 'the regime for sentenced prisoners shall be designed to enable them to lead a responsible and crime-free life'. EPR 102.2 makes clear that prison is the punishment and prisoners should not receive further punishments: 'Imprisonment is by the deprivation of liberty a punishment in itself and therefore the regime for sentenced prisoners shall not aggravate the suffering inherent in imprisonment.'

However the Rules also cover a number of very specific areas central to prison life including medical care, access to resources and physical conditions. They prohibit corporal punishment, inhuman and degrading punishment for disciplinary offences and they stipulate that prisoners should be permitted to communicate with their families and friends (EPR 60.3, EPR 24.1). Other provisions include the requirement for inspection and monitoring, the separation of children and adult prisoners, and the provision of appropriate facilities for persons detained through mental illness (EPR 92, 93.1, 11.1, 47.1, 47.2.) There are also provisions relating to health care and a stipulation that prisoners shall not be subjected to any experiments without their consent (EPR 39, 40, 48.1). Sentence plans should be formulated for sentenced prisoners and these plans should be regularly reviewed. In addition there are specific rules relating to the treatment of remand prisoners (EPR 94–101). For example, the rules also stipulate that remand prisoners should be allowed to wear their own clothes (EPR 97.1), should have access to facilities to prepare their case for trial (EPR 98.2) and be offered work but are not required to work (EPR 100.1).

The European Committee for the Prevention of Torture

The European Convention on the Prevention of Torture and Inhuman or Degrading Treatment or Punishment, was adopted in 1987 by the Committee of Ministers of the Council of Europe and came into effect in 1989. The Convention sets clear limits on what is acceptable in prison regimes. It established a Committee to conduct visits and publish standards for the treatment of those in detention, including prisons, police stations, immigration centres and psychiatric hospitals.[4] Its mandate is set out in Article 1 of the Convention: 'The Committee shall, by means of visits, examine the treatment of persons deprived of their liberty with a view to strengthening, if necessary, the protection of such persons from torture and from inhuman or degrading treatment or punishment.' The act of depriving a person of their liberty means that there is a correlative duty to safeguard their physical and psychological welfare until they are released. While the European Prison Rules are general rules, the CPT Reports are much more specific, highlighting problems within states and making appropriate recommendations.

The Committee visits member states periodically and issues Reports on the basis of these visits as well as making ad hoc visits if there are particular concerns. As well as Reports on specific states based on its visits, it also publishes annual General Reports and the result of its Reports and Reviews is the publication of a Code of Standards for detention which is then used as a benchmark when it visits member states of the Council of Europe. These detention standards cover a wide range of issues, including health care, the treatment of women, juveniles and foreign nationals. The standards on prisons cover access to fresh air and light, to work, education, medical services, access to the outside world, as well as issues of safety, staff–inmate relations and grievance and inspection procedures. By the end of April 2010, the CPT had conducted 284 visits, which consisted of 171 periodic visits and 113 ad hoc visits, and published 236 Reports. The emphasis in recent Reports has been on prison overcrowding which it sees as amounting to inhuman and degrading treatment.

The Committee's role is to review the treatment of prisoners to strengthen their protection from torture, inhuman or degrading treatment or punishment. The Convention on Torture and the European Convention on Human Rights are intended to supplement each other, as the former is preventive, to prevent torture and to improve standards of detention, while the latter is adjudicative, dealing with individual complaints. Unlike the European Court of Human Rights, the CPT does not have a judicial function and its recommendations are not binding on states. Nevertheless, the Reports and comments on particular states provide some jurisprudence on the Committee's understanding of torture, inhuman and degrading treatment.

However, as the number of states of Council of Europe has expanded to the current figure of 47, it means that there are pressures on resources and the initial aim of four yearly visits is difficult to maintain.[5] The CPT's approach has been described by Evans and Morgan as a 'variable geometry' approach, in the sense that the it formulating and seeking to apply a common standard, but whether it is achieved will depend on local and national resources (Evans and Morgan 1999). Pressure from the Committee may exert some pressure on prison authorities to modify their regimes but in practice the minimum that may be achieved is prevention of torture rather than good-quality prison regimes, so these standards may in the prison context remain largely aspirational. Some of the states it visits cover vast territories. For example, the

Russian Federation which joined the Council of Europe in 1996 has the second highest incarceration rate in the world at 585 per 100,000 of population and contains a huge number of prisoners and extensive prison estate (ICPS 2010). As Piacentini (2004) has shown, Russian prisoners are held in poor physical conditions, but also suffer from poor health and have high rates of self-harm. While membership of the Council of Europe increases pressure on states with the poorest conditions and extreme punishments to improve their penal regimes, this may be difficult to enforce. Periodic Visits and the subsequent Reports will inevitably be selective as only a small sample of the facilities will be visited. It is also dealing with a broad range of states in terms of what is seen as acceptable treatment and in terms of the amount of financial resources available for improving places of detention. It has found the use of torture, the deliberate infliction of pain, usually by the police, widespread in Turkey, where detainees have been subjected to the use of electric shocks and beating of the soles of the feet, and treatment amounting to torture and inhuman and degrading treatment in Bulgarian prisons. The CPT has treated torture and inhuman and degrading treatment as distinct forms of ill-treatment, whereas within the European Convention jurisprudence they are seen as lying on a continuum, although it may be difficult to find the exact point of transition. The Committee has also become increasingly concerned with overcrowding and medical care.

UK prisons, like other prisons in Europe, have also been inspected by the CPT. Its Report was critical of the conditions in English prisons, specifically Leeds, Wandsworth and Brixton on its visit in 1990 (Council of Europe 1991). It concluded that the cumulative effect of overcrowding and slopping out meant that the conditions amounted to inhuman and degrading punishment. But the UK Government rejected this assessment of conditions. It acknowledged that the conditions were poor, but argued that they were not so poor that they could be described as inhuman and degrading. The CPT's visit was undertaken just after the riots and included Holloway and Bullwood Hall although it did not visit the 'rioting' prisons. The impact of the CPT Report was overshadowed by the Woolf Report, but it nonetheless provided corroboration of the poor conditions and added to the impetus for change (Woolf and Tumim 1991).

But, as Shaw notes, the CPT covered two issues not raised by Woolf, the use of body belts as restraints which the CPT saw as potentially dangerous and recommended ending their use and the treatment of mentally disturbed violent prisoners in Brixton's F wing (Shaw 1999). The CPT Report observed that the prison did not have the appropriate resources to deal with these prisoners who had an adverse effect on the prison as a whole (Council of Europe 1991: para 59). Its Report strengthened the case for closure and the wing was subsequently closed.

Subsequent UK visits have included an ad hoc visit to Northern Ireland holding centres for individuals detained under the Prevention of Terrorism Act which was critical of the failure to record interviews and psychological ill-treatment. The Report following the second Periodic Visit to the UK in 1994, which included police stations and immigration centres as well as prisons and Rampton special hospital, was critical of treatment of those detained in police stations in Liverpool and of the detention of prisoners in police cells because of overcrowding. It recommended ending this practice and the Government did stop this in five instances but this has resumed at times of severe overcrowding. This visit also included a return to Leeds and Wandsworth prisons where it was found that conditions had improved, but there were still problems regarding sanitation, overcrowding and provision of activities. The Committee was concerned at the increase in prison numbers and its implications for the quality of prison regimes. The most recent Report, based on its visit in late 2008, focused principally on overcrowding in adult prisons, and expressed concerns over plans for larger prisons, the treatment of indeterminate public protection (IPP) sentenced prisoners and conditions in Young Offender Institutions (Council of Europe 2009).

Shaw argues that the CPT's impact in the UK has been less significant because of the existence of other modes of inspection and monitoring available in the UK and given the gap between visits (1999). However, because of its emphasis on day-to-day prison life, it can offer a more practical approach than the European Convention and produces very specific recommendations. This is important because there are relatively few cases brought by detainees under Article 3 of the European Convention compared to the extent of the problems highlighted by the Committee's Reports across Europe. The CPT Reports can also focus on quite specific practices which may not be brought to the attention of the Strasbourg Court in the absence of a specific complaint. They also focus on the general conditions affecting large numbers of detainees and have expressed concern over the psychological effects of imprisonment.

Whether the CPT's recommendations are implemented will depend on how far governments are committed to human rights or how deeply entrenched they are within the legal culture of member states, so clearly the CPT will have the most impact where governments are receptive, such as the Netherlands. The CPT first visited the Netherlands in 1992 and published its Report in 1993 (Council of Europe, 1993). It has made further regular periodic visits since then. As might be expected, given the Netherlands' reputation on prison conditions, there were no examples of inhuman or degrading treatment found within Dutch domestic prisons. But concerns have been raised over prisoners being detained in police cells and access to lawyers while detained by the police. Concerns were also raised over the use of handcuffs in high security units on both visits, but this did not reach the level of inhumane treatment. There have also been concerns over the isolation of those detained under terrorist legislation.

Because the Dutch government has been supportive of the CPT's aims, it has implemented its recommendations and has also approached it for guidance on the implementation of its standards when introducing new prison accommodation (van Reenan 1999). Some of its recommendations, for example on complaints procedures, have also been referred to in the decisions of the Dutch Prison Appeal Board.

It has also visited the Dutch overseas territories of the Netherlands Antilles and Aruba since 1994. The most recent visit was in 2007 (see Council of Europe 2008) which was critical of poor physical conditions in the Netherlands Antilles, including dilapidated accommodation, overcrowding and health care issues.

The European Convention on Human Rights

Within Europe, the Convention has been the key source of the developing prison law. The European Convention on Human Rights came into force in 1953, although there were relatively few prisoner cases until the mid-1980s. Because of the cumbersome admissibility procedures conducted by the European Commission in the past, many cases were screened out early on and the time scale made it impracticable for shorter serving prisoners. The Commission earned a reputation for conservatism in ruling prisoners' claims inadmissible and when applications did reach the Court, the Commission and the Court sometimes took different positions.[6] The Commission was abolished in 1999. Moreover, even when cases passed this hurdle of admissibility and reached the Court, it was often reluctant to uphold claims relating to prisoners' conditions unless they were very harsh, but more willing to acknowledge procedural rights and sometimes seemed to take a hands-off approach similar to that found in the USA and UK's domestic courts. However, over the last decade, the Court has become more interventionist and critical of prison regimes and has scrutinized very closely rights' infringements, applying the principle of proportionality robustly, examining whether the infringements meet legitimate aims and whether they are necessary or could be achieved by less restrictive means. This proportionality test is similar to the approach already well established in public law, in for example, *R v Secretary of State for the Home Department ex parte Leech (No.2)* [1994] QB 198, where the Court of Appeal referred to limiting rights only where the need was pressing and by the minimum necessary to meet that need.

The Strasbourg Court is now less willing to accept rights infringements on public interest, security or cost grounds. The Court's scrutiny provides a further oversight of the operation of the prison system and means that international human rights standards are being brought to bear more closely on the practice of punishment. It is clear from the Convention jurisprudence that prisoners retain rights despite imprisonment and the extent of punishment should be the loss of liberty rather than further humiliations inside prison. The rights prisoners have under the Convention follow them into prison, although the scope of these rights may be limited by the prison context. Because of the limitations of public and private law, the European Convention has for long been viewed positively by prisoners as a means of dealing with their grievances, but with the enactment of the Human Rights Act, its value and use has increased further.

Although in the past, the Court has resisted prisoners' claims in favour of prison security and public interest considerations, it is true to say that recently the Strasbourg Court's tolerance of poor prison conditions has decreased, so Article 3 has been used increasingly in relation to substantive conditions of treatment, principally the right to a minimum standard of living within prison, which also could be interpreted as evidence of a move towards recognition of social rights. While the notion of rights within the Convention is individualistic, encompassing primarily civil and political rights, rather than social rights, in contrast to the European Social Charter, in recent years the Court has tried to impose positive obligations on states to provide a minimum standard of living in relation to prisoners and other groups which reflects a greater willingness to read social rights into the Convention.

With the enactment of the Human Rights Act, the potential to rely on Convention rights relevant to the context of imprisonment is greatly enhanced. The protection of the Human Rights Act and the rights under the Convention has also been extended to those prisoners held in prisons under the control of British forces in Southern Iraq in *Al-Skeini and others v Secretary of State for Defence* [2007] UKHL 26, a decision welcomed by civil rights lawyers and human rights campaigners.

When the HRA was passed in 1998, the official view was that the prison regime was Convention compliant. It was clear that the government would defend any infringements by arguing that they were necessary for the smooth running of the prison which given the tenor of past Convention jurisprudence, was a reasonable assumption. But at the same time there was optimism on the part of prison reformers and campaigners, that there would be more scope for rights claims and, as we shall see, there have been several successful challenges since then and in fact the success of these claims has arguably contributed to the backlash against the Human Rights Act.

The Strasbourg Court has stressed that the European Convention is a 'living document' which can take account of changing conditions and expectations. In this respect it resembles the Bill of Rights in the US Constitution. But each may evolve in a different direction, reflecting its own social and political context. Both rights instruments face the problem of protecting rights, both are potentially limited by the qualifications and narrow interpretations and by countervailing arguments, which give more weight to the public interest and to the administrative needs of prison regimes. The Court has had to adapt its reading of the Convention to twenty-first century conditions, at a time of political, economic and constitutional changes in Europe, and has also faced a considerable rise in its workload because of an increase in Convention challenges (Greer 2006).

Both the Strasbourg Court and the US Supreme Court have acted to uphold prison standards, although this commitment has varied depending on the political climate. But while the Supreme Court's concern to subject prison life to judicial scrutiny was stronger in the 1960s than the 1980s and 1990s, as we saw in Chapter 2, for the Strasbourg Court, the reverse was the case. There has been increasing scrutiny of prison life and activism on the part of the Strasbourg Court in the past decade and less toleration of inadequate prison conditions, expressed in a greater willingness to find breaches of Articles 2, 3, 5 and 6.[7] The Court has also become more critical of appeals to public opinion as a reason for limiting rights[8] and rejected blanket limitations on rights which do not assess properly the situation of individual prisoners.

Although offenders inevitably lose their right to liberty on incarceration, they enjoy the protection of all the rights under the Convention but clearly the key Articles for prisoners are Articles 2, 3, 5, 8, 9, 10 and 12. The implications of these rights for prisoners will be considered in more detail in subsequent chapters but will be highlighted here. The right to life, protected by Article 2, has been especially important to prisoners, including those imprisoned abroad. States are obliged to do all that could reasonably be expected to avoid an immediate risk to life of which they are or should be aware.[9]

There are no specific or explicit provisions on prison conditions in the European Convention but Article 3, which prohibits torture, inhuman or degrading treatment or punishment, is clearly the most relevant provision so prisoners have the right not to be subjected to such treatment or punishment. Moreover the right under Article 3 is absolute, so breaches cannot be justified even in times of war and public emergency and competing state interests cannot be balanced against the right. The Court made clear in *A and others v UK*, Application No. 3455/05 (19 February 2009) that even when states face the threat of terrorist violence, torture and inhuman and degrading treatment or punishment are not acceptable. Article 3 also has implications for extreme overcrowding, as this may constitute degrading treatment if it is excessive, as well as for conditions in segregation and full body searching. In the UK prisoners have brought Article 3 claims on a wide range of issues, including the failure to provide appropriate medical care.

Although prisoners inevitably lose their right to liberty by the fact of incarceration, they retain the right to challenge their detention in certain circumstances, under Article 5, which states that everyone deprived of his liberty by arrest or detention is entitled to take proceedings to challenge the lawfulness of detention and to do so speedily. So this has been used by prisoners to challenge the lawfulness of their detention and to limit the intervention of the Secretary of State in sentencing and release decisions, and to strengthen the procedural rights of prisoners. It has also been used to challenge detention in psychiatric hospitals. The ECHR has also had an impact in relation to the reading of letters, access to lawyers, and to challenges to the continuing detention of discretionary lifers and mentally disordered offenders. Many of the issues raised by the Woolf Report related to the processing of grievances and the conduct and impact of disciplinary hearings, an area where there was an established Convention jurisprudence on Article 6, the right to a fair trial. Article 6 has been used by prisoners with some success to deal with deficiencies in disciplinary proceedings and to secure their right of access to the courts (see Chapter 5). Although the right is not qualified, limitations may be implied into it, but they will be assessed on the principle of proportionality.

Article 8, the right to respect for the individual's private and family life, home and correspondence, has also been successfully used by prisoners to challenge transfers, restrictions on prison visits and without success, to challenge the denial of conjugal visits. These issues will be considered in Chapter 6. However, the qualifications in Article 8(2), which allow infringements in the interest of national security, public safety, the prevention of disorder or crime, the protection of health or morals, or the protection of the rights and freedoms of others, may limit its usefulness for prisoners. Prisoners have also used Article 9, their right to freedom of religion, and Article 10, the right to freedom of expression, although again restrictions are permitted under Articles 9(2) and 10(2).[10] However, the state will need to be able to justify limits on the freedom of expression. Article 10 has implications for censorship of prisoners' speech and their access to the media. Article 12, which protects the right to marry and found a family has also been used by prisoners to obtain temporary release to marry and for access to artificial insemination.[11] The issues raised by the jurisprudence on Articles 8, 9, 10 and 12 will be considered in more detail in Chapters 6 and 7.

Article 13, the right to an effective remedy when a Convention right is violated by a national authority, has also been used by prisoners. In *Keenan v UK* Application No. 27229/95 (3 April 2001), the Court held that the lack of a remedy to the parents whose son had committed suicide in prison constituted a breach of Article 13. The Strasbourg Court also found a breach of Article 13 in *McGlinchey v UK* Application No. 50390/99 (29 April 2003). Article 14, the right not to be subject to discrimination also has implications for the equal treatment of female and ethnic minority prisoners, foreign national prisoners, and those detained under immigration law and prisoners with disabilities, and will be considered in Chapter 7. The obligation on states to hold free elections under conditions which will ensure the free expression of the people in the choice of the legislature, stipulated in Article 3 of Protocol No. 1 as also been used to successfully challenge the loss of voting rights for convicted prisoners in *Hirst v UK* (*No. 2*) Application No. 74025/01 (6 October 2005) as we shall see in Chapter 8.

In the Netherlands there have been fewer prisoner cases brought under the Convention but the conditions in Dutch prison in many respects have exceeded international standards. For example, the Netherlands wanted independent inspection included in the European Prison Rules in 1973, but this was rejected at the time although it is now included. However, the Court has been critical of routine strip-searching in a high security prison in *van der Ven v the Netherlands* and *Lorse v the Netherlands* Application Nos. 50501/99, 52750/99 (4 February 2003) and the failure to transfer prisoners to a psychiatric prison in *Morsink v the Netherlands, Brand v the Netherlands*

Application Nos. 48865/99, 49902/99 (11 May 2004). To comply with the Court's judgments the Dutch Parliament has made relevant changes and the Strasbourg decisions in these cases have been cited in the decisions of the Prison Appeal Board. In the Netherlands prisoners have become increasingly aware of international standards. Like the CPT, the Court has been critical of the regimes in Dutch overseas territories, for example, in Curaçao, in *AB v the Netherlands* (2003) 37 EHRR 48.

However, the advances made by prisoners and other claimants has contributed to a backlash against the Convention and the Human Rights Act in the UK. The Act has been seen as a source of unmeritorious claims, inhibiting the work of prison authorities by the Government, the Opposition and by some sections of the press and the public. One issue which has aroused particularly negative comment has been the fact that damages have been paid to prisoners. If a breach of a Convention right has been proven, then the applicant is entitled to 'just satisfaction' under Article 41 of the Convention. However, this does not necessarily mean financial compensation will be paid. In *Ocalan v Turkey* Application No. 46221/99 (12 May 2005), where the Court found violations of Articles 3, 5 and 6, it deemed its finding of these breaches as sufficient to provide just satisfaction and paid only the costs and expenses for Ocalan's lawyers. Similarly in *Hussain v UK, Singh v UK* Application Nos. 21928/93, 23389/94 (21 February 1996), the Court awarded costs and expenses only, and said the judgment gave just satisfaction for the non–pecuniary damage claimed by the applicants. The Court will also consider the context of the breach. In *A and others v UK* Application No. 3455/05 (19 February 2009), for example, where the Court found breaches of Article 5, in the detention of the claimants under anti-terrorist legislation, the Court gave awards lower than in previous cases of unlawful detention, because the detention scheme was set up in the context of a public emergency. The state was seen as trying to reconcile the protection of the public against terrorism with an obligation not to send the detainees back to countries where there was a real risk of ill-treatment, so the applicants received less than EUR 4,000 but did receive a large award for legal costs.

But even if an award for damages is made, the level of compensation may vary considerably and often the level of damages awarded under Article 41 in prisoner cases is modest. Deductions are usually made where legal aid has been received. However, the quantum of damages paid to prisoners has been very negatively reported in the press and subject to adverse comment by leading politicians from all parties, for example in the case of Abu Qatada although he received only £2,500 for being unlawfully detained without trial under anti-terrorist legislation in breach of Article 5, but had asked for £170,000. The level was reduced by the Court because of the emergency at the time after 9/11. But regardless of the level of damages, the view that prisoners should receive *any* compensation for poor conditions has been questioned by some sections of the public. Yet without the prospect of compensation for costs and expenses, prisoners are unlikely to proceed with an application to the court and few prisoners would have the financial resources to mount an application themselves. Even in Article 3 cases, the payments have not been substantial, for example in *van der Ven v the Netherlands* and *Lorse and others v the Netherlands* Application Nos. 50501/99, 52750/99 (4 February 2003), Mr. van der Ven was awarded EUR 3,000 for non-pecuniary damage, and Mr. Lorse received a payment of EUR 2,195 which was for costs and expenses, following a finding of an Article 3 breach for unnecessary and repeated strip-searching. In *Doerga v the Netherlands* Application No. 502109/99 (27 April 2004) the prisoner received damages for costs and expenses only (EUR 2,500). However, in *Moisel v France* Application No. 67263/01 (14 November 2002) where the prisoner was subjected to inhuman and degrading treatment as he was handcuffed on his way to hospital for treatment for cancer, the prisoner received EUR 15,000 for non-pecuniary damage. In *McGlinchey and others v UK* Application No. 50390/99 (14 April 2003) the Court found breaches of Articles 3 and 13 and because the prisoners had no right to compensation for their inhuman and degrading treatment within the internal prison complaints procedure, the applicants were awarded EUR 22,900 for non-pecuniary damage and EUR 7,500 for costs and expenses.

In *Blackstock v UK* Application No. 9152/00 (21 June 2005) where the Court found breaches of Articles 5(4) and 5(5), the rights to liberty and security, the prisoner was awarded EUR 1,460 for non-pecuniary damage and EUR 8,756 for costs and expenses. But the claimants in *Ezeh and Connors v UK* Application Nos. 39665/98, 40086/98, (9 October 2003) were awarded EUR 44,000 for breaches of Article 6(3)(c) although this reflected the additional days added to their sentence. In *Stafford v UK* Application No. 46295/99 (28 May 2002), the Court found breaches of Articles 5(1) and 5(4), because the lawfulness of the prisoner's continued detention was not reviewed by a body with the power of release or under a procedure with the necessary safeguards. Stafford was awarded EUR 16,500 for pecuniary and non-pecuniary damage and £17,865.10 sterling for costs and expenses. In *Dickson v UK* Application No. 44362/04, (4 December 2007) a breach of Article 8 resulted in damages of EUR 5,000 for non-pecuniary damage and EUR 21,000 for costs and expenses. In *Wainwright v UK* Application No. 12350/04 (26 September 2006), a case concerning the strip-searching of prison visitors, the Court found breaches of Articles 8 and 13 the awards were EUR 6,000 for non-pecuniary damage, and EUR 17,500 for costs and expenses. However, the attack on the Convention extends beyond these payments and has led to demands for rejection of the Human Rights Act and drafting of a replacement British Bill of Rights. Yet what is less often reported is the problems prisoners face in bringing claims or succeeding with them.

The limits of the Convention

Despite fears in some quarters of the floodgates opening to prisoners' claims with the enactment of the Human Rights Act, it is clear that there are barriers to success. Reviewing the history of prisoners' claims in Strasbourg, we find that cases have failed to progress for a variety of reasons, because they were out of time, or because not all available internal domestic remedies were exhausted before proceedings were instituted, or failed on their merits, or because of the weight given to countervailing considerations. Before the HRA, the cumbersome and lengthy procedures for going to Strasbourg, and passing the admissibility hurdle of the Commission, meant that Convention rights were most likely to be used by those serving longer sentences. The lengthy procedures are likely to deter those on shorter sentences from initiating proceedings. With the abolition of the Commission in 1999, procedures have been speeded up and under the HRA, of course, it is possible to pursue a human rights claim in the domestic courts, although the complainant may still go to Strasbourg if he is dissatisfied with the domestic courts' treatment of the case.

Notwithstanding the progress made through the Convention, its use and value has been limited in the prison context, because many of the demands and exigencies of prison life, to protect security and maintain good order within the prison, can be accommodated within the qualifications to the relevant Convention rights. As these include the prevention of crime and disorder, the protection of health or morals, the protection of the rights and freedom of others, the interests of national security and public safety, this still allows considerable discretion for the prison authority. These qualifications which limit the impact of the rights may be used extensively within the prison context. The tension between rights and discretion discussed in relation to public and private in Chapter 2 has also coloured Convention jurisprudence. Moreover, despite its status as a rights Convention, it is clear that the provisions are tempered by a strong strand of utilitarianism with public interest considerations playing an important role. This may mean that like the domestic courts, the prison authority's assessment of security issues will be given considerable weight which may make the courts reluctant to intervene. However, as well as the hurdle of the qualifications to overcome, the definition of breaches may be narrow. For example, some of the earlier Strasbourg jurisprudence suggested that conditions had to be very poor to amount to a breach of Article 3 but this has now changed. Derogations may also be permitted from Convention rights under Article 15, but these are extremely rare and permitted only in times of emergency where they are strictly required by circumstances and the measures must not be inconsistent with other international law obligations.

The doctrine of the margin of appreciation has been used to the advantage of states in limiting rights. States have also been accorded a wide margin of appreciation by the Strasbourg Court in interpreting and implementing the rights granted under the Convention within their jurisdictions, particularly in areas where there is no consensus among states or the issues are politically sensitive for states, because they concern religious or sexual matters or where the law is changing on an issue and generally where the Court does not feel confident in questioning the judgement of states on particular domestic matters. As Letsas notes the margin is also an alternative way of applying the proportionality principle; if the state does not strike the right balance between the individual's rights and the public interest, the Court will see them as outside, but if the measure is deemed proportionate, it will be seen as within the margin of appreciation (Letsas 2006). But it is precisely the focus on the balancing exercise which is problematic for those who hold a Dworkinian approach to rights as trumping collective interests (Dworkin 1977). For Dworkin it is clear that external preferences should not be used to limit rights. However, as the Court has become more activist it has been less willing to invoke the doctrine in relieving states of their obligations, and has intervened in areas where there is evidence of divergences between states, for example in relation to voting rights for prisoners, in *Hirst*.

Moreover, as the states who have signed the Convention encompass a wide range of prison standards with varying degrees of human rights protection, the Court, like the CPT, assumes a key role in exerting pressure on the regressive states to raise their standards. With the expansion of the membership of the Council of Europe since the early 1990s, the possibility of raising prison standards across Eastern Europe has increased as the penal systems of the new members are subject to review. The Court hears claims from a broad spectrum across Europe, including Eastern and Southern Europe, including Greece and Turkey, where prison standards fall below the UK and Dutch standards, and Russia where prisons are very overcrowded.

The rights within the original structure of the Convention are primarily civil rights rather than social rights, when the latter may be more valuable to prisoners. For rights to be effective in a prison context as in the wider society, they need to include social rights, as well as civil and political rights, to address the problem of social exclusion. For prisoners, this would include a right to a minimum standard of living and the right to rehabilitation with an obligation on states to provide prisoners with the opportunity to reform. However, recent decisions in Strasbourg and the UK do suggest a greater willingness by the courts to impose positive duties on the state, for example to avoid discrimination, even though this may seem to conflict with the fundamental liberal foundations of the Convention (see Fredman 2008). However there is some scope, as we shall see, for construing Article 3 as generating a social right insofar as it has been used to achieve a minimum standard of living for prisoners. We also find a shift towards imposing positive as well as negative duties on states in Article 3 jurisprudence, so states should provide sufficient resources to avoid rights infringements in the context of prison overcrowding. The Strasbourg Court has said that lack of resources is insufficient reason for failure to respect and protect rights.[12]

While rights claims have become more common and have achieved some success, we still need greater willingness on the part of Governments to comply with the Court's findings as there have been considerable delays, in some areas, for example, the extremely slow response of the UK to the Court's judgment in *Hirst v UK* (see Chapter 8).

Conclusions

Because of the limitations of public and private law discussed in Chapter 2, the rights protection in the Convention offers a better means of securing humane and fair conditions of internment, notwithstanding the problems highlighted above. Taken together with the work of the CPT, the Strasbourg Court offers a rich source of case law and principles to govern the practice of imprisonment. We also find increasingly a 'cosmopolitan jurisprudence' in the interpretation of prisoners' rights, with a cross-fertilization of ideas, drawn from the various sources of prison law. The Committees and the Court will refer to each others' findings and decisions. The work of the CPT was cited by the Commission and Court in, for example, *Delazarus v UK* Application No. 17525/90 (16 February 1993) and more recently in *Peers v Greece* Application No. 28254/95 (19 April 2001) and *Dougoz v Greece* Application No. 40907/98 (6 March 2001). However, because the Court's findings are binding rather than mere recommendations, governments are more likely to respond to the Court's findings than to the CPT. However, if an applicant can refer to conditions criticized in the CPT Report then this will strengthen his or her case. The Convention is also an importance guiding principle for European Union law and has also influenced the UN Human Rights Committee in its deliberations. So we can find a developing rights jurisprudence which reflects these different sources and at a formal level provides a framework for humane imprisonment. Its application to specific conditions in prison will now be considered.

4   Prison conditions

Introduction

Prison conditions are clearly a key area for prisoners' rights as these impact most directly on prisoners' experience of imprisonment. Yet, as we saw earlier, the courts here and in the USA have been more reluctant to become involved in overseeing conditions compared to other areas of the prison regime. However, the European Convention has been a major source of protection for prisoners in the UK challenging the conditions of their detention. This chapter will discuss the implications of Articles 2 and 3 of the European Convention for prisoners' treatment and the problems in maintaining prison conditions while prisons are under extreme pressure from the pressure on prisoner numbers. Although states have been accorded a wide margin of appreciation in applying the requirements of the Convention, the Court is now scrutinizing prisoners' applications very closely and is more willing to criticize state practice on punishment. Since the early 1990s, the Strasbourg Court has become less tolerant of poor conditions and more willing to classify them as inhuman or degrading treatment and to require a minimum standard of living for prisoners. The Court is also more reluctant to accept 'blanket' provisions or rules which are applied to prisoners indiscriminately, without a full examination of individual circumstances for example in assuming levels of risk. This approach has also been reflected in the domestic courts' criticism of blanket approaches.[1]

As the Strasbourg Court has become less tolerant of poor prison conditions, Article 3 has been used increasingly in relation to substantive conditions of treatment, such as overcrowding and medical care, both of which could be seen as signifying a move towards the recognition of social rights. The Court will also look closely at whether the conditions are an inevitable consequence of punishment or go beyond this.

Adoption of the European Prison Rules also means that there are specific requirements for states in terms of their physical conditions, such as space per prisoner, as well as access to light. Under the EPR, prisoners should have reasonable accommodation, three meals a day and adequate health care. There are also provisions on work, education, recreation, disciplinary measures and complaints. But a breach of the European Prison rules per se will not constitute a breach of Article 3.

In addition, of course, the UK Prison Rules published under the Prison Act 1952 do cover basic conditions as well as disciplinary matters and visits. However, breaches of the Prison Rules may not be sufficient to support a breach of statutory duty claim.

The recommendations of the European Committee for the Prevention of Torture (CPT) have also had some impact on conditions and on the jurisprudence of the Strasbourg Court. The CPT has been very critical of the conditions in which individuals are detained and has also focused on specific aspects of imprisonment which have received less attention in Strasbourg, such as the psychological impact of punishment.

But while the Strasbourg Court is taking a more robust approach to conditions in prisons, the domestic courts have been more tolerant of poor conditions. For example, in *R (on the application of BP) v Secretary of State for the Home Department* (2003) EWHC 1963 (Admin) where a 17-year-old offender who had previously self-harmed and attempted suicide had been placed in segregation while in a Young Offenders Institution, this was deemed not to breach Article 3. The Court referred to the duration of the time spent in segregation, his access to visits and the aim of confinement. In *Broom v Secretary of State for the Home Department* (2002) EWHC 2401 where the poor conditions included failure to provide a modesty screen in the cells and walls stained by cigarette smoke, this did not reach the threshold for degrading treatment.

However, it is widely accepted that prison conditions in the UK have improved substantially over the past 20 years, although some individual institutions do still have poor conditions and have been criticized by the Inspector of Prisons and by the Courts, most notably Barlinnie Prison in Scotland,[2] where slopping out did not end until 2002, and Pentonville, which was criticized by the Independent Monitoring Board in its Annual Report in 2007, for its poor physical conditions which included infestations of rats and cockroaches (Independent Monitoring Board 2007).

There have been National Operating Standards for prisons in England and Wales since 1994 as part of the Woolf Reforms as well as Key Performance Indicators and Targets to measure and encourage progress. Reports on prison service performance are published annually by the National Offender Management Service (NOMS) and the Ministry of Justice.[3] But if a target is not met, this is a problem for managers rather than prisoners as there is nothing prisoners can do to ensure a target is met or to seek redress if it is not. Targets may also be set relatively low because of the costs implications. The introduction of League Tables has identified those performing least well, but obviously knowing the conditions in individual establishments is of little help to prisoners who have no control over their allocation and entering prison is hardly comparable to checking in to a hotel. UK prisoners have no input to the allocation process, although EPR 17.3 states that: 'As far as possible, prisoners shall be consulted about their initial allocation and any subsequent transfer from one prison to another'. For most prisoners. the key issue in their allocation will be proximity to their local area. Allocating prisoners to facilities near their homes has positive benefits as maintaining regular contact with families may defuse the stresses of prison life and have implications for good order within prisons, but also facilitate the offender's reintegration on release. Nonetheless, the league tables published quarterly by the Ministry of Justice do highlight an important issue, namely variability of conditions. There are currently no prisons at the lowest level.[4]

While there are examples of good practice within the prison regime, the problem is that this is not uniform. For example, remand prisoners often face the worst conditions because training and work opportunities will be geared towards long-serving prisoners especially when resources are limited and may be held in local prisons where there are fewer facilities and which are more likely to be overcrowded. The experience of imprisonment may also vary between different groups of prisoners, for example, between UK and foreign national prisoners, men and women, older and younger prisoners, and different ethnic groups, and between prisoners with and without disabilities which will be discussed in Chapter 7 below.

The quality of prison conditions is crucial in ensuring a regime which complies with Article 3 of the European Convention on Human Rights, but also prepares prisoners for release in the community with appropriate skills and allows them to address their offending behaviour, and in order to prevent re-offending. So the provision of constructive activities, including work, education and recreational activities, has been seen as crucial in this process and stressed by the Woolf Report and by the Committee for the Prevention of Torture. Some of the key issues relating to prison conditions will now be considered. The focus will be primarily on adult prisons rather than other forms of detention, such as juvenile institutions, or immigration holding centres, although clearly similar issues may arise in those contexts.

Deaths in custody

This issue is relevant to prison conditions as the number of deaths in custody is clearly an important indicator of the quality of a prison regime, as is the review mechanism following a death. Prisoners clearly retain the protection of Article 2 of the Convention, the right to life, while inside prison which means obligations are imposed on the prison to protect the prisoner from any foreseeable risks by, for example, providing appropriate medical care, suicide prevention measures and protecting inmates from harm from other prisoners.

Some of these deaths in custody may be self-inflicted. The number of self-inflicted deaths in prison custody in 2009 was 60, which consisted of 57 males and 3 females. Five deaths were in the 18–20 group and the remainder in the over 21 age group.

This compared with 61 suicides in 2008 and 95 in 2004. Deaths in custody raise Article 2 issues if the state knows or ought to have known of a real or immediate risk to life, but failed to take measures to avoid it, and there have been several cases on the provision of appropriate medical treatment, for example, *R (Wright) v Secretary of State for the Home Department* [2001] EWHC Admin 520. In considering whether the duty under Article 2 has been breached, the courts will consider whether prison staff have done all that can be reasonably expected in monitoring a prisoner. But even if the prison authority has met that minimum in terms of monitoring, the failure to provide adequate health care may amount to degrading treatment in breach of Article 3. So in *Keenan v UK* (2001) Application No. 27229/95 (3 April 2001), where the prisoner committed suicide while in custody, the Court took the view that the prison had done all that could reasonably be expected in monitoring the prisoner, but it had failed in providing appropriate care for his mental illness. He had been placed in a segregation unit while suffering from mental health problems and this use of segregation to discipline a prisoner with medical problems breached Article 3.

Many of the cases have raised issues on appropriate medical treatment, but there have also been deaths resulting from assaults by fellow prisoners which raises the question of whether dangerous prisoners should be sharing cells. This issue arose in the cases of *Edwards v UK* Application No. 46477/99 (14 March 2002), *R (Amin) v Secretary of State for the Home Department* (2003) 4 All ER 1264 and Zahid Mubarek where prisoners were killed by their cellmates. The level of overcrowding in prison may be relevant to the issue of deaths in custody, as housing prisoners in single cells may be safer if there is a risk of violence, an issue stressed in the Mubarek Report although potential suicides may be more at risk in single cells (see Keith 2006). The prison authority still bears some responsibility in failing to provide a safe environment even if the assault is committed by a third party.

The use of excessive control and restraint by officers may result in death as in the case of Alton Manning where an inquest found that he had been unlawfully killed when restrained by an illegal necklock.[5] To comply with Article 2, no more force should be used in restraining prisoners than is absolute necessary, which is a stricter test than at common law.

Moreover, where a death occurs in custody, Article 2 also imposes an obligation on the state to provide a proper review and effective official investigation of that death, to identify the circumstances leading to the death and the way in which the prisoner was treated while inside. An inquest alone may be insufficient and there are clear procedural requirements for investigations set out in *Jordan v UK* (2001) 11 BHRC 1 where an individual was killed by agents of the state, and in *Edwards* and *Amin*. An effective investigation should be able to give a satisfactory explanation of the death, it should be independent and not conducted by persons implicated in the death, and the next of kin of the deceased should be fully involved. In addition, it was stressed in *Amin* that there is a requirement for prompt and reasonable expedition as this is essential in promoting public confidence in the procedure. As well as an independent inquiry, it must be possible for families to attend the whole proceedings and to examine witnesses directly or via representatives. In the *Edwards* case, the prisoner's parents had only been allowed to attend when giving evidence themselves. The Court in *Edwards* also found a breach of Article 13 in the failure to provide an effective legal remedy.

If a prisoner refuses to eat, the position in the UK is that this is a matter of choice for the individual, and force feeding is seen as degrading and unlawful, as stated in *R v SSHD ex parte Robb* [1995] 1 All ER 67. Although hunger strikes to the point of death are relatively rare, in 1981 Bobbie Sands died after 66 days on hunger strike in pursuit of the recognition of Irish nationalist prisoners as political prisoners. While force feeding would constitute degrading treatment and potentially breach Article 3, refraining from feeding may conflict with the state's obligations under Article 2. In *X v Germany* (1985) 7 EHRR 152 the Strasbourg Court, said that that while force feeding may potentially be degrading there had not been a breach in this case and the state was meeting its obligations under Article 2.

Torture

Clearly torture is prohibited in the prison system, but cases have arisen which raise the question of the borderline between torture and inhuman treatment and obviously the definition of torture is crucial here. Although under the original Bill of Rights of 1689, torture meant barbarous punishments such as disembowelling, it is now interpreted as the deliberate imposition of extreme mental and physical suffering. In the USA torture is defined as cruel and unusual punishment and clearly prohibited by the Eighth Amendment to the US Constitution. The UN definition is given in Article 1.1 of the Convention Against Torture, which is an act intentionally inflicted on a person causing severe pain or suffering, physical or mental, in order to extract information or to punish, and inflicted by a person acting in an official capacity or with the consent or acquiescence of a public official or person acting in an official capacity. But the treatment has to reach a sufficient level of severity to constitute torture, and there has to be intentional ill-treatment causing intense mental or physical suffering. Torture will always involve inhuman and degrading treatment.[6]

The CPT has distinguished between inhuman and degrading treatment on the one hand and torture on the other, as distinct forms of ill-treatment. So in the context of prison, degrading treatment would include slopping out and overcrowding and the use of substandard accommodation, whereas torture is reserved for the deliberate imposition of extreme mental and physical suffering. However, for the European Court of Human Rights inhuman and degrading treatment and torture are seen as lying on a continuum. The borderline may not always be clear for example, in cases of prolonged segregation. Since the 1970s, there have been several cases brought against the UK under Article 3, including a challenge to the treatment of detainees in Northern Ireland in *Ireland v UK* (1978) 2 EHRR 25. Here the detainees were forced to wear hoods over their heads, to stand up for long periods and were subjected to sensory deprivation, severe mental stress and deprived of food and sleep. However, while the Commission thought this amounted to torture, the majority of the European Court of Human Rights concluded that use of these techniques constituted inhuman and degrading treatment and did not reach the level of intensity needed for torture.

The threshold for torture was reached in the later case of *Aksoy v Turkey* Application No. 21987/93 (18 December 1996) where a person detained by the police had been suspended by his arms, leaving his arms paralysed for some time. Similarly in *Akkoc v Turkey* Application Nos. 22948/93 (10 October 2000) where the applicant detained in police custody was given electric shocks, hot and cold water punishments and her children were threatened, the Court thought this did amount to torture. In *Selmouni v France* Application No. 25803/94 (28 July 1999), where the detainee was assaulted by police officers and threatened with a blowtorch, the Court made it clear that it was taking a stronger line on breaches and conditions which in the past were seen as inhuman and degrading might be in future be classed as torture.

Inhuman and degrading treatment

Inhuman and degrading treatment may cover a broad range of physical conditions, including overcrowding but also isolation, shackling and in some cases strip-searching and excessive security, but not the length of the sentence itself, unless it is grossly disproportionate (see Chapter 5).

Overcrowding and poor physical conditions

In England and Wales, overcrowding is measured in terms of the number of prisoners held in a cell designed for fewer prisoners. On this criterion prison overcrowding is currently running at 24 per cent. The target for 2009–10 was 26 per cent but 24 per cent was achieved (Ministry of Justice/NOMS 2010c). In the past the definition used was 'doubling', so this referred to two prisoners in cell designed for one, but the new definition could include three in a cell designed for two. Efforts to reduce overcrowding have been hampered by the substantial increase in the prison population. The projections for 2016 suggest the highest figure will be 93,600 and the lowest 83,100 (Ministry of Justice 2010d). This shows a slight decline from the 2009 projections (Ministry of Justice 2009b). In England and Wales changes in sentencing law and policy have been a significant factor in penal expansion (Piper and Easton 2006/7).

Clearly a target for overcrowding is less effective than a statutory right not to be overcrowded which the Woolf Report recommended, but this has not been implemented (Woolf and Tumim 1991). In August 2009 Shrewsbury Jail was the most overcrowded prison holding 79 per cent more prisoners than it was designed for, according to the Prison Reform Trust, although this figure was questioned by the Independent Monitoring Board's chair who said some prisoners had now been transferred.

In England and Wales the practice has been to continue with the admission of prisoners into the system notwithstanding the pressure on places in contrast to some other European societies, for example, in France and Italy where amnesties or collective pardons have been used to deal with pressures (see Kensey and Tournier 1999). An end of custody licence scheme was introduced in 2007 as a temporary measure to relieve pressure on places by releasing eligible prisoners up to 18 days early but this ended in March 2010. Eligible prisoners were those who were serving determinate sentences of more than four weeks but under four years and were not sex offenders or convicted of violent crimes.

Overcrowding can have both physical and mental effects and can contribute to friction between prisoners and between prisoners and staff, affecting the whole atmosphere of the prison. Overcrowding can contribute to ill-health but also increase the risk of assaults as occurred in the Mubarek case. Both the Committee for the Prevention of Torture and the European Prison Rules stress that where possible single cells should be used (EPR 18.5), or at least that prisoners should have a choice whether to share or not (EPR 18.7). Overcrowding may also increase tensions within prison and the risk of disorder. It may also have implications for Article 8 if it means a lack of privacy in relation to sanitation and washing facilities. Prisoners should have proper access to sanitation and at least two baths a week but if possible daily (EPR 19.3, 19.4).

For cases on overcrowding to succeed in Strasbourg, the overcrowding will need to be severe or an additional element is needed, such as a loss of privacy or aggravation of a health problem, but overcrowding will usually have implications for privacy. The more excessive the overcrowding, the more likely it is the court will find it inhuman and degrading. For example, in the case of *Kalashnikov v Russia* (2003) 36 EHRR 34, each bed was used by two or three prisoners so that it was necessary for them to sleep in shifts. A similar situation arose in *Babushkin v Russia* Application No. 67253/01 (18 October 2007), where overcrowding in prison dormitories meant that the prisoners could not all sleep at the same time and in *Gusev v Russia* Application No. 67542/01 (15 May 2008) where prisoners did not have their own sleeping space. In Russia and Eastern Europe, prisoners are usually held in dormitories (Piacentini 2004). In the UK prisoners are usually held in cells and overcrowding does not reach such extremes. The Court has made clear that financial pressures are not sufficient to justify inhuman and degrading conditions and this is also written into the European Prison Rules: 'Prison conditions that infringe prisoners' human rights are not justified by lack of resources' (EPR 4).

In *Denmark, Norway, Sweden and Netherlands v Greece* (1969) 12 YB 1 the Court said that overcrowding may amount to degrading treatment but it also focused on a range of other factors. It also referred to poor hygiene, food deprivation, poor medical care, lack of exercise, and where prisoners are held in solitary confinement, lack of contact with the outside world, in deciding whether Article 3 had been breached.

In *Peers v Greece* (2001) 33 EHRR 51, the Court found that the very poor conditions in which the prisoner was held undermined his dignity and engendered feelings of humiliation, even if this was not intended. The prisoner had been held in cells without natural light, or ventilation and lacking privacy when using the toilet facilities. Prior to this, the Court had taken the view that the treatment needed to be imposed intentionally to be inhuman and degrading.

In *Price v UK* (2002) 34 EHRR 53 a wheelchair-bound woman with severe disabilities was held in a police cell in conditions which were found to be degrading because of the problem of access to toilet facilities without assistance from male officers. The Court accepted that there was no intention to degrade or humiliate, but the conditions still breached Article 3.

The Courts will also consider the length of time the prisoner has to spend in those conditions so if the individual is serving a longer sentence, this is more likely to conflict with Article 3 so this may mean that remand prisoners held for a short period are unlikely to succeed with a claim. If a prisoner spends only one night in very poor conditions this may not be sufficient to breach Article 3. In addition, in *Delazarus v UK* Application No. 17525/90 (16 February 1993) the Commission held that while the conditions, including overcrowding and poor sanitary arrangements, had been very unsatisfactory, and had been criticized by the CPT, the fact that the prisoner had the cell to himself made this less problematic and therefore his application failed.

If a lack of privacy does not reach the level of degradation required for Article 3, it might breach Article 8 and in many cases it would be difficult for the prison authority to justify it as necessary under Article 8(2). In *Napier v Scottish Ministers* (2005) 1 SC 229 a successful challenge was brought in the domestic courts by a prisoner using Articles 3 and 8 relation to conditions in Barlinnie Prison in Glasgow. The prisoner had been held with another prisoner in a cell designed for one. The living space was inadequate and he was held there for at least 20 hours a day. The court was very critical of the fact that there was no access to a toilet overnight or at weekends and the prisoners were forced to slop out. Because of the squalid conditions, the prisoner's pre-existing skin condition worsened, a factor which influenced the Court of Sessions in finding a breach of Article 3. The Court also found a breach of Article 8, the right to respect for private life, because of the poor sanitary arrangements which could not be justified under Article 8(2). Steps should have been taken to improve the regime and, particularly, to end slopping out. A subsequent appeal by the Ministers failed. *Napier* may indicate a greater willingness by the domestic courts to review and criticize prison conditions using the prisoners' right jurisprudence from Strasbourg. However, success for prisoners' claims or an interventionist approach by the courts is by no means guaranteed as cases will turn on their own facts and weight will still be given to the needs of the prison administration. The Commission has also said that if the poor conditions are self-inflicted, as in the case of the 'dirty protest' of Irish nationalist prisoners, this would not amount to a breach of Article 3, in *McFeeley v UK* (1981) 3 EHRR 161.[7]

European Prison Rule 20.2 states that clothing should not be degrading or humiliating. While the ordinary prison clothing used in the UK is not degrading per se, if prisoners refused to comply, then it would breach Article 3 to punish prisoners by making them eat in the cells.[8]

As we have seen degrading treatment needs to be 'grossly humiliating' to breach Article 3. However, cases have also been brought in relation to degrading punishments which infringe Article 3 by attacking a person's dignity and physical integrity. So in determining whether there is a breach, the Court will consider the surrounding circumstances, the nature and the context of the punishment, and the way it is carried out, as well as the person's age and state of health. For example, in *Tyrer v UK* [1978] 2 EHRR 1 the birching of a 15-year-old boy in the Isle of Man was found to breach Article 3 because it was degrading. The Strasbourg Court emphasized that a punishment could be degrading even if it was supported by the public and carried out in private, deterred crime and caused no lasting physical damage, and was used to punish violent crimes.

The degrading nature of punishment has also been considered in relation to death penalty cases. Although the death penalty was not prohibited by Article 2 of the Convention, it is now prohibited by Protocols 6 and 13 for those states which have ratified them, and Turkey abolished the penalty in August 2002. While such extreme punishment is no longer used within Europe, with the exception of Belarus, the issue may arise in cases of extradition to countries where it is still practised. Article 3 has been used successfully used in death penalty extradition cases, if there are substantial grounds to show that a person being extradited faces a real risk of being subjected to torture, inhuman or degrading treatment or punishment in the requesting country. In *Soering v UK* (1989) 11 EHRR 439 the court did not focus on the execution itself, but the fact that the applicant would very likely be waiting on Death Row for several years before the execution if extradited to the United States.

Security and control

As well as issues relating to overcrowding and poor physical conditions, the courts have considered the use of restraints, full body searching, cell searching and segregation, issues which arise as part of the process of control of prisoners. So the Woolf Report (Woolf and Tumim 1991) stressed the way in which security and control is handled within prison may be crucial in terms of the maintenance of good order but also in terms of how prisoners perceive their treatment. Obviously the public needs security so prisoners do not escape and prisoners themselves need security from assault, so the prison authority needs to maintain good order within prisons. But the way in which security is achieved is crucial in achieving legitimacy for the prison authority and should not be subordinated to justice. If the balance between security, control and justice is not achieved, this is likely to generate more disorder. Escapes have not been a serious problem within the prison regime in the UK, although there was a series of high-profile escapes in the 1990s which led to an intensification of security measures. Dealing with disruptive or difficult prisoners and controlling the problem of contraband, notably drugs and mobile phones in prison are now the major security issues, which have become more difficult with the expansion of the prison population. The emphasis now is, or should be, on dynamic security, that is, building up good relations within the prison between staff and prisoners so that staff are aware of possible problems and tensions do not escalate or can be resolved without the use of force. If staff know the prisoners well, they are able to deal with grievances rather than simply relying on electronic surveillance and security. Dynamic security is also strongly recommended in the European Prison Rules: 'The security which is provided by physical barriers and other technical means shall be complemented by the dynamic security provided by an alert staff who know the prisoners who are under their control' (EPR 51.2).

The European Prison Rules specific that security measures should be the minimum necessary to achieve secure custody (EPR 51.1) and prisoners should be held in security conditions appropriate to their level of risk and this should be reviewed regularly during the term of imprisonment (EPR 51.4, 51.5). So special high-security measures should be used only in exceptional circumstances (EPR 53.1). Prisoners being searched should not be humiliated by the searching process (EPR 54.3) and intimate examinations should only be made by medical practitioners (EPR 54.7). The Rules also specify that solitary confinement should be used only in exceptional cases and for a specified period (EPR 60.5).

Under the UK Prison Rules force should only be used as a last resort where it is necessary to prevent harm to officers and others, and its use is reasonable and proportionate (PR 47, PSO 1600). The use of weapons, handcuffs or body belts must be legally justified (PR 49). The use of force has implications for both Articles 2 and 3 if prisoners' lives are threatened or if they are shackled. EPR 64.1 provides that 'Prison staff shall not use force against prisoners except in self-defence or in cases of attempted escape or active or passive physical resistance to a lawful order and always as a last resort'. Moreover, 'the amount of force used shall be the minimum necessary and shall be imposed for the shortest necessary time' (EPR 64.2).

The most disruptive or highest escape risk prisoners will be allocated to high-security regimes or special units. Prisoners especially vulnerable to attack will be held on Rule 45 regimes in vulnerable prisoner units, but the experience of violence in prisons shows that ordinary prisoners not on special regimes may be at risk, as in the case of Zahid Mubarek (see Keith 2006). These issues do need to be considered in the context of overcrowding as cell sharing will be more frequent and obviously identifying prisoners who present a risk to others and passing on information is crucial, and failure to do so can have catastrophic consequences, as they did in that case.

If a prison has secure external boundaries, a more relaxed regime inside those boundaries should be compatible with security from escapes, even for category A prisoners. But of course threats to prison security may come from internal tensions between prisoners and between prisoners and staff, so a relaxed regime may be difficult to achieve. If a prison houses prisoners requiring different levels of security, then usually a higher level of security will be imposed which prisoners from less intense regimes may find difficult. The CPT has been critical of regimes which rely on intense security rather than dynamic security.[9]

If it is necessary to physically restrain a prisoner, than this should be done for the minimum time necessary. The European Court of Human Rights in *Mathew v the Netherlands* Application No. 24919/03 (29 September 2005) said that the use of handcuffs was legitimate provided they were used appropriately, for example, where there was a risk of absconding, although the fact that the prisoner had been held in solitary confinement did breach Article 3.

Excessive security for seriously ill prisoners may also amount to inhuman and degrading treatment. In *Moisel v France* Application No. 67263/01 (14 November 2002), for example, the Strasbourg Court found a breach of Article 3 because the use of handcuffs was disproportionate to the needs of security when a prisoner suffering from Hodgkin's disease and leukaemia was handcuffed in transit as he went to hospital for treatment. While shackling per se does not breach Article 3, the inappropriate use of shackles may constitute inhuman or degrading treatment. In attending hospital appointments, prisoners should not be routinely handcuffed or this would also breach Article 3. Prisoners should be assessed for their escape risk first before such measures are employed (see *R (Graham) v Secretary of State for Justice*; *R (Allen) v Secretary of State for Justice* [2007] EWHC 2910 (Admin)).

Prisoners may be isolated if they are disruptive or for security reasons and held in segregation units or care and separation units as they are referred to in some prisons. The impact of segregation on prisoners' mental health may be traumatic, especially if they already have a history of mental illness (Edgar and Rickford 2009). In the past the Strasbourg Court in the past was reluctant to treat prolonged segregation as a breach of Article 3. Cases on prison conditions failed in the past, even when the conditions of segregation were so severe that they were criticized by the Committee for the Prevention of Torture. For the CPT segregation may amount to inhuman and degrading treatment and should be used only where necessary and for as briefly as possible. But the Strasbourg Court has been more tolerant than the CPT on this issue in the past.

Some of the earlier cases on Article 3 such as *Ensslin, Baader and Raspe v Germany* (1978) 14 DR 64 suggested that treatment would have to be quite severe to amount to a breach; for example, segregation as such would not reach this level, but there would have to be complete isolation and sensory deprivation. In *Kröcher and Möller v Switzerland* (1982) 34 DR 25 the Court declined to find a breach of Article 3 even though prisoners were isolated, had no contact with other prisoners and were kept in harsh conditions for one month, and could not see out because the windows were frosted over, and were subject to constant surveillance, in cells which were permanently lit and were denied papers, radio, television and watches. The Court noted that in subsequent months some of these conditions were relaxed, but the prisoners did not take advantage of the limited opportunities for outside contact.

A key issue for the Strasbourg Court in deciding whether segregation amounts to a breach of Article 3 is its duration. The court will also consider the aim of the segregation and its impact on the prisoner.[10] Issues of sensory deprivation will also be considered. The decision to segregate has to be based on good reasons and there should be regular reviews of a prisoner's case to see whether he can be returned to normal conditions. Confinement has to be justified, based on reasons and not applied arbitrarily, and the prisoner should be regularly monitored to see if continued segregation is necessary.[11]

Segregation in England and Wales is governed by Prison Rules 45 and 46 and PSO 1700. PR 45 states that prisoners can be removed from association by the governor for reasons of good order or discipline or in the prisoner's own interests. Prisoners should be given reasons for these decisions. The initial period they can be held on segregation is 72 hours, but any further extension must be authorized by a review board and can be unlimited. Disruptive prisoners may also be removed to a Close Supervision Centre under PR 46 where it is necessary for the maintenance of good order or discipline, or to ensure the safety of prisoners, officers or others although conditions in these centres, have been criticized for their harshness by the Chief Inspector of Prisons and others (Clare and Bottomley *et al.* 2001). The CSC at Woodhill was strongly criticized by the Chief Inspector of Prisons in 2000 but has improved since. If necessary disruptive prisoners may be transferred to other prisons, but prisons are expected to try to deal with difficult prisoners themselves first.

However, the European Court has been more critical of strip- or full body searching than segregation. Strip-searching as such does not breach Article 3 but the way in which the search is conducted may constitute inhuman or degrading treatment in the view of both the Court and the CPT. The Court was critical of the routine use of systematic strip-searches which the state is unable to justify which breached Article 3 in *van der Ven v the Netherlands* and *Lorse v the Netherlands* Application Nos. 50501/99, 52750/99 (4 February 2003). These cases show how much the respect for prisoners' rights in Europe has progressed as in some of the earlier Convention cases failed. In *McFeeley v UK* Application No. 8317/78 20 DR 44 (1980) the Commission decided that routine strip-searching did not breach

Article 3. The Court has also been very critical of the strip-searching of prisoners' relatives on visits, in *Wainwright v UK* Application No. 12350/04 (26 September 2006) as we shall see in Chapter 6.

In England and Wales there are clear guidelines for procedures to follow in conducting searches of prisoners by officers set out in the UK Prison Rules (PR 41). The European Prison Rules are also clear that the prisoner should not be strip-searched by a member of the opposite sex (EPR 54.5). The search should be conducted in a way that respects the dignity of the prisoner and intimate searches should only be conducted by medical personnel (EPR 54.7).

Prisoners may also be subject to searches of their cells but these should be conducted with prisoners present (see *R (Daly) v Secretary of State for the Home Department* [2001] 2 AC 532). Although cell searches might raise Article 8 issues, intruding on the prisoner's private life, if private letters are read when there are grounds for suspicion, they would usually fall within the qualifications in Article 8(2) (see Chapter 6).

In other areas Article 3 claims have been less successful. Mandatory drug testing, which was introduced in all prisons in England and Wales by March 1996, does not breach Article 3 unless a prisoner is forced to give a sample in public (see *Galloway v UK* [1999] EHRLR 119). While routine urine testing for drugs may breach Article 8(1) it may be justified under Article 8 (2) as made clear in *Galloway v UK* and *Peters v the Netherlands* Application No. 21132/93 (6 April 1994).

Health care issues

A failure to provide proper facilities for prisoners with serious medical problems may also breach Article 3 as the Courts are now much more critical of the failure to provide medical care, illustrated for example in *R (Wright) v Secretary of State for the Home Department* [2001] EWHC Admin 520). In *McGlinchey v UK* Application No. 50390/99 (29 April 2003) the Court found a breach of Article 3 when a heroin addict suffering from withdrawal symptoms, died in hospital having suffered severe dehydration and vomiting and was not treated appropriately, nor admitted to hospital early enough to prevent deterioration. The Court took the view she had not been given appropriate treatment while in prison.

There is a duty on the prison authority to provide treatment for heroin withdrawal symptoms (see PSO 3550) but this is controversial when methadone treatment is provided, as it has been argued that it perpetuates the problems. But on the principle of equivalence, treatment will follow appropriate Health Department guidelines. Healthcare staff will work together with Counselling, Assessment, Referral, Advice and Throughcare services (CARATs) to provide advice and treatment. Prisoners suffering withdrawal symptoms in prison should be given appropriate treatment and failure to provide such care may raise Article 3 as well as Article 2 issues if the prisoner were to die as a result, which happened in the cases of *Keenan v UK* (2001)

Application No. 27229/95 (3 April 2001) and *McGlinchey v UK* Application No 50390/99 (29 April 2003).

The principle which should govern health care in prison is that it should match the standard of care outside, that is, the principle of equivalence of care. This is required by the CPT and under the European Prison Rules: 'Prisoners shall have access to the health services available in the country without discrimination on the grounds of their legal situation' (EPR 40.3). The principle covers psychiatric health care as well as physical health care. Under EPR 12.1 prisoners with mental illness should not be held in ordinary prisons. However, in practice many are held in prison while awaiting assessment and some prisoners may develop mental health problems for the first time inside prison. Prisoners' complaints about the quality of health care can be made through the normal NHS procedures and complaints on ancillary matters may go through the normal prison complaints procedure.

Health care in UK prisons has been criticized for failing to match the standard of health care outside prison in the NHS and there have been successful recent challenges under the Human Rights Act. Health care has improved since the responsibility shifted to the NHS Health Care Trusts in partnership with the Prison Service. Health care is a key issue within prisons as prisoners suffer higher levels of illness than are found in the wider community and the number of prisoners with mental problems entering prisons has increased. The problems of identifying, assessing, diverting and treating prisoners with mental health problems and learning disabilities have been highlighted by the Bradley Report. This Report recommends further research on these problems as well as on the links between mental health and learning disability issues and imprisonment for public protection, greater coordination between agencies and continuity of care for prisoners leaving prison and registering prisoners with general practitioners while in prison (Bradley 2009). Within sentenced prisoners IPP prisoners appear to suffer more from mental health problems (Jacobson and Hough 2010: 15).

There is concern at the continuing availability of illegal drugs within prison which may lead to prisoners using drugs for the first time in prison, as well as increased prescription drug use. Achieving equivalence in health care may also be a particular problem for female prisoners given their higher rates of morbidity (see Prison Reform Trust 2003 and Chapter 7). However in some cases the health of prisoners may actually improve during their time in prison, particularly if they are malnourished and receive a poor diet outside and if they habitually use drugs and alcohol will benefit from refraining from them inside. Moreover, if they need prescribed medicine, they will benefit from the fact that it will be administered regularly inside prison.

One area of prisoners' health care which is has been contentious is the appropriate treatment of prisoners who are HIV positive or living with AIDS. This may be a particular problem in prisons where there is high level of illegal drug use, including using shared needles, and a high risk of rape or sexual assault. The question has been raised of whether prisoners should be compulsorily tested and segregated if they are positive and whether the state should provide condoms to HIV positive prisoners and clean needles to drug users, as the use of shared needles poses a serious risk of transmission of both AIDS and hepatitis (Valette 2002). However, it is difficult to argue that the state has a positive obligation to provide a rapist with condoms to use in the course of his felonies, and it may be unlikely that rapists would be so conscientious in using them or that victims or perpetrators would come forward if the crime is unreported, but in cases of consensual sex, then at least prisoners would then be protected. It is also a particular problem if the crime is unreported.

The UN Programme on HIV/AIDS has published recommendations for the treatment of prisoners with HIV/AIDs and the World Health Organisation has published guidelines. UNAIDs is critical of compulsory testing although mandatory testing takes place in some states of the USA and Australia. WHO recommends voluntary testing and confidentiality to avoid stigmatization of prisoners or discrimination against them.

Compulsory medical examinations have been treated by the European Court of Human Rights as a breach of Article 8, the right to respect for private life which includes the right to respect for bodily integrity, rather than as a breach of Article 3 in *X and Y v the Netherlands* (1986) 8 EHRR 235. Although the case did not deal with HIV/AIDS specifically, it might be easier to justify HIV testing under Article 8(2) given the public health considerations of protecting prisoners and their future partners, as well as prison staff. However, the UN guidelines do not include public health or security justifications for HIV testing of prisoners, not least because of the time gap between infection and showing sero-positive on the test. Furthermore, if the test reveals a false positive the prisoner could be segregated unnecessarily which could be psychologically damaging.

There are also problems concerning the circulation of information on HIV status even if the purpose is to protect others. In *Z v Finland* Application No. 220093/93 (25 February 1997), the access to information on the prisoner's HIV status by prison and medical staff was seen as infringing Article 8. If prisoners know or suspect that information will be passed on they may be reluctant to seek advice.

There may also be problems in segregating prisoners on these grounds and especially if it means they are confined to a restrictive regime and it clearly raises rights issues.[12] The segregation of HIV prisoners was challenged successfully *X and Y v State of Western Australia* (1996) HREOCA 32. In European Convention jurisprudence, segregation would not constitute inhuman and degrading treatment if justified on security grounds, but it should not be aimed at humiliating the prisoner, the Commission said in *Peters v the Netherlands* Application No. 21132/93 77-A DR 75 (1994). Segregation of immune-depressed prisoners could make outbreaks of other illnesses more likely and more severe without reducing the incidence of transmission and it should be possible to manage this risk within the normal environment.

On the principle of equivalence, prisoners should have access to the same health care and health information as in the community. So the provision of condoms and clean needles could also be seen as part of health care to which prisoners have a right under Article 3, and may engage Article 2 if we are dealing with the prevention of transmission of life-threatening illnesses. In some jurisdictions, but not the UK, prisoners do have access to condoms and clean needles. Condoms were made available in New South Wales following a successful legal challenge in 1994 and no adverse effects have been reported. A trial provision of machines was halted, however, in Queensland when it was found prisoners had been using flavoured condoms to sweeten their milk. In England and Wales condoms are available on prescription only where the prison doctor believes that there is a genuine risk of HIV transmission, but are available in Scotland. This restrictive policy was challenged in *R v Home Secretary ex parte Fielding* (1999) COD 525, but the Court rejected this claim and decreed the policy was lawful.

Some prison systems, including Switzerland, Germany, Spain and Scotland, provide an exchange for clean needles. Others, including England and Wales, provide bleach or disinfectant instead as the UK government has taken the view that provision of syringes may increase drug use and that they may also be used as weapons (see PSI 05/2005). However, WHO does not see disinfectant as an effective alternative. A report by UNODC, WHO and UNAIDS on AIDS prevention in prison in 2006 recommended that measures available in the community to prevent aids, including sterile needles, should be available to prisoners, to satisfy the principle of equivalence and to ensure compliance with Articles 2 and 3 (UNODC, WHO and UNAIDS, 2006).

The Strasbourg Court considered a challenge to the UK policy in *Shelley v UK* Application No. 00023800/06 (4 January 2008). Here the prisoner argued that the failure to provide needles breached Articles 2, 3 and 8, as well as Article 14, as it discriminated against prisoners as a group. The Court rejected these arguments as the prisoner had not shown that he was under a real or specific personal risk, or that the policy had an adverse effect on his private life. The state had a number of preventive policies and measures that were being taken, such as the provision of disinfectant, and the state's response was proportionate and reasonable and fell within the margin of appreciation. If prisoners choose to engage in risky behaviour, then this should be distinguished from the question of obligations on the state to provide health care. However, although the prisoner could not establish a breach under these rights, the Court acknowledged that prisoners do form a distinct legal group even if membership is involuntary and temporary, so that does suggest Article 14 claims might succeed where breaches of other Convention rights have been found.

The US Federal Bureau of Prisons tests some prisoners regularly, some randomly and all prisoners 60 days before release. The rates for HIV and AIDS are higher in prison than outside. Many states in the USA have compulsory testing. In Alabama and South Carolina prisoners with HIV are segregated and Mississippi stopped segregating prisoners with HIV in 2010. Apart from the fact that such treatment is inherently discriminatory, it may also mean that prisoners end up serving their sentence in higher-security conditions than necessary and also with limited access to resources.

There are also issues of confidentiality and privacy. In *Woods v White* 689 F. Supp. 874 (W.D.Wis.1988) the Court ruled that the right to privacy extends beyond the prison door, so the prisoner's HIV status should be protected from non-consensual disclosure. However in *John Doe v Joan Delie* 257 F 3d 309 (3rd Cir 2001) the prisoner's medication had been discussed by nurses with the door open so that other prisoners and officers could hear the details. The Court held that while the Fourteenth Amendment protects a prison's right to privacy in medical matters, it is subject to legitimate penological interests and will consider whether the interference is proportionate:

> We acknowledge, however, that a prisoner does not enjoy a right of privacy in his medical information to the same extent as a free citizen. We do not suggest that Doe has a right to conceal this diagnosed medical condition from everyone in the corrections system. Doe's constitutional right is subject to substantial restrictions and limitations in order for correctional officials to achieve legitimate correctional goals and maintain institutional security (at para 32).

Some prisons in the USA, including state prisons in Vermont and Mississippi and some county jails do allow condoms to be distributed to prisoners. Some critics oppose this because it is seen as condoning sexual activity and may be used to conceal evidence of the crime in rape cases. A review of the evidence concluded that the concerns over the dangers were not supported by evidence and were largely political objections (see Sylla 2008).

Similar objections have been made to distribution of needles, namely that they condone drug use but also that they may be used as weapons. There was a case in Australia where a prison officer, Geoffrey Pearce, was killed with a needle which the prisoner concerned had filled with his HIV infected blood, the virus was transmitted and the officer died subsequently died of an AIDS-related illness.

Work, training and education

When we talk of prison conditions, provision for work, training and education form an important element of constructive regimes. These activities are crucial in terms of making prison life tolerable and providing prisoners with key skills to assist their reintegration in society. The provision of constructive regimes may also contribute to security and good order within the prison. In the UK sentenced prisoners are required to work, but remand prisoners are not, although of course many prefer to as it makes the time pass more quickly. One problem is that access to programmes of work and training is geared towards longer-serving prisoners, so remand prisoners and prisoners serving shorter sentences may have fewer opportunities to work. However the amount of work available has increased since the 1990s. Work should not be used as punishment as penal servitude in Europe has long since been abolished.

Prisoners do not have a clear-cut right to work but under EPR 26.2 'prison authorities shall strive to provide sufficient work of a useful nature'. The prison regime for sentenced prisoners should include, work, education, other activities and preparation for release (EPR 103.4). But of course these Rules are not enforceable and in practice it may be difficult to provide appropriate work for all who are eligible. There may also be problems for specific groups of prisoners who may find it harder to obtain access to work, such as remand prisoners, foreign national prisoners, older prisoners or those with health problems or disabilities. There are also provisions relating to provision of educational programmes and libraries.

The European Prison Rules also stipulate that 'In all instances there shall be equitable remuneration of the work of prisoners' (EPR 26.10). However in practice it is very low in the UK with a minimum of £4 per week. The amount will vary depending on where the prisoner is placed on the Incentives and Earned Privileges Scheme. This would seem to be one area where the principle of less eligibility prevails as wages are much lower than outside. If work is not available then prisoners may claim unemployment benefit which has led to much criticism in the popular press, although this amounts to only £2.50 a week.

Prisoners should also have access to exercise, leisure, and recreational facilities under both the European and the domestic Prison Rules (PR 30, 32). Access to education and training should be available for adults and is compulsory for young offenders below the school-leaving age. Clearly education offers possibilities of retraining, and reintegration. Education has been treated as a fundamental right, see Article 2 of Protocol No. 1, but this provision is primarily aimed at children and in practice provision for adults varies across states (see UNGA HRC 2009). The CPT have emphasized that education is part of the process of normalization. A wide range of courses may be available including Open University degree courses. Given their particular interest in and experience of crime and punishment, courses on criminology are often popular with prisoners following academic courses. However, most of the educational work in prison is at a much more basic level with the focus on literacy and numeracy.

The Strasbourg Court is unlikely to treat absence of recreational facilities per se as a breach of Article 3 unless it is part of a regime which is deficient overall. Under the domestic UK Prison Rules adult prisoners are entitled to one hour a week of physical education (PR 29). Prisons should prepare the offender for release and this is included in the European Prison Rules: 'All prisoners shall have the benefit of arrangements designed to assist them in returning to free society after release' (EPR 33.3).

As well as formal education and training, prisoners may be required to complete Offending Behaviour Programmes in order to become eligible for consideration for parole and to reduce the risk of reoffending which will be a key element of their risk assessment. Problems may arise where there are insufficient courses available which will be discussed in Chapter 5. The Coalition Government announced in July 2010 that a major review of prison education will be conducted to assess cost-effectiveness and its implications for reducing reoffending.

Prisoners should have access to exercise outside in the fresh air for at least one hour a day under the European Prison Rules (EPR 27.1) and on the CPT recommendations, and denial of such access would amount to degrading conditions. A similar requirement was found in the UK Prison Rules until 1996, but now the revised PR 30 is less specific: 'If the weather permits and subject to the need to maintain good order and discipline, a prisoner shall be given the opportunity to spend time in the open air at least once every day, for such period as may be reasonable in the circumstances.' For a prisoner with no work or classes then he could lawfully remain in his cell for as long as 23 hours a day.

A recent report of the National Audit Office is critical of the fact that between half and one-third of prisoners serving short sentences spent most of the day in their cells and were not involved in training or rehabilitation programmes, because of the lack of availability of courses and pressures from overcrowding (NAO 2010). The majority of prisoners serving short sentences are serving less than three months. The Report stressed the adverse implications of this inactivity for the prospect of reoffending as this group is most likely to reoffend. The NAO questions the cost-effectiveness of these sentences and stresses the need for sufficient activity spaces to be made available and in the interim for more purposive activities to be available in cells.

Prison conditions in the Netherlands

Dutch prison conditions have the reputation of being generally more humane than other European countries and prisoners' rights were well developed there relatively early and have been held out as a model for other European societies. The reasons for this humanitarianism include the tradition of Dutch tolerance and more specifically the influence of the so-called Utrecht school, associated with the Institute of Criminology at Utrecht University and originally headed by Willem Pompe and later by Ger Kempe, which rejected positivistic criminological approaches in favour of a rehabilitative and humane and anti-punitive approach. The current cost of Dutch prisons is now running at 1bn euros per annum, although this figure includes closed centres for asylum seekers, while in England and Wales the UK the running cost is in excess of £2bn per annum.

However, because of the smaller numbers in Dutch prisons, the level of spending per prisoner is approximately three times higher than in England

and Wales. Yet the incarceration rate, the number of persons in prison per 100,000 of population, increased from 20 in 1970 to 45 in 1990, then increased dramatically to 128 in 2006, but had fallen to 94 by the end of April 2010 (International Centre for Prison Studies 2010). In 1984 there were 45,000 prisoners in England and Wales and 4,000 in the Netherlands, so the contrast has been marked for decades. From 1951 to 1977 the Dutch prison population was halved, despite an increase in the crime rate from 1966–75, while the UK prison population doubled.

Although the numbers in prison have increased since the early 1990s there has been a recent fall to 12,000 in 2009 so these figures are clearly modest compared to the UK. This expansion increased pressures on prison budgets and has led to more attention being given to making prisons more cost-effective and this concern with costs remains strong despite recent falls in the incarceration rate. One element of cost-effectiveness is ensuring that the time spent in detention and any treatment programmes are appropriate to the individual so there is now more focus on sentence planning and evaluation, just as in the UK. There is also increasing reliance on technological means of surveillance rather than dynamic security to cut staffing costs and to control prisoners, for example, through electronic tagging of prisoners, CCTV cameras and giving prisoners a touch screen to plan activities. As in the UK, rewards and privileges are used to control prisoners' behaviour.

The Dutch Deputy Minister of Justice has announced plans to close prisons in the Netherlands because of overcapacity. However discussions are underway to transfer Belgian prisoners to Tilburg prison in the Netherlands to prevent closure.

Dutch prison conditions are framed by the European Prison Rules and of course prisoners have the protection of the European Convention and the domestic law of the Penitentiary Principles Act 1999 (PPA) and Penitentiary Rules. The PPA gives prisoners minimum rights to certain activities and resources and operates on the assumption that the prisoner should be subject to as few restrictions as possible beyond the loss of liberty. The rights encompass both substantive and procedural rights and include access to visits, classes, complaints procedures and access to libraries.

The Prison Appeal Board hears prisoners' appeals and is strongly influenced by the Convention jurisprudence in deciding whether rights exist or whether limits on rights may be justified (see de Jonge 2007). Prisons are less crowded than in the UK and during periods of high demand in the past a waiting list was used to prevent overcrowding, but this ended in 1994 because the expansion of the prison population led to a backlog. However, prisoners may not serve sentences immediately but report to prison on a set date. This not only allows time for a suitable place to be found but also means the offender can plan his affairs properly before entering prison to avoid disruption.

A major comparative study of Dutch and English prisons was conducted by Downes in 1988 in *Contrasts in Tolerance*. It reviewed postwar penal policy in the Netherlands and England and Wales to see how each state responded to common problems of rising crime and pressures on prisons. Downes interviewed judges, public prosecutors, administrators and criminologists in the Netherlands and prisoners in both Dutch and English prisons, who in some cases had sampled both regimes. Although he did not interview English judges and the sample of prisoners was quite small, consisting mostly of drug offenders, his research nonetheless provides insights into the differences between the prison regimes at that time. What Downes found was greater coordination between agencies in formulating criminal justice policies and a wider range of options for dealing with drug offenders than in the UK. Prosecutors had powers to formulate and implement policies, to decide which cases should be prosecuted, and to waive prosecutions on policy grounds. Their views were also fed into the development of sentencing guidelines. Senior prosecutors met regularly to review criminal justice policy.

Downes also found evidence of a distinctive culture among Dutch judges and prosecutors in which a low value is placed on incarceration, an awareness of criminological research findings and a more critical attitude to the value of imprisonment and a strong commitment to the rehabilitative ideal. He contrasts this with English judges who sought and were obliged to keep policy objectives out of the sentencing process. The Dutch judiciary, he argues, also insisted on high standards within prison and resisted pressures to lower them. So overall he found the Dutch system more humane and not simply because sentences were generally shorter. There was a higher staff-prison ratio than England, better relations between staff and prisoners, better leave arrangements and a procedure whereby less serious offenders were allowed to arrange their own reception into prison. There were also better facilities for work, education, welfare and recreation and better grievance procedures. At the time of his research, the Dutch system was still committed to individual cells while the English system was experiencing increasing overcrowding. This review of Dutch penal and drugs policy shows greater levels of coordination and integration of policy than the UK, and less reliance on piecemeal policies, in response to media pressure, public opinion or political pressure.

The Dutch prison regime at that time reflected the view that humane conditions and relatively short sentences for most offences other than drugs offences, are most likely to promote the reintegration of the prisoner into society and thereby reduce recidivism. A range of welfarist and preventive strategies were also used to deal with drug users but also heavier sentences for traffickers. While Downes found no evidence to suggest the recidivism rate for Dutch prisoners was better than England, it was no worse. When he interviewed the prisoners themselves, some of whom had sampled prison life in both regimes, he found that they also saw the Dutch system as more humane, less repressive and less psychologically damaging than the English system. Issues referred to were the amount of time spent in cells and the excessive rules and restrictions in English prisons. There was a lack of privacy because of overcrowding which made it hard to maintain good relations between prisoners. However, English prisons were deemed to be superior ·in the treatment of remand prisoners and the educational facilities then available. The Dutch prisons also had relatively high suicide rates, armed guards around the perimeter and poor physical conditions in some of the older prisons and in some respects remand prisoners were treated more harshly than in the UK.

However, since Downes' work there has of course been considerable change in both Dutch and English prison regimes, in the quality of the English prison regime, particularly changes in response to the Woolf Report on the UK prison riots of 1990 (Woolf and Tumim 1991). When Downes was writing the Crown Prosecution Service had only recently begun operating, in 1986. The CPS is able to filter prosecutions in the public interest and the Code has recently been revised to clarify further factors relevant to this filtering process.[13] There are also now routes to feed research findings into the sentencing process through the Sentencing Council (Easton and Piper 2008: 47–55). While there may be greater scepticism on the use of custody among English criminal justice professionals and more awareness of prison overcrowding, even in the early 1980s, there was some awareness of these problems. For example the Lord Chief Justice, Lord Lane said in *Bibi* [1980] 1 WLR 193 that sentencers should be aware of the problem of prison overcrowding in reaching a decision. More recently, in *Kefford* [2002] EWCA Crim 519, the Court of Appeal stressed that sentencers must acknowledge the reality of prison expansion and where possible should use community punishment and fines instead of short prison sentences.

There have also been a number of changes in the Dutch prison system which have been charted by Tak and others (Tak 2003, Tak 2008, Boone and Moerings 2007). Prison building in the Netherlands has expanded to meet the increased population, but this also reflects a move away from the use of psychiatric disposals. The Netherlands has a higher proportion of remand prisoners than England and Wales, but they will often be released at trial because of the time served. It also has a high number of prisoners detained indefinitely under mental health provisions, known as TBR. There are also increasing numbers of foreign nationals with large numbers detained for drugs and immigration offences. Sentence length has increased for long and short sentences.

The pressure of prison expansion has meant financial pressure on prison budgets with fewer resources in prison, and more cell sharing. New prisons have been built to meet demand for places and formal limits on prison capacity have been removed. The quality of prison regimes has declined with fewer activities and the degree of penal austerity has increased. There are fewer rehabilitative programmes which are now limited to specific offenders and as in USA and the UK, the rehabilitative ideal has declined but not disappeared as rehabilitation has been combined with more punitive regimes. Faced with more prisoners serving longer sentences and more prisoners with drug and mental health problems, as well as more aggressive prisoners, there is now more emphasis on security and preventing escapes but also on individualized treatment and detention.

There are 20 adult prisons with separate wings for women in 9 prisons although they may participate in activities alongside men. Life in modern Dutch prisons has been well documented by Tak (Tak 2008). Prisons will vary in security level from very low, low and normal to extended security and extra high security. At lower levels of security where prisoners are approaching the end of their sentence, security is more relaxed and prisoners have far more freedom and are allowed home leave one weekend a month. In fact burglars broke into Het Keern prison to steal prisoners' televisions while they were on weekend leave in March and April 2010.

However, at higher levels of security, regimes are obviously more restricted. Following some high-profile escapes, a new Extra High Security unit was built at Vught prison and here the prisoner has no contact with prisoners from other parts of the prison, is limited to closed visits and is handcuffed if he leaves his cell. However, inmates do have access to recreational activities and sport, so while the conditions are more austere than those of Dutch prisoners on lower security levels, they are not as severe as the American supermax prisons. Vught also includes the special wing for prisoners convicted of terrorist offences, who are kept apart from other prisoners because of the fear of radicalization of other inmates and held on a very restricted regime and unable to work. A similar wing is found at De Schie prison.

The increase in the number of prisoners and changes in the composition of the prison population since the early 1990s has led to changes in the Dutch system. As de Jonge (2007) notes in the late 1980s and 1990s, the government was committed to the view that all prisoners should be given work to help them become law-abiding citizens and make them self-supporting, but it has been difficult to achieve this with prison expansion and budget cuts. *The New Prison*, a ministerial paper published in 2004, stressed the need to cut prison budgets to enforce sentences more cheaply and to do so through closing down workshops, cutting education classes, and reducing time spent outside cells. During that period police cells were also used when necessary. However, there have also been new measures to detain persistent drug offenders. As in the UK, there are pressures on politicians to reduce the financial burdens of imprisonment on the public purse, but this will inevitably have implications for the quality of the regime and ultimately its effectiveness in reducing reoffending.

Every prisoner has the right to work but in the past few years there have been fewer opportunities to work, reflecting budgetary constraints and increased demand. Increasingly security, economy and public safety have assumed more importance in prison priorities. Prisoners should have at least 18 hours of activities and 26 hours of work a week. The aim is that prisoners should be outside their cells for over 59 hours per week, including work and other activities, depending on their level of security and the availability of resources. So as well as work, there may be sports and other recreational activities. All prisoners have a right to spend one hour a day outside and to six hours of recreation per week. Prisoners can also wear their own clothes.

The increase in prison numbers in recent years has meant that demand has outstripped supply of programmes as well as budget cuts which has meant more time spent in cells. The Implementation of Sanctions Inspectorate reported on work conditions in the Over-Amstel Penal Institution, including Demersluis, De Weg and Het Schouw prisons, in 2009 and found there were particular concerns over cancellation of work for prisoners because of insufficient supervisors as well as concerns about library provisions and visits (ISS 2009). If work is unavailable, prisoners should attend other activities including sport, education and creative education, that is art or craft activities, but education is no longer available to all and for those who are working, access to education will be limited. In the past some prisoners have received student grants during their time in prison but this was curtailed in December 2008. Access to activities is also intended to relieve pressure when prisoners are sharing cells so they will attend activities at different times. The right to rehabilitation of sentenced prisoners enshrined in the Penitentiary Principles Act has now been limited to specific groups. Only a limited number of prisoners now have access to work and education and not all of these will have access to rehabilitative programmes (see Boone 2007). Remand prisoners no longer have access to work although they are not obliged to work if work is available. For sentenced prisoners, access to education and work is limited to those serving longer sentences. These limitations on access to activities may conflict with EPR 25 which emphasizes the need to provide a balanced programme of activities and EPR 6 which stipulates that detention shall be managed to facilitate the reintegration of offenders into society.

Usually prisoners want to work but if asked to work and if they refuse to do so they may be subject to sanctions. Earnings are usually very low as in the UK and like the UK, longer-serving prisoners are given priority for education, training and work, although some education and training is available for shorter-serving prisoners. Access to resources such as work, education and recreation is limited for those convicted of drug trafficking offences. There are also problems in finding suitable work because of the lack of skills of the prisoners, including language skills, in some cases. There may also be mental health problems, which make organizing work difficult. Work may be undertaken to service the needs of the prison, but may also involve working in a range of industries. Prisoners may also serve part of their sentence in the community attending classes or drug treatment and other programmes.

Cognitive behavioural training programmes are widely used to develop cognitive skills, including problem solving and impulse-control. There are some indications that CBT based programmes have an effect on recidivism (see McGuire 1995). Behavioural programmes are assessed by an independent Accreditation Panel which uses similar criteria to those in England and Wales and which reports to the Minister of Justice.

In 2007 the Inspectorate criticized the reduction of prisoners' daily activities which had led to a more austere regime and the fact that owing to more intense schedules, prison staff had less time to talk to prisoners which meant fewer opportunities to identify potential problems. There were also concerns about passing on information between institutions and for this reason the Inspectorate conducted a thematic review of information transfer in 2007.[14] Prison resources have been stretched by budget cuts and increasing importance is given to security and public protection. The Annual Report of the Council for the Administration of Criminal Justice and Youth Protection in 2005 noted a reduction in education and work activities and less contact with staff and prisoners which also had implications for resettlement as it would be harder to find work without skills.

The entitlement to single cells was phased out at the end of 2003, beginning with remand prisoners at Tilburg and those serving shorter sentences in detention centres. Initially shared cells were allocated on a voluntary basis. The use of shared cells was later extended to Rotterdam, Breda, Utrecht, Limburg-Zuid, Achterhoek and Vught and became compulsory. Newly built prisons have been designed for multi-occupancy cells on the assumption that cell sharing is available in all penal institutions. In addition, use has been made of two boats in Rotterdam to hold those detained for breaches of immigration rules. Prisoners may share cells if they are serving short sentences, or are on remand, or prefer to share (Kelk 2007). However pressure has meant that some remand prisoners have been sharing with convicted prisoners which conflicts with EPR 18.8a (de Jonge 2007). However, recent reductions in the population have made it easier for prisoners to regain single cells. If prisoners are required to share, they will first be assessed for risks, for example, of aggression and for any medical or other problems.

Prisoners have clear-cut rights to visits, and other benefits such as physical education. Prisoners also have the right to medical care under s 42 of the Penitentiary Principles Act and EPR 39 and this health care inside prison should be as close as possible to the care citizens receive outside prison. There is a special complaints procedure for medical care in the Dutch system and a developing body of case law on prison medical law. Prisoners may also take complaints to the Ombudsman. The CPT has praised the medical care in Dutch prisons, saying that that it does satisfy the principle of equivalence. Prisoners on hunger strike may not be force fed by prison doctors because of the conflict with Article 3 unless there is a life-threatening emergency. The issue arose in 2002 when Volkert van der Graaf, the prisoner convicted of murdering Pim Fortuyn, went on hunger strike for 69 days in protest over his prison conditions, including camera surveillance in his cell. Doctors acting on Dutch Medical Association Advice refused to force feed him but van der Graaf abandoned the hunger strike when some of his demands were met.

The Netherlands has a well-established system of detention for mentally ill offenders, called TBS. Offenders who have committed serious offences while suffering from a mental illness may be given a prison sentence in combination with TBS, that is a placement under a hospital order, in order to protect society. The hospital order may entail compulsory treatment so the individual will be held in a custodial clinic for that treatment. Hospital orders may also be conditional, so the individual will not be detained in a clinic provided certain conditions are met, such as not using drugs or alcohol, or undergoing treatment, but the Order can be changed to a compulsory order if the conditions are breached. There are eight custodial clinics and four Forensic Psychiatric Clinics in the Netherlands. There has been a decline in the use of psychiatric prison sentences, or TBS, since 2004, leading to some clinics being closed. It has been a concern of lawyers for some time that those given TBS serve longer sentences.

As the key principle governing prison health care is equivalence, patients with a psychiatric disorder who are detained in a penal institution, should receive care which is equivalent to care outside, including compulsory treatment, but if long-term compulsory treatment is needed, then the prisoner should be referred to an appropriate psychiatric institution. The number of prisoners with mental illness has increased and these prisoners may be transferred to forensic clinics or to psychiatric hospitals.

Concerns have been voiced regarding the level of care in TBS wards within the prison system in a recent Report of the Council for the Administration of Criminal Justice and Protection of Juveniles (CAJ 2010). There are five prisons with TBS wards at the present time. The Report recommended that three of the smaller wards within the prison system should be closed because of insufficient facilities or skills available and overall the level of care was lower than that in TBS clinics. Originally these wards were used because of pressure on places in TBS units outside, but the waiting list for those places is decreasing. The facilities have also been criticized by the Implementation of Sanctions Inspectorate and the Healthcare Inspectorate as patients in the units have less freedom of movement than in ordinary clinics outside as well as worse patient care than outside.[15]

Cases have been brought to Strasbourg by Dutch prisoners challenging aspects of prison conditions within the Netherlands and its overseas territories. Dutch prisoners have access to generous legal aid provision which is not means tested. As in the UK, the prisoners' rights claims have achieved mixed results. A challenge to the treatment of prisoners in a Dutch maximum security prison failed in *Baybasin v the Netherlands* Application No. 13600/02 (6 July 2006) on issues other than routine strip-searching. However, in the key case of *van der Ven v the Netherlands* and *Lorse v the Netherlands* Application Nos. 50901/99, 52750/99 (4 February 2003), the applicants were routinely and regularly strip-searched regardless of whether there had been contact with the outside world or any reason to suspect possession of objects which might compromise prison security and a refusal to comply resulted in punishment. The Court found clear breaches of Article 3. The cases also followed criticism by the CPT of the regimes in high security units in the Netherlands in its reports on 1997 and 2001 visits. After *van der Ven* and *Lorse* the rules were modified and prisoners are no longer routinely strip-searched.

Most of the concerns of the CPT and the European Court of Human Rights have focused on the Dutch overseas territories which have much worse physical conditions, funding and resources. The CPT has been very critical of conditions in the Netherlands Antilles, including the amount of food provided (Council of Europe 1996: para 87). It criticized the poor physical conditions, the lack of physical space and raised concerns over the impact of such conditions on prisoner's mental health and found conditions in Curaçao's prisons were inhuman and degrading. In *Mathew v the Netherlands* Application No. 4919/03 (29 September 2005), the segregation of prisoners in Aruba was deemed inhuman treatment in breach of Article 3.

When the CPT examined the high security regime in Demersluis Prison High Security Unit, in the early 1990s it found insufficient time outside cells, insufficient activities for prisoners and poor staff–prisoner relations (Council of Europe 1993: para 91). In response the Government announced it would build two further units. When the CPT returned for another visit in 1997 it criticized the fact that only one unit had been built (Council of Europe 1998). In its Report on Vught maximum security prison, the Committee was critical that not enough progress had been made giving prisoners time outside cells, and the regime was still humiliating for them. While the Committee said that medical care had improved, there were still concerns over the prisoners' mental health and the psychological impact of the regime and it therefore requested a study of inmates' mental health.

Following this criticism, an independent review of prisoners' mental health in Dutch extra high security prisons and the unit for prisoners with restricted association (BGG) in Vught prison was conducted.[16] The research carried out at Nijmegen University for the Research and Documentation Centre of the Ministry of Justice in 2000 examined the effects of high-security regimes on prisoners' mental health and the long-term effects on inmates of the regime, but found no causal evidence of a link between the regime and the prisoners' mental health and made only a few minor recommendations. They found that medical and nursing care was adequate although more empirical research was needed to see the impact on mental health over time. The Ministry of Justice's conclusion was that while prisoners at this prison suffered more stress than prisoners elsewhere, it was not sufficient to justify major changes to the regime.

In its 2002 Report the CPT found no evidence of torture or inhuman or degrading treatment in the prisons it visited, but did recommend offering more work and education activities in high security prisons (Council of Europe 2002). It also wanted clearer criteria for allocation to high-security prisons. It has subsequently expressed concern at increased pressure on staff with the number of prisoners although the government responded with a commitment to increase staff recruitment and training, but as the emphasis now is on electronic monitoring and surveillance there may be less contact between staff and prisoners. If a prisoner is disruptive he can be held in isolation for two weeks during which time he cannot work or take part in recreational activities, but must still have access to fresh air for one hour a day, be allowed to attend religious services and have access to visits unless the disruptive behaviour is related to visits.

In its latest report, based on its visit in 2007, the CPT expressed some concern about the use of double cells and recording of disciplinary sanctions in prison, the lack of provision for recreation and other facilities for short-term prisoners and the problems with the gowns provided for prisoners who were in isolation (Council of Europe 2008). Although it found no instances of ill-treatment it did refer to allegations of ill-treatment relating to the expulsion of illegal immigrants. Concerns were raised about the isolation of prisoners in the terrorist wings and the CPT recommended regular reviews for prisoners placed there and that the selection should be based on individual risk. Other issues raised were handcuffing during medical examinations which the CPT recommended should be avoided. It also criticized the physical conditions, the lack of activities and overcrowding in prisons in Aruba and ill-treatment and medical care in the prisons of the Netherlands Antilles. In its response published in 2009, the Government provided more information on cell sharing, referred to a review of the regime on the terrorist wings, and to the refurbishment of prisons in Aruba and the development of programmes in the Netherlands Antilles.[17]

The Dutch government has said that it is committed to modernization of the prison system. This modernization agenda 2007–10 focused on reoffending and aftercare, better treatment of prisoners with psychiatric and addiction problems but also increasing the efficient use of prison capacity to reduce the costs, but also to a more individualized approach. The emphasis was on achieving cost-effectiveness through cell sharing, and simplification of detention regimes, improved screening for mental health and risk factors, and improved allocation procedures to ensure that prisoners serving short sentences and those nearing the end of longer sentences can be housed near their local area. The system of care is also being reorganized with additional care places and to deal with drug dependency. Violence prevention is regularly reviewed in Dutch Prisons by the Inspectorate for the Implementation of Sanctions and there are clear protocols for managing violence.

A survey of 10,000 prisoners was conducted in 2003 with a response rate of 60 per cent. The average age of the prisoners surveyed was 33. Fifty-seven per cent of respondents were born in the Netherlands, 9 per cent were Surinamese, 8 per cent from the Netherlands Antilles, 6 per cent from Morocco and 5 per cent from Turkey (Netherlands, Ministry of Justice 2003). Prisoners were questioned on whether they felt safe, on whether prison rules and rights were enforced, future prospects, and contact with staff and other prisoners. The majority of prisoners felt safe from assault or sexual assaults but were concerned over theft of their goods. Many prisoners thought that prison rules were often unclear and that they were not sufficiently informed about their rights and were critical of the handling of complaints. For the most part relationships with prison staff were good, and prisoners felt that they were treated well by officers, although they were less positive about their relationships with other prisoners. There were complaints about too much time spent in their cells and boredom particularly at the weekends and in the evenings. Remand prisoners were the most dissatisfied prisoners. Not surprisingly the majority of respondents disagreed with the statement that prisons are like hotels.

As in the UK, a large number of prisoners are drug users and drugs are smuggled into prisons despite a range of preventive measures including sniffer dogs, redesigning visitors' rooms and drug testing. Penalties for violating drugs policies have increased and prisoners may face prosecution as well as disciplinary measures. Some prisons have drug-free wings to help prisoners seeking to avoid drugs. Methadone may be given to prisoners who are heavy drug users. HIV prevention measures include the distribution of condoms, but not as yet clean needles. Prisoners cannot be tested for HIV without their consent.

An indication of possible future developments in Dutch penal policy was given in June 2009 when the deputy justice minister Nebahat Albayrak announced that the government plans to close eight prisons to achieve financial savings, as there is capacity for 14,000 prisoners, but only 12,000 places are needed. The change was attributed to a lower crime rate, meaning less demand for prison places. However, it also reflects the increased use of community sentences since 2001 when the law was amended so that a community sentence could be used for offences punishable by six months imprisonment (van Langendonck 2009). Judges can now give community sentences for offences which carry up to a six-month sentence and they now amount to 30 per cent of all sentences. It also reflects the awareness that prison does not prevent reoffending and the reoffending rates from some groups of prisoners released from Dutch prisons can be as high as 70 per cent within seven years. Community sentences are seen as a cheaper and more humane alternative to prison. Other factors contributing to the reduction are changes in criminal justice policy and sentencing, including focusing on drug traffickers leaving Curaçao so that they can be detained at the airport of origin, rather than on arrival in Amsterdam.

Prison conditions in the United States

In contrast to the Netherlands, the prison system in the United States has a reputation for penal austerity. However, while prison sentences may be longer than in the Netherlands and conditions harsher, the quality of conditions may vary. The harshest conditions are in the so-called 'supermax', maximum security prisons for dangerous, disruptive and violent prisoners, where solitary confinement is the normal mode of containment and prisoners are confined to their cells for the majority of the time with very little contact with others, especially as security is controlled by technology (King 1999, Kurki and Morris 2001, Ross 2007, King and Resodihardjo 2010). The cells are small and the lights are on all the time, which raises serious concerns for prisoners' mental health. Prisoners are isolated from other prisoners, and their access to resources available to other prisoners is limited. These prisons house dangerous disruptive and violent prisoners. They have very secure external perimeters and lethal force can be used against those who try to escape and prisoners' access to the prison outside their cells is very limited.

King and Resodihardjo (2010) compare the American approach to dealing with high-security prisoners of the supermax prison with the alternatives chosen in the UK and the Netherlands. All three states faced similar problems in the 1990s including concerns over managing high-risk prisoners and preventing escapes, although with the Northern Ireland peace process pressure for high-security prisons receded. The supermax model was rejected in the UK in favour of using High or Special Secure Units and Close Supervision Centres within high-security prisons and which rely more on high staff–prisoner ratios for security, than on the physical separation of staff and prisoners. Special security units were built in the Netherlands at Vught prison as we have seen. There is more freedom for prisoners in Vught than in the US supermax prisons, but less access to activities than in lower-security Dutch prisons.

Although the emphasis is often placed on American exceptionalism in terms of the modes of punishment and severity of punishment, there is variation between states and between institutions. The American penal estate is not a homogenous entity but includes a wide range of correctional facilities, including state and federal, public and private prisons. There are higher rates of imprisonment in the states with lowest welfare spending and variations in the levels of overcrowding between states (see Beckett and Western 2001). States have been subjected to budget cuts over the past few years but the budget for federal prisons has increased since 2009. The development of mass incarceration has also meant substantial business opportunities for private companies in supplying goods and services to the prison industries, benefiting from prison labour and of course in running private prisons (Herivel and Wright 2008). There are now business opportunities undreamt of when Jessica Mitford published her study of the American prison business in 1973 (Mitford 1973).

In the United States there is a wide range of institutions and obviously the number of prisons is much greater. There are over 1500 prisons, of which 95 per cent are run by state or federal institutions and 5 per cent by private companies, so conditions may vary and the prison building programme is continuing to meet demand. Although prisons conditions in the majority of prisons in the USA are harsher than in the UK or the Netherlands, prisoners now have more formal rights and improved conditions compared to the early 1960s, reflecting as we have seen, the increasing activism of the courts in the landmark cases of *Monroe v Pape* 365 US 167 (1961), *Cooper v Pate* 378 US

546 (1964) and *Wolff v McDonnell* 418 US 539 (1974). However, concerns remain over the harsh conditions within the prison estate and the treatment of prisoners held in Guantanamo Bay.

Moreover, there is a long tradition of prison reform in the United States. The demand for reform and for prisons to be used for rehabilitation existed alongside some of the worst conditions, as well as some of the most progressive, for example in women's reformatories (Zedner 1995, Rotman 1990, Rothman 1995). Some of the most progressive attitudes towards imprisonment in the eighteenth century were found in the United States, where the Quakers played a key role in prison reform, just as they did in the UK, and were influential in the Philadelphia Society for Alleviating the Miseries of Public Prisons. This Society was established in 1787 to campaign for improvements in Walnut Street jail in Philadelphia and many of their demands were implemented. Although some of these 'advances' such as solitary confinement and hard labour would be unacceptable to modern reformers, at the time they were radical and some of these measures did alleviate for a period the overcrowding and poor conditions in the jail and brought the indignities and abuses suffered by prisoners to the attention of the public. The Society later became the Pennsylvania Prison Society and continued to campaign and to visit prisons regularly and is still active today in fighting for social justice for prisoners.

The prison population expanded rapidly in the 1990s from 1,295,150 in 1992 to 2,297,400 in mid-2009 which increased pressure on prisons and made it harder for regimes to provide conditions which respect prisoners' rights and fostered rehabilitation (ICPS 2010). The expansion reflects the war on drugs, increase in sentence lengths, and cuts in parole. At any time, about one-third of admissions into prison will be parole violators returning to custody.

In 2009 the number of prisoners in state prisons declined by 0.4 per cent.[18] However, the prison population as a whole increased because of the increase in the federal prison population, although the rate of increase has slowed down. There are still over 1.6 million people in state and federal prisons and a further 700,000 in local jails. The fall in the state prison population has been attributed to a number of factors including greater availability of non-custodial options to sentences, greater use of technology including GPS monitoring to avoid custodial sentences, better risk management procedures and fiscal pressures on states. There is also evidence of more public support for non-custodial options for non-violent offenders. However, increasing awareness of the social and economic costs of prison may encourage consideration of alternatives and there were strong expectations that President Obama would address some of these issues and the federal budget for prisons has increased.

In *Coleman v Schwarzenegger* US District Court, No. Civ. S-90-0520 (4 August 2009) the California District Court ordered the state to reduce prison overcrowding within two years. The claimants argued that their constitutional rights were violated by the overcrowding in California's prisons and the only way of remedying the constitutional violations was a prisoner release order, that is, an order for release of a prisoner or non-admission to prison where the purpose is to reduce or limit the prison population. The case has been running since the early 90s. All parties accepted that overcrowding existed and a state of emergency had been declared by the governor in 2006 because of severe overcrowding and was still in effect. The court had previously held that the state had failed to provide mental or physical health care which was constitutionally adequate. The issue reviewed here was whether overcrowding was the primary cause of the failure to provide adequate health care. There were insufficient medical personnel or officers to ensure that prisoners received appropriate treatment and there was a risk of increase in infectious diseases because of the overcrowded conditions. These included prisoners being housed in triple bunks in gyms and other areas not intended to be used for housing. By 2008 prisons were operating at 200 per cent capacity. The Court issued an interim order demanding that it be reduced to at most 120–45 per cent capacity within two to three years and for prisons with clinical programmes reduced to 100 per cent. It proposed that funds could be diverted to community rehabilitative programmes and the earned credit and parole systems could be reformed to address the problems. Public safety would benefit as there would be more scope for rehabilitative programmes. The Court argued that prison could be reformed through measures which would not threaten public safety and that overcrowding is itself a public safety issue because of the increased risk of infectious diseases. This was an interim order and the court has invited responses on the percentage and dates to be included in the final order and on measures to address public safety concerns. An appeal against the order has been made and will be heard by the Supreme Court in due course.

There is a system of prison accreditation run by the American Correctional Association so prison and probation facilities for adults and juveniles which meet the appropriate standards may be accredited. The accreditation process includes reviews and audits. However, some of its decisions to accredit particular institutions and failure to consider key rights issues such as reviews of segregation have been subject to criticism.[19] By 2006, less than half of American prisons were accredited and ensuring that accreditation standards are applied regularly in practice may be more difficult (Gibbons and Katzenbach 2006). However, the courts have played an important role in the governance of prison regimes. As we saw in Chapter 2, the role of the courts in prison supervision shifted from a hands-off to a hands-on approach in *Coffin v Reichard* 143 F 2d 443 (6th Cir 1944), but the court's commitment to overseeing and improving prison conditions has since wavered. In *Union County Jail Inmates v. DiBuono*, 713 F.2d 984 (3d Cir. 1983), the court said that prisoners are entitled to a 'minimal civilized measure of shelter'. Prisoners should not be subjected to arbitrary punishment, or physical restraints, although they can be restrained if a danger to themselves or others and placed in solitary confinement if necessary. They should have adequate space, food, clothes and sanitation.

If the Court is concerned over conditions, it may appoint a court monitor to oversee conditions. The monitor appointed in *Ruiz v Estelle* 503 F. Supp. 1295 (1980) was retained for 20 years, before the court released him from his role and even then there were still problems, including assaults in the prison. *Ruiz v Estelle* was a class action brought by Ruiz and others who claimed that prison conditions in Texas violated prisoners' constitutional rights and which involved protracted reviews and litigation over a number of years. The case began in 1972 and resulted in the District Court taking on a supervisory role overseeing prison conditions in Texas, in *Ruiz v Lynaugh*, 811 F. 2d 856 (5th Cir. 1987). Subsequently, the Court ordered the parties to negotiate with a view to ending the court's supervisory role. In 1992 the court withdrew from supervision of the majority of areas, apart from overcrowding. But the arguments continued including issues such as the implications of the Prison Litigation Reform Act 1995 in *Ruiz v Estelle v Culberson and Brown*, No.97–21003 (5th Cir. 1998).

We still find within American prisons a range of problems including disorder, violence and arson, assault, rape and racial abuse.[20] Since the Attica riot in 1971, there have been riots in Sante Fé, New Mexico, in 1980, where several prisoners were murdered and staff injured and the prison set alight, over two days of extreme violence and disorder (Colvin 1992). There were riots in the Cimarron Unit of the Arizona State Prison Complex in Tucson in 1986, and in Atlanta, Georgia, in 1987. In Lucasville, Ohio, in 1993, prisoners occupied the Southern Ohio Correctional Facility, and the siege lasted 11 days with officers taken hostage, and ended with nine prisoners and an officer murdered (Lynd 2004). There was a riot at Pelican Bay State Prison in California in 2000 and riots at Reeves County Detention Center in Pecos, Texas, a privately run facility in 2008 and 2009. There were also incidents of disorder in August 2009 at the medium-security Northpoint Training Center in Burgin, Kentucky, and at the California Institution for Men in Chino, California.

The levels of violence, including deaths at the hands of fellow prisoners increased in the 1980s, and paradoxically this has been attributed in part to the expansion of prisoners' rights and the impact of legislation addressing prisoners' rights claims which limited the powers of prison officers and the use of prisoners to control other prisoners which was an issue in *Ruiz v Estelle* 503 F. Supp. 1295 (1980). Some prisoners felt safer when this practice ended, but it created a space for gangs within the prison to take over this controlling role. There have also been many incidents of prisoners being assaulted and shot by officers. There is still a high incidence of rape in prisons, as well as problems of physical and racial abuse. The high levels of assault, both physical and sexual, are reported in a major review of violence by the Commission on Safety and Abuse which found violence widespread with prisoners subjected to violence from gangs, sexual assault, violence from officers and both officers and prisoners living with a constant fear of assault (Gibbons and Katzenbach 2006). Yet, as the Report points out, there is a range of violence prevention strategies which can and should be used including better supervision, reduced overcrowding, more recreational facilities, support for family and community bonds, and better oversight of prisons, the use of force as a last resort, and obtaining more information on the extent of the problems of violence. What is also needed is a change in prison culture to promote mutual respect between prisoners and officers, and stronger protection of the vulnerable and mentally ill.

Challenging prison conditions

Challenges to prison conditions have been brought by prisoners, individually and by means of class actions, and by the ACLU who have been active on a wide range of prisoners' rights issues and their campaigns have achieved improvements in prison conditions as well as bringing actions, for example in *Clement v California Dept of Corrections* 220 F. Supp. 2d. 1098 (N.D.Cal. 2002).

To bring a claim challenging prison conditions, a prisoner has to find a clear source for the right in question and use has been made mostly of the Eighth Amendment prohibition on cruel and unusual punishment and Fourteenth Amendment due process rights. A civil action for deprivation of civil rights under the Constitution may be brought under 42 U.S.C. section 1983 of the Civil Rights Act 1871. This Act removed the immunities of government bodies if they violate constitutional rights and has been used against prison wardens. Remedies available to prisoners include damages and injunctions.

Most challenges to prison conditions rely on the Eighth Amendment prohibition on cruel and unusual punishment, adopted in 1791 which was based on the provision in the English Bill of Rights in 1689. Originally applicable to federal law, it now applies to states and a substantial body of jurisprudence has focused on arbitrary, unnecessary and disproportionate punishments, and punishments imposing severe suffering. While originally intended to prohibit torture and barbaric punishments such as beheading and disembowelling, the Court has emphasized, for example, in *Trop v Dulles*, 356 US 66 (1958), that it should be interpreted in the context of evolving standards of decency, so punishments which might have been acceptable in the past would not be acceptable today. In death penalty jurisprudence this has led to a progressive narrowing of methods of execution to lethal injections and of the class of offenders on which the punishment may be used to those over 18 and fully competent adults.[21] Within the context of imprisonment, it has been used to successfully challenge corporal punishment in prison in *Jackson v Bishop* 404 F. 2d. 571 (8th Cir. 1968) and it is now well-established that corporal punishment is unconstitutional. Although a prisoner can be lawfully shot if he tries to escape, the Court in *Whitley v Albers* 475 US 312 (1986) said that excessive force should not be used, so if a prisoner is caught and restrained and then assaulted by guards, this would offend common standards of decency and breach the Eighth Amendment. However the jurisprudence suggests that the Eighth Amendment affords prisoners less protection than the European Convention or the Conventions against Torture.

In considering constitutional challenges on prison conditions, the courts will review the 'totality of the circumstances', so if conditions are poor and there are no rehabilitation programmes, then the living conditions as a whole may amount to cruel and unusual punishment. Since the early 1990s, the case law indicates that it has become harder for prisoners to succeed in cases on prison conditions. In *Wilson v Seiter* 501 US 294 (1991), the prisoner proved assault, overcrowding, poor sanitation and other problems which in the past would have been deemed to violate the Eighth Amendment. However the Court said the prisoner had to prove not just defects, but 'deliberate indifference' on the part of the prison authority, that is, to show that they knew and disregarded all those problems. This is clearly a more onerous burden as it would be hard for the prisoner to obtain such evidence.

Attempts have also been made to use the Fourth Amendment, the right not to be subjected to unreasonable searches and seizures, to challenge cell searches and strip-searches, but without success. The court has said that prisoners have no Fourth Amendment rights in prison, so strip-searching (including searches of body cavities) is not an unreasonable search, as the prison is entitled to search for contraband (see *Bell v Wolfish* 441 US 520 (1979)). Privacy issues may also arise if a woman prisoner is searched by a male officer (see Chapter 7). In *Hudson v Palmer* 468 US 517 (1984) the Court said a cell search would be unconstitutional if it is done only to harass the prisoner but even so, this would be a violation of the Eighth Amendment prohibiting cruel and unusual punishment rather than of the Fourth Amendment. The prisoner also has no right to be present while his cell is searched, the court said in *Bell v Wolfish*. The due process clause of the Fourteenth Amendment has been used with some success in relation to procedural justice as we shall see in Chapter 5. However in *Parratt v Taylor* 451 US 527 (1981) where the prisoner brought a claim arguing that the loss of his hobby materials sent to him by mail through the negligence of the prison did not succeed. The court concluded that the procedure available for filing tort claims could have been used to seek compensation.

Prisoners' health care

All prisoners are entitled to access to health care. Cases on medical negligence, the involuntary administration of psychotropic drugs, coerced medical treatment, the failure to provide rehabilitation programmes and poor health care have been brought under the Eighth Amendment. In *Estelle v Gamble* 429 US 97 (1976) the Supreme Court ruled that if the prison authority is 'deliberately indifferent' to the prisoner's medical needs and this results in the prisoner suffering unnecessary pain which is not linked to the goals of incarceration, this would amount to cruel and unusual punishment. However, in practice the standard of care does not need to be very high to move beyond indifference, so provided that some medical care is given, then this may be sufficient to cross the threshold for indifference.

However, in *Todaro v Ward*, 565 F. 2d 48 (2nd Cir. 1977) the Court of Appeals ruled that the prison's failure to provide adequate and appropriate health care was unconstitutional. Here female prisoners from the Bedford Hills Correctional Facility brought a class action against the New York State Department of Corrections in the District Court using 42 U.S.C. s 1983, arguing that their constitutional rights had been breached by poor medical care. The District Court found the medical care constitutionally inadequate and this was upheld by the Court of Appeals. A physician and psychiatrist were later appointed by the court to monitor the prison's progress in improving care in a range of areas including referrals, care of the chronically ill and record keeping, because of concerns over the prison's compliance and the monitoring continued until 2004. In *Madrid v Gomez* 190 F. 3d 990 (9th Cir. 1999) prisoners in Pelican Bay supermax state prison did succeed because of the prison's indifference to their medical needs and the prison was forced to improve conditions.

The right to medical treatment includes psychiatric treatment for serious mental health problems, as the federal Court of Appeals made clear in *Bowring v. Godwin*, 551 F. 2d 44 (4th Cir. 1977), and a failure to provide it would be unconstitutional and breach the Eighth Amendment. However, it does not extend to the right to rehabilitation for drug use for habitual users, as the Court affirmed in *Marshall v US* 414 US 417 (1974) which is significant as high numbers of drug users are incarcerated. As in the UK, US prisoners have higher rates of mental illness and suicide compared to the wider community. In the landmark case of *Ruiz v Estelle* (1980) 503 F Supp 1295 (1980) the treatment of mentally ill prisoners was criticized and the Court stressed the need to provide appropriate treatment and to exercise care in prescribing psychotropic drugs. The prisoner has the right not to be given psychotropic drugs without his consent. However, this can be overridden if there is a risk to others or to the prisoner himself if treatment is withheld, as the court made in clear in *Washington v Harper* 494 US 210 (1990). But the treatment imposed on the prisoner has to be appropriate to be justified, according to *Riggins v Nevada* 504 US 127 (1992).

Prisoners' work, training and education

Prisoners work on farms, in prison industries and in providing prison services and chain gangs are still used in some states. As in the UK there is limited work in prison industries and insufficient work for all prisoners and much will depend on the prisoner's skill and security level. The availability of work varies between states and prisons. However, where prisoners work in private programmes they may be paid prevailing local pay rates from which deductions will be made for food and board, restitution to victims and family support. If prison industries pay below the minimum wage they would undercut other workers so this has been a concern. However, there is a wide range of state, federal and local programmes.

Like the UK, the prison population constitutes a potential workforce; for the most part it is low skilled and requires high supervision which pushes up costs for potential employers although wage levels commanded will not be higher than other comparable workers. It has been argued that private companies have profited greatly from prison labour as well as from their increased involvement in the process of punishment through privatization of prisons. If wages are low there are concerns about the exploitation of labour and whether prison work has become a new form of penal servitude. Federal Prison Industries, which operates as UNICOR, employs prisoners selling goods including furniture and clothing to other government departments which has raised questions about issues of competition and undercutting of other workers and businesses.

As prisoners have high levels of illiteracy the consensus among those working in the prison system is that education is ultimately a key means of crime prevention. Prisoners are entitled to basic education and skills training to meet the problem of illiteracy. In addition, there is a range of sporting and recreational programmes. While it is accepted that basic skills training is an important element of prison education, the issue of access to and support for higher education for prisoners able to benefit from it is more politically contentious. The supply of educational courses varies between prisons but some facilities offer access to college level education.

This is illustrated by the arguments in the 1990s over Pell grants for prisoners pursuing higher education. These grants had been available since the mid-1960s but their use expanded in the mid-1970s when education was seen as part of the process of rehabilitation in reducing recidivism. Inmates had been allowed to apply for financial assistance to follow college courses since 1965, and this was widely seen as helping to reduce crime by giving offenders advanced skills to obtain work on release. So the grants, administered by the US Department of Education, were seen as valuable in terms of rehabilitation and public protection. The grants were not given to Death Row inmates or to prisoners serving life sentences without parole. The grants enabled those with few resources to receive support for postsecondary correctional education and were not given directly to prisoners, but to the programme providers. So when they were cut by Congress in 1994, by an amendment to the Violent Crime Control and Law Enforcement Act, this led to the loss of many programmes.

The debate highlighted the tensions between the different strands of penal policy, including rehabilitation and reform on the one hand and the principle of less eligibility and penal populism on the other. Politicians appealed to the principle of less eligibility and penal austerity and in doing so sought to satisfy what they saw as the public's punitiveness. The Pell grant debate reveals a further dimension of the social death of the prisoner considered in Chapter 1 and emphasises the gap between the law-abiding citizen and the prisoners. Loss of the grants can be seen as another expression of the weakening support for the rehabilitative ideal.

Page examines this shift in terms of appeals to white middle- and working-class voters struggling to pay their children's college fees, fears about street crime, economic fears, and ways in which lawmakers obtain political support for punitive policies (Page 2004). He argues that:

> lawmakers, in concert with the popular media, produced a legislative penal drama – complete with heroes and villains, action and suspense and colorful imagery – in which they spoke to key audiences (specifically white working and middle class voters) mistrust of penal practitioners and criminal justice experts, prejudices towards (black and brown) street criminals, fears about crime and anxiety about the economy, the transformed labor market and access to higher education. (ibid at 360)

Page notes that critics argued that the funds for prisoners diverted them from ordinary law-abiding students, that it was a waste of money as it was unlikely to change offenders in most cases, and that there was already sufficient spent on prisoner rehabilitation and it was also insulting to victims of crime. Some critics even suggested that some individuals committed offences in order to go to prison to obtain the funding. Defenders emphasized that the grants were available to ordinary students who were not disadvantaged and that the total funding was very small, less than 1 per cent of the funding allocated for Pell grants, and that it had positive benefits in reducing reoffending and ultimately in protecting the public. There is some evidence that following higher education programmes did contribute to a reduction in reoffending. A study by the US Department of Corrections calculated that every dollar spent on education resulted in a return of more than 2 dollars in reduced prison costs and prison education cut the risk of reincarceration by almost one-third (Steurer, Smith and Tracy 1999). This longitudinal study surveyed 3,600 offenders after release for three years, in Minnesota, Ohio and Maryland.

Prisoners may also be offered offending behaviour programmes, which as in the UK, rely mostly on cognitive behavioural programmes and include specific programmes for female prisoners. However, prisoners do not have a right to rehabilitation and the Court would not see a failure to secure a place on an offending behaviour programme as a violation unless this was part of the 'totality of the circumstances', or the treatment was a crucial element of the sentence and if it was not provided, this might raise such a right. However, while a wide range of rehabilitative programmes was used in prison in the post-war period, the number of programmes has declined, partly because of the loss of support for the rehabilitative ideal in response to Martinson's paper (Martinson 1974). But it also reflected criticisms of coerced treatment and increased demands for due process rights and in recent years, the impact of budgetary constraints. While rehabilitation should be a crucial element of a prison regime, especially where there are high levels of recidivism, as high as 70 per cent for some groups of offenders, in practice we find limitations on the availability of programmes and variations between prisons.

Rape in prison

One of the most widespread, persistent and serious problems in men's prisons in the USA is rape. It is a crime which is under-reported so official figures on incidence are likely to be underestimates and more accurate figures are usually based on self-reporting by prisoners. Under the Prison Litigation Reform Act, if a prisoner is bringing an action relating to violence or sexual assault there are special provisions within the Act to allow these to proceed speedily. But victims may be reluctant to report rape for fear of being seen as a grass and being further victimized, or because of shame or embarrassment, or because they do not think it will be dealt with seriously. Even when it is reported to prison officials, it rarely ends up in court which suggests a degree of toleration. There have also been reports of prisoners who claim to have been 'set up' by prison officers to be raped or attacked by other prisoners.[22] In *Farmer v Brennan, Warden et al.* [1994] 511 US 825 the US Supreme Court held that a prison official may be liable under the Eighth Amendment if he acts with 'deliberate indifference' to prisoners' health and safety, if he knows that there is a substantial risk of serious harm and disregards that risk and fails to take reasonable measures to reduce it. Deliberate indifference here means subjective recklessness rather than negligence. The ACLU took on the case of Roderick Johnson, a prisoner held in a Texas prison, who claimed he had been repeatedly raped and subjected to what was essentially sexual slavery and sold to other prisoners for sexual services. Johnson argued that that the officials knew he was vulnerable as a gay man and failed to protect him but he did not succeed in establishing their complicity in court (*Johnson v Johnson* 5th Circ. Court of Appeals No. 03-10455 (2005)).

The Rape Elimination Act 2003 is the first major law to address this problem. It imposes a duty on prison officials to monitor the problem and to prevent it and ultimately to eliminate it. It was set up following pressure from agencies and the Human Rights Watch Report in 2001, *No Escape: Male Rape in US Prisons* which estimates that 13 per cent of the inmate population in the USA has been subject to sexual assault and that over the past 20 years, more than one million inmates have suffered abuse (Human Rights Watch 2001). Those most at risk are young offenders and offenders with mental health problems. The survey studied over 200 prisoners, across 34 states, and included personal interviews with rape victims. Their evidence testifies to the routine occurrence of rape and the victimization of young and vulnerable prisoners, the fear of reporting crimes in case of violent retribution from attackers, and lack of support from staff when incidents are reported and evidence of HIV transmission. Some studies estimate the incidence is as high as 1 in 10 (see Struckman-Johnson and Struckman-Johnson 2000). As well as forced sexual activity, prisoners may be intimidated into cooperating or 'agreeing' to sex with one prisoner, in order to receive protection from other predatory inmates.

The 2003 Act suggests measures to reduce prison rape including obtaining more information on the problem, and developing national standards for the detection, prevention, reduction and punishment of prison rape in order to eliminate this problem. The aim of the Act is to ensure zero tolerance of rape. It imposes a duty on the Department of Justice to conduct annual surveys of the problem and to identify the causes and to draw up guidelines. Hearings should be held to collect evidence and grants awarded to help states and local government achieve the purposes in the Act. Prisons themselves must also develop ways of reducing the risk. The Act covers all public and private institutions for adult and juvenile offenders and immigration centres.

A Panel was set up under the Act to examine the impact of rape, the National Prison Rape Elimination Commission. The Commission has conducted hearings, visited prisons and talked to survivors, to assess the extent of the problem and its impact. Its Final Report was published in June 2009 and expressed particular concern over overcrowding and its implications for abuse. It found variation in the incidence of abuse between facilities, refers to a survey showing that 4.5 per cent of prisoners had experienced non-consensual sexual contact, and the percentage was higher among younger offenders (National Prison Rape Elimination Commission 2009: 400). Perpetrators of assaults included staff and other prisoners. Although it found good practice in some facilities it was not uniform across the prison estate. It notes that less research has been conducted on assaults on female prisoners by staff but the problem clearly persists (see Girshick 2003, Amnesty International 1999). The District Court in the case of *Women prisoners in the District of Columbia Department of Corrections v District of Columbia* 877 F. Supp. 634 (DDC 1994) recognized the systematic sexual abuse of women in prison as a violation of the Eighth Amendment prohibition on cruel and unusual punishment.

The Commission's Report recommends clear policies, better training and education for both staff and prisoners, the need to identify the most vulnerable individuals, to develop rigorous internal monitoring and external oversight of this problem, to improve reporting procedures for assaults to give prisoners confidence that complaints will be dealt with properly and the use of skilled investigators. Segregation should be used as a last resort because of the stresses it imposes. Victims should be supported with better access to mental heath and support services. Policies should also be tailored towards the special needs of particular groups such as young offenders and immigrants.

The Attorney General is required to respond to the Report and proposed standards from the Commission within one year and to promulgate national standards for the detection, prevention, reduction, and punishment of sexual abuse in detention facilities. The Department of Justice is now reviewing national standards and has solicited responses from the public which were due in by May 2010, before drafting final standards.

The impact of rape may be devastating, leading to suicide and psychological damage but also to health problems if perpetrators are HIV-positive and there may be a substantial risk of acquisition of HIV for victims of rape in prison as safe sex is unlikely to be practised and violent rape may cause bleeding which will aggravate the risk (Pinkerton *et al.* 2007).

The reasons for the high incidence of rape are discussed by Wyatt who notes that while overcrowding and cell sharing exposes prisoners to risk, the problem existed before recent overcrowding (Wyatt 2006). It is also hard to explain it in terms of sexual frustration as research on rapists shows the exercise of power and the subordination of the victim are more important issues, whether the victim is male or female. In an environment without women, rape may also be used to assert an expression of masculinity. There may also be specific cultural factors (O'Donnell 2004). One measure which has been suggested to deal with the problem is to permit conjugal visits, but while there may be good grounds for allowing these visits, rape in prison persists in states where it is permitted. The arguments for and against conjugal visits will be considered in Chapter 6.

The problem of prison rape highlights dramatically the gap between prisoners' rights at a formal level and the reality of prisoners' lives. The problem is not unique to the United States and seems to be a recurring feature of prison regimes around the world. A study by Banbury in 2004 of 432 respondents in British prisons found that 1 per cent of the sample had been sexually coerced at some point in prison and often subjected to repeated abuse (Banbury 2004). A figure of 119 reported instances of sexual assault in prisons in England and Wales in 2008 was given by Maria Eagle in response to a parliamentary question.[23]

Conclusions

The steady stream of prisoners' rights cases in the USA has yielded some significant improvements in prison conditions but as we have seen, not all these claims have been successful. Moreover, there has been a shift in recent years towards greater penal austerity in terms of conditions and treatment with increased control and internal discipline and more overcrowding, despite the expansion of the prison estate. Moreover, following the enactment of the Prison Litigation Reform Act there are more obstacles to litigation as prisoners are required to show physical injury as mental suffering is insufficient, and required to pay court filing fees and to exhaust internal remedies and grievance procedures before bringing an action.

Similarly, in the UK and the Netherlands prison conditions have been under pressure due to expansion although these problems are now receding in the Netherlands. Improvements in prison conditions and enhanced respect for prisoners' rights has led to public concern and demands for increased penal austerity. Legal aid for prisoners' claims has also come under pressure at a time of wide-ranging cuts in legal aid budgets. But prison conditions are not the only concern for prisoners. An important element of prison life is procedural justice which will now be considered.

5 Procedural justice

Introduction

This chapter will consider procedural fairness in the context of the right to challenge unlawful detention and in relation to disciplinary hearings and complaints procedures. The advances in procedural justice and due process rights for prisoners can be seen as a result of a number of factors, including the expansion of judicial review, the impact of the Woolf Report and more recently, the Human Rights Act. The 1970s and 1980s also saw an expansion of the use and scope of judicial review in the UK which enhanced procedural justice within the prison system and prisoners contributed to the expansion by bringing a number of key cases. There was also greater use of the European Convention to assert prisoners' rights in the 1980s, when one of the most pressing issues for prisoners was a failure to respond to grievances and a refusal to inform prisoners of the reasons for decisions which affected them. The Woolf Report was also influenced by public law discourse (Woolf and Tumim 1991). The review of decisions of the prison authorities and the Secretary of State was further enhanced by the Human Rights Act 1998.

However, considerable weight has been accorded by the courts to the needs of the prison management for efficiency and good order in running the prison, which allows plenty of scope for decision making by the authority. In the 1970s and 1980s, more weight was given to the institutional needs of the prison, but in recent years some progress has been made, particularly in relation to the right to an independent adjudicator in disciplinary matters where days may be lost and in relation to reviews of detention.

The issue of access to offending behaviour courses has also been subject to challenges, albeit with mixed results, as prisoners serving sentences imposed for public protection find that there are insufficient available courses, but successful completion of such courses is a key step in establishing the reduction of risk to the public.[1] With the increase in the number of IPP prisoners in recent years, and in the context of the expansion of the prison population, access to programmes is becoming a more important issue where assessments based on performance on those programmes is taken into account in reaching decisions on parole.

Procedural rights, including natural justice, are also very significant in the prison context so it is important that prisoners have access to an impartial and fair complaints procedure and that they perceive those complaints mechanisms as just. Clearly this will have implications for good order in prison, and a sense of unfairness was seen by the Woolf Report and a key contributory factor in the prison riots in 1990 (Woolf and Tumim 1991). Fairness in dealing with prisoners has been stressed by the Committee for the Prevention of Torture who have stressed the need for fair procedures in dealing with prisoners' offences against prison discipline. Procedural justice in disciplinary matters has also been advanced by the European Court of Human Rights.[2]

Procedural fairness is also incorporated into the European Prison Rules. EPR 50 stipulates that 'Subject to the needs of good order, safety and security, prisoners shall be allowed to discuss matters relating to the general conditions of imprisonment and shall be encouraged to communicate with the prison authorities about these matters.' EPR 70.1 provides that 'Prisoners, individually or as a group, shall have ample opportunity to make requests or complaints to the director of the prison or to any other competent authority.'

An important element of procedural justice is that prisoners should be given reasons for decisions which affect them. This was highlighted in the Woof Report and in subsequent decisions and is relevant to issues such as categorization, re-categorization, transfers and segregation. In *R v Secretary of State for the Home Department ex parte Peries* [1997] EWHC 712 (Admin) the Administrative Court stressed that prison authorities should give prisoners reasons for recategorization into higher-security categories, and that prisoners should be given an opportunity to make representations before the decision is finalized. If a life sentenced prisoner is transferred to a higher-security prison then he must notified in writing that they can make representation regarding this within 28 days of notification. Similarly there are clear procedures relating to the process of segregation of disruptive prisoners in PSO 1700. This is not simply a matter of procedural justice but the risk of suicide may be higher for prisoners on segregation. So segregation should be used only as a last resort when necessary to deal with disruptive prisoners. The reasons for the segregation should be recorded, the prisoner informed of the reason and told when the segregation will be reviewed. They should also be told the reasons if they are to be transferred to another prison.

In the past the use of transfers as a punishment was widely resented by prisoners and a significant issue in prison unrest in the 1980s and 1990s. Transfers may be made for behavioural and disciplinary reasons, concerns over escape attempts, or to enable a prisoner to be nearer home. But the expectation is that prisons should make an effort to manage difficult prisoners first. Obviously if prisoners are frequently transferred because of behavioural problems or other reasons, it may make it difficult for them to attend courses and programmes which assist their rehabilitation. However, sometimes they may be transferred to allow them to attend vocational courses or for accumulated visits or inter-prison visits The Chief Inspector of Prisons has been very critical of the practice in some prisons of transferring difficult prisoners before visits to improve the assessment of the prisons (Owers 2010).

Procedural rights for prisoners are protected by Articles 5 and 6 of the European Convention. Article 5 has been used to challenge initial and continued detention and refusal to grant early release and to limit the role of the Secretary of State in reviews in these processes. Under Article 5(1), everyone has the right to liberty and security of person, save for specified cases, and no one shall be deprived of liberty unless in accordance with a procedure prescribed by law, which includes conviction by a competent court. Under Article 5(4), everyone who is deprived of his liberty by arrest or detention shall be entitled to take proceedings by which the lawfulness of his detention shall be decided speedily by a court and his release ordered if the detention is not lawful.

If individuals are detained this must be done with due regard for the law and not arbitrarily. Article 5 has clear implications for the detention of remand prisoners as well as for sentenced prisoners subjected to indeterminate periods of detention. Article 5 challenges have also been used by those detained under mental health law, to establish the right to regular reviews of their detention under a mental health order, as in *Winterwerp v the Netherlands* (1979) 2 EHRR 387.

Article 6 has been used to challenge the procedures and outcomes of disciplinary hearings. Article 6(1) provides that everyone is entitled to a fair and public hearing within a reasonable time by an independent and impartial tribunal established by law. Article 6(2) refers to the right to be presumed innocent while Article 6(3) states that everyone charged with a criminal offence has certain rights including the right to be informed of the charge, to have time to prepare a defence, to defend himself in person or through legal assistance of his own choice and if he has insufficient means to pay for legal assistance to be given it free when the interests of justice so require, the right to examine witnesses against him and to obtain the attendance and examination of witnesses on his behalf and to have the free assistance of an interpreter if necessary.

As we saw in Chapter 2 some improvements in procedural justice for prisoners were achieved through judicial review and use was made of the European Convention decades before the Human Rights Act came into force, for example in *Golder v UK* Application No. 4551/70 (21 February 1975).

Procedural rights are also important in relation to the conduct of parole hearings and there have been numerous challenges demanding procedural safeguards and participation in these hearings. The Parole Board was set up by the 1967 Criminal Justice Act and its powers increased by the 1991 Criminal Justice Act and then the Crime (Sentences) Act 1997. Over the past 20 years the role of the Parole Board has moved closer to a court-like body following interventions by the courts. Prisoners have been given the right to see and make comments on papers considered by the Board and to be provided with reasons for decisions when parole is declined.

Recent challenges have focused on whether the Board is independent from the executive. Before 2007 the Board was sponsored by the Home Office and it is now sponsored by the Ministry of Justice.

In *Weeks v UK* (1988) 10 EHRR 293 and *Hirst v UK* Application No. 40787/98 (21 March 2000) the Strasbourg Court thought the Parole Board was independent. However, the domestic court in *R (Brooke) v Parole Board and others* [2008] EWCA Civ 29 said the Parole Board did not have the degree of independence from the executive or the parties necessary for its judicial role in determining whether prisoners should be released on licence and did not satisfy Article 5(4).

The conduct of proceedings is set out in the Parole Board Rules. The basic procedural requirements are that the prisoner should be informed in advance of the panel's meeting, to receive copies of documentary evidence in advance unless there are grounds for withholding them, for example, national security, prevention of disorder or crime, and to have the opportunity to make representations. If the panel decides the prisoner is unsuitable for release, then the prisoner may request an oral hearing. If there is an oral hearing, then the prisoner may call witnesses and ask questions. Following the hearing the prisoner should be informed of the decision and the reasons for the decision.

Throughout the 1980s, the role of the Home Secretary in the sentencing process was also subject to repeated challenges because the Minister was not seen as independent or impartial, in relation to life sentences, prisoners detained at Her Majesty's Pleasure and the decisions regarding the recall of mandatory life prisoners released on licence.

Sentence length

The Strasbourg Court has said that supervising the sentencing process is not part of the Court's role and is not explicitly governed by the Convention. Such matters would normally be a matter for states and fall within the margin of appreciation. So the Court has been reluctant to comment on the sentencing process or sentence length unless a sentence is grossly disproportionate, in which case it could breach Article 3. Issues of unlawful detention would usually be dealt with under Article 5 rather than Article 3.

Article 3 challenges have been mounted in both the domestic courts and Strasbourg in relation to sentence length but with mixed responses. In *Weeks v UK* (1987) 10 EHRR 293 it was held that a disproportionately severe sentence could constitute inhuman punishment, especially if there is no prospect of release. But life sentences for serious offences are not themselves arbitrary or disproportionate. In *Weeks* the Court said that it might be justified to impose an indeterminate sentence on public protection grounds, but if it were on the grounds of punishment, then it would be concerned about proportionality, and potentially this could breach Article 3. However, it has said that an excessively long minimum period of detention imposed on a juvenile might amount to inhuman treatment in *T v UK, V v UK* Application Nos. 24724/94, 24888/94 (16 December 1999).

A life sentence without any prospect of release would breach Article 3 if the recipient is a child or young person under 18 and breach the UN Convention on the Rights of the Child. In *Einhorn v France*, Application No. 71555/01 (16 October 2001) which concerned an adult, the Court stated: ' ... it is not to be excluded that the extradition of an individual to a State in which he runs the risk of being sentenced to life imprisonment without any possibility of early release may raise an issue under Article 3 of the Convention'.

When the Human Rights Act was passed it was thought that an Article 3 challenge might be mounted in relation to automatic life sentences for a second serious offence under s 2 of the Crime Sentences Act 1997[3] but in *R v Offen* [2001] 1 WLR 253, the Court of Appeal rejected a claim that this amounted to inhuman and degrading treatment. It also rejected a claim that mandatory life sentences are disproportionate and therefore inhuman and degrading, because a life sentence rarely means life and the offender's case is considered on an individual basis, in *R v Lichniak* [2001] EWHC Admin 294. So most of the successful cases have been brought been under Article 5.

The system of sentencing and early release available to prisoners is extremely complex and worthy of extensive scrutiny in itself. It has developed through a series of complex statutes, clarified by cases and overlaid by the jurisprudence of the Strasbourg court, as the UK has sought to comply with these judgments. The basic rights and principles will be highlighted in relation to both indeterminate and determinate sentences.[4]

Challenging indeterminate sentences

Indeterminate sentenced prisoners include prisoners sentenced to life imprisonment and those sentenced to imprisonment for public protection and in both cases the prisoners serve a minimum period of imprisonment to satisfy the requirement for retribution and deterrence. This punitive period is calculated as half of the length of the appropriate determinate sentence and is stated by the trial judge in open court and must be served before release can be considered. But at the end of this period release is not automatic as it depends on the Board's assessment whether the risk of harm the prisoner poses to the public is no more than minimal. The release of indeterminate prisoners is solely a matter for the Parole Board and is binding upon the Secretary of State. As Judge Caflish observed in *Hirst v UK* (No. 2) Application No. 74025/01 (6 October 2005), retribution 'is no longer relevant, therefore, as soon as a person ceases to be detained for punitive purposes' (at para 4). If release is granted it will be on licence and supervised by the Probation Service and prisoners can be recalled to prison at any time to continue serving their sentence if it is deemed necessary to protect the public.

The power to set the punitive period is now the responsibility of the courts rather than ministers. This shift has evolved gradually since 1983 but in

(R) Anderson v Secretary of State for the Home Department [2002] 4 All ER 1089 in 2002 the House of Lords ruled that setting of what used to be called the 'tariff' for mandatory lifers was an exercise that must be made by a judge rather than the Secretary of State and this was given a statutory basis in the Criminal Justice Act 2003.

There are three types of indeterminate sentences available to the court: mandatory life sentences, discretionary life sentences and imprisonment for public protection. Mandatory life sentences relate only to the offence of murder and include imprisonment for life, the mandatory sentence for those who are aged 21 or over at the time of the offence, custody for life, which is the mandatory sentence for those aged 18–21 at the time of the offence, and detention during Her Majesty's Pleasure, which is the mandatory sentence for those convicted of murder and aged over 10 but under 18 at the time of the offence.

Discretionary life sentences include imprisonment for life, which is the maximum sentence for those convicted of serious offences, that is offences listed in Schedule 15 of the CJA 2003 including manslaughter, attempted murder and rape, who were over 21 at the time of the offence, and custody for life, which is for those between 18 and 21 who commit serious offences where a discretionary life sentence would have been given if they were an adult, and detention for life, the equivalent for those aged 10–18. The punitive part of the sentence for discretionary lifers will reflect the seriousness of the offence and not the risk.

While not rejecting indeterminate sentences per se, the Strasbourg Court has emphasized the need for regular access to a court to review their detention and that the use of indeterminate sentences falls within the scope of Article 5. Prisoners detained because of the risk to the public arising from their dangerousness, who are in preventive detention, must be entitled to challenge their detention regularly through regular reviews to ensure they are detained for the minimum period necessary. Prison regimes should also still try to prepare offenders for release notwithstanding the fact that the release date is indeterminate. A large number of prisoner cases have been brought by prisoners who are detained beyond the minimum period.

Imprisonment for Public Protection

The use of indeterminate sentences has increased with the new Imprisonment for Public Protection (IPP) sentences introduced by s 225 of the CJA 2003 which came into effect in 2005. An IPP sentence may be given where the offender is convicted of a 'specified' violent or sexual offence which is serious, which means one of the many offences specified in Schedule 15 of the Act, for which the maximum sentence is 10 years, or more, and where the offender in the view of the Court, poses a significant risk of serious harm to the public through the commission of a further specified offence. A distinction is drawn between the punitive minimum part of the sentence, and the indefinite subsequent period where the offender is detained because of the risk to the public and can be released only when the Parole Board decides that the offender no longer represents such a risk. However, in practice in some respects it is similar to a life sentence although the tariff is usually shorter. IPP prisoners can also apply to have their licence cancelled after 10 years in the community. A minimum two-year tariff for IPP prisoners, subject to certain exceptions, was introduced by the Criminal Justice and Immigration Act 2008. However, this was not retrospective and many IPP prisoners if sentenced now would receive a determinate sentence. But it also means that the IPP cannot now be imposed unless the tariff is set at a minimum of two years.

The number of prisoners being held on IPP sentences is higher than anticipated when the sentence was introduced and it is now estimated that about one in ten of sentenced prisoners is serving an IPP sentence. By June 2010 6,189 prisoners had been sentenced to an IPP sentence and 2,468 of IPP prisoners were are being held beyond the expiry of the punitive part of their sentence in January 2010 (PRT 2010: 15). Only 133 IPP prisoners have been released and 33 of these have been recalled.

As Jacobson and Hough argue, this sentence has created problems, as apart from adding to the numbers in prison, the release of these prisoners has been impeded for a number of reasons, including the difficulty facing prisoners in demonstrating that they are no longer a risk, the workload of the Parole Board which has meant delays in hearing applications, and the problems of access to courses, as well as the deeper problems of predicting dangerousness (Jacobson and Hough 2010). The authors recommend an urgent review of the sentence to consider whether it should be abolished, or used less frequently but focused on individuals where there is a real risk of serious reoffending. If the IPP sentence is retained, then, they argue, resources should be increased to expedite release from it.

Normally, these prisoners would be required to take, and complete satisfactorily, offending behaviour courses and ideally these should be completed before they reach the end of the punitive part of the sentence, but in practice insufficient resources have been provided to meet the demand by that date. Cases have been brought by IPP prisoners challenging lack of access to courses relevant to parole decisions under Article 5, although the results have been disappointing. The Administrative Court in *R (Wells) v Parole Board; R (Walker) v Home Secretary* [2007] EWHC 1835 (Admin) found the Secretary of State had acted unlawfully in failing to provide sufficient courses for prisoners to demonstrate to the Parole Board that they were no longer a risk by the time the punitive part of their sentence expired. Similarly, in the case of *R (James) v Secretary of State for Justice* [2007] EWHC 2027 (Admin), the Court deemed the failure to provide courses was unlawful and that the prisoner should be released, but the release order was stayed while awaiting the outcome of an appeal.

The two cases were conjoined on appeal in *R (Walker and James) v Secretary of State for Justice* [2008] EWCA Civ 30. The Court of Appeal agreed that the Secretary of State had acted unlawfully. There was an obligation to provide enough courses to allow prisoners to show that they were safe to be released. But the Court of Appeal thought that ultimately whether the detention was lawful depended on the risk posed by the prisoner, rather than the provision of courses used to assess the risk. The Court did say that if the prisoners' detention was extended further without regular reviews then it might amount to arbitrary detention under Article 5(1). It set aside the release order for Mr. James and the case then went to the House of Lords.[5]

In the House of Lords in *Secretary of State for Justice v James (formerly Walker and another)* [2009] UKHL 22, the Court held it was irrational in a public law sense to introduce the IPP sentence without adequate resources, but the fact that it was irrational in public law did not mean that Article 5(1) had been breached. Article 5(1) requires a link between the original sentence and the continued detention and this remained in this case because the detention was based on risk, the prisoner was still deemed dangerous and his continued detention was subject to regular reviews. Article 5(4) would be infringed if there were no courses provided to such prisoners, so there was no possibility of showing to the Board that the prisoner was no longer dangerous. Here there were some courses available and there were regular reviews so procedural justice under Article 5(4) was satisfied. This outcome was disappointing as the review body needs all the relevant information to arrive at a fair assessment. It is important that all prisoners have equal opportunities to meet requirements for parole. Now IPP prisoners with short tariffs are being given priority access to offending behaviour courses.

Discretionary lifers and mentally disordered offenders

Initially the Strasbourg Court was only willing to intervene in relation to discretionary life sentences which raise the issue of whether a dangerous offender's detention should be reviewed at regular intervals by an independent body. Article 5 challenges to discretionary life sentences were brought in *Weeks v UK* (1987) 10 EHRR 293 and in *Thynne, Wilson and Gunnell v UK* (1990) 13 EHRR 666. In *Weeks v UK* (1988) 13 EHRR 435, the Strasbourg Court said the sentencing decision must be taken by an independent body. The same applies if a life prisoner is released but has breached conditions and is returned to prison. In *Thynne* the Strasbourg Court said that discretionary life sentence prisoners should be entitled to an oral hearing by any independent court-like body with the power to direct release if continued detention was not justified. So the 1991 Criminal Justice Act reflected this decision. Following this case, new law was introduced by s 34 of the 1991 Act which removed powers from the Home Secretary to make decisions about the release of a discretionary life sentence prisoner, because the Minister was not seen as independent by the Strasbourg Court.

Section 34 provided that the judge at the point of sentencing should state the minimum part of the sentence for punitive purposes. When that has been completed, the prisoner may ask the Home Secretary to refer his case to the

Parole Board for review and if the Board decides that he should be released because he is no longer a threat to the public, the Home Secretary should order his release. The review is conducted by a Panel who will hold an oral hearing and under the Act, the lifer has the right to see the reports on which the Panel relies in reaching its decision. Discretionary life sentence prisoners have the right to require the Secretary of State to refer their case to the Parole Board at any time after the tariff or punitive part of the sentence has been served.

In *Blackstock v UK* Application No. 59512/00 (21 June 2005) a discretionary lifer challenged the delay in reviews of his detention. After the expiry of the tariff part of his sentence, he applied to the Parole Board to be transferred to an open prison. But it took nearly two years before the Secretary of State accepted this recommendation. The Strasbourg Court decided that Article 5(4) was breached because of the failure to deal with the issue speedily. Article 5(5) was also breached because it was not possible for him to obtain compensation for this failure.

A similar approach was taken in *Benjamin and Wilson v UK* Application No. 28212/95 (26 September 2002) in relation to discretionary life sentence prisoners detained in a mental hospital. The Court again stressed the importance of the separation of powers between the executive and the body reviewing the sentence. The Court was critical of the Home Secretary's role in the release of the prisoners because of his lack of independence from the executive and could not avoid this charge by saying that he acted on the recommendations of the Mental Health Review Tribunal. The Court said that 'This is not a matter of form but impinges on the fundamental principle of separation of powers and detracts from a necessary guarantee against the possibility of abuse' (at para 36).

In *Hutchison Reid v UK* Application No. 50272/99 (20 February 2003) the Strasbourg Court reviewed the legality of detaining a patient convicted of homicide, who had a personality disorder which was untreatable in a psychiatric hospital. The Court held that the continued detention of a patient could be justified, not only on the basis of the patient's need for medical treatment, but also because the patient needed supervision to prevent him or her harming himself or others, so Article 5(1) was not breached here. However, Article 5(4) was breached by placing the burden of proof on the patient to prove that he no longer suffered from a mental disorder.

The Strasbourg Court also said in *Aerts v Belgium* (1998) 29 EHRR 50 that mentally ill prisoners should be detained in hospital to receive appropriate treatment, rather than in prison although in practice many mentally ill offenders are detained in prison and prisoners may become mentally ill while in prison. The Strasbourg Court has been very critical of the UK's procedures and this has led to changes in mental health law with decisions on restrictions being transferred to Mental Health Review Tribunals.

A prisoner suffering from a mental disorder may be transferred from prison to a mental hospital for treatment provided that appropriate medical treatment is available.[6] These prisoners can apply to the Tribunal at regular interviews to review their detention in hospital.

The power to hold oral hearings and to order release for discretionary life sentence prisoners has been extended to juvenile prisoners detained during Her Majesty's pleasure and to prisoners given an automatic life sentence for a second conviction for a serious sexual or violent offence under the 1997 Crime (Sentences) Act[7] in the light of the Strasbourg Court's rulings on these issues.

In *Hussain v UK* and *Singh v UK* Applications Nos. 21928/93, 23389/94 (21 February 1996) the applicant Hussain had been detained at Her Majesty's Pleasure. He was not given any reasons for the decisions taken by the Parole Board, or the decision by the Secretary of State to reject the Parole Board's recommendation that he be transferred to an open prison. Singh was also denied access to probation and police reports submitted to the Parole Board, in the course of considering whether to recommend his release. The key issue for the Strasbourg Court was whether the sentence of detention during Her Majesty's Pleasure should be treated as similar to a mandatory or to a discretionary life sentence. The original sentences contained a fixed period for the purposes of punishment and an indeterminate period which could only be justified by the risk to the public. The Court thought that they were closer to discretionary life sentences than mandatory ones, and that applicants had a right under Article 5(4) for their continued detention to be considered by a court. The limited powers of the Parole Board did not satisfy Article 5(4) which requires that prisoners are able to challenge their continued detention in a hearing with procedural powers and guarantees. This means an oral hearing with a proper adversarial procedure, where the prisoner has legal representation and is able to call and question witnesses. Because the Parole Board lacked these procedural safeguards, it did not function like a court and being able to pursue judicial review was not sufficient to satisfy this.

In *T v UK, V v UK* Application Nos. 24724/94, 24888/94 (16 December 1999) the Strasbourg Court concluded that setting the minimum term for a young murderer detained at Her Majesty's Pleasure is a sentencing exercise and not within the power of ministers. For those detained during Her Majesty's Pleasure the starting point for the minimum is usually 12 years. However, this will be subject to periodic reviews to see if the figure is appropriate given the person's behaviour in custody.

In the subsequent case of *Curley v UK* Application No. 32406/96 (28 March 2000) where the applicant was convicted of murder and detained at Her Majesty's Pleasure, the Secretary of State rejected the Parole Board's recommendation for release and he was refused leave to apply for judicial review to challenge the Secretary of State's rejection of his submission against that decision. This was after the judgment in *Hussain* and *Singh*. His case was referred back to the Parole Board and the recommendation for release was then accepted. The Court accepted that Article 5(4) had been breached because he did not receive a review of his continued detention by a body with the power to order his release, or a review which reached a decision speedily. He also had no enforceable right to compensation for a breach of Article 5(4). However, the Court rejected his argument that this extended detention without the proper procedures amounted to inhuman and degrading punishment under Article 3.

Mandatory life sentences

Most of the Strasbourg Court's decisions have been on discretionary rather than mandatory lifers, and the Government and the Courts in the past have sought to maintain a sharp distinction between them. The House of Lords in *R v Secretary of State for the Home Department ex parte Doody* [1994] 1 AC 531 distinguished between mandatory and discretionary life sentences noting that they were very different, so it was appropriate for the Home Secretary to set the offender's tariff for murder (at 558). However, Lord Mustill stressed that procedural fairness or natural justice was still required and the court referred to key elements of fairness in the process of decision making by public bodies, including the presumption that public bodies will act fairly, that an individual affected adversely by a decision should be allowed to make representations preferably before the decision is made or if that is not feasible as soon afterwards as possible so that the decision could be changed, that reasons and evidence on which the decision is based are disclosed so that the individual may make representations on an informed basis.

A similar approach was taken by the Strasbourg Court in *Wynne v UK* (1994) 19 EHRR 353, where the Court said Article 5(4) was not engaged when a prisoner who receives a mandatory life sentence for murder is recalled as this is part of the original sentence. So Wynne, a convicted murderer was not entitled to the same protection as would have been appropriate if he had been serving a discretionary life sentence. So there was no right to review at that time, but this was reconsidered by the Stasbourg Court in *Stafford v UK* Application No. 46295/99 (28 May 2002).

In *Stafford*, the offender had been originally convicted of murder and given a mandatory life sentence, with a minimum tariff and further indefinite period for public protection. He was released conditionally on licence but reconvicted of a dishonesty offence and then recalled to prison for breaching his licence conditions. In 1997 the Secretary of State rejected the Parole Board's recommendation to release him. Stafford commenced a judicial review of the lawfulness of the decision to continue his detention, arguing that the decision to detain him after his prison term for the fraud offence was unlawful, as it bore no relation to the original rationale for his detention. The House of Lords said the 1991 Act afforded the Secretary of State a wide discretion which allowed him to arrive at such a decision. However, the Strasbourg Court found that his detention after 1997 was not justified and Article 5(1) had been breached as the decision regarding his continuing detention had to be taken by an independent body and not the Secretary of State. Article 5(4) was also breached because of the absence of procedural safeguards. Lifers in the post-tariff period could only be detained if it was necessary for public protection and the justification for continued detention must be reviewed regularly by a court-like body conducting an oral hearing and with the power to direct the prisoner's release if no longer justified.

So to comply with Article 5(4) the decision has to be made by a court, considering both elements, whether the term of imprisonment to satisfy punishment for the offence has been completed, and whether the person is still a danger to society. The discretion of the Secretary of State which may be exercised in response to public opinion or political pressures is not sufficient. The Court said that it 'may now be regarded as established in domestic law that there is no distinction between mandatory life prisoners, discretionary life prisoners and juvenile murderers, as regards the nature of tariff-fixing. It is a sentencing exercise' (at para 79). So once the punishment part of the sentence has been met, the grounds for continued detention in relation to mandatory life sentence must be risk and dangerousness just as it is for discretionary life and juvenile murderer cases. The Court was concerned at the continuing role of the Home Secretary in tariff-fixing and in determining when the prisoner should be released once the tariff has expired which was 'increasingly difficult to reconcile with the notion of separation of powers between the executive and the judiciary' (at para 78). The Court found that the approach in *Wynne* could no longer be seen as reflecting the real position of the mandatory life prisoner. Similarly, in *Waite v UK* Application No. 53236/99 (10 December 2002), the Court said that Article 5(4) requires that the body must be independent and the prisoner must be allowed an oral hearing under Article 5(4) if released on licence and recalled to prison.

So following *Stafford* decisions on whether the prisoner should be released at the end of the minimum term or should be returned to prison after release must be a matter for a court and this must be decided on the basis of risk as the sentence for punishment purposes is already completed. The same principles apply to all prisoners given life sentences, including mandatory life sentences, so the domestic courts are now more willing to challenge the decisions of the Home Secretary on the tariff for mandatory life prisoners.

The requirement for an independent and impartial tribunal is also required by Article 6(1) of the Convention. So the House of Lords in *(R) Anderson v Secretary of State for the Home Department* [2002] 4 All ER 1089, ruled that the Home Secretary should play no part in fixing the tariff and that the minimum term for mandatory life prisoners under s 29 of the Crime (Sentences) Act 1997 breached Article 6(1) because the Home Secretary was not an independent and impartial tribunal and their Lordships issued a declaration of incompatibility.

The principles governing the fixing of tariffs and the procedures to be followed are now in the CJA 2003 which establishes a new framework for the release of murderers given a mandatory life sentence. The court which gives the life sentence also determines the minimum term which the offender must serve before he can be considered for release on licence and gives its reasons. The principles to guide its decision are specified in Schedule 21 of the Act. Once the offender has served that minimum term, he can then apply for release. If the Parole Board decide that the prisoner should be released, then the Secretary of State must comply. So the Secretary of State will not be involved in determining the minimum term or the decision to release the prisoner on licence, whereas prior to the 2003 Act the Secretary of State was allowed to take part in the decision whether a mandatory life prisoner should be released. Prisoners convicted of murder seeking release have to be given reasons for the recommendations of the Parole Board and these should be disclosed to the prisoner. If the Board does not recommend release, it should indicate when the next review will be.

With fixed term sentences which are not life sentences, the Strasbourg Court is unwilling to get involved in reviewing the sentencing process or release arrangements. So with a fixed term sentence it is sufficient that decisions are made by the Parole Board rather than the court. The House of Lords said in *R v Parole Board ex parte Smith; R v Parole Board ex parte West* (2005) UKHL 1 that determinate prisoners on licence are entitled to an oral hearing to consider the prisoner's recall. This procedural fairness is required to satisfy Article 5(4) of the Convention but their Lordships said that Article 6 was not engaged. For prisoners serving determinate sentences over 12 months they are released automatically halfway through their sentence when they are released on licence and subject to supervision, but the Parole Board will be involved in reviewing recall decisions of these offenders.

Terrorist offences

Article 5 has also been used to challenge the detention of suspected international terrorists held in Belmarsh under anti-terrorism legislation in *A and others v UK* Application No. 3455/05 (19 February 2009). The Government issued a notice of derogation under Article 15 of the Convention because it thought the detention might conflict with Article 5. Some of the applicants suffered serious mental health problems and were transferred to Broadmoor. When the individuals were released, they were then subject to control orders under the Prevention of Terrorism Act 2005. The Strasbourg Court found the detention of the prisoners breached Articles 5(1), 5(4) and 5(5). Although the Court found no breach of Article 3 regarding the conditions in which they were held, there was a clear breach of Article 5(1) by their internment and indefinite detention in the absence of a valid derogation under Article 15. The Court accepted that there was a public emergency and the life of the nation was under threat, following the July 7 bombings, but the Court thought the measures were disproportionate and discriminated without justification between foreign nationals and nationals. The Court also found that some of the applicants had been unable to challenge effectively the claims made against them so there was a breach of Article 5(4) and Article 5(5) was breached because they could not bring an enforceable claim in the domestic courts.

Access to the courts

The right of prisoners to seek access to the courts is well established in the UK and is required by Article 6(1) the prisoner's right to a fair trial. The issue was aired in the Strasbourg Court in the 1970s in *Golder v UK* Application No. 4551/70 (21 February 1975). There had been an incident of disorder in the prison where Golder was held, and it was suspected that he had been involved and had assaulted a prison officer. Golder wrote to his MP and to a Chief Constable about the incident and the problems he was facing as a result, but these letters were intercepted and stopped by the prison governor, on the ground that the prisoner had not raised the issue through the appropriate procedures. Golder complained about the interference with his letters, as well as the refusal by the Home Secretary to allow him to consult a solicitor. The Court held that denial of access to a solicitor for the purpose of bringing a civil action against a prison officer breached his right of access to the courts guaranteed by Article 6(1). The Court also considered the issue in relation to Article 8, but concluded that if the refusal to allow him to contact his solicitor regarding a possible libel action against a prison officer was a breach of Article 8, it could be justified under Article 8(2). The Court stressed the needs of the prison but said limits on the right under Article 8 could only be justified if they were necessary and proportionate. Following *Golder*, new Prison Service Instructions were issued to allow prisoners to contact their solicitors for the purpose of bringing a legal action.

The issue of prisoners' letters to lawyers and others was reconsidered by the Court in *Silver and others v UK* Application No. 5947/7 (25 March 1983) where the court found the requirement that a prisoner receive permission from the Home Secretary to seek legal advice was incompatible with Article 6 (1) in denying access to the courts. There had also been a breach of Article 8 in the interference with his correspondence.

In *Campbell v UK* Application No. 13590/88 (25 March 1992) the Court ruled that all letters to lawyers were privileged and protected by Article 8, whether or not those letters related to potential litigation. The court also ruled that such correspondence should not be opened unless there is reasonable cause to believe that prison security may be endangered and then only in the presence of the prisoner. If correspondence is interfered with, the court in considering infringements of Article 8, will apply the principle of proportionality to consider whether that interference was lawful, whether it had a legitimate aim and whether the interference was necessary in a democratic society. Although private correspondence may also be protected under Article 8, as we shall see in Chapter 6, letters to lawyers are given greater protection by the court than ordinary correspondence and the courts are less willing to accept limits on the right to correspondence in such cases.

Disciplinary proceedings

Disciplinary proceedings are a very important issue for prisoners as the outcome may mean days added to their sentences. The Prison Rules are very wide ranging and generate a large number of disciplinary offences. A high number of disciplinary charges are brought in prison in England and Wales. In 2008, there were 135 proven offences against discipline for every 100 prisoners. Female prisoners had higher rates than male prisoners. Punishments consisted mostly of loss of privileges, cellular confinement and loss of earnings. There has been a decline in the use of days lost since 2003. The overall rate of punishment in 2009 for male and female prisoners was 218 punishments per 100 of population (Ministry of Justice 2010e: 132). So the conduct and perception of the fairness of disciplinary proceedings is very important.

The offences and procedures are set out in Prison Rules 51–61. Under the pre-1999 Rules there was a catch-all offence, where 'the offender in any way offends against good order and discipline'. This clearly was potentially very broad but was removed by the 1999 Rules, but while the offences are now more specific but there is still considerable scope for falling foul of these Rules.

The conduct of prison hearings raises procedural and human rights issues. Fair procedures for dealing with discipline, complaints and requests all contribute to good relations between officers and prisoners so they can promote a perception of fairness and legitimacy which contributes to dynamic security. In *Leech v Deputy Governor of Parkhurst Prison* [1988] AC 533, it was decided that any prison disciplinary hearing can be reviewed on the grounds of unfairness, procedural defects or irrationality.

There are also provisions relating to disciplinary procedures, in EPR 59, namely that prisoners should be informed promptly of the accusations and have enough time to prepare their defence and be allowed to defend themselves in person or have legal assistance when the interests of justice require and be allowed to call witnesses, and examine them or have them examined on their behalf and access to an interpreter if necessary. So these Rules give effect to Article 6(3) of the Convention. The CPT also recommends that disciplinary procedures embody due process rights, so a prisoner has the right to be heard and the right of appeal.

Before the 1980s, disciplinary hearings were closer to military court martials which meant the accused had few rights even though the outcome could be loss of remission, that is, a further punishment, which clearly moves it closer to a criminal hearing than an administrative procedure.[8] It is difficult not to see the loss of days as punishment on any definition of punishment.

The disciplinary system before 1992 left much to be desired, as even serious charges were dealt with by the Boards of Visitors with considerable powers to punish. Many of the cases brought in the 1980s and early 1990s concerned the conduct of adjudications. The role of the Boards of Visitors in the adjudication of disciplinary cases led to resentment by prisoners and was subject to several challenges in the courts and criticized by the Woolf Report. Their adjudicative function ended in 1992 although the Boards, now called the Independent Monitoring Boards, retain their scrutinizing functions and are able to hear complaints by prisoners. Once the Boards lost their powers to adjudicate or punish, the focus of prison litigation shifted towards the role of the Governor and independent adjudicators. Until 2002, the power to award additional days was vested in the Prison Governor.

Whether disciplinary hearings constitute 'criminal proceedings' for the purpose of Article 6 claims, has been a contested issue for the domestic courts and prison authorities with a substantial jurisprudence on this subject. If disciplinary hearings are seen as similar to a criminal trial then offenders would be entitled to full procedural due process rights demanded by Article 6 of the Convention, including the right to representation. The claim that disciplinary proceedings constitute hearings was vigorously challenged in the past in the domestic courts, for precisely for this reason. One reason why the claim is resisted, of course, is that offences against prison discipline may include many relatively minor offences as well as much more serious offences. So the preferred approach was to treat them as administrative tribunals. However, given that the outcome of hearings may be added days, it is hard to justify this position, and if they are effectively criminal proceedings, then this raises the issue of whether a Prison Governor is an impartial adjudicator.

The judicial function of hearings was recognized in the *R v Board of Visitors of Hull Prison ex parte St. Germain (No. 1)* (1979) QB 425. In this case, which arose out of riots at Hull Prison, the House of Lords ruled that Boards of Visitors' disciplinary decisions were reviewable and that the Boards should be seen as a quasi-judicial body when adjudicating on disciplinary matters. Since then, the impact of judicial review of disciplinary hearings has meant that the conduct of disciplinary hearings has moved closer to ordinary court hearings. In *R v Board of Visitors of Hull Prison ex parte St. Germain (No. 2)* (1979) 3 All ER 545 the Court of Appeal held that prisoners should be able to call and cross-examine witnesses.

The Strasbourg Court considered the issue of whether disciplinary proceedings amounted to a criminal trial in *Campbell and Fell v UK* (1984) 7 EHRR 165. Campbell and Fell were both involved in a protest at Parkhurst. In the scuffle they suffered injuries for which they wished to obtain compensation for injury. They were initially denied permission to contact a solicitor and when they did speak to a lawyer, they were not allowed to do so in private. They were also subjected to disciplinary proceedings before the Board of Visitors, which resulted in a substantial loss of remission and privileges. Campbell lost 450 days remission for the 'offence' of prison mutiny and 120 days for the violence offences. Campbell and Fell argued that their case should not be heard by the Board because the Board was not independent or impartial and the proceedings were not held in public and were therefore unfair. Instead the matter should have been dealt with by a court of law.

The Strasbourg Court's approach in deciding whether proceedings were disciplinary or criminal was to look at the penalty and seriousness of the offence. An attack on an officer was clearly at the top end of seriousness of disciplinary offences and the penalty substantial, so if guilty the prisoner's release date would be much later than he would have expected. This brought the hearing within the ambit of Article 6. The Court said it was not necessary that the proceedings should be held in public as this would be too onerous, but the decision should be made public and failure to do so breached Article 6(1) and the fact that they were denied legal representation to defend these charges at the hearing breached Article 6(3). The Court ruled that they should have been given legal representation, given the nature of the proceedings and the potential loss of remission. Article 6(1) was also breached by the refusal to allow access to a solicitor regarding the claim for their injuries. The delay in granting them access to legal advice denied them access to justice, and the fact that the discussion with the lawyer was not in private also breached Article 6(1). However, the Court rejected the claim that the Board was not independent or impartial.

After *Campbell*, disciplinary system procedures were changed and eventually, following the recommendations of the Woolf Report, the Boards relinquished their adjudicative role. The recommendation that they should lose this role had in fact been made in 1985 by the Report of the Committee on the Prison Disciplinary System.[9] But they were not removed until the 1991 Criminal Justice Act and this change came into force in 2002. The Act also substituted 'added days' for 'loss of remission'. So after *Campbell and Fell*, there were some improvements in disciplinary procedures.

The question of legal representation was also considered in the domestic courts in *R v Secretary of State for the Home Department ex parte Tarrant* [1984] 1 All ER 799. Here the Divisional Court said that there is no general right to be represented at the adjudication but it is a matter for the adjudicator's discretion and in making the decision, the adjudicator should consider the seriousness of the charge and the possible penalty, the ability of the prisoner to present his case, whether there are any difficult points of law, and any procedural problems which might arise and the need for fairness between the prisoner and prison staff. It also confirmed that the standard of proof in adjudications is the criminal standard. However, even after the Human Rights Act, the domestic courts held in *R (Carroll) v Secretary of State for the Home Department*, *The Times* (16 August 2001), that the right to representation under Article 6(1) would be no greater than at common law, as enunciated in *Tarrant*. The Court of Appeal also said in that case that disciplinary hearings before a prison governor were not criminal proceedings but the imposition of 21 additional days was moving close to the borderline of criminal proceedings.

A major breakthrough came with the Article 6 case of *Ezeh and Connors v UK* Applicant Nos. 39665/98, 40086/98 (15 July 2002) where the status of disciplinary hearings was resolved. Ezeh and Connors were charged separately with disciplinary offences, using threatening language and assault, and found guilty at hearings before the Governor at which they were not represented. Ezeh received 40 additional days and Connors 7 additional days. They argued that Article 6(3)(c) had been breached by the failure to allow representation.

Here the Court decided that Article 6 did apply to the disciplinary proceedings brought against the applicants and that they should have been represented. The failure to allow representation breached Article 6(3)(c). Although the penalties were imposed lawfully and the extra days did not extend beyond their original sentences, the additional days were significant and the charges should be seen as effectively criminal charges. While the offences in question in this case were less serious and resulted in fewer days lost than in *Campbell*, given the charges they faced and the extent of the penalty, the court still treated them as a criminal matter, which fell within Article 6 because of the added days. The Court ruled that additional days given as punishment for disciplinary offences may be imposed only by independent adjudicators and not by prison governors.

Following the decision by the Chamber in this case in 2002, the Government appealed to the Grand Chamber. The Government had argued that the need to refer to an independent adjudicator imposed costs and further delays and argued that judicial interference undermines prison discipline. However, in *Ezeh and Connors v UK* Application Nos. 39665/98, 40086/98 (9 October 2003) the Grand Chamber affirmed that Article 6 did apply to the proceedings against the prisoners, in view of the nature of the charge and severity of the penalties and that Article 6(3)(c) had been breached. The Court said that practical cost issues could not be used to justify denial of rights.

Since that decision, the relevant Prison Rules have been amended.[10] Now adjudications may be conducted by either governors or independent adjudicators depending on the seriousness of the charges (PR 53(2)), but the Governor should decide whether the charge is so serious that it could lead to additional days if the prisoner is found guilty (PR 53A(1)). If so, the governor can refer the case to an independent adjudicator, in which case the prisoner must be offered the opportunity to seek legal representation (PR 54(3)). These independent adjudicators are district judges. Otherwise, the Governor can conduct the adjudication (PR 54A(2)(b)). If the Governor does proceed, but it becomes clear that additional days should be awarded, the Governor should refer the case to an independent adjudicator, during the hearing or after the hearing, and before imposing punishment (PR53A(3)). The independent adjudicator can award up to 42 additional days for adult prisoners and 21 additional days for young offenders. Further punishments can also be imposed including cellular confinement, the stoppage of earnings and removal from the wing. However, any punishment for offences committed in prison should not be degrading, so it should not involve physical punishments, and should not entail reductions in family visits.

Following the *Ezeh* decision, the Prison Service remitted all additional days given as punishment by prison governors, since the Human Rights Act came into force. Challenges to days imposed prior to the Human Rights Act coming into force, have failed in the Court of Appeal in *Rogers v Secretary of State for the Home Department* [2002] EWCA Civ 1944 where the Court of Appeal held, following the decision of the House of Lords in *R v Lambert* [2001] 2 WLR 206, that the Act was not retrospective. In the later case of *R (Greenfield) v Home Secretary* (2005) UKHL 14, the House of Lords said that even if the conduct of disciplinary hearings does breach Article 6, the remedy may consist only of a declaration and not an award of damages.

In *R (Bannatyne) v Secretary of State for the Home Department* (2004) EWHC 1921 (Admin) the argument that prison disciplinary hearings should be held in public again had failed under Article 6 in the domestic courts. The court noted that the issue had already been considered and rejected by the Strasbourg Court, because if permitted, it would impose a disproportionate burden on the public and would raise issues of public order and security as well as infringing the privacy of witnesses.

Independent monitoring of prison disciplinary hearings is undertaken by the Independent Monitoring Boards and by the Prisons and Probation Ombudsman, which compensates for the fact that they are not held in public. Moreover, prisoners are entitled to legal representation where necessary and to receive a record of their adjudications which could be made public. If charged with disciplinary offences, prisoners should be asked whether they wish to have a McKenzie friend, that is, a person who is not legally qualified to assist them, or consult a solicitor, and if refused to be told why. If they lose at the disciplinary hearing prisoners can appeal to prison service headquarters and then to the Ombudsman unless the matter has been dealt with by an independent adjudicator, in which case they could seek a review of the punishment by the senior district judge or judicial review if appropriate.

The right to complain

It is crucial that prisoners should feel able to raise concerns, and complaints, and to know that their concerns will be taken seriously and dealt with fairly. A complaints procedure recognized by prisoners as fair is an important source of legitimacy and security. The problems with the complaints procedure were seen by the Woolf Inquiry as a key issue in prison disorder in the UK. If prisoners do not feel their complaints are being taken account of they may resort to extreme actions, as for example, in the case of Michael Hickey who spent three months on the roof of Gartree Prison in the winter of 1983–84 to draw attention to the fact that he had been wrongfully convicted. Moreover, if complaints are addressed, this can raise standards and the solutions can provide a model of good practice for other prisons. It is also important that prisoners' relatives have access to procedures to express complaints and concerns, especially in cases where prisoners die in custody, as we saw earlier.

However, it is important that not only are prisoners aware of the procedures but also know that if they do raise a complaint this will not cause problems for them, otherwise they may be reluctant to bring claims. An effective complaints procedure can contribute to stability and allow problems to be resolved before they become more contentious. Many complaints and requests may be dealt with informally before the formal complaint system is used. The fairness of the complaints procedure is an important indicator of the quality of a prison regime and recognition of this is well established in international penal law. The CPT have stressed that prisoners must be made aware of the procedures and have confidential access to them. Under the UN Standard Minimum Rules (SMR): 'Every prisoner shall be allowed to make a request or complaint, without censorship as to substance but in proper form, to the central prison administration, the judicial authority or other proper authorities through approved channels' (SMR 35.3). The European Prison Rules (EPR) also place considerable weight on the right to complain so prisoners should have ample opportunity to make requests or complaints to the prison director or other competent authority (EPR 70.1). If their complaint or request is rejected they should be given reasons and also have the 'right to appeal to an independent authority' (EPR 70.3). So as well as procedures for dealing with day-to-day concerns, there should be access to an independent body such as the Ombudsman.

There are various avenues for prisoners to bring complaints, both informal and formal within the UK prison system. Prisoners can also take complaints to the Independent Monitoring Board, the Prisons and Probation Ombudsman and to the Parliamentary Commission for Administration. If the complaint relates to injustices arising from maladministration, prisoners can contact the Parliamentary Commissioner for Administration (PCA) via their MP at any stage of the complaints process and this should be dealt with within 12 months. The PCA will seek to resolve the matter or undertake a statutory investigation. The PCA's recommendations are not binding but usually they are accepted. Complaints can also be taken to the Inspector of Prisons and to Members of Parliament. Access to the media may also be permitted on matters of concern to prisoners, subject to certain limits, which will be discussed in Chapter 6. They can also petition the House of Commons through their MP or the House of Lords, through a member of the House, and may petition the Queen.

In addition there is the framework of public law and as we have seen, judicial review has been well used by prisoners. Discretion should not be exercised unreasonably in the *Wednesbury*[11] sense and the administrative body, or prison authority, should not act unlawfully, or unfairly or in a way which infringes the prisoner's rights under the Convention and where that infringement cannot be justified. So any infringements will be assessed on the principle of proportionality. The prisoner could also bring a civil action against a member of staff or if appropriate a private prosecution.

The prisoner can also, of course, take complaints relating to breaches of Convention rights to the European Court of Human Rights in Strasbourg, although this may be a lengthy process and the Court will usually expect the prisoner to have gone through the internal remedies first. Moreover, since the Human Rights Act came into force in 2000, human rights issues may be raised in the domestic courts. Discrimination issues may also be raised with the Equality and Human Rights Commission (see Chapter 7).

Under Article 13 of the European Convention, there must be an effective remedy for breaches of Convention rights, so if there is a complaint over a rights violation then it is essential that there is access to a national authority to make a decision on it and to provide an appropriate remedy. Breaches of Article 13 have been found by the Court in several cases including *Silver and others v UK* Application No. 5947/7 (25 March 1983), because the Board of Visitors could not make binding decisions, and in *Keenan v UK* Application No. 27229/95 (3 April 2001), because the prisoner had been unable to challenge added days imprisonment imposed in the course of disciplinary proceedings.

Internal complaints procedures

A prisoner who has a particular request or complaint usually will discuss the problem first with an officer on his wing or his personal officer, and then make an oral or written application. But he can make a formal application without a prior informal discussion. However, the Prison staff try to deal with complaints and requests internally where possible. Most complaints are resolved at the early stages. Complaint forms are available on prison wings and complaints can be posted into sealed boxes. Complaints may cover a wide range of matters from trivial to allegations of mistreatment, and requests could include requests for artificial insemination, or a place in a mother and baby unit.

Complaints should be submitted within three months of the relevant incident. Prisoners who have literacy problems, or for whom English is not their first language, should be given assistance to make a complaint. When boxes are emptied, complaints should be answered by prison officers, ideally the personal officer or wing officer. Most complaints will be resolved at that stage but if the prisoner is not satisfied, he or she can appeal to the prison management and if still not happy, to the Governor. Responses to complaints should state the reasons for the response and deal with the points made, whether the complaint is accepted or rejected. If the complaint raises the issue of racism this must be brought to the attention of the Race Equality Officer. Complaints relating to bullying must also be dealt with under anti-bullying and violence reduction procedures (PSO 2750). If the prisoner is still not satisfied, he can complain to the Prisons and Probations Ombudsman.

Confidential or sensitive matters can be sent direct to the Governor, the Area Manager, Prison Service headquarters or the Chair of the Independent Monitoring Board. Complaints dealing with reserved subjects will be made directly to area managers or the Prison Service headquarters, and if the prisoner is not satisfied then he can also take the matter to the Prisons and Probation Ombudsman. Most of the issues relating to Category A prisoners and life sentence prisoners' requests and complaints are reserved subjects and will be dealt with by Prison Service headquarters. Reserved subjects also include appeals against adjudication decisions which should be made within three months of receiving the decision, early release due to illness, and allegations against the prison governor.

Independent Monitoring Boards

The Independent Monitoring Boards can also receive complaints from prisoners though, as noted above, they have not always been seen by prisoners as independent or receptive to complaints. Complaints can be made to the Board at any stage of the internal process. Each prison and immigration removal centre has an Independent Monitoring Board, members of whom have open access to local prisons and detention centres and can interview prisoners in private. If a prisoner has a complaint which has not been resolved internally, he or she can make a confidential request to see a member of the IMB. These complaints may cover a range of problems including visits, lost property and more serious issues. The Board can ask the Governor to reconsider or bring the matter to the attention of the Area Manager or to the Secretary of State. The Board also monitors the system of dealing with complaints and will review complaints logs and statistics regularly. The IMB also attend prisons following deaths in custody or incidents of disorder to observe how they are handled. The Boards play an important role in monitoring standards in the prison. The Boards are constituted by unpaid, ordinary members of the public and are independent. They publish annual reports on individual prisons.

The Prisons and Probation Ombudsman.

Prisoners may also take their complaints to the Prisons and Probation Ombudsman, a body established in 1994 on the recommendations of the Woolf Report. The work of the Ombudsman covers prisons, accommodation run by the Probation Service and immigration removal centres. Although the Ombudsman can only make recommendations rather than decisions which bind the prison, the Prison Service is required to issue a response within four weeks of receiving those recommendations. Internal procedures should be exhausted first and the prisoner should contact the Ombudsman within one month of receiving the Prison Service's decision.

The Ombudsman can hear complaints from prisoners who are not satisfied with the outcome from the Prison Complaints systems in state and contracted-out prisons, or if a prisoner has not received a response from the prison service to a complaint within six weeks. The Ombudsman deals with complaints within 12 weeks of the acceptance of the complaint. The role of the Ombudsman is to give an independent, impartial and accessible means of resolving complaints, and to investigate deaths in custody. It is sponsored by the Ministry of Justice, but independent of it. A complaint to the Ombudsman should be made within one month of the response of the Prison Service to complaints raised within the internal complaints procedure.

The Ombudsman deals with a wide range of complaints, including lost property, decisions on categorization and adjudication, and now has the power to investigate deaths in custody but he cannot deal with questions relating to appeals against conviction or sentence, complaints already subject to civil or criminal legal proceedings, or review the policy decision of ministers. As internal complaints procedures should be exhausted first so the process can be lengthy. The Ombudsman can look at the merits of a decision as well as the adequacy of the procedure by which it was reached and can also investigate decisions taken by the IMB, as well the Prison Service, and omissions as well as actions, relating to the management, supervision, care and treatment of prisoners by staff. Before the final report on the investigation is published, a draft is sent to the Director General of the Prison Service to allow any staff involved to make representations. When the investigation is complete, if the prisoner's complaint is upheld, recommendations will be made to the Director General of the Prison Service and the Secretary of State for Justice and the prisoner will be informed of the response. An Annual Report on the Ombudsman's work is submitted to the Secretary of State which includes details of complaints, recommendations and responses. If the complaint is not upheld, there is no right of appeal against the Ombudsman. In dealing with deaths in custody, the Ombudsman will consider whether any policy changes are needed and provide explanations to the prisoner's relatives. Clinical issues relevant to deaths in custody will be dealt with in conjunction with the NHS.

The Reports of the Ombudsman provide a further source of information on prison conditions. During the period 2008–9 the Ombudsman received 4,288 complaints, of which 89 per cent (3,818) related to prisons, 9 per cent (388) to the Probation Service and 2 per cent (99) were from detainees in immigration removal centres. During the period 1,515 investigations were conducted; 181 deaths were investigated, of which 164 were from prisons, 2 were offenders recently released from prison, and 11 were from Probation Service approved accommodation. Of the 1,515 completed complaints investigations the Ombudsman found in favour of the complainant in 29 per cent of these (436) and mediated settlements were achieved in 117 complaints (Prisons and Probation Ombudsman for England and Wales 2009). The majority of complaints received were ineligible, usually because they had not gone through the internal procedures, others were out of time or raised issues not within the Ombudsman's remit. In that period the complaints related to a wide range of issues including regime activities and adjudications, but mostly related to general conditions, lost property and cash.

Given the time involved in these procedures the Ombudsman may be an option only for those serving longer sentences, but it is less effective for those on shorter sentences, and in some cases the prisoners have been released by the time the investigations are complete. To bring a case requires both a clear understanding of the Ombudsman's powers and remit and a certain level of literacy. However, it has enhanced the protection of prisoners, particularly in relation to lost property claims and to deaths in custody.

External inspections

As well as the complaints process, there is also a process of external scrutiny. The European Prison Rules stipulate that prisons should be shall be subject to regular government inspection and independent monitoring. (EPR 92, 93.1). In addition, as we saw in Chapter 3, the CPT makes occasional visits but more frequent inspection is carried out by the Prison Inspectorate. This is a well-established system of prison inspection. The Chief Inspector of Prisons reports to Parliament and has been a major source of critiques of prisons in England and Wales and is very effective. The Reports carry considerable weight and many of its recommendations have been followed. Anne Owers, the Chief Inspector from 2001–10 was very critical of a number of aspects of the prison regime and offered constructive and practical suggestions for improvement which were grounded in respect for human rights.

The Inspectorate provides independent scrutiny of the conditions in which prisoners are held and their treatment in England and Wales as well as Northern Ireland, the Channel Islands and the Isle of Man. The Inspectorate inspects a wide range of custodial establishments for adults and juveniles. It also visits immigration removal centres and short-term holding facilities, the military corrective training centre in Colchester, and has now begun inspections of police custody suites. Inspections may be announced or unannounced. The Inspectorate also publishes thematic reviews on specific issues and specific groups of prisoners such as women, mentally ill prisoners and prisoners with disabilities.

Adult prisons are given a full inspection every five years and those holding juveniles every three years. Inspection reports are published and the prisons then draw up an action plan and follow-up inspections are made where there are concerns. Its most recent Report noted that 72 per cent of the assessments of the Inspectorate were positive but the figure was lower in closed male prisons (HMCIP 2010a: 5). The Report referred to the fact that prison system 'remains caught between the irresistible force of an increasing population and the immovable object of actual and threatened budget cuts' (ibid: 7). It also expressed concern over segregation and the fact that reviews of prisoners in segregation in most male adult and young adult prisons 'were perfunctory: with little emphasis on reintegration to a normal residential unit or meaningful target setting to challenge and address poor behaviour. Sometimes prisoners were not routinely present at their reviews' (ibid. 24). Moreover, in some cases prisoners were being held outside formal segregation units which were not following the protocols for segregation in PSO 1700. However, in relation to the adjudication process, it found that adjudications were well conducted although in some male adult prisons there was 'insufficient enquiry into disciplinary offences'. Moreover, issues raised during adjudications by prisoners were not always followed up and in some cases minor offences were referred to the district judge for added days. The Report also noted that in young adult establishments 'the proceedings and documentation in adjudications were not age-appropriate' (ibid. 25). The Inspector also highlighted the problem of IPP prisoners being held beyond their tariff owing to problems in accessing offending behaviour programmes as well as parole delays. These iusses will no doubt be followed closely by Owers' successor, Nick Hardwick.

Procedural justice in the Netherlands

In the Netherlands there is also a well-established system of complaints. Prisoners have access to an independent complaints committee from which they can then appeal to a central body, and these bodies make decisions which affect not only the complainants individually but affect prisoners more generally in providing a source of standards and recommendations. The original Dutch penitentiary law was found in the Dutch Prison Act 1886 and Rules published under the Act. The system was reformed after the war by the 1953 Principles of Prison Administration Act which set up a Central Board for the Administration of Criminal Justice to give advice to the Ministry of Justice. This role is now performed by the Council for the Administration of Criminal Justice and the Protection of Juveniles. The 1953 Act also allowed prisoners to appeal against selection and transfers, which gave concessions to prisoners decades in advance of those given to prisoners in England Wales and which in some cases have yet to be secured.

In 1977 the Prison Act was amended giving prisoners the formal right to complain about disciplinary punishments imposed by the Director, as well as interference with correspondence or visits, and any other measures taken by Director which infringe prisoners' rights under the Prison Rules. Prisoners also were given the right to complain about other aspects of their detention in 1977. Downes found that the procedures to deal with grievances in Dutch prisons in the 1980s were more transparent and effective than in England and Wales (Downes 1988). Despite recent pressures on the system, it is fair to say that the Dutch complaints and appeals procedure is still well regarded. The current procedures are found in the 1999 Penitentiary Principles Act and prison directors are bound by this Act. The Act allows considerable room for mediation to resolve complaints.

Complaints are sent to the Complaints Committee, elected by the Minister of the Supervision Board, and both the Director and the prisoner can appeal against their decision. Complaints should be made within seven days of the incident. So prisoners can complain about being sent to a particular prison or being transferred to a particular institution (Tak 2008). As well as complaints over disciplinary sanctions, they can complain over refusals relating to prison visits, controls on letters, or any measures which breach the prisoner's statutory rights. Complaints should be made in writing within one week of receiving the decision and the Committee should respond within four weeks. The Complaints Committee meets in private and both parties can give their views to the Committee in person and the prisoner has the right to legal assistance, if required. If the Committee finds in the prisoner's favour it can quash the decision, order the Director to take a new decision, reject a complaint, or award compensation. Appeals against the Committee's decision may be made by either party to the Appeal Committee of the Council for the Administration of Criminal Justice and Youth Protection. There are different Appeal Boards for prisoners, mental health law and medical law in which prisoners can challenge decisions and bring complaints. The Appeal Committee is the final stage of appeal within domestic law, and while prisoners could go to the European Court of Human Rights, and also to the Ombudsman they are rarely used.

The complaints submitted cover issues including disciplinary sanctions, denial of leave, or medical issues, so in practice this means that prisoners can complain about every decision which implies an infringement or the absence of a decision, but not about the actual rules themselves (Serrarens 2007). Prisoners may also receive financial compensation for a failure to transfer them to a psychiatric prison from an ordinary prison. However, the prison complaints system is under increasing pressure with prison expansion and the complaints regime was suspended for drug traffickers for a period; this has now been reinstated but only partially, so they have fewer rights than other prisoners. The impact of prison expansion means there is less contact with staff and greater emphasis on technological control and surveillance which may impede the complaints process. However, in the Netherlands, like the USA and UK, the view has been expressed in some quarters that the balance has shifted too far in the prisoner's favour as literally thousands of complaints are made every year and that there should be further limits on the right to complain.

Disciplinary measures can be imposed on prisoners by the governor for behaviour which undermines the security, good order or discipline of the prison. The sanctions may range from loss of access to activities for up to two weeks, loss or restrictions on leave, fines which will mean loss of wages, loss of visits if the misbehaviour related to visits and where necessary, segregation (Tak 2008). The prisoner has the right to be notified of the governor's decisions and reasons for it and the prisoner can if he wishes take the matter to the Complaints Committee.

As well as the formal complaints procedures there are also prisoner councils or prisoner committees which provide a useful framework of meetings to discuss problems and in this sense contribute to dynamic security (see van Zyl Smit and Snacken 2009).

All Dutch prisons have an Independent Supervision Board whose members can enter the prison at any time. In addition the Implementation of Sanctions Inspectorate, set up in January 2005, is responsible for the supervision of probation, prison and all national institutions and services which fall within the Custodial Institutions Services. It reviews performance and compliance with regulations and relevant law. It is independent but part of the Ministry of Justice and Reports to the Minister of Justice. It conducts both general and thematic investigations. The full inspection programme began in 2006 when inspectors made 56 inspection visits to penal institutions and 57 visits to probation and after care organizations.

So a new system of conditional early release was introduced in 2008 in the Netherlands allowing prisoners release after serving two-thirds of a sentence of two years or more, but the conditions may include restrictions on movement, electronic tagging and participation in programmes, for example, for drug treatment. The decision to release may be postponed, because of the prisoner's conduct in prison or because of disciplinary sanctions but the decision in such cases should be taken by the court (Tak 2008). For prisoners serving less than two years, the release point would be one year and one-third of the remaining term.

Procedural due process challenges in the United States

The source of procedural rights in the United States is obviously the Constitution and the court may also read these rights into statutes or find them inherent in particular contexts of imprisonment. If the government intends to deprive the citizen of his life, liberty or property, then he possesses due process rights under the Fourteenth Amendment: 'Nor shall any State deprive the person of life, liberty or property without due process of law, nor deny any person within its jurisdiction the equal protection of its laws.' Procedural due process rights would involve those rights implicit in the right to a fair hearing, such as being informed of the case against the prisoner and the right to call witnesses. If a prisoner is challenging his conviction or sentence and has exhausted all the available appeals procedures, he may seek access to the courts through a writ of habeas corpus and the court may order his release. But this is likely to happen only in rare cases where his constitutional rights have been breached. In the United States, as we have seen, there has been a retreat from the high point of prisoners' rights and more weight is being given to the interest of the prison in maintaining security and the courts are more willing to see the loss of prisoners' rights as an inevitable consequence of imprisonment.

Prisoners' right of access to the courts is constitutionally protected by the due process clause of the Fourteenth Amendment. In *ex parte Hull* 312 US 546 (1941) the Court ruled that a rule in state prisons preventing prisoners applying to the federal court for a writ of habeas corpus was invalid. The issue of access to the courts has always been given great weight by the courts because it is clearly crucial that the prisoner should be able to contact the courts to clear his name or raise questions about his case. In *Bounds v Smith* 430 US 817 (1977) the Supreme Court affirmed that this right of access to the courts also entails access to law libraries and to persons with legal training in order for prisoners to prepare their cases. In the later case of *Lewis v Casey* 518 US 343 (1996), which raised questions about the shortcomings of the prison library and prison assistance programme, the court limited this right, saying that the inmate has to show that these shortcomings caused actual harm in mounting his case. Justice Scalia also said that *Bounds* did not give prisoners a guarantee that they will be given the facilities to file any type of legal claim, but only that they have the tools to challenge their sentences or conditions of confinement.

The right of access is overlaid by lawyer–client privilege so the prisoner should be able to contact his lawyer without the prison first reading or interfering with his mail. The prison should also provide stamps, paper, and allow visits from lawyers. *Wolff v McDonnell* 418 US 539 (1974) made clear that the prison authority should only open legal correspondence if illegal contraband is suspected and this has to be opened in the presence of the prisoner, as in the UK. Officers should not listen to the conversations between the lawyer and the prisoner. They should also make provision for access to legal advice or assistance as the Supreme Court made clear in *Johnson v Avery 393* US 483 (1969). However, legal help might mean just help from law students or paralegals as the Court said in *Bounds v Smith*. Access to help from these sources should be permitted and a prohibition in the California prison regulations on interviews with paralegals and law students was an unjustified limit on prisoners' access to the courts and constitutionally invalid, the Supreme Court said in *Procunier v Martinez* 416 US 396 (1974).

Procedural rights also arise in the context of reductions of sentence for good behaviour. Prisoners may be given credit for their good behaviour and their sentence length reduced. The term used is a meritorious 'good time' allowance and most but not all, states do make some provision for this. The exact calculation varies from state to state. For example, it might be one day of good time credit for three days' good behaviour. If a prisoner loses his 'good time credits' then he is entitled to be informed of this and entitled to a hearing before the prison board and to put evidence to support his case. So disciplinary matters clearly have implications for continued detention and this detention on disciplinary grounds does raise a liberty interest. So in the landmark decision *Wolff v McDonnell* 418 US 539 (1974) the Supreme Court was critical of the prison authority for removing the prisoner's good time without procedural protection. The Court did not say that there is a constitutional right to good time, but if the state creates such a provision and sets out when it might be removed, then a protected liberty interest has been created. In this case prisoners would be entitled to expect advance notification, a statement of reasons for disciplinary action, and have the opportunity to call witnesses and present evidence unless restrictions are necessary. But the court said that there was no right to counsel for the prisoner unless the prisoner was illiterate or unable to conduct the case himself. In this case the court said that moving the prisoner to solitary confinement raised a due process issue. The prisoner had argued that the prison disciplinary proceedings violated his due process rights, that regulations governing inmates' mail were unconstitutionally restrictive and that the legal assistance programme did not meet the standards demanded by the due process clause. Following this case, states had to conduct disciplinary hearings with procedural protections where loss of days or segregation might result, although this would not be required for minor infractions. However, subsequent cases have limited the impact of *Wolff v McDonnell* and even when it was still good law, prisoners were sceptical how much due process was built into proceedings in practice.

In *Sandin v Conner* 515 US 472 (1995) the court was critical of the expansion of prisoners' rights cases and critical of claims which sought to elicit rights from the statutory language of privileges. It said that the courts had become too lenient in accepting prisoners' rights claims. The court restricted due process rights in segregation to cases where the move is an atypical significant deprivation or hardship, rather than where the prison authority is simply carrying out the normal day-to-day business of the prison. The impact of this case is that it became harder for prisoners to challenge their treatment on constitutional grounds. So where the segregation is administrative or punitive, the court is unlikely to find due process rights protection.

The Courts have also declined to find that transfers raise due process rights for prisoners, even when the effect of the transfer is to make it difficult for families to visit because it is further away from home or has fewer facilities. In *Meachum v Fano* 427 US 215 (1976) the court said that there is no right to be held in a particular prison, no liberty interest is raised, although this was criticized by the dissenting judges who argued that the liberty interest existed here apart from statute or positive law and was therefore inalienable. But if no due process rights are raised then the prisoner has no right to be told of reasons for transfer or to a due process hearing. However, if the prisoner is being transferred to a mental hospital as in *Vitek v Jones* 445 US 480 (1980) then due process rights demanding the procedural protections specified in *Wolff* would also arise. Furthermore, if a prisoner is reclassified then procedural rights are engaged and he should be notified of that and the reasons for the decision.

The court's role in intervening in sentences which are excessive has been limited. While making clear that sentences which are grossly disproportionate would breach the Eighth Amendment, the majority of the Court in *Ewing v California* 538 US 11 (2003) thought that a sentence of life without possibility of parole for the first 25 years, under California's Three Strikes law, for a repeat offender who stole a set of golf clubs was not precluded by the Eighth Amendment. However, in a recent important decision in *Graham v Florida*

Case No. 08–7412 (May 17 2010) the US Supreme Court ruled that a life sentence without parole for juveniles in non-homicide cases violated the Eighth Amendment. The use of this sentence has attracted considerable criticism. However, the sentence remains constitutionally valid for juveniles convicted of homicide.

Conclusions

Procedural justice comprises a significant element of prisoners' rights and we have seen an expansion of procedural justice in England and Wales and the USA. Advances have been made in relation to access to the courts, reviews of detention and disciplinary hearings which have enhanced the protection of prisoners. Nevertheless, some of the advances made in procedural justice in the United States in the 1970s have been reined in by recent decisions. However, procedural rights and procedural justice which includes the right to be treated fairly, for example, in the context of disciplinary hearings, may be distinguished from substantive rights and substantive justice, which would include rights to a minimal standard of living and access to resources issues discussed in Chapter 4. But a further key element of substantive justice is contact with the outside world and this will now be considered.

6   Contact with the outside world

Introduction

Contact with families and access to the normal sources of information, including the media, are important elements of the normalization of prison life. This contact prepares prisoners for life when they return to the community, may assist the process of rehabilitation and ultimately the reintegration into the community and weaken the process of prisonization whereby prisoners adapt to life in prison and negotiate the pains of imprisonment by adopting the values, customs and mores of the prison subculture (Clemmer 1940, Sykes 1958). For individuals confined within a total institution where all activities are undertaken within the prison walls, any contact with the outside world can reduce the impact of isolation on the prisoner's sense of self and also assist the process of rehabilitation (Goffman 1961). So states should assist prisoners to maintain or create links with the outside world as part of the process of rehabilitation and prepare them for resettlement. Access to work and education which could take place outside the prison walls, where appropriate, can also assist with retraining and ultimately resettlement.

The problems prisoners face in maintaining contact with the outside world, including their families, will be considered in relation to the right to correspondence, contact with the media, temporary release, prison visits, access to artificial insemination and conjugal visits. Free speech issues have arisen in relation to the publication of 'memoirs' and materials relating to offenders' criminal histories. Apart from the inherent value to prisoners of maintaining contact with their families, links to the outside world also provide a key element of security for prisoners in protecting against poor conditions or poor treatment inside prison, as access to the media and to the legal profession may be crucial in drawing attention to problems, assisting with prisoners' campaigns, or in ensuring appropriate treatment for ill or disabled prisoners.

Contact with the prisoner's family engages Articles 8 and 12 of the European Convention on Human Rights, the right to private and family life and the right to marry and found a family, while the right to publish and to contact with media would *prima facie* be protected by Article 10, the right to freedom of expression. However, the qualifications to Articles 8 and 10 clearly set limits on their value to prisoners. In the context of imprisonment, infringements of Articles 8 and 10 have been justified by states and the courts in terms of security and safety, pressure on resources, and the prevention of crime, what constitutes a breach has been narrowly defined. So prisoners asserting these rights have faced a number of hurdles in bringing claims and succeeding and states have been accorded a wide margin of appreciation in applying the Convention in this area of law and practice. While some Article 8 claims have failed because they have been seen as justified under Article 8(2), nonetheless Article 8 is valuable in protecting privacy, access to family, visits and telephone calls, and contact between women prisoners and their children. More account is being taken of the right to family life under Article 8 and respecting family ties in transfer and allocation decisions, but of course security considerations may still be invoked.

Under the European Prison Rules, contact with the outside world is essential: 'Prisoners shall be allowed to communicate as often as possible by letter, telephone or other forms of communication with their families, other persons and representatives of outside organizations and to receive visits from these persons' (EPR 24.1). The visiting arrangements 'shall be such as to allow prisoners to maintain and develop family relationships in as normal a manner as possible' (EPR 24.4).

Prisoners also have the right to be kept informed of public affairs, so this means that they should have access to newspapers and radio or television unless there is a specific prohibition on this made by a judicial authority for specified period (EPR 24.10). So this would also mean providing foreign language newspapers where possible for foreign national prisoners. Prisoners do spend some of their free time reading newspapers and watching television and some may attend classes on current affairs. Perhaps this is unsurprising as prisoners have a direct interest in the political issue of the relation between the citizen and the state, having experienced the consequences when the social contract is breached.

The UK Prison Rules also emphasize that 'A prisoner shall be encouraged and assisted to establish and maintain such relations with persons and agencies outside prison as may, in the opinion of the governor, best promote the interests of his family and his own social rehabilitation' (PR 4(2)). Particular attention should be given to the maintenance of family bonds where this is in the best interest of the prisoner and the family. Prison visits also contribute to good order within the prison in reducing tensions.

Maintaining family contact is linked to the reduction of reoffending as the work of Ditchfield and others has shown, and is of benefit to both prisoners and family members (Ditchfield 1994). Strong family links may reduce the pains of imprisonment, but concerns about families, particularly the fate of children outside, will also add to the stress experienced by prisoners. However, in cases of abusive relationships, then family members may well be safer without contact and their lives may be improved by the absence of a violent parent or partner.

Isolation is one of the most destructive aspect of imprisonment and breaking down that isolation will benefit prisoners and the wider society. Lippke, for example, argues that prison should be more 'permeable' that is, open to the outside world in terms of allowing prisoners access to the outside world through outside visits, work and education and other forms of communication (Lippke 2007). For example, German prisoners are allowed time outside to attend courses but the number of absconders is low, although the fear of absconding is one of the main reasons for limiting physical access to the outside world. Allowing family visits to take place outside prison would be less daunting for visitors, and generate a better atmosphere which would be consistent with retributivism:

> Again, retributivism requires that legal punishment be structured so that it treats and addresses offenders as rational moral beings. This entails that the losses or restrictions punishment imposes must not be permitted to erode or destroy offenders' capacities for responsible citizenship.
>
> (Lippke 2007: 183)

Contact with families and friends outside the prison, he argues, would strengthen 'prisoners' commitments to becoming and remaining responsible citizens' (ibid 184). This is particularly important given that many offenders are aged under 35. Isolating offenders at a younger age level will make it harder to develop a capacity for responsible citizenship. His analysis of prisons is based mostly on American prisons, where visits are conducted behind glass and are far less open than those in the UK, and where visits have been limited because of the pressures of prison expansion.

Lippke advocates what he describes as Minimal Conditions of Confinement which means imposing the minimal restrictions compatible with prisoners' confinement, so they should be allowed and encouraged to maintain social bonds and given access to paid work with proper working conditions, and to recreational facilities and should retain full civil rights including voting. Promoting such a humane and permeable regime will have benefits in terms of promoting prisoners' sense of responsibility and also make the management of prisons easier. He argues that punishment should be devised 'so that it is possible for offenders to respond as autonomous beings to the sanctions imposed on them' (Lippke 2007: 115). But it is unlikely that the more extreme conditions of confinement found in supermax prisons, where prisoners have very limited time outside their cells, or access to such facilities, will facilitate this.

Consideration of prisoners' right to family life under Article 8 also raises questions of third party impact. There has been more interest recently on prisoners' families and third party impact, particularly on the question of whether family responsibilities should be used in mitigation (Piper 2007, Easton 2008). However, the European Court of Human Rights has demonstrated an understanding of the impact of imprisonment for third parties in recent judgments such as *Dickson v UK* Application No. 44362/04 (4 December 2007). Questions about prisoners' rights to artificial insemination and conjugal visits highlight the problem of whether prisoners' reproductive rights and those of their partners are inevitably reduced by imprisonment. Any policy which has an effect on family bonds clearly affects the rights of family members as well as the prisoner, even if this is unintended.

On retributivist theory any punishment should be imposed only on the culpable individual and avoid or minimize the impact on the partners and children of offenders. However, we shall see, the rights of prisoners' families may also be infringed in practice by policies on visits, searches and other areas of prison life. Third parties may also be treated in ways which imply that they are 'tainted' or share responsibility for their partners' crimes. At the same time, however, impact mitigation on the grounds of family responsibilities is problematic for retributivism because it would mean variation in sentencing between offenders on external grounds.

Codd (2008) argues that prisoners' families have been marginalized and stigmatized by their association with the prisoner. Although the focus in penal policy has been on the role of the family to help prevent reoffending, there has been less interest in the problems faced by female partners of male prisoners. The social exclusion of prisoners is shared by their families and research findings suggest that children of prisoners are more likely to become offenders themselves (Murray and Farrington 2005, Bernstein 2005). Intervening variables here may include the children's experience of deprivation, involvement in criminal subcultures and being taken into care.

For example, in the USA like the UK, women may find it hard to maintain family bonds while partners are in prison especially with the high costs of telephone calls and visits which may be particularly difficult if prisoners are housed out of state. If county jails are underused they may sell places to other states so prisoners in the USA could be housed some distance from home. Although prisoners can make outside calls and receive them, they pay premium rates, which means huge profits for phone companies and a burden on families. Similarly in the UK prisoners who make outgoing calls pay far more than they would outside prison and the contracts are awarded to private companies. In the USA prisoners who live in public housing and are convicted of drug crime, lose that housing so their families will also be evicted.

Incarceration can adversely affect the wider community as well as families. The impact of 'mass imprisonment' on poor urban communities has received considerable attention in recent years from criminologists. Wacquant's work has drawn attention to the ghettoization of communities, and the ghettoization of prison with a concentration of black males (Wacquant 2001, 2007). The incarceration of young black males in prison in the USA has dramatically affected the quality of life in black urban communities. As Mauer and King note: 'One of every 14 black children has a parent in prison on any given day; over the course of childhood, the figures would be much higher' (Mauer and Scott King 2004: 5). Communities are affected by high levels of incarceration and an absence of black adult males. In parts of Washington D.C., they point out, there is a gender ratio of 62 males for every 100 women. The deeper implications of this incarceration for voting patterns and the democratic process will be considered in Chapter 8, but it clearly also will affect family life and lead to housing and work problems in the communities.

Clear has shown how changes in sentencing law have meant a concentration of imprisonment on young black males from poor urban neighbourhoods with implications for the human and social capital of those areas (Clear 2007). The effect of this has been to weaken families and parental control, change social attitudes and increase rather than reduce crime. Mothers are rearing families with a father in prison, children have siblings in prison and 'Prison is thus woven into the fabric of these communities, with its stark implications for social networks, social capital and, ultimately, informal social control' (ibid. 10). These communities suffer from poor social cohesion as the residents become isolated from each other, and there are also economic effects as the local labour market is depressed, which makes it harder for those released from prison to find work. Because of higher rates of disenfranchisement among these groups, they are also excluded from the political process and less able to influence the acquisition and distribution of resources. Clear argues that the effect of high incarceration in these impoverished communities may generate more crime because of the disruption of family structure, parenting and informal social controls: 'There is good evidence that high rates of incarceration destabilize families, increase rates of delinquency, increase rates of teenage births, foster alienation of youth from pro-social norms, damage frail social networks, and weaken labour markets' (ibid. 173). The strategies he advocates to address the problem are community justice, improving jobs and housing, and promoting restorative justice in communities and sentencing reforms, including removing mandatory sentencing and reducing sentence length.

Interference with correspondence

Regular letter writing is seen as an important way of maintaining the prisoner's links with family and friends which will ultimately assist his resettlement. Interference with correspondence has been a key concern for prisoners', especially if that correspondence relates to legal matters arising out of their conviction and here of course Article 6 issues may also be raised, as denying access to the courts may prejudice the prisoner's right to a fair trial. The Strasbourg Court has ruled that interference with prisoners' correspondence has infringed both Articles 8 and 6. In considering infringements in relation to the qualifications in Article 8(2), the court will apply the proportionality principle although what is seen as a legitimate infringement may change depending on the political climate, the prevailing policies and political objectives.

Before the Human Rights Act, a number of successful cases were brought by prisoners in relation to interference with their correspondence to lawyers which led to changes in the Prison Rules to comply with Article 8. The European Court of Human Rights has robustly protected prisoners' rights to correspond with their legal advisors in cases such as *Silver and others v UK* Application No. 5947/7 (25 March 1983), *Campbell v UK* (1992) 15 EHRR 137 and *McCallum v UK* (1990) 13 EHRR 596. The CPT has taken a similar position to the approach of the European Court of Human Rights in these cases and has criticized the censorship of prisoners' mail in the UK and this was also criticized by the Woolf Report (Council of Europe 1991,Woolf and Tumim 1991). The European Prison Rules also require that prisoners should be allowed to communicate as often as possible with their families by letter, telephone or other means (EPR 24.1).

Ordinary correspondence to family and friends is less likely to be protected by the Court, than letters to lawyers, but there still must be some grounds, such as the prevention of crime, to justify interference. In considering whether there is a sufficiently pressing need to justify the interference with a fundamental right, the Court will give considerable weight to the prison authority's risk assessment which will make it harder for prisoners to succeed. In the past the prison authority has been reluctant to cede ground to prisoners, but the increasing influence of rights jurisprudence, including the judgments of the Strasbourg Court, has forced a modification of its position.

Restrictions on the number of letters which may be sent and the reading of prisoners' letters may be permitted under Article 8(2), provided that they are proportionate to the aims of prevention of crime and protecting the rights of others (see *Boyle and Rice v UK* (1988) 10 EHRR 425). The Court will also consider whether these aims could be prevented by less restrictive means.

The justifications in Article 8(2) are incorporated into the UK Prison Rules. PR 34(2) allows the Secretary of State to impose restrictions or conditions on the prisoner's communications, provided it does not interfere with the Convention rights of any person or is necessary on the grounds of national security, the prevention of crime, interests of public safety or the protection of rights and freedoms of others. Communications may be intercepted if necessary on these grounds and that the interception is proportionate to the aim (PR 35A). This mirrors the qualification in Article 8(2).

Prison Rule 35 on personal letters and visits provides that remand prisoners can send and receive as many letters as they wish, while convicted prisoners can send one letter once a week. As well as the basic 'statutory' rights to correspondence, further correspondence may be allowed under the privileges scheme. So prisoners can then send as many privilege letters as they wish and special letters, when they are about to be transferred or immediately after conviction, to settle their business affairs, or in relation to legal proceedings, or to contact the Ombudsman. In *AB v Netherlands* (2003) 27 EHRR 48, the Court said that allowing a prisoner to send 2–3 letters a week with unlimited incoming mail was compatible with Article 8.

There are no limits on the number of letters they receive in prisons where correspondence is not monitored, but where it is monitored then if an excessive number of letters are received they may be returned and prisoners may be asked to limit themselves to 4 sides of paper when they send out letters. Correspondence with any person or organization can be disallowed if there is reason to believe the person or organization is planning or engaged in activities which threaten the security or good order of the prison. Again, this would fall within the justifications in Articles 8(2) and 10(2). If the prisoner is deemed to be a risk to a child then he will have to apply for permission to correspond with a child. Correspondence with legal advisers and the courts is privileged, so should not be opened, read or stopped except in special circumstances, that is, where the governor has reasonable cause to believe the contents of the letter would endanger prison security, the safety of others or is otherwise of a criminal nature. Letters to Members of Parliament and Members of the European Parliament are also privileged when the recipients are acting in a constituency capacity.

The rules governing restrictions on correspondence are set out in PSO 4411 *Prisoner Communications: Correspondence* (05/09/2007). The guidance was revised considerably in the 1980s following the case of *Silver and others v UK* Application No. 5947/7 (25 March 1983) and has been further revised to comply with Articles 8 and 10. Correspondence should not contain material which is indecent, offensive, obscene or threatening, contain escape plans or could damage national security. Correspondence may be routinely read only in high-security prisons and for Category A prisoners or for those on the escape list.

All letters to lawyers and the courts are privileged and this privilege has now been expended to legal papers. PR 39 states that such correspondence can only be interfered with if the governor has reasonable cause to believe it contains an illicit enclosure, or its contents endanger the security of the prison or the safety of others, or is otherwise of a criminal nature. It should normally be opened in the presence of the prisoner. The Strasbourg Court has been less willing than the domestic courts to accept interference with prisoners correspondence with lawyers or with their families and recognizes the importance of correspondence in preparing for legal proceedings as well as in the context of the right to family life.[1]

Access to lawyers and letters to lawyers are protected by legal privilege and in the key case of *Raymond v Honey* [1983] 1 AC 1, which concerned letters to a solicitor, the court stressed that letters to lawyers where the prisoner is a party to legal proceedings cannot be interfered with. If the letter relates only to proceedings which are contemplated rather than ongoing, these communications are still protected by Article 8, according to the Strasbourg Court. In *Campbell and Fell v UK* (1984) 7 EHRR 165 the court found a violation of Article 8 when one letter was opened because it inhibited correspondence regarding a proposed legal action. So these communications should be only read or stopped if there is reason to believe that legal privilege is being abused.

In the past, until the mid-1970s, interference with and monitoring of prisoners' letters was widespread. One of the first cases on this issue was

Golder v UK Application No. 4551/70 (21 February 1975) where the Court found a breach of Article 8 in the interference with Golder's letters to his MP and to the Chief Constable, in relation to a disturbance in which he was involved and to a claim he had assaulted a prison officer. Golder was contemplating bringing a libel claim against a prison officer. At that time there was a prior ventilation rule which required that the prisoner try to resolve the issue through internal procedures before seeking legal advice, but the Court ruled this breached Article 8 and it could not be justified under Article 8(2) in the interests of security. The Court also found a breach of Article 6(1) as he was refused permission to contact a solicitor.

A prisoner must be able to seek legal advice to enforce his or her rights. In *Silver and others v UK* Application No. 5947/7 (25 March 1983) sixty-two of Silver's letters and six letters of other prisoners were subject to interference for a variety of reasons, but the interference in most cases could not be justified under Article 8(2). The Court affirmed the decision of the Commission in 1980. Silver had died by the time the case came to court but it was decided to pursue the case. In *Silver*, the right of access to the courts protected by Article 6(1) was also violated as Silver had been refused leave to consult a solicitor. After *Silver* the prior ventilation rule was removed. This was initially replaced by a simultaneous ventilation rule which required that complaints be made simultaneously through internal procedures as well as external ones, but this was also removed in 1984 in the domestic courts in *R v Secretary of State for the Home Department ex parte Anderson* [1984] QB 778. Here the Divisional Court was critical of the restraints on prisoners' right of access to the courts by means of secondary legislation and stressed that any limitations should be by primary legislation.

In *McCallum v UK* (1990) 13 EHRR 596 the Court found a breach of Article 8 when restrictions were imposed on correspondence, following a prison disciplinary hearing. The Court ruled that examining letters to lawyers in the absence of the prisoner could not be justified. Legal correspondence may only be read if there is reasonable cause to believe it will affect the security or safety of others. This case on Scottish prisons placed Scottish prisoners in the same position as those in England and Wales following *Silver*.

The issue of interference with correspondence also arose in *Campbell v UK* Application No. 13590/88 (25 March 1992) where a prisoner's letters to his lawyer as well as letters to MPs and family members, were read. The Strasbourg Court was critical of the rules on prisoners' access to legal correspondence then in place, as knowing that letters would be read would prevent prisoners from communicating freely to their legal advisers. Any interference amounts to a prima facie breach of Article 8 so it would have to be justified under Article 8(2). To justify an infringement under Article 8(2), the state would need to show some grounds for concern over the specific correspondence, rather than simply routinely opening and reading the prisoner's mail. If there was good reason to believe that the mail contained an illegal enclosure, for example, then the mail could be opened and checked without having to read it as well. The UK restrictions were far too broad and not Convention compliant. Campbell's case had also raised Article 6 issues as we saw in Chapter 5. The Strasbourg Court also found a breach of Article 13 because of the absence of an effective remedy. By the time the case reached the Court, the Rules had been revised following *Silver v UK*.

Following *Campbell*, in the case of *R v Secretary of State for the Home Department, ex parte Leech* [1994] QB 198, the Prison Rules were changed to strengthen the protection of privileged correspondence and to comply with the Convention. Here the Court of Appeal made clear that correspondence to lawyers is protected by legal privilege, otherwise the prisoner's access to the courts will be impeded and the expectation is that this would only rarely be restricted. The burden is on the Secretary of State to show that any restrictions are necessary and should be the minimum possible.

The principle of proportionality now applies when assessing any restrictions on the key right of access to the courts as the House of Lords made clear in *R v Secretary of State for the Home Department ex parte Daly* [2001] UKHL 26 where the prisoner's letters to lawyers were read in the course of a cell search in his absence. Furthermore, if there are grounds to suspect illicit enclosures, the letters should be opened in the prisoners' presence. Since the Human Rights Act came into force, several Article 8 cases have been brought by prisoners in the domestic courts, using the proportionality test, arguing that restrictions on correspondence are disproportionate, and therefore unlawful, but the domestic courts may be more willing to accept restrictions than the Strasbourg Court, as can be seen in the case of *Szuluk*. Here a prisoner who had suffered a brain haemorrhage was in correspondence with a medical specialist to discuss the appropriate treatment. The Prison Governor decided that his correspondence should be read by the prison medical officer, before passing it on to the specialist. Szuluk was a category B prisoner but held in a high-security prison so was subject to the higher level of security appropriate to category A prisoners. He sought judicial review and the High Court quashed the Governor's decision but this was reversed on appeal. The Court of Appeal again stressed that letters can be read if it is necessary for the prevention of crime, and the protection of the rights and freedoms of others, the least invasive method is used and the restriction is not excessive.[2] So reading Szuluk's letters to his NHS consultant, was not based on a rigid application of a policy and the risk of abuse was reduced by allowing only the medical officer to read them. However, the Strasbourg Court found that Article 8 had been breached. In *Szuluk v UK* Application No. 36936/05 (2 June 2009) the Court acknowledged that in some cases control of correspondence is compatible with the Convention, but there must be some exceptional circumstances to justify this. Given the seriousness of Szuluk's medical condition, the Court concluded that 'uninhibited correspondence with a medical specialist in the context of a prisoner suffering from a life-threatening condition should be afforded no less protection than the correspondence between a prisoner and an MP' (at para 53). The Court thought that the Government had failed to provide sufficient justification of any risk of abuse in the correspondence with the medical specialist, as the correspondence was to a named person whose *bona fides* was not in question and there was no likelihood of the specialist being tricked by the prisoner. The Court also referred to the CPT Standards, specifically that medical secrecy should be followed in prison as in the community on the principle of equivalence.

Of course prisoners may also communicate by phone. The Court in *AB v the Netherlands* (2003) 27 EHRR 48 said that Article 8 does not give a right to telephone calls where there are facilities for correspondence in place, but where telephone calls are permitted, the principles governing Article 8 will apply. So restrictions may be imposed provided that they are proportionate.[3] In *R (Taylor) v Governor of HMP Risley* [2004] EHWC 2654 (Admin) the prisoner was limited to 20 phone numbers he could contact and which were monitored by the prison. Given concerns over illegal drug use in the prison the Administrative Court thought this infringement of Article 8 was proportionate. Maintaining contact by phone may be an important element of maintaining family bonds and contact with the outside world, but obviously there are concerns over prisoners' involvement in illegal activities outside the prison. Prisoners are not permitted use of mobile phones but mobile phones and SIM cards are smuggled into prison in body orifices. Special body scanners and new mobile phone detectors have been introduced to control the problem. Blocking signals is not possible because it would affect users in the immediate vicinity of the prison.

Recent concerns have been focused on prisoners' access to social networking sites including Facebook. Although access to the internet is normally limited to educational purposes and closely supervised, some prisoners have been updating their Facebook pages from prison using smuggled mobile phones, including observations on prison life and in some cases taunting their victims. The relevant pages have been removed from Facebook following requests from the Ministry of Justice.

In the Netherlands sentenced prisoners are entitled to send or receive an unlimited number of letters and this should only be restricted if justified on the grounds of good order in the prison or safety issues. Letters to MPs, the courts or the Ombudsman are unrestricted. Remand prisoners' letters are more heavily controlled and all their incoming and outgoing post is checked. Prisoners have been able to challenge the Prison Director if he refuses to send letters or pass them on, or refuses to allow the visits of certain people, since the late 1970s. Prisoners are allowed reading materials including when on segregation. The principle of proportionality will be applied by the courts in dealing with these issues. So most of the Dutch cases on access to correspondence have related to the Dutch overseas territories. For example, the Strasbourg Court found a breach of Article 8 because of the interference with prisoners' post in the Netherlands Antilles in *AB v the Netherlands* (2003) 37 EHRR 48. The CPT was also critical of the failure to give prisoners in Aruba stamps and paper to maintain contact with the outside world

(Council of Europe 1996: para 259). Prisoners should be able to maintain contact with the outside world subject to security requirements.

There are also provisions against tapping prisoners' phones in the Netherlands as there must not be any arbitrary interference with prisoners' phone calls. The court will look closely at the limits on the interception and tapping of telephone calls. In *Doerga v Netherlands* Application No. 50210/99 (27 April 2004) the applicant successfully brought an Article 8 claim in relation to phone tapping of his conversations inside prison. One of the phone conversations was instrumental in a subsequent conviction. The Court acknowledged that there are circumstances in which monitoring prisoners' contact with the outside world, including tapping prisoners' calls might be necessary, but it concluded that the rules governing the monitoring of prisoners' calls in the Netherlands were insufficiently clear or detailed to protect prisoners against arbitrary interference by the authorities with the applicant's right to respect for his private life and correspondence and did not meet the criteria of being in accordance with law required by Article 8(2). So telephone calls were protected by the right to privacy.

Prisoners in the Netherlands have the right to make phone calls for a minimum of 10 minutes per week, which should not be monitored unless there are concerns over safety, good order in the prison or prevention of crime and the prisoners should be informed of this monitoring in advance. They also have the right to unlimited calls to lawyers, MPs, the Ombudsman and judicial bodies which should not be intercepted.

In the United States freedom from censorship of mail and contact with the media have been addressed mostly under the First Amendment right to freedom of speech and the due process clause of the Fourteenth Amendment. However, the courts in addressing First Amendment issues whether inside or outside prison, balance the free speech right against the public's interest in speech suppression, considering issues such as national security and the public interest in safety, and if there is a clear and present danger, in a similar fashion to European Convention jurisprudence. Within the prison context these interests may be given more weight, as the safety of the public as well as other prisoners will be very important. As we saw in Chapter 1, the courts in the United States accept that the prisoner retains some constitutional rights inside prison, but these will be balanced against the need for security. So while prisoners retain the right to freedom of expression, it can be interfered with where there are security issues. As in the UK, a distinction is drawn between mail to lawyers and other mail. Communication with lawyers should be not be read by prison officers or restricted but is protected by the Fourteenth Amendment due process clause.

Although the courts in the early 1970s took a robust approach to prisoners' right to correspondence, notably in *Procunier v Martinez* 416 US 396 (1974), subsequent cases showed more deference to the prison authorities. In *Procunier* the Supreme Court invalidated the Californian prison regulations concerning prisoners' correspondence. These rules allowed the authorities to ban letters in which prisoners expressed complaints or inflammatory political, racial, religious or other views. The Court ruled that these vague standards infringed the First Amendment rights of prisoners and the recipients. Prisoners had the right to send or receive mail without censorship of their content which had been critical of the prison. The Court said it would subject infringements to strict scrutiny, so a compelling governmental interest should be shown and the infringement must be strictly tailored to that interest. For letters to be read, there has to be a legitimate governmental interest, and a suspicion that it contains a threat to security. Prisoners are also entitled to private visits from their lawyers so while prison officers can supervise and remain in the room, they cannot listen to what is said which is protected by lawyer client privilege and calls to lawyers cannot be monitored.

In the later case of *Turner v Safley* 482 US 78 (1987) the Court diluted this strict scrutiny test, and said instead there had to be a reasonable or rational relationship between the restriction and the state interest. Here the case concerned two prisoners writing to each other in different prisons. The prison authorities thought they might discuss escape plans, or plans for assault or the promotion of gang activities, so the Court upheld the ban. However, the prison authorities have to show that if a right is asserted it would be burdensome on the prison and a drain on prison resources to meet it.

Prisoners also have a right to access to publications and the prison would have to show grounds for restrictions, the Court said in *Thornburgh v Abbott* 539 490 US 401 (1989). A similar approach was taken in *Clement v California Dept of Corrections* 220 F. Supp. 2d 1098 (2002). In this case which the ACLU brought on behalf of a Pelican Bay prisoner, the prisoner won the right to mail containing material printed from the internet.

Freedom of expression

Free speech issues may arise in prison in relation to contact with the media, the prisoners' own writings and access to material. The right to freedom of expression in UK prisons is protected by Article 10 of the European Convention which states: 'Everyone has the right to freedom of expression. This right shall include freedom to hold opinions and to receive and impart information and ideas without interference by public authority.' However, the right is qualified in Article 10(2):

> The exercise of these freedoms, since it carries with it duties and responsibilities, may be subject to such formalities, conditions, restrictions or penalties as are prescribed by law and are necessary in a democratic society, in the interests of national security, territorial integrity or public safety, for the prevention of disorder or crime, for the protection of health or morals, for the protection of the reputation or the rights of others, for preventing the disclosure of information received in confidence, or for maintaining the authority and impartiality of the judiciary.

To use Article 10(2), the State would have to show good grounds for such interference. This framework of exceptions is mirrored in the Prison Rule 34 (1) which states that restrictions can be imposed on communications between the prison and any other person provided that the restriction does not interfere with the Convention rights of any person, is necessary on the grounds in para 44(3) and reliance on those grounds is compatible with the Convention right to be interfered with and the restriction or condition is proportionate to what is sought to be achieved. The grounds are the interests of national security, prevention, detection, investigation or prosecution of crime, the interests of public safety, the protection of health or morals, maintaining the authority and impartiality of the judiciary, or the protection of the rights and freedoms of any person, so they reflect the qualifications in Article 10(2). Any limits must be directed at one of the aims in Article 10(2) and implemented in a way proportionate to those aims.

The intensity of review of decisions under the proportionality principle is greater than under the *Wednesbury*[4] principle, because the doctrine of proportionality requires the Court to assess the balance the decision maker has struck and not merely whether it is within the range of rational or reasonable decisions.

The current rules on contact with the media in England and Wales are set out in PSO 4470 *Prisoners' Access to the Media* (02/09/2005) and PSO 4410 *Prisoner Communication: Visits* (05/09/2007). These provisions seek to ensure a balance between protecting freedom of expression and ensuring that access to the media does not mean a risk to the public, prison order or national security and were revised following the cases of *Simms and O'Brien* and *Hirst*. Access to the media may be by letter, phone or visits.

Prisoners do not need permission from the Governor in advance to send letters or receive letters from the media, but need to apply in writing to the Governor for permission for telephone calls or visits. However, there are limits on what can be sent out. Letters to the media cannot contain material on the prisoner's own or others' offences, unless it contains serious representations about convictions or serious comment about crime, the justice process or penal system, and should not refer to prisoners or staff in ways which allow them to be identified (PSO 4470: para 2.2). Visits from the press are permitted only at the governor's discretion, and only if the governor is satisfied it is to enable the prisoner to highlight an alleged miscarriage of justice and he needs the assistance of a journalist to challenge the safety of a conviction, the prisoner has exhausted all appeals and has no further access to publicly funded legal aid, a visit is the only appropriate method of communication and the press intend to investigate the prisoner's case and allowing the visits poses no threat to security and good order. Permission must be sought in advance for visits from the media and it will only be given in exceptional circumstances. If permission is given for a visit, the visits themselves cannot be filmed or broadcast. The journalists and prisoner will be asked to sign an undertaking that they will comply with any conditions set, including that the interview may not be broadcast, and payment will not be made to the prisoner for interviews or material arising from the interview.

Permission should also be obtained from the governor for telephone calls to the media and again it will only be given exceptionally where the prisoner will be making representations about matters of legitimate public interest affecting prison or prisoners, including alleged miscarriages of justice. Although it is harder for prison authorities to control telephone conversations, compared with written communication, telephone conversations with the media will be monitored and should not make gratuitous reference to victims or make any statements likely to cause them or the public distress, allow the identification of prisoners or officers or breach any other requirements.

In *Simms* the journalists in question declined to sign the undertaking and this requirement was challenged. The Divisional Court found the requirement did infringe the prisoner's right to freedom of expression and could not be justified. The Court of Appeal disagreed, finding the restrictions reasonable as the prisoner inevitably lost the freedom to communicate with journalists on imprisonment. But the House of Lords in *R v Secretary of State for the Home Department, ex parte Simms and O'Brien* [2000] 2 AC 115 thought the fact that the prisoners wanted to communicate to raise issues about their alleged wrongful convictions meant that a blanket ban on interviews with prisoners is unlawful. Freedom of expression applies to all and the case for restrictions must be clearly established, which had not been achieved here. The court ruled that a blanket ban on access to the media was not acceptable and that where a prisoner wishes to address issues relating to the safety of a conviction that is, a possible miscarriage of justice, or make serious representations about matters relating to prisons, then access should be allowed. Lord Steyn said that:

> Not all types of speech have an equal value. For example, no prisoner would ever be permitted to have interviews with a journalist to publish pornographic material or to give vent to so-called hate speech. Given the purpose of a sentence of imprisonment, a prisoner can also not claim to join in a debate on the economy or on political issues by way of interviews with journalists. In these respects the prisoner's right to free speech is outweighed by deprivation of liberty by the sentence of a court, and the need for discipline and control in prisons. But the free speech at stake in the present case is qualitatively of a very different order. The prisoners are in prison because they are presumed to have been properly convicted. They wish to challenge the safety of their convictions. In principle it is not easy to conceive of a more important function which free speech might fulfil. (ibid. at 127)

While acknowledging the rationale for restrictions, the House of Lords stressed these cannot be used to deny access to justice which was the effect in this case. Lord Millett said the approach to prisoners' rights under English law and Convention jurisprudence is the same. The consequences that imprisonment has on the exercise of human rights are justifiable provided that they are not disproportionate to the aim of maintaining a penal system designed to punish and deter. If a prisoner wants to contact the media because he believes his conviction to be unfair and wants the press to establish his case for wrongful conviction, then he should be able to do so. The prison authority cannot have a policy which denies all prisoners the right to contact the media by phone to comment on matters of legitimate public interest relating to prison.

In the subsequent case of *R (Hirst) v Secretary of State for the Home Department* [2002] EWHC 602 (Admin) in 2002 a prisoner gave a radio interview by phone despite being ordered not to do so by the prison governor. He was speaking in his capacity as the General Secretary of the Association of Prisoners and therefore as a self-appointed representative of prisoners' interests. He was willing for the content of any interviews to be checked by the Governor before transmission. Hirst argued that his right to freedom of expression was infringed and that the restriction was disproportionate. His purpose was to comment on matters of legitimate public interest relating to prisons and prisoners. The Court thought that discussion of issues affecting the rights of prisoners as a group fell within the same area as debates on the economy or political issues referred to by Lord Steyn in *Simms* and therefore any restrictions had to be proportionate and a blanket prohibition on contact with the media by telephone is unlawful.

However, publications of prisoners' memoirs may include details of crimes which would upset the families of the victims. The issue of prisoner memoirs was considered in the case of Dennis Nilsen, a notorious serial killer, who is believed to have killed 15 males and dismembered their bodies, and is serving life sentences for six homicides. Nilsen has brought several Article 10 challenges, including an unsuccessful claim that denial of access to gay pornography violated his rights under Article 10. In 1993 he was interviewed in Albany prison and filmed by Central Television, describing his crimes. The interview was undertaken by a clinical psychologist accompanied by the police and a film crew, and permission had been given by the prison governor for the interview for training purposes. The Home Office obtained an injunction to prevent it from being broadcast as part of a programme on serial killers because of the suffering it would cause to the families of their victims and argued that it, rather than the TV company, had the control of the film. In *Secretary of State for the Home Department v Central Broadcasting Ltd.* [1993] EMLR 253 the Court approved the general Home Office policy which was designed to prevent causing distress, or enhancing his notoriety or encouraging sensationalist journalism.

In 2003 Nilsen sought judicial review of the refusal of the Prison Governor at Full Sutton Prison and the Secretary of State to return a 400-page manuscript of his autobiography. Nilsen had given the copy to his lawyer who then returned it, informing the governor of the contents, but the prison governor refused to pass it on to Nilsen, because he assumed that the final copy would be destined for publication. The Governor concluded that publication would breach the Prison Service rules on prisoners' general correspondence which should not contain material intended for publication or use on radio or TV which is about the inmate's crime, except where it consists of serious representations about conviction or sentence or forms part of serious comment about crime, the processes of justice or the penal system. The works contained details of his grisly crimes. The Administrative Court in *R (Nilsen) v Governor of HMP Full Sutton and Secretary of State for the Home Department* [2003] EWHC 3160 (Admin) was satisfied that the decision of the Secretary of State did meet the demands of proportionality and the test of *Wednesbury* rationality. The Secretary of State was entitled to take account of likely effect on victims' families and survivors. It is also quite clear that the manuscript falls outside the serious comment or serious representations. The work included pornographic material and lurid and explicit descriptions of the crimes and its publication, which if permitted, would cause great distress to the surviving victims and to victims' families, and would lead to public outrage. In these circumstances the Court thought the withholding of the manuscript was proportionate. Nilsen also tried to rely on Article 1 of the First Protocol, the right to peaceful enjoyment of one's possessions. But as the Court noted, this right was also qualified. It would be different if the prisoner was making representations about his sentence or conviction, or making a serious comment on the process of justice, but that was not the case here. Rather the work was intended to justify his conduct and denigrate others. The court held that it was not disproportionate to entail some restrictions on freedom of expression under Article 10(2) taking account of the views of the public and victims who would be very angry about the prospect of Nilsen publishing it from his cell.

These cases make clear then that the prisoner's right to freedom of expression may be limited in the case of criminal autobiographies, but not if the prisoner is making serious representations relating to his conviction or sentence, or on the processes of justice.

In the United States, prisoners have the right to contact the press and media, but not to be visited by the press, as the Supreme Court made clear in *Turner v Safley* 482 US 78 (1967). Although contact with the media is protected by the First Amendment the courts have taken the view that where there are alternative means of contact, face-to-face contact is not necessary and provided there is no blanket ban and prohibitions or restrictions can be justified, if reasonably related to a legitimate penological interest. The press have no constitutional right to access to prison over and above the ordinary public as the Supreme Court made clear in *Pell v Procunier* 417 US 817 (1974) and *Saxbe v Washington Post* 417 US 843 (1974). So agreement for face-to-face interviews would rarely be given and most First Amendment applications by prisoners and the media have been unsuccessful.

The right to family life

The right to family life has arisen in relation to a range of issues in prison including allocation, temporary release, visits and the right to marry and have children. These issues have been considered in relation to Articles 8 and 12 of the European Convention and highlight the tensions between the principles of normalization and less eligibility. As Diver notes, the right to family life of prisoners has often been rather viewed by the state and the courts as a privilege to be earned or lost by the prisoner's behaviour, rather than a right (Diver 2008).

Prisoners' allocation

The right to family life protected by Article 8 has also been invoked by prisoners in relation to the allocation and transfer of prisoners, as clearly where prisoners are placed within the prison estate will have implications for family visits. Allocation of sentenced adult male prisoners will be based on the needs of security, including control, the need to make maximum use of available spaces in training prisons, and the needs of individual prisoners. Account must also be taken of the prisoner's suitability for particular types of accommodation including factors such as the prisoner's age, medical and psychiatric needs, the need for offence-related behavioural programmes to confront the assessed risk, the person's home area or that of his likely visitors, and education or training needs (PSO 0900: para 1.6.4). So being near home is only one of many factors considered during allocation.

Before prisoners are allocated, they are first categorized into the appropriate security category level, which will affect their ultimate location within the prison estate. Procedures and classifications are set out in PSO 0900. The categories for male adult prisoners are A, for prisoners whose escape would be highly dangerous to the public, the police or the security of the state and for whom the aim must be to make escape impossible; B, prisoners for whom the very highest conditions of security are not necessary but for whom escape must be made very difficult; C, prisoners who cannot be trusted in open conditions but who do not have the resources and will to make a determined escape attempt; and D, prisoners who can reasonably be trusted in open conditions. Remand prisoners, other than those categorized A, are unclassified. Female prisoners are categorized either as A, or as suitable for closed, semi-open or open conditions.

So the key criteria here are likelihood of escape and the risk to the public if they do escape. Although every prisoner should be placed in the lowest category possible, in some cases prisoners may be allocated a higher level of security than otherwise necessary because of their behaviour in custody. The prisoner's current offence, sentence, previous convictions and custodial sentences, previous escapes, escape attempts and absconds, are used to calculate the appropriate level in an objective way. These categories are regularly reviewed, to assess the risk of escape and risk to the public if the prisoner did escape. If the prisoner's domestic circumstances have become more stable, this may be seen as making it less likely he will escape, so family bonds will be an important element in making an assessment. Category A prisoners are dealt with by the Category A Section at Prison Service Headquarters.

The same principles should be applied in recategorizing prisoners. Recategorization will also be on the basis of current risk to the public compared with when first categorized and whether the prisoner is now more or less likely to abscond. So to move to semi-open conditions, prisoners will have to show a change in the risk to the public and the risk of absconding.

An Article 6 challenge to changes in the classification of prisoners failed in *R v Secretary of State for the Home Dept ex parte Sunder* [2001] EWHC Admin 252 because the process of classification was deemed not to be comparable to a criminal charge. In *R (Vary and others) v Secretary of State for the Home Department* [2004] EWHC 2251 (Admin) where 22 prisoners had been recategorized from D to C so they could no longer remain in an open prison, the Administrative Court held that the decision of the Secretary of State was unlawful because the prisoners' circumstances had not been considered on an individual basis.

Once categorized, the prisoner can then be allocated. Closed conditions are for prisoners for whom the highest-security conditions are not necessary, but who present a high risk for open conditions, cannot be trusted in open conditions or for whom open conditions are not appropriate. Semi-open conditions are for prisoners who present a low risk to the public but who require a level of physical perimeter security to deter them from absconding. Open conditions are for low-risk prisoners who can reasonably be trusted in open conditions and for whom they are appropriate (PSO 0900, para 6.1).

Prisoners are allocated within the prison estate accordingly and for female prisoners significant issues would include facilitating visits from children or other family members, enabling childcare arrangements to be sorted out, completing any necessary offending behaviour work and facilitating resettlement needs (para 6.4.2). If prisoners suffer from psychiatric problems, they will be allocated to closed conditions initially until they can be given a proper assessment by medical staff. In some cases prisoners may be allocated to a prison with higher security than necessary to retain proximity to home or to make it easier for children to visit. It is also recommended that women prisoners and young offenders should be held as close to home as possible (PSO 4800: 14). While the prisoner has no right to be held in a prison near his home, Article 8 imposes obligations on the state to enable prisoners to keep in contact with their families. Article 8 jurisprudence suggests that only in very exceptional circumstances would it be breached by the fact that the prisoner is not held near his home, so the distance would have to be considerable, or some additional factor such as disability of the family members would be needed.

Although the European Prison Rules stipulate that prisoners should be allocated 'as far as possible, to prisons close to their homes or places of social rehabilitation' (EPR 17.1) in practice this may not be achieved. In the 1980s there was a well-organized campaign by Irish republican prisoners held in England and Wales for repatriation to Northern Ireland but their applications asserting their right to be transferred nearer home were deemed inadmissible by the European Commission in *Kavanagh v UK* Application No. 19085/91 (9 December 1992) and *McCotter v UK* (1993) 15 EHRRR 98.

However, the Commission did hold in *Wakefield v UK* Application No. 15817/89 (1 October 1990) that the right to respect for family life under Article 8 was infringed when the prison authority refused to transfer a prisoner to Scotland which meant that his fiancé would be unable to visit him, but this could be justified under Article 8(2) by security concerns. In the domestic courts, in *R (Gilbert) v Secretary of State for the Home Department* [2002] EWHC 2832 (Admin), the Administrative Court held that while Article 8 was applicable, the refusal to transfer the prisoner from a Close Supervision Centre at Woodhill to a prison nearer his family was not disproportionate in the particular circumstances. While his parents were elderly and in poor health and unable to visit him at Woodhill, the facilities in the CSC would not be available at the prison nearer the family home. Here the court applied the principle of proportionality following *R v Secretary of State for the Home Department ex parte Daly* [2001] UKHL 26 and rejected the prisoner's claim that the refusal was disproportionate.

Temporary release

Prisoners may be granted temporary release on compassionate grounds, for example, to deal with urgent family matters or to attend funerals of close family members. Temporary release may also be granted to allow prisoners to receive necessary medical treatment, or to assist the police with their inquiries, or for access to work or training and for resettlement purposes. Prisoners may be released in the day for work, education and training purposes, which is clearly important in assisting with rehabilitation and reintegration when the prisoner returns to the community. The rules and procedures governing temporary release are set out in PSO 6300. Temporary release may raise serious security issues if there is a threat of absconding or there is a risk of harm to witnesses or the community, so usually Category A prisoners or those on the escape list would not be entitled to it. Lifers would be allowed temporary release only if they were being held in open or semi-open conditions. All prisoners will be subject to a risk assessment and the decision will be matter for the discretion of the prison governor and the Secretary of State. Article 8 was not breached by a refusal to allow a prisoner to attend a family funeral in *X v UK* [1973] 42 CD 140 because of security considerations.

There is a well-established system of temporary release in the Netherlands but the system came under scrutiny following the Saban B case, when a notorious human trafficker involved in the sex industry was granted temporary release to visit his newborn daughter in September 2009 but disappeared. Temporary release arrangements have been reviewed and are limited to exceptional personal circumstances, for example, to attend the funeral of a close family member. So it is likely that leave will be refused where there is a risk of absconding, in the case of foreign national prisoners, confrontation with victims or a risk of social unrest.[5] Whether temporary release is given will depend on how long the prisoner has served and how much of his sentence remains and his release date and will be a matter for the governor. In controversial cases where there may be particular public concern, the decision will rest with the Justice Minister (Tak 2008). Temporary release may be given for urgent family matters or to attend medical appointments or for educational purposes.

However, Dutch prisons have a generous system of leave including weekend leave for low-security prisoners. Leave may given for up to 60 hours every two months during the last year of the sentence. Certain groups are excluded from the leave arrangements including those on high or extended security and foreign nationals. Prisoners on low security may have weekend leave once a month and on very low security it may be every weekend. Obviously, issues such as the risk of absconding and any threats to contact victims, will affect the decision to grant or withhold leave.

Prison visits

Prison visits may also engage Article 8, as they clearly have implications for family life. Visits from family members are protected under Article 8 and any limitations on visits will be assessed against the justifications required under Article 8(2), but Article 8 cannot be invoked in relation to visits from friends. Remand prisoners in the UK can receive as many visitors as they wish, within such limits and conditions as the Secretary of State may direct (PR 35(1)). Remand prisoners should be allowed visits on at least three days a week, including weekends (PSO 4410). Sentenced prisoners are entitled to a minimum of two visits per month, but this may be reduced to one per month if the Secretary of State so directs (PR 35(2)(b)). However, in practice prisoners may receive more than the statutory minimum. As well as these basic or statutory visits, additional visits may be granted where it is deemed necessary for the welfare of the prisoner or his family, for example, to sort out any personal or business affairs, or where the prisoner is seriously ill (PR 35(3)). They may also be granted under the Incentives and Earned Privileges Scheme. In *R(K) v Home Secretary* [2003] EWCA Civ 744 the court declined to treat the basic level of visits as an unjustified breach of Article 8. In *Boyle and Rice v UK* [1988] 10 EHRR 425, limits of visits to 12 one-hour visits a year were held not to breach Article 8 and the fact that the number of visits had fallen, because of a transfer, did not constitute a breach.

Visits for remand and sentenced prisoners should normally last a minimum of one hour, but in practice it will depend on the staff resources for supervision. Up to three adults and any accompanying children should be permitted at each visit. If close relatives are both in custody, but held in different prisons, arrangements may be made for inter-prison visits. There may be problems for families in arranging visits to distant locations if there are cost or childcare issues. Relatives can apply for assistance from the Assisted Visitors scheme administered by the Assisted Prison Visits Unit. Prisoners located far from home can accumulate visits and then ask for a transfer to a prison nearer home for a temporary period (PSO 4410: para 1.13–1.25). The quality of visiting facilities varies considerably between prisons and this means transfer may become very contentious for prisoners as it will impact on both the quantity and quality of visits. Children may find the prison environment very intimidating and clearly it is important to make the environment as welcoming as possible. While prisoners may maintain family contact through telephone calls clearly this can also be very expensive. Prisoners in England and Wales have been paying seven times the normal cost of phone calls. A complaint to Ofcom in 2008, which was upheld, led to an order to BT to reduce prices, but they are still higher than calls outside prison.

Ordinary social visits take place within both the sight and hearing of a prison officer. As well as visits from families and friends, they can also receive visits from their lawyers, MPs, or ministers of religion (PR 15). Prisoners should be able to discuss any ongoing or potential legal proceedings in which they are involved with their lawyers out of hearing but within sight of prison officers (PR 38(1)). Similarly, visits from priests should also be held out of hearing.

The Governor has the discretion to refuse visits or impose conditions on visits, on the grounds of security, maintenance of good order and discipline, prevention of crime or if there is reason to believe that the visit would be detrimental to the prisoner's best interests, or impede the prisoner's rehabilitation. Visits may only be stopped if an attempt is made during the visit to pass an unauthorized article, there is violence or a threat of violence or verbal threats, or escape plans are overheard, or if there is any incident which threatens the smooth running of the visits session. Any letters handed over by prisoners during visits are subject to the same monitoring procedures as posted letters, so letters to legal advisers can be opened but not read in the prisoner's presence. Visitors are not permitted to take recording devices or cameras with them into the visits. Reasonable physical contact is permitted. Isolation may be particularly severe for foreign national prisoners, for whom visits and family contact may be difficult and infrequent, and telephone costs will be high and in these cases provision for extra long visits may be needed.

If the prison authority is reluctant to allow family visits or imposes conditions upon them, then the refusal will be subject to judicial review and will inevitably engage Article 8. However, restriction on visits will not be seen as breaching Article 8 unless they are excessive and any conditions or prohibitions on visits will be considered on the principle of proportionality.[6] Visits by close relatives should be refused only in exceptional circumstances.

Under PR 73 visitors may be prohibited or restricted by the Secretary of State for such time as he considers necessary if such a prohibition is necessary on the grounds specified in PR 35A(4) which include the interests of national security and prevention of crime, public safety and maintaining good order and discipline in the prison, and the prohibition is proportionate to the aim of the prohibition. Usually issues of security can be dealt with by closed visits and this is the preferred procedure in most cases and visitors may be searched if there are grounds for suspicion.

Visits may also raise child protection issues. Restrictions may be imposed on visits from children if they are deemed to be at risk. Concerns on this issue were highlighted by the case of an eight-year-old child taken to visit her sex offender father in Ashworth special hospital, where it was clear that the child was being groomed for sexual abuse. A report on the Personality Disorder Unit at the hospital was highly critical of the regime, operating in the hospital in the late 1990s (Fallon *et al.* 1999). Applications for visits from children to prisoners assessed as posing a risk to children are considered under procedures in the Safeguarding Children section of the Public Protection Manual (PSI 08/2009). Risk assessments should also be conducted for any prisoner who wishes to take part in visits or other events involving children. For example, if there is a history of physical or sexual abuse, then there is no presumption of contact with the parent in prison. While contact centres might be used outside prison if it is deemed in the child's interest to maintain contact with the absent parent, there is less scope for this in prison. Where the rights of the child conflict with the rights of the prisoner then the rights of the child will clearly trump the prisoner's right under the Convention as the Strasbourg Court made clear in *Yousef v Netherlands* [2002] 3 FLR 577. Restrictions on children visiting patients at high-security hospitals were held not to breach Article 8, in *R v Secretary of State for Health, ex parte L* [2001] 1 FLR 406.

Constraints on prison visits will also be imposed in the Netherlands on similar grounds. Challenges to limits on contact with the outside world in a Dutch high-security regime failed under Article 8 in *van der Ven v the Netherlands* and *Lorse and others v the Netherlands* Application Nos. 50501/99, 52750/99 (4 February 2003). The conditions included visits with a glass partition in place and open visits (without partition) allowed only once a month with close relatives but with no physical contact, other than a handshake. The court ruled that the prison authorities were entitled to consider that there was a risk of escape, and a risk to the public if the prisoners did escape, given the crimes that they had committed. The limits could therefore be justified under the qualifications to Article 8 and satisfied the proportionality principle. However, the Strasbourg Court did find a breach of Article 3 in the routine strip searching to which prisoners were subjected (see Chapter 4 above).

However, the CPT was critical of those conditions imposed on prisoners' visits in its Report on its visit to the Netherlands in 1997 and recommended changes to allow open visits (Council of Europe 1998: para 66).

Sentenced prisoners in the Netherlands are entitled to a minimum of one hour of visits each week. Potential visitors have to obtain permission to visit in advance and as in the UK, visitors may be denied access if there are concerns about safety and public order, the prevention of crime or protection of victims, or threats to good order within the prison. The right to visits may not be suspended for disciplinary reasons, for more than four weeks, and only if the disciplinary sanction is related to behaviour on visits, for example, smuggling contraband. Remand prisoners do not have an automatic right to visits, but will be allowed visits only if the prosecutor or examining judge, issues a direction giving permission.

Visits usually take place in the presence of other prisoners and prison officers. If officers want to monitor what is said during the visit, then prisoners are informed in advance. Visitors who are not on high security will not have to speak through a screen. Before and after the visit, visitors may be searched. In addition to ordinary visits, inmates are entitled to visits from lawyers. Some prisoners may also be permitted conjugal visits.

Similarly in the United States, restrictions and prohibitions on visits may be legitimately imposed for security grounds. In *Block v Rutherford* 468 US 576 (1984) the Supreme Court upheld a ban on contact visits, that is on visits without a screen separating the prisoner and visitor, for remand prisoners on security grounds. The Court has also endorsed limits on particular visitors. In *Orerton v Bazetta* 439 US 213 (2003) the Supreme Court concluded that regulations issued by the Michigan Department of Corrections prohibiting visits from younger brothers, sisters, nieces and nephews and other minors, were rationally related to a penological aim and did not breach the due process clause of the Fourteenth Amendment. Temporary limits on visits for those with substance abuse violations did not breach the Eighth Amendment prohibition on cruel and unusual punishment. The Court decided in *Meachum v Fano* 427 US 215 (1976) that the due process clause does not protect a convicted prisoner from transfer to or from a particular prison even if that may make home visits more difficult.

Prison visits also raise issues of third party impact. Prisoners' families may themselves be made to feel like prisoners, subject to prison rules, head counted and searched, a process which might be seen as a 'secondary prisonization' of families into the prison culture. The difficulty of meeting the costs of visits and phone calls makes it more difficult for poorer families to maintain contact. Furthermore, in the USA visitors may be strip-searched but this has been challenged in the UK.

Prisoners' families in the UK do not have access to the normal complaints procedure available to prisoners or the Prisons and Probation Ombudsman unless they are dealing with a death in custody. However, they do have access to judicial review and may bring human rights challenges. A successful

Article 8 challenge was brought by family visitors in *Wainwright v UK* Application No. 12350/04 (26 September 2006). This case is very significant because it focuses on the rights of visitors themselves and highlights the problem of third party impact and the way in which prisoners' relatives may be stigmatized. Mrs and Mr Wainwright (a mother and son) had been strip-searched because of concerns that the prisoner they were visiting had been involved in drugs trafficking in HMP Leeds. The Court recognized that given the drugs problem inside the prison, the searching of visitor might be legitimate in preventing crime, but it needed to be conducted with respect for visitors' dignity. Here the procedures were very sloppy, as Mrs Wainwright had been visible through a window during the procedure. Mr Wainwright had cerebral palsy and arrested development, so he was not able to consent to the procedure. He was extremely upset by it and had suffered from post-traumatic stress disorder following the search. Medical evidence was accepted which supported the adverse effect of the search on both the visitors.

Mrs Wainwright was unable to obtain a remedy in the House of Lords. However, the Strasbourg Court concluded that while the search was humiliating, it did not reach the level of severity required for a breach of Article 3 but did breach Article 8. There was a legitimate aim for the search but the Strasbourg Court was not convinced that the searches were proportionate to that aim and the appropriate safeguards needed for such searches were not complied with. The Wainwrights had been subjected to a humiliating and invasive search, even though they had committed no offences, their dignity was not protected and the searches could not be viewed as necessary in a democratic society.

The right to marry

All prisoners, whether convicted or on remand, retain their right to marry under both the Marriage Act 1983 and Article 12 of the European Convention and unlike Article 8 this right is not qualified. In *Hamer v UK* (1979) 24 DR 5 the Commission ruled that the UK's refusal to grant a prisoner temporary release to marry his girlfriend breached Article 12. As marriage did not require that the parties live together, but was simply a legal relationship, there were no security issues involved in allowing marriage. If there are concerns about release, these can now be met by allowing the marriage to take place inside the prison or through providing secure escorts. So in *Draper v UK* (1980) 24 DR 72 the Commission recognized the right of prisoners serving long sentences to obtain temporary release from prison to get married. The demand of the right to marry was one of the key demands of the prisoners' rights group PROP in the 1970s.

The right to marry can now be exercised inside or outside prison, and the procedures are governed by PSO 4450 Marriage of Prisoners (18/10/07) and the Marriage Act. Category C prisoners are allowed to marry outside prison, unless there is a strong likelihood that the prisoner will try to escape and Category D prisoners are also usually allowed to marry outside. But Category A and B prisoners and prisoners on the escape list are not allowed to marry outside. Guests will be allowed into the prison for the ceremony subject to security checks. Other prisoners will be granted temporary release to marry outside, or if not eligible for temporary release, may be escorted (PSO 6300 29/11/2005). These rights now include civil partners under the Civil Partnership Act 2004. Prisoners are permitted to register a civil partnership and the same security considerations will apply, so registration may take place outside prison for Category C and D prisoners, unless there are concerns the prisoner will seek to escape, and inside prison for those in higher categories (PSO 4445 18/10/07).

In the Netherlands, prisoners' right to marry is clearly protected by Article 12 and in the United States, the constitutional right of prisoners to marry was upheld in *Zablocki v Radhail* 434 US 374 (1978).[7] A ban on marriages between prisoners was rejected by the Court in *Turner v Safley* 482 US 78 (1967). The state had argued that prisoners did not have the same right as ordinary citizens and there were security concerns. But the court ruled that prisoners can marry each other, but not write to each other. The court held that restrictions on correspondence between prisoners could be justified under the First Amendment right to freedom of expression if they were linked to legitimate penological aims and prison security issues.

Access to artificial insemination

Apparently neutral penal policies and prison rules may have a disparate impact on women so in this sense penal policies may be gendered. This has been highlighted by the issue of prisoners' access to artificial insemination which has focused attention on the rights of prisoners' families. It is clear from recent European Convention jurisprudence that the decision whether or not to become a parent falls within the right to respect for private life protected by Article 8 and Article 12, the right to found a family.[8] Prisoners may apply for permission to the Family Ties Unit for permission to artificially inseminate their partners. The policy prior to the decision of the Strasbourg Court in *Dickson v UK* Application No. 44362/04 (4 December 2007) was to consider requests for AI on the basis of individual merit and to grant permission only in exceptional circumstances. Issues which have been taken account by the Unit in reviewing applications, are whether AI is the only route to conception, whether the couple are in a well-established relationship which will survive the prisoner's release and whether the prisoner will be in a position to assume the role of a parent, and the arrangements for the welfare of the resulting child, and whether or not, given the prisoner's history and antecedents, it is in the public interest to grant permission. In effect the right to reproduce has been treated as closer to a privilege than a right.

The policy also effectively imposes a form of secondary liability as the prisoner's partner is deemed to be undeserving of her reproductive rights unless there are exceptional circumstances and it may also depend on the gravity of the offence committed by her husband, which as Jackson notes, stands in contrast to support given to bereaved women requiring assisted reproduction, such as Diane Blood (Jackson 2007). Yet the spouse of the prisoner can hardly be said to have voluntarily assumed the risk of forfeiting reproductive rights through marriage to the offender.

Refusal can, and has been, challenged by judicial review and proceedings under the Human Rights Act and the policy has been tested in the cases of *Mellor* and *Dickson*. In *R v Secretary of State of the Home Department ex parte Mellor* [2001] EWCA Civ 472 a prisoner challenged the refusal to meet a request for artificial insemination. The Court of Appeal decided that the prisoner has no right under Article 12 or Article 8 to give a semen sample to artificially inseminate his wife, and said that the decisions of the Strasbourg Court establish that lawful imprisonment can constitute a justifiable interference with the right to respect for family life, by virtue of Article 8(2). Mellor argued that there was no threat to the good order of the prison raised by granting the request which could be justified by Article 8(2). The Court of Appeal stressed that the aim of punishment is to deprive him of rights and pleasures he would enjoy outside in the community, including the enjoyment of family life. It was also concerned about public attitudes if permission were given, as well as the problems which might be raised by creating a single parent family. This left his partner the only options of finding another partner or sperm donor outside the prison.

However, the issue was raised again with some success in *Dickson v UK* Application No. 44362/04 (4 December 2007) where the case was brought to the Strasbourg Court by Mr and Mrs Dickson, rather than the prisoner alone, and focused on her rights as well as his. Here Dickson's wife was much older than Mellor's partner and would be 51 by the time of his release in 2009, so postponing childbearing until then could mean that the chance to have a child would be lost. The applicants argued that there were no security grounds or costs arising from application, so the only possible reason for refusal was punitive.

Mrs Dickson was a former prisoner who met her husband through a prison pen pal arrangement. The Dicksons were married in 2001, but had never lived together because of the imprisonment. The request for permission for artificial insemination was refused by the Secretary of State for a number of reasons, including the fact that the relationship had never been tested and concerns over the welfare of the child. Mr Dickson was serving a life sentence for murder and given the nature of his crime, kicking a man to death, it was thought that the punitive and deterrent elements of the sentence might be undermined if permission was given and this might also lead to public concern.

Following an unsuccessful appeal against the decision, the Dicksons brought a Convention challenge arguing that refusal of access to AI facilities breached their right to respect for family life under Article 8 and their right to found a family under Article 12. The applicants failed in the High Court, the Court of Appeal and initially in the Chamber of the Strasbourg Court but succeeded in the Grand Chamber. The state argued that loss of the chance of a family may be an inevitable consequence of imprisonment, so restriction on AI is an appropriate punishment and states should be given wide margin of appreciation on this issue because there is no clear consensus on it within Europe.

The Chamber of the Court of Human Rights agreed that decisions on this matter fell within the margin of appreciation and applicants were considered on the basis of individual merit and Articles 8 and 12 were not breached. The Chamber acknowledged the importance of the welfare of the child and that maintaining public confidence is an important issue in penal policy. Given the margin of appreciation accorded to states, the decision was reasonable and struck an appropriate balance between competing interests, although the dissenting judge thought it was paternalistic.

However, the Grand Chamber held by a 12:5 majority that there was a breach of Article 8 and did not find it necessary to review the complaint under Article 12. Article 8 does include the right to respect the decision to become a genetic parent. The Strasbourg Court focused on whether the right balance had been struck between the public and private interests in the case. It referred to the case of *Hirst v UK* (No. 2) Application No. 74025/01 (6 October 2005) where it had previously said that the prisoner enjoys all rights and freedoms except the right to liberty, does not forfeit his Convention rights simply because of his prisoner status and that there is no place under the Convention for automatic loss of Convention rights, just because recognizing those rights would offend public opinion (at para 68). Of course the welfare of the resulting child should be considered, but it was clear that Mrs Dickson could take care of the child herself. The state has to strike a fair balance between competing public and private interests, but it had not been struck in this case and Article 8 was breached. Here there was no realistic prospect of the Dicksons having a family by normal means and there were no security or cost issues involved. While public confidence in the penal system has a role to play in the development of penal policy, this is not the only factor and the rehabilitative goal of imprisonment should also be considered as a crucial element of the prison sentence. The loss of the right should not be seen as an inevitable consequence of the fact of imprisonment. The government's policy of 'exceptionality' meant that there was a very high barrier for applicants to transcend. One would in effect have to show that the refusal would mean the loss of the chance to have any children and only about a quarter of applicants succeeded.

The UK had exceed the margin of appreciation because the issues of proportionality or Convention compliance had not been considered in formulating the policy, as it was in place before the Human Rights Act. The competing interests had not been addressed, but a restriction had been imposed on all prisoners regardless of the gravity of offence or individual circumstances. In response the Government argued that only minor changes were necessary to comply and removed the exceptional circumstances requirement, so that now the Secretary of State can take account of any factor considered relevant in reaching a decision. However, in practice it may still be difficult to obtain permission.

Elsewhere, in Europe there have been more generous concessions to prisoners to fulfill their reproductive rights. In Spain a 47-year-old female prisoner, Elena Beloki, a member of a Basque separatist group, sentenced to 13 years for ETA terrorist offences, was released on conditional bail in June 2009 to allow her to undergo a course of IVF treatment funded by the Spanish state. She argued that it was her last chance to have a child. The contribution of the state in *Dickson* and *Mellor* fell far short of this in terms of costs and administrative burdens. It is possible that future challenges may be mounted in the UK on access to IVF which will raise the question whether there is a positive obligation on states to assist in the right to found a family. If male prisoners are allowed AI, it could be argued that female prisoners on grounds of equity should also be permitted access to assisted reproduction. However, clearly the costs involved in IVF are substantial and it is difficult to obtain NHS funding for this procedure outside prison, so this may well influence future decisions by the courts on this issue.

Dickson is very significant for the recognition of the rights of partners' families. While *Mellor* marginalized the right of the prisoner and the wife, *Dickson* does recognize the right of the partner. AI arguably offers a cheap and easy way of respecting prisoners' rights under Articles 8 and 12, without the cost or security implications of conjugal visits. The prisoner could be taken to a clinic just as he is taken to a hospital visit or donate a sample at the prison. The case is also interesting in taking account of the interests of the unborn and unconceived child in making the decision as Jackson observes (Jackson 2007).

In the United States there is a blanket ban on AI and constitutional challenges to the ban failed in *Goodwin v Turner* 702 F Supp 1452 (W.D.Mo.1988) and *Gerber v Hickman* 273 F 3d. 843 (9th Cir. 2001). The Court of Appeals in *Gerber v Hickman* reversed its earlier decision which had ruled in favour of Gerber's application to artificially inseminate his wife. This strict policy has led to a problem of sperm smuggling in prisons and has generated considerable discussion of the question of the judicial control of procreative decisions (Sutherland 2003, Codd 2007).

Conjugal visits

One way of dealing with the problem of access to AI suggested in *Dickson* would be conjugal visits which, as the Grand Chamber commented, are allowed in half of the Council of Europe states. The Court approved the move towards accepting conjugal visits found in 30 members states, albeit subject to certain restrictions, although it also accepted that there was no duty on states to make provision for them. The CPT also favours conjugal visits if they are conducted in conditions which respect dignity and good facilities are provided. The EU Resolution on Improvements and Alternative Penalties for Prison Conditions also advocates encouraging family visits and conjugal visits.

Many European countries allow them including the Netherlands, France, Sweden, Spain and Belgium, where they are seen as strengthening family bonds, improving prisoner rehabilitation and security within prison and as contributing to a fall in recidivism and as part of the humane treatment of prisoners. In the Netherlands the eligible prisoners are allowed non-supervised visits which may be used for conjugal visits once a month so the issue of AI has been avoided. This privilege is usually only given to prisoners serving longer sentences and would rarely be given to prisoners serving shorter sentences or to remand prisoners unless they are detained for long periods. In the UK, in contrast to many other states, there is no right to conjugal visits, and this has been justified in terms of security, public opinion and the argument that loss of the family life is an inevitable consequence of imprisonment. Prisoners' rights groups have also campaigned on this issue and this was one of the demands of PROP in the 1970s. In one sense conjugal visits would not be a new development in the UK. In the eighteenth century debtors' prisons, debtors would take their families to live with them inside the prison and family members would have considerable freedom to move in and out of the prison (McGowen 1995: 82).

However, past challenges to the refusal to allow conjugal visits failed in Strasbourg in *X v Germany* (1970) 12 YB 332, *X v United Kingdom* (1975) 2 DR 105, *X and Y v Switzerland* (1978) 13 DR 241 and in *ELH and PBH v UK* Application Nos. 32094/96, 32568/96 (22 October 1997). In *ELH and PBH v UK* the Commission held that while the refusal of prison authorities to allow conjugal visits is an interference with respect to a prisoner's right to respect for family life, this can be justified under Article 8(2) of the Convention and the UK government successfully argued that security grounds justified the policy. These challenges have also failed under Article 12 as the point was made in *ELH and PBH v UK* that prisoners could apply for permission to use AI if they want to found a family although, as we have seen, permission may not be given. The Commission also acknowledged that some other European countries allow conjugal visits, but said that the refusal of visits could still be justified as preventing disorder or crime. The Strasbourg Court has treated the decision on conjugal visits as a matter for states, but in recent cases, such as *Dickson*, has been more supportive of these visits. So it is possible that there may be a stronger ruling on this in future and ultimately states may be required to change their policies to comply.

Arguments have been advanced for and against allowing conjugal rights. While they may raise more costs and security issues than AI, these visits may also have benefits.

The denial of conjugal visits in European societies is difficult to justify under the qualifications in 8(2). To provide privacy to prisoners would clearly have some security implications, but these may be managed without too much difficulty. The fact other countries allow them without resulting in disorder or crime suggests this would not be an inevitable result. They may strengthen family bonds and thereby assist in the rehabilitation of the prisoner.

Conjugal visits are well established in some states of the USA, namely New York, California, Washington, New Mexico and Mississippi. They are seen as a means of promoting family relationships, reducing male rapes and as an incentive for good behaviour in prison and the visits have received public support according to public opinion polls. In California, families and parents can visit as well as spouses, so the aim is to promote family bonds rather than merely sexual contact. However, visits are limited to these states and no legal or constitutional right to such visits has been upheld by the courts.

Mississippi was the first state in the USA to introduce conjugal visits in 1918, initially to reduce sexual tensions, but they are now primarily aimed at encouraging family bonds. The privilege was first granted to black males and extended to white males in 1940 and later to female prisoners. Originally prostitutes were brought into Parchman Prison, the state penitentiary, but later common law partners and spouses were allowed. By the late 1950s only family visits were permitted and prostitutes were banned. In Mississippi prisoners who are who are legally married and held on minimum and medium-security conditions, but not in high-security units, and who have a record of good behaviour are entitled to one visit lasting up to three days every two weeks and are housed in cottages inside the prison.

It has been argued that conjugal visits will reduce the problem of sexual violence and rape within prison which, as we saw earlier, is a key issue in US prisons and this may also have implications for the reduction of HIV transmission. Whether conjugal visits will solve the problem of male rape and violence in prisons is debatable. The evidence is inconclusive as it is difficult to isolate causal links and clearly there are many intervening variables involved, although more research is needed on this (Hensley *et al.* 2000, Wyatt 2006). It is hoped that the Prison Rape Elimination Act may generate some research findings through the Data Collection process under the Act. These findings will be of interest to prison systems elsewhere, including the UK, and may assist in strengthening the case for conjugal visits. The causes of rape are complex and raise issues relating to power, aggression and assertions of masculinity. But the goal of rape prevention through the reduction of sexual tensions is one reason why visits are allowed in the USA. However, it could also be argued that visits would spread HIV outside the prison and put partners at risk, although condoms are usually given to prisoners where these visits are allowed. While prisoners could be tested, the time lag between infection and showing up sero-positive on the test would be a problem.

In the UK, the argument in favour has focused principally on the benefits in strengthening family bonds. Allowing these visits, it is argued, would also reduce the negative impact of imprisonment on prisoners and bring prison life closer to life in the community so it would be justified on the principle of normalization. If visits were permitted on grounds of good behaviour, this could be used to encourage prisoners to comply with the prison regime and offer another means of control of prisoners and could be incorporated into the Incentives and Earned Privileges Scheme. It would mean that there would be an opportunity for longer and more private visits for families irrespective of the sexual issues; so in Canada they are included within family visits and perhaps the emphasis should be on family visits rather than conjugal visits.

In the USA it is believed by prison officers and the public that these visits encourage good behaviour and family bonds and there is some evidence to support this (see Bales and Mears 2008). Given that families find it hard to renew family bonds at the end of their sentence and marriages often end during imprisonment or on release, it is clearly important to support families during imprisonment. A study of the Family Reunion Program in a New York State prison found that prisoners on the programme who received conjugal visits were closer to their families than prisoners not on the programme. The research surveyed 63 prisoners and 39 wives. The programme involved family visits every two to three months (Carlson and Cevera 1991). Further research is needed to explore the link between visits and recidivism.

Arguments raised against conjugal visits include the conflict with the principle of less eligibility. Loss of family contact and sexual relationships would be seen by many as an inevitable element of punishment. So the public may be offended or hostile to this concession and favour penal austerity instead. It may well upset victims' families who are deprived of their loved ones. There might be concerns about the welfare and financial burdens of children resulting from such visits. There would also be cost implications in providing suitable private accommodation.

However, if the benefits could be explained to the public in terms of the the contribution to rehabilitation and the importance of maintaining contact with the outside world, they may be more willing to accept it. The fact that other states allow such visits without security problems needs to be communicated, and limiting the visits to prisoners on lower-security regimes may reassure the public. It seems likely, however, that some sections of the media would sensationalize conjugal visits just as the provision of televisions has been viewed negatively by the press, although they are a privilege and linked to good behaviour. The public would have to be convinced that visits are an important element of rehabilitation and ultimately cost-effective by reducing reoffending through supporting family life and partnerships.

There are obviously cost implications in providing safe and private facilities at a time when budgets are under pressure, and there would be security concerns about visitors passing drugs, weapons or phones, but these could be met by the usual searching arrangements for prison visits discussed earlier.

Special accommodation would need to be available inside the prison perimeter which could be expensive and there would need to be supervision by staff of those checking and leaving the unit which would add to the cost. In New York, partners are allowed to stay overnight in dedicated accommodation in the prison grounds. There might also be concerns relating to violence against visitors and a woman was killed by her partner during a conjugal visit to a German prison in 2010.[9]

A decision also would have to be made regarding access to visits, for example whether it should be limited to married couples or include cohabitees, civil partners and others, and whether those who have committed sexual offences or violent offences should be excluded. In the United States conjugal visits are limited to common law or legal spouses and usually sex offenders are excluded. In California conjugal visits include gay partners. Granting visits to selected prisoners may lead to resentment by other prisoners although Hensley *et al.* found no significant difference in attitudes towards the Conjugal Visit programme in Mississippi between participants and non-participants (Hensley *et al.* 2000). However, in Paraguay in June 2008 prisoners rioted when permission for visits was confined to periods in the day when many prisoners were working.[10]

Conclusions

As we have seen, there are a number of ways in which prisoners' access to the outside world may be promoted, including correspondence, visits and leave. While some of the measures to promote contact have been widely accepted and approved by the Courts, there are also some initiatives which have been more problematic and controversial. However, the consensus is that contact, subject to security considerations, is beneficial to prisoners, to good order in the prison and can promote rehabilitation, and assist the prisoner in returning to society. The rules relating to contact also highlight in some cases the gendered nature of penal policy and practice and this will discussed in more detail in Chapter 7.

7 The right to equality

Introduction

This chapter will consider efforts to eliminate discrimination in the criminal justice system in the context of imprisonment. The impact of recent developments in equality law will be discussed. The prison regime is now circumscribed by a range of equality laws and all policies need to be assessed for their impact on race and gender. Prison authorities are required to pay particular attention to women's needs, as well as the needs of foreign national prisoners, ethnic and religious minorities. There is also now greater awareness of the duty to take account of the needs of disabled and older prisoners. These issues are particularly important given the changes in the composition of the prison population which includes older, disabled prisoners, ethnic minority prisoners, religious minorities, gay and transgender prisoners. In considering equality issues, the focus now is broader than race and gender but also encompasses sexual orientation and disability. The disparate impact of policies on particular groups of prisoners and ways of achieving equality of impact in the prison context will be reviewed.

Prisoners have a right not to be subjected to less favourable treatment on the grounds of gender, race, religion, age, disability or sexual orientation. This means that they should have equal assess to resources in prison, including work, accommodation, education, exercise and library resources and prison authorities also have a positive duty to promote equality. Anti-discrimination law is well established in UK domestic law. Prior to the Equality Act 2010, it was possible to bring discrimination cases under the Sex Discrimination Act 1975, the Race Relations Act 1976, the Race Relations (Amendment) Act 2000 and the Disability Discrimination Act 2005. So if female prisoners can show that they have been treated less favourably than men in an analogous position, then they could succeed with a discrimination claim, but it may be hard to find a comparator and to proceed with a discrimination case as male and female prisoners in the UK are usually imprisoned separately. The European Prison Rules and the UK prison rules require that male prisoners should be detained separately from female prisoners (EPR 18.8, PR 12). Although one prison, Peterborough, holds male and female prisoners they are held in separate units within the precincts of the prison. Any contact between them would obviously raise safety issues for women as well as concerns over the use of female prisoners as part of the re-socialization of male prisoners.

To bring a case a claimant would need considerable information on the comparator prison, and it would be possible for the prison to argue that they provide different courses tailored for women. There is also considerable variation between prisons in the prison estate, as illustrated by the league tables and the results of prison inspections, so it would not be difficult to find, for example, a male prisoner who has problems accessing a course, and, as we have seen, the key cases on this issue were brought by men. But in the past when women were more frequently housed on the same sites as men, it was found that they had less access to the available resources.

Apart from the problems of finding a comparator among other prisoners, and obtaining sufficient information, even if differential treatment is established, it might be easier for the prison authority to justify the difference if it provides special facilities in women's prisons tailored to women. Furthermore, the majority of women are serving shorter sentences so like male prisoners in that position they may decide it is not worth pursuing a claim or also fear victimization if they do. Although the anti-discrimination legislation includes protection against victimization for bringing complaints, there may still be a perception of being seen as a troublemaker.

Discrimination issues might arise in relation to differential treatment in any area of prison life, access to education, training, accommodation, visits, racist and sexual abuse and harassment. Research has also been undertaken on racism experienced by staff from colleagues. Because of the disproportionate number of black and ethnic minorities in prison compared to their proportion in the wider population, attention has also focused on the earlier stages of the criminal justice process to explain this situation.

Racism and sexism can be expressed at an individual level in racist or patriarchal attitudes and differential treatment, but also may operate indirectly so that apparently neutral policies may have a disparate impact on particular groups. Both direct and indirect discrimination have been covered by the Race Relations and Sex Discrimination Acts. Moreover, the Strasbourg Court has recognized indirect discrimination and imposed positive duties and obligations on states to prevent discrimination. Some of the earlier research on racism in prison focused on attitudes and access to accommodation and work within the prison, but recent work is more concerned with institutional practices and with racial harassment. Racism may also be institutionalized in the sense that it is built into the culture, practices and policies of an organization.[1] Prisoners with disabilities have been protected by the Disability Discrimination Act 1995 which makes it unlawful to discriminate in the provision of goods, facilities or services on grounds of disability. Reasonable adjustments should be made to meet the needs of disabled prisoners.

The framework of equality law

Section 95 of the 1991 Criminal Justice Act requires the Secretary of State to publish information considered expedient to allow those involved in the criminal justice system to avoid discriminating against any person on grounds of race, sex or any other improper ground. So ethnic monitoring has been undertaken in prisons in England and Wales since 1994 and statistical data on race and gender and the criminal justice system is published regularly. The latest statistics on women and the criminal justice system were published in January 2010 and race and the criminal justice system in June 2010.[2] But this was only a requirement to obtain information, rather than to actively develop policies to combat sexism, racism or homophobia.

Further information on the experience of imprisonment of particular groups is available from empirical studies from independent researchers and prison reform groups and official reports highlighting the problems of women and ethnic minority prisoners, notably the Corston Report and the Mubarek Report (Corston 2007, Keith 2006). In addition we have thematic reports from the Prisons Inspectorate.

There have been significant developments in equality law in the past five years. The Equality Act 2006 established the Equality and Human Rights Commission which replaced the Equality Opportunities Commission, the Commission for Racial Equality and the Disability Rights Commission. The expectation was that a large equality body would be more effective in promoting equal opportunities and challenging discrimination. It also broadened discrimination to encompass discrimination in the treatment of prisoners as it imposed on public authorities, including prisons, an 'equality duty' to take positive action to eliminate unlawful discrimination on grounds of sex, race, disability, religion, sexual orientation, age and gender reassignment, and imposed a clear duty to promote gender equality (Part 4, s 84). The parts of the 2006 Equality Act relating to the operation and functioning of the Equality and Human Rights Commission remain in force after the new Equality Act 2010 which aims to simplify and strengthen equality law, replacing existing anti-discrimination laws with one single Act, and harmonizes definitions and exceptions and imposes a duty to promote equality of opportunity. The new Act comes into force in October 2010.

The Equality Act 2010 imposes a duty to eliminate discrimination and promote equality and expands the protected characteristics which now cover age, disability, gender reassignment, marriage and civil partnership, race, sex, sexual orientation and religion or belief. It prohibits age discrimination in public functions and enhances the duty to make reasonable adjustment for the disabled. It repeals *inter alia* the Equal Pay Act 1970, the Sex Discrimination Act 1975, Race Relations Act 1976 and the Disability Discrimination Act 1995. It increases the power of tribunals to make recommendations to employers to improve their practices. It introduces a new duty on public bodies to consider reducing socio-economic inequalities and integrates the Equality Duty on public bodies.

Under the Equality Duty, all public bodies have a duty to develop and publish action schemes, including action plans, on the steps they are taking over three-year periods to achieve equality outcomes and to promote equality. They are prohibited from discriminating in carrying out any of their functions. The race equality duty was originally introduced by the Race Relations (Amendment) Act 2000. It imposed a statutory duty on public authorities to promote race equality and applied to prisons. This duty included ethnic monitoring, assessing the impact of policies on particular ethnic groups and taking positive action to meet the needs of particular groups. It required them to promote equality and improve race relations. It covered direct and indirect discrimination and required authorities to set up Race Equality Schemes, and to monitor the impact of policies and the effectiveness of these schemes. Under section 1 of the Act it is unlawful for the authority to discriminate in relation to any of its functions. So this could cover all aspects of prison life and access to resources, including work, recreation and training, as well as policies relating to transfer, segregation, the privileges scheme and visits. This was followed by the imposition of a disability equality duty which came into effect in 2006 and the gender equality duty which came into force in 2007, both of which imposed similar duties.

Prisons have an equality duty under the Equality Act not to discriminate against prisoners and prison staff on grounds of race, sex, but also, age, disability, religion, gender reassignment, marriage and sexual orientation. Issues may arise in relation to the treatment of ethnic minorities which may include foreign national prisoners. There are well-established procedures for monitoring compliance with equality law and the equality duties which are set out in PSI 40/2007 and PSO 2800. Although some prisons had already moved towards implementing gender-specific standards by early 2008, all prisons were required to do so by October 2008.[3]

This means that prison authorities can no longer simply monitor discrimination, but must actively develop policies which promote equality and all new policies need to be tested for equality impact in individual prisons and at the level of NOMS. The performance of public authorities is monitored and reviewed by the Commission. Prisoners who wish to bring a complaint to the Commission must bring a claim within six months of the incident in question. A prisoner may request a visit from a representative of the Commission for Equality and Human Rights (PSO 4410, para 4.21). The governor can also invite representatives of the CEHR to visit the prison to interview prisoners (para 4.22). These visits can take place out of the hearing but within sight of a prison officer.

Equality is also a key principle underpinning the application of the European Prison Rules. EPR 13 states that: 'These rules shall be applied impartially, without discrimination on any ground such as sex, race, colour, language, religion, political or other opinion, national or social origin, association with a national minority, property, birth or other status'.

The right to equality is also protected within the framework of European Union and European Convention law. Within European Union law the key provision is the new Article 13 introduced by the Treaty of Amsterdam, which came into force in May 1999. This establishes a general principle of non-discrimination which prohibits discrimination on the grounds of sex, racial or ethnic origin, religion, disability, age or sexual orientation, The new Directive 2000/78/EC of 27 November 2000 sets out a general framework for equal treatment in employment and occupation and prohibits discrimination on the grounds of religion or belief, disability, age, or sexual orientation in relation to employment and occupation.

Scope for affirmative action in EU law is also found in the EC Treaty 141(4). Positive action has received more support in EU law than European Convention law, for example in the cases of *Marschall v Land Nordrhein-Westfalen* C-409/95 [1997] ECR I-6363, *Kalanke v Freie Hansestadt Bremen*, Case C-450/93 [1995] IRLR 660 and *Lommers* C-476/99 [2002] ECR 1–3231.

In addition, Article 21 of the EU Charter of Fundamental Rights prohibits discrimination on any ground such as sex, race, colour, ethnic or social origin, genetic features, language, religion or belief, political or any other opinion, membership of a national minority, property, birth, disability, age or sexual orientation and also discrimination on the grounds of nationality. As well as including provisions on torture, inhuman and degrading treatment and a prohibition on the death penalty, the Charter of Fundamental Rights also requires that penalties must not be disproportionate to the offence (Article 49 (3)). The Charter is made directly applicable by the Lisbon Treaty.

Under the European Convention on Human Rights, protection against discrimination is provided by Article 14 which states that:

> The enjoyment of the rights and freedoms set forth in this Convention shall be secured without discrimination on any ground such as sex, race, colour, language, religion, political or other opinion, national or social origin, association with a national minority, property, birth or other status.

However, this not a free-standing right but is contingent on other rights being breached so a prisoner would first need to establish that he or she has been discriminated against in relation to another right under the Convention, on one of the grounds specified in Article 14, that he or she has been treated differently to a person in an analogous situation and that the discrimination cannot be justified. To establish justification it would be necessary to show that the differential treatment had a legitimate aim and that the differential treatment was proportionate to that aim. In reviewing infringements on Convention rights, the court will focus on whether the infringement falls within any express or implied exception and apply the principle of proportionality. As we saw in Chapter 6 the exceptions to Articles 8 and 10, including national security and the public interest in the prevention of crime, may give some scope for the prison authority to justify differential treatment. However, in dealing with discrimination, differential treatment would have to be both reasonable and objectively justified and the measure used proportionate to the aims.

Relatively few prisoners' rights cases have been brought under Article 14. But in *R (Clift) v Home Secretary; R (Hindawi) and another v Home Secretary* [2007] 1 AC 484, foreign national prisoners successfully argued that they had been excluded from an early-release scheme. It was clear that this was based on the prisoners' national origin and the House of Lords found that this could not be objectively justified. Here the prisoners used Article 5, but it may also be possible in some circumstances to argue that racist treatment is degrading under Article 3. In the earlier case of *Hilton v UK* [1976] 4 DR 177 the European Commission said that the verbal and physical abuse including racist abuse suffered by a prisoner was admissible as the basis of an Article 3 challenge, because he suffered stress and degradation as a result. Discrimination was seen as degrading under Article 3 in *East African Asians v UK* (1981) 3 EHRR 76 and as breaching Article 8 in relation to discrimination against gays, lesbians and transgender individuals in *Goodwin v UK* Application No. 28957/95 (11 July 2002) although these were not cases specifically involving prisoners.

The fact of being a prisoner has been accepted by the Strasbourg Court as placing the individual in a distinct legal category, albeit involuntarily and for a temporary period, which means that Article 14 may be used, the Court said in *Shelley v UK* Application No. 23800/06 (4 January 2008). In this case, the applicant was challenging the failure to provide needle exchanges in prison, claiming breaches of Articles 2, 3 or 8, arguing that prisoners as a group were treated less favorably than individuals in the wider community. However, the Court ruled that the health care policy already being used was within the margin of appreciation of states.

Although Protocol 12 to the Convention, if ratified, would allow a free-standing discrimination claim to be brought so it would not be necessary to show that other Convention rights were engaged, the UK has not yet ratified it. The Labour Government made clear that it did not intend to ratify it and it seems unlikely that the Coalition government will take a different position. It has been ratified by the Netherlands, so clearly there is more scope in the Netherlands for bringing discrimination cases.

The value of Article 14 has been debated by discrimination lawyers. Some are sceptical because it is not free-standing and because of the scope for justification of discrimination within the Convention and the fact that the margin of appreciation granted to states may be used to weaken its potential. Others see it as valuable because the grounds of discrimination are very wide under Article 14 as 'any other status' may be used for sexual orientation, and any discrimination will need to be objectively justified. The court has dealt robustly with discrimination on sexual orientation in recent cases, for example, in *EB v France* Application No. 43546/02 (22 January 2008) where the Grand Chamber of the Strasbourg Court construed a refusal to allow single people to adopt as being based on the applicant's sexual orientation where this was not explicit.

Furthermore, as O'Connell argues, in recent years, Article 14 jurisprudence has developed its potential in the protection against discrimination, as the ambit of Article 14 has been interpreted broadly and the Court has acknowledged and challenged indirect discrimination and favoured positive action (O'Connell 2009). The Court has in some cases treated Article 14 as autonomous and found a violation even where the other Article in question has not been breached, for example the *Belgian Linguistic Case* (1979–80) 1 EHRR 252 and *Stec and others v the UK* Applications Nos. 65731/01 and 65900/01 (12 April 2006). So it has treated Article 14 here as if Protocol 12 were in effect. In doing so it has moved beyond formal equality to substantive equality and focused on effects rather than simply intention.

Although in the past, Strasbourg jurisprudence resisted widening its scope to indirect discrimination, since *Thlimmenos v Greece* (2001) 31 EHRR 411, the court has acknowledged problems of indirect discrimination, for example, in *Abdulaziz, Cabales and Balkandali v UK* (1985) 7 EHRR 471, in *Zarb Adami v Malta* (2007) 44 EHRR 49 and *DH v Czech Republic*, Application No. 57325/00 (7 February 2006), where the Grand Chamber stressed the importance of differential treatment to achieve equality although these were not cases involving prisoners. The need for positive action was recognized in *Thlimmenos v Greece* (2001) 31 EHRR 411, and *Connors v UK* (2004) Application No. 66746/01 (27 May 2004) which has enhanced the potential effectiveness of the Convention in ensuring equality (de Vos 2007, Fredman 2008.) In the domestic courts the issues of positive duties have been discussed mostly in tribunal cases.[4] The Court has also stressed the positive duty on states to investigate discrimination and racism involved in the ill-treatment of suspects in *Petropoulou-Tsakiris v Greece* Application No. 44803/04 (6 December 2007). So clearly Article 14's potential value has increased but prisoners have made relatively little use of it. In any case the court will often resolve the primary issue and not find it necessary to consider the Article 14 implications.

The issue of equality has also been considered by the CPT in its 10th General Report, which has criticized the failure to provide women prisoners equal access to constructive activities including work, education and training but which offer instead activities based on traditional female stereotypes while male prisoners have access to more vocational courses:

> Women deprived of their liberty should enjoy access to meaningful activities (work, training, education, sport etc.) on an equal footing with their male counterparts. As the Committee mentioned in its last General Report, CPT delegations all too often encounter women inmates being

offered activities which have been deemed "appropriate" for them (such as sewing or handicrafts), whilst male prisoners are offered training of a far more vocational nature. In the view of the CPT, such a discriminatory approach can only serve to reinforce outmoded stereotypes of the social role of women. Moreover, depending upon the circumstances, denying women equal access to regime activities could be qualified as degrading treatment. (Council of Europe 2000: para 25)

The equality issues facing particular groups of prisoners will now be considered.

Gender equality

There has been an increase in the number of women prisoners since the early 1990s in the UK. Although the number of women in prison has increased since the early 1990s, the numbers are still very small compared to the male population and over the past few years have ranged between 5 per cent and 6 per cent of the prison population. The proportion of female prisoners in the prison population in 2004 reached 6 per cent but had fallen to 5.3 per cent in 2008. By July 2010 the proportion was 5 per cent. On 2nd July 2010 there were 85,074 prisoners in total, of whom 80,822 were male and 4,252 were female. Nearly two-thirds (64 per cent) of custodial sentences given to women in 2008 were for less than six months, compared to 54 per cent for men. Of women 4 per cent were sentenced to four years or more, compared to 8 per cent of men (Ministry of Justice 2010a: 10). The increase in women prisoners reflects the impact of increased punitiveness which has affected both male and female offenders so they are more likely to receive a custodial sentence and to serve a longer sentence compared to the early 1990s. Women are also now more heavily involved in drugs crimes which attract custodial sentences. Twenty eight per cent of women in custody in 2008 were serving offences for drugs offences. Female offenders have been subject to increased punitiveness, and because women have committed more drugs offences which attract longer sentences, this has pushed up the population. Female offenders, like male offenders, are now more likely to receive a custodial sentence than in the early 1990s and have experienced harsher sentences for drugs-related offences. The question of whether women are more or less likely to be given a custodial sentence because of their role as prime carers and particularly whether they are seen as good or bad mothers, has been subject to considerable debate (see Carlen 2003). But as women receive shorter sentences than men on average and are less likely to receive a custodial sentence, it is difficult to argue that women are treated more harshly than men at the sentencing stage. However, they may face problems in gaining access to community programmes or residential drug detoxification programmes because of childcare responsibilities. Although the Criminal Justice Act 2003 increased the range of community penalties, some women may find it very hard to comply with them because of childcare problems so they run the risk of ending up in custody for breach. The Corston Report found that large numbers of women were in prison for this reason (Corston 2007). There has been more interest in recent years on women in prison and as the expansion of prisons has increased financial burdens on the state, the prospect of removing women from penal custody has become more attractive to governments. Questions have also been raised whether imprisoning women who are not convicted of offences of violence meets the aims of punishment, as it is hard to justify imprisonment on the grounds of risk. On retributivist grounds, it might also be argued that punishing women through custody is disproportionate because women suffer more than male prisoners if they are the prime carers of young children.

In 2010 there were 14 women's prisons. Standards may vary considerably between prisons, but there are currently no women's prisons at the lowest level on the league tables, although in the past some of the worst prisons in the prison estate were women's prisons, notably Holloway. Because there are fewer female than male prisons, women are more likely to be housed further away from home than male prisoners. Some former women's prisons, such as Cookham Wood, have been converted to men's prisons because of the pressure on prison places from the expansion of the male prison population so the number of women's prisons has declined in recent years, making it even harder in some cases to allocate women to prisons near their home.

Women as a group commit fewer offences than men, including violent and sexual offences, which raises the issue of whether the majority of women offenders should be incarcerated. Women prisoners are most likely to be serving sentences for drugs and property offences and the female prison population contains relatively few dangerous prisoners. Although female prisoners, like male prisoners, have a background of social exclusion, so homelessness, health problems and deprivation, unemployment are worse for women than for men (Corston 2007, Social Exclusion Unit 2002). Female prisoners also have higher rates of mental illness than male prisoners and higher rates of self-harming so they have specific needs for mental health care although the suicide rate has fluctuated over the past few years.

However, there is no therapeutic prison specifically for women, although there are therapeutic units within women's prisons at Send, Styal and Eastwood Park, although the Inspector of Prisons has criticized the declining support for women at risk at Send (HMCIP 2010a: 60). However, in some cases, women's health like men's, may improve in prison as they receive more support, eat properly and generally lead better organized lives.

The understanding of the problems facing women prisoners has increased in recent years with the publication of research studies and major reviews. Thematic reviews of female prisoners have been undertaken by the Chief Inspector of Prisons in 1997, 2001 and 2010 (HMCIP 1997, 2001, 2010b). In addition, the Wedderburn and Corston Reports have reviewed women's prisons (PRT 2000, Corston 2007). The 1997 Report by the Chief Inspector of Prisons was critical of the excessive security used on female prisoners particularly on antenatal visits and medical procedures. This should be based only on individual risk assessment and should not be used during the medical examination. The 2010 Report found that the majority of women's prisons were performing well with good staff–prisoner relations, but raised concerns over bullying and the use of segregation in some establishments (HMIP 2010). It noted variations between women's prisons and expressed concerns over Holloway where women felt unsafe and over the response to women with mental heath problems at Styal (HMCIP 2010a). Women as a group may also be adversely affected by imprisonment as third parties, as female partners of male prisoners may suffer loss of income, housing problems and stigmatization as we saw in Chapter 6.

Inequalities between female and male prisoners may arise in terms of access to accommodation, visits, work and other resources. However, the question is whether women's right to equality in terms of imprisonment means the right to be treated the same as male prisoners, in terms of access to resources, or whether equal treatment is achievable only by treating women differently. However, under domestic law and European Convention law, equality may mean both treating the parties the same and differential treatment when it is necessary to achieve equality. So cuts in home leave, for example, may be more significant for women if they are primary carers of young children.

The right to treatment as an equal may not necessarily mean receiving the same treatment. Given that women serve shorter sentences than men, then they may have fewer opportunities for certain work or rehabilitation programmes or training. Until recently they were provided with offending behaviour programmes and skills programmes originally designed for male prisoners, but this is no longer the case and skills provision has also improved. However, the Inspector noted that there are still not enough opportunities for women prisoners to gain vocational qualifications.

Apparently neutral policies may have a disparate impact on women. In many cases injustices have arisen where women have been subjected to similar penal requirements and a common criticism of the female prison regime has been that it has been largely based on the male prison regime, without sufficient acknowledgement of the differences between male and female experiences of offending and imprisonment. For example, when instances of disorder, absconding and escape occur, this usually results in an increase in levels of security and may have implications for home leave which affect all prisoners even though women were not involved in the prison riots and are less likely to abscond. So women may be adversely affected by the behaviour of male prisoners.

Women may also find the loss of privacy in prison very stressful especially when observed by male officers and find cell sharing difficult and this may engage Article 8 which protects the right to privacy. Under PR 41(3) women prisoners should only be subjected to full search by female officers and no male officers should be present. Women have been subjected to full body searches even though as a group they pose less of a security risk. The use of full body searching in women's prisons was criticized by the Prison Inspectorate in its 1997 Report but this had improved by the time of the follow-up report in 2000 (HMCIP 1997, 2001). This use of strip-searching was criticized by the Corston Report (Corston 2007: para 3.18). Routine full searching for women prisoners, for example on entering prison, has now ended. Many female prisoners have been subject to sexual abuse so they find this particularly humiliating. Visitors have also been subjected to full searches as we saw in the *Wainwright* case.

To bring an Article 14 claim an interference with another right must be proved, so it is possible that use might be made by female prisoners of Article 8 in the future but it would be quite difficult to overcome the potential defences in Article 8(2) in the prison context. To bring a discrimination case under Article 14, a female prisoner would have to show she had been treated differently from a male prisoner which may be difficult. Article 8 potentially could be used by women to increase contact with their families and could be raised if they show that women prisoners received less home leave than men, especially if based on assumptions about security risk, although they would face the hurdles discussed above.

However, as the majority of women are serving shorter sentences, then the incentive and opportunity to bring a case may be lessened. Because prisoners are for the most part deprived of responsibility and in many ways treated like children, this may be harder for women as they are used to running a home and organizing children. Female prisoners are also more likely than men to be subject to disciplinary charges and to be punished. There were 180 punishments per 100 female prisoners compared to 133 per 100 male prisoners in 2008/09 (Ministry of Justice 2010a: 64).

Female prisoners are also likely to have poor health before entering prison and high levels of prescription drug use inside prison. Although health care in prisons has improved, there are still problems in providing mental health care within prison. While mentally ill offenders ideally should not be dealt with in prison, in practice many will enter prison with a mental illness or develop mental health problems for the first time during imprisonment. However, if the emphasis is on refining mental health care within prisons this may reduce the impetus to divert these women to alternative provision.

Female prisoners have high level of self-harming and the latest report from the Prison Inspectorate found that levels of self-harm were still high in women's closed prisons. The Report refers to over 1,700 incidents of self-harming reported in three women's local prisons in 2008–9 and 2,256 in Holloway (HMCIP 2010a: 23). The Bradley Review of people with mental health problems or learning disabilities in the criminal justice system did not focus specifically on the problems female prisoners, but clearly they would benefit from the Report's recommendations for improved assessment, cooperation between agencies and continuity of care (Bradley 2009).

Prison reformers have frequently argued that women should be diverted from custody where possible and more use made of temporary release to deal with family problems. The Corston Report recommended using custody for women only where it was necessary to protect the public but otherwise diverting non-violent offenders from custody. It has also been argued that the impact of a prison sentence on the children of female prisoners should be given more weight in mitigating their sentences (see Piper 2007). Others have argued that women should be given more access to home leave to deal with children and more family-friendly policies should be developed, for example, in relation to family visits (Easton 2008).

Gender-specific standards

Campaigners have been arguing for many years for feminist penologies and gender-specific standards and policies which recognize that women may find imprisonment harsher because of their roles as prime carers, that they have different needs from male prisoners, principally because of these roles and that they need differential treatment. But the prison system has been designed around male prisoners which has often left women at a disadvantage and the lion's share of resources in terms of courses and facilities has been found at men's prisons. It is now widely accepted that women prisoners experience prison differently and that, in many cases, the pains of imprisonment are more severe, because of their role as carers of young children and of elderly relatives. The right to family life is therefore very important for female prisoners, yet they are likely to be held further from home than men. So this raises issue of whether women should have more access to home visits, temporary release to deal with children and generally more access to the outside world. It may be necessary to develop separate regimes for male and female prisoners governed by separate prison rules.

However, the need to reduce the differential impact of imprisonment has received more acceptance by government in recent years. In response to the Wedderburn and Corston Reports, the Labour Government accepted that women prisoners need gender-specific policies and standards which recognize the differential impact on women as carers, the need for better access to health services and development of community based programmes for women and the development of specific offending behaviour programmes for women. Some of these programmes have now been introduced, so it easier now for women to obtain temporary release to deal with problems at home. There is a separate Women and Young People's Group which oversees gender equality issues. Gender-specific standards have been developed by the Prison Service to promote equality so at a formal level, there has been commitment to improvements. But there are concerns over the resources available for improvement in the current climate of national austerity and swingeing budget cuts as well as concerns whether sentencing reforms are likely to increase the numbers of women entering prison.

Reformers have argued for more decarceration, better community programmes and bail hostels, as well as hostel accommodation for sentenced prisoners in smaller units held near their homes rather than large-scale prisons. The Labour Government favoured larger Titan prisons to achieve economies of scale, although smaller units would be held within these prison. Although development of the Titan prisons has been postponed because of the substantial costs, it is possible that this could return to the political-penal agenda to the detriment of female prisoners.

More constructive regimes will also reduce the differential impact of imprisonment, for example, programmes dealing with women's drug and alcohol abuse, and mental health problems, and which address the high levels of abuse experienced by women prisoners, as well as better work opportunities, and improved home leave and extended visiting arrangements. Women need access to work which will increase their work opportunities on release. Support groups working with women prisoners are usually voluntary and find it hard to get funding, and their work may also support families outside prison and improving visiting conditions to make them more welcoming for children. While the Coalition Government is committed to making more use of voluntary groups in the rehabilitation process this needs to be supported by adequate resources.

Under the European Prison Rules, 'the authorities shall pay particular attention to the requirements of women such as their physical, vocational, social and psychological needs when making decisions that affect any aspect of their detention' (EPR 34.1). This might also mean taking particular account of the needs of women who have suffered physical, mental or sexual abuse (EPR 25.4).

If women are given special privileges such as extra home leave, this may be construed by male prisoners as discrimination against them. In the case of *Spence* [1993] NILR 97 a male prisoner in Northern Ireland brought a differential treatment case because women were eligible for pre-release home leave earlier than men, but the Court rejected his claim because women had more family responsibilities which could justify the difference. Where women prisoners have been given concessions in some jurisdictions male prisoners have raised equality claims, for example, in Canada in the case of *Weatherall v Canada* [1993] 2 S.C.R. 872, an unsuccessful constitutional challenge was brought relating to the use of female officers to patrol and search male prisoners. The Court noted that the right to equality protected by s 15(1) of the Canadian Charter of Rights and Freedoms does not necessarily mean identical treatment, so that while such practices might be forbidden in relation to male officers guarding female prisoners, the historical, social and biological differences between male and female prisoners means that cross-gender searching may be different and more threatening for women than for men. But it may be that a more generous policy on home leave for women as prime carers, for example, could be extended to men in that position.

Once in prison women may lose their children, as female prisoners are less likely than male prisoners to have their children looked after by their partners. Very few children of female prisoners will remain in the family home so the 'third party impact' here will be exacerbated for female prisoners. If the woman's close female relatives are unable to take on the children, then they will go into the care system. So women prisoners will experience anxiety over what is happening to their children. Women may lose their home while in prison which will then make it harder for the family unit to survive or for prisoners to be reunited with their children on release. Codd uses the metaphor of a shadow to illustrate the way in which these families' lives are affected by their parent's imprisonment to an extent not found in other modes of punishment (Codd 2008).

The small size of the women's prison estate also has negative implications for women. It may be harder to find prisons with the right facilities for women with special needs. Because there are fewer women's prisons, women are more likely than adult males to be housed far from home and this may make resettlement more difficult. Most importantly, this distance from home makes family visits harder and if the mother is in prison there is also the problem of escorting children to prison for visits and the expense involved. So this may make it harder for those women to maintain contact and some women may also be worried about the effect on their children of visiting them in prison. Fathers in prison generally receive more regular visits from their children than mothers in prison.

Nonetheless, family contact could be improved by more assisted visits, weekend visits, more access to home and most importantly, housing women nearer their homes whenever possible, as well as by the use of intermittent custody. The Corston Report favoured small multi-functional centres providing a range of services for majority of prisoners although some would need to be held in secure conditions.

However, in some respects women in prison fare better than men. Women's prisons usually have better visiting facilities than men's prisons and obviously a key difference is that women have access to mother and baby units and may have better access to home leave. Moreover, the report of the Inspector of Prisons has found that in terms of access to purposeful activities, including education, women's prisons generally performed well allowing a reasonable amount of time outside cells (HMCIP 2010a, HMCIP 2010b). Women also have the advantage that they may be permitted to keep their children in prison with them, which fathers are denied.

Mother and baby units

Women who give birth in prison may, if permitted, have their children with them in a mother and baby unit for up to 18 months in some units and 9 months in others. Under PR 12(1) the Secretary of State may a permit a woman to have her baby with her in prison subject to any conditions he sees fit. In England and Wales there are seven units, including those at Holloway and Askham Grange. Antenatal care should be provided at any female prison up to 32 weeks, following which the prisoner may seek a transfer to a mother and baby unit. The factors to be considered in deciding an admission are set out in PSO 4801 and include the best interests of the child, the mother's behaviour and attitudes, whether there are implications for the safety and wellbeing of others, and the good order of the prison. Category A prisoners are not allowed access to mother and baby units and a refusal to allow access in such cases was unsuccessfully challenged in *R v Secretary of State for the Home Department ex parte Togher* 1 February 1995 (unreported).

In England the maximum time is 18 months, but in some European states, children remain with their parents until they are much older. In Germany, for example, women may live in accommodation in the community where they are locked up at night but the children go to a day nursery while their mothers have access to prison work and education. In Europe there is considerable variation in practice. In the Netherlands babies are allowed to stay with their mothers for up to nine months and in one prison, Ter Peel, there is a special unit where children can remain up to four years. In Spain and Switzerland children can remain until they are three years old and in some German prisons it can be as high as six years old. Usually the facilities are concentrated in open prisons and Ter Peel is set in acres of woodland so it is much less forbidding than a closed prison, or in separate units held just outside the prison. Crèche facilities are provided in Ter Peel to allow mothers to work. In the Netherlands women comprise 7.4 per cent of the prison population and as in the UK, many of these prisoners will be carers of young children.

In England and Wales, competition for places is intense and there are insufficient places to match demand for access to mother and baby units and there are likely to be more actions brought on this by women prisoners in future. One way of dealing with the problem would be to establish hostels outside prison where prisoners and babies can be held under supervision. There have already been several cases relying on Article 8 since the Human Rights Act was enacted as the right to family life of women prisoners has been given more weight by the domestic courts. In considering whether the state's interference with Article 8 is justified, the court will consider factors including the need for prison security and the need to avoid discrimination, and the more serious the interference with Article 8, the more compelling the justifications need to be. So in cases where the separation has an adverse effect on a child, the court may intervene.

In *R (P,Q and QB) v Secretary of State for the Home Department* [2001] EWCA Civ 1151, the rule prohibiting prisoners remaining with babies over 18 months was challenged. The Court of Appeal found in favour of Q but it upheld the separation of the child from P. The court said that in the past under public law it would be clear that the authority was entitled to have general policy in the exercise of its public law functions. But now following *R v Secretary of State for the Home Department ex parte Daly* [2001] UKHL 26, the court will examine closely whether the infringement of the right is necessary and proportionate, to achieve a legitimate aim. The Court deemed it appropriate for the Prison Service to have such a policy but it should not be applied rigidly and greater flexibility was needed. As the purpose of the policy is to promote the child's welfare, if applying the policy rigidly has catastrophic effects, then the policy is not meeting its objectives. Moreover, any interference with the child's family life must be justified under Article 8(2). Clearly the welfare of the child is a key issue, but in applying Article 8 there may be rare exceptions where the interests of mother and child coincide and might outweigh the fact of the mother's imprisonment or the implications of the policy being relaxed. The importance of the decision is that cases are now considered with much more attention to individual circumstances and may even extend beyond 18 months in appropriate cases.

In *CF v Secretary of State for the Home Department* [2004] EWHC 111 (Fam) the baby was separated from the mother at nine months. The mother wanted to move to a different unit where the child could stay for 18 months. But the judge was critical of the sloppy procedures by which the application was dealt with. The court stressed the importance of Article 8 in considering the issues concerning the children of prisoners and prisoners' families, although the separation was upheld in this case.

These cases illustrate that family issues are becoming more important, that the court will review the decision-making procedures, and that the courts will reject a blanket approach in favour of an individualized assessment of the needs of the mother and the child and of the risks involved. *CF* contrasts with the earlier case of *R v Secretary of State for the Home Department ex parte Hickling* [1986] 1 FLR 483, where a refusal to send a woman to a unit based on the mother's conduct and the impact on other women in the unit, was seen by the court as sufficient reason to reject an application. Today more attention will be paid both to the right to family life and to alternative ways of managing the risk. Under PSO 4801 the decision will take account of the mother's behaviour and risk to others, but the response must be proportionate to the seriousness of the problem. The court will look at whether if there is a risk to others and if so, whether the risk could be managed in other ways than removing the woman from the unit. In *R (CD) v Secretary of State for the Home Department* [2003] EWHC 155 (Admin) a decision to separate mother and baby was quashed. There were concerns about the risk posed by the mother to others in the unit, but the risk to others could be managed and had to be weighed against the impact of separation on the child. Under the UN Convention on the Rights of the Child which the UK has ratified, the Court must give priority to the best interests of the child.

Third party issues also arise in relation to the treatment of children born to mothers in prison and children's rights are becoming much more important. Whether it is in the interest of the child to remain in prison or some form of custodial unit has been debated (Caddle 1998). While being raised in a prison environment may not be ideal, in the long term, being in close contact with the mother in the first few months of life is generally crucial for development and in most cases would be in the child's interest. While there are some indications that the baby's cognitive and locomotor development may fall behind in prison, the research suggests that this will quickly catch up once outside. There are also issues over contact with other family members as the units may be even further away, making family visits difficult and there is also the problem of maintaining contact with the child's father and there have been several contested applications for contact in these circumstances. Alternatively periods of extended leave in school holidays or extended family visits would provide some means of facilitating family contact with other siblings.

The CPT standards are also clear that babies should not be born in prison and the overriding principle should be the child's welfare. Any medical care provided to the mother and child should be equivalent to that in the community and where babies are held in prison the aim should be to provide a child-centred environment where there are no obvious signs of incarceration, such as uniforms or jangling keys. In the UK the unit at Styal Prison is run by staff from Action for Children and has been highly praised by the Chief Inspector of Prisons (HMCIP 2010a).

Sexual orientation

Prisoners have a right not to be discriminated against or harassed on the grounds of sexual orientation. The Report of the Inspector of Prisons found that the provision for prisoners who were gay or bisexual was overall poor in male prisons, apart from Hull and Wakefield and the issue of sexuality was given little recognition in diversity policies (HMCIP 2010a: 35, 61). In some prisons, but not all, there are gay prisoner forums.

In *R v Home Secretary ex parte Fielding* [1999] COD 525 a gay prisoner challenged a policy of issuing condoms to prisoners only in cases of a known risk of HIV infection. In rejecting his claim, the court took the view that the Prison Service should not be seen to encourage homosexual activity in prison which, it said, might be the message which would be given to the prison population, and the public at large, if condoms were available on demand. This decision is problematic, however, as if prisoners decide to have a sexual relationship they may not wish to give this information to the medical officer and clearly the risk of transmission may be increased. One of the problems is that the prison environment is more homophobic than outside which may make it harder to obtain information on sexual orientation which can be used to monitor treatment. There is also no formal policy in the Prison Service specifically for dealing with sexual orientation issues or special complaints system to deal with homophobic complaints comparable to that for racist incidents, so this needs addressing. Gay prisoners also need to be incorporated in equality impact assessments.

Transgender prisoners

The gender equality duty includes elimination of unlawful discrimination against or harassment of transsexuals whether as users of services or employees. Enhanced protection for transgender prisoners is found in s 7 of the Equality Act 2010. Discrimination in the provisions of goods, facilities and services to transgender prisoners prior to the Act was prohibited by the Sex Discrimination (Amendment of Legislation) Regulations 2008. The NOMS Equality Review referred to the need to develop a more coherent policy on transgender prisoners (NOMS 2009).

By transsexual or transgender is meant an individual who has undergone, is undergoing or intends to undergo gender reassignment surgery. The rights of transsexuals in prison have recently been considered by the courts when a refusal to allow a pre-operative transgender prisoner to transfer to a women's prison was subject to judicial review. In *R (on the application of AB) v (1) Secretary of State for Justice (2) Governor of Manchester Prison* QBD (Admin) (4 September 2009), the prisoner argued that she should be transferred to a women's prison, claiming that her Article 8 right to private life had been infringed. The prisoner's identity was concealed by a court order. She was serving a sentence for manslaughter and attempted rape and unlikely to be released for some time. The prisoner argued that the change of sex was a way of dealing with her offending behaviour as the prisoner's original crimes were linked to his/her gender identity. The process of sex reassignment began in prison with hormone and other treatments and the prisoner was legally a woman under the Gender Recognition Act 2004 and had undergone some physical changes. But she was not allowed to wear women's clothes in the male prison. Before she could have the necessary surgery to complete the changes, she had to live as a woman which was clearly impossible in a male prison. The Secretary of State's refusal was based on the fact that women prisoners would not want a pre-operative transsexual in their prison and that a lengthy period of segregation would be needed, which will mean additional costs and there were concerns over the risk to other prisoners. However, male prisoners would not accept her because of her feminine appearance, so she was held in a Vulnerable Prisoner Unit within a male prison. The Court decided that Article 8 was engaged as the decision to keep the prisoner in a men's prison prevented her from qualifying for the surgery and moving to full gender reassignment and interfered with her personal autonomy and could not be justified on the ground of risk or cost. If B still posed a risk this could be managed and the period in segregation may not be great. The decision to keep B in the men's prison violated the principle of proportionality and could not be justified under Article 8(2). The decision was also *Wednesbury* unreasonable and therefore was quashed.

The problem of dealing fairly with transgender prisons has been addressed in the United States and in other European states. In Italy a special prison for transgender prisoners is being prepared near Florence. It will house about 30 prisoners who previously have been held in women's prisons usually under segregation for their own protection. In the United States there are now separate units for transgender prisons in some prisons, although allocation is still based on anatomical changes rather than physical appearance.

Age and disability discrimination

Prisons also have an equality duty towards older prisoners and as the number of older prisoners increases, then it is possible that cases may be brought by older prisoners in future challenging their treatment. As the prison population ages, then the number of disabilities may increase, although of course there are younger disabled prisoners and problems faced by older prisoners which do not reflect disabilities, such as the lack of availability of employment, so age and disability issues may be distinguished. The treatment of prisoners with disabilities is regulated by PSO 2855 which includes provisions on older prisoners. Older prisoners will tend to have higher morbidity rates. In extreme cases where prisoners are terminally ill they should be cared for in a hospice if appropriate or may be given compassionate release, as in the case of former train robber, Ronnie Biggs, and the Lockerbie bomber, Abdulbaset Ali al-Megrahi.

Older prisoners should have treatment appropriate to their needs as the Strasbourg Court said in *Papon v France* Application No. 64666/01 (7 June 2001). Here the prisoner in question was a 90-year-old former official of the Vichy regime, convicted of complicity in crimes against humanity during the German occupation, namely signing deportation orders sending over 1500 French Jews to concentration camps. Here it was noted that while in certain circumstances, extended detention could breach Article 3, the court would not accept Papon's argument that any imprisonment of a person of this age breached Article 3. But, appropriate care should be available for elderly prisoners. However, prisons are designed primarily for younger and able-bodied prisoners despite the fact that the prison population is ageing (see Howse 2003). The Chief Inspector of Prisons has criticized the lack of progress in this area in the UK (HMCIP 2008).

In domestic law disabled prisoners are protected by the Equality Act and formerly by the Disability Discrimination Act. The equality duty under the Equality Act applies to disabled prisoners so prisoners should be proactive in eliminating inequality and these duties may be enforced by the Equality and Human Rights Commission. Disabled prisoners should also have treatment appropriate to their needs to comply with Article 3. The court was very critical of the treatment of a disabled woman in police custody in the case of *Price v UK* (2002) 34 EHRR 53 where she was held in inappropriate and degrading conditions without a proper consideration of what her needs required.

Prison authorities in England and Wales are required to make reasonable accommodation to meet the needs of disabled prisoners and their visitors. If a reasonable adjustment is feasible then the authority would be open to an action if it did not pursue that adjustment. Prisons have to make appropriate provision to accommodate visitors with disabilities or special requirements and reasonable adjustments should be made to accommodate any special requirements, to avoid challenges under disability law (PSO 4410 para 2.15).

So if a prisoner is unable to take part in prison activities because no reasonable accommodation is made for him, for example, by providing him with a suitable wheelchair, then a claim could be brought. Under the 1995 Act the scope of the legislation was limited to access to education, and other programmes but did not extend to key functions such as allocation, but this is now covered by the DDA 2005 and the Equality Act. A prisoner could also bring a claim under Article 14 if other rights are engaged, for example an Article 8 claim, if he had problems with visits because of his or his visitor's disabilities. To justify its action, the prison would need to show that the differential treatment was proportionate.

Equality for disabled prisoners, as in the case of female or ethnic minorities, may mean differential treatment in order to achieve equality. Prisoners with special needs need appropriate accommodation and access to resources, so these will be important issues in the allocation and transfer of disabled prisoners. Problems can be raised initially with the Disability Liaison Officer or the prisoner can make a formal complaint through the internal complaints procedure, go to the Ombudsman or bring civil proceedings. The number of claims brought by disabled prisoners is increasing.

There are variations between prisons in terms of their suitability for disabled prisoners. Much of the prison estate is inaccessible to prisoners with mobility problems and buildings may have been constructed before the statutory duty was imposed. New prisons will be purpose-built with appropriate access but this may be harder in older prisons. So in providing accommodation, the prison authority will need to consider these issues, but the needs of disabled prisoners will also arise in relation to access to activities, work and education. Although disabled prisoners have been overlooked by researchers until relatively recently, there is now more interest in the treatment of disabled prisoners. While the needs of prisoners with physical disabilities may be easier to identify and meet, it may be harder for prisoners with learning disabilities to have their needs addressed or to be recognized. Identifying these needs may become harder with overcrowding and the pressure on prison staff. The recent Report of the Chief Inspector of Prisons noted that 5 per cent of prisoners with disabilities were recorded by prisons, but surveys in which prisoners themselves reported on this showed 15 per cent of prisoners with disabilities (HMCIP 2010a: 36). The Bradley Report made a number of recommendations, including more research to improve identification and screening at the point of entry into prison (Bradley 2009).

Loucks found that prisoners with learning disabilities spent more time in their cells and had worse treatment and less access to activities (Loucks 2007). Clearly such prisoners may find it harder to complain because they lack the necessary resources. They may also find it very difficult to adapt to imprisonment and if they become disruptive, may be more likely to be segregated. Research for the Prison Inspectorate found that half of prisoners with disabilities felt unsafe at some time during their imprisonment compared to one-third of those without a disability (HMIP 2009a). This review is based on inspection reports and surveys from 2006–8. Approximately one-third of respondents with disabilities reported being victimized and young adult prisoners with disabilities were more likely to report the use of force against them compared to other young adults. Although the prisons had disability liaison officers, two-fifths of the officers reported they did not have time to deal with their tasks and received insufficient training and support.

The Inspectorate found that the experience of imprisonment for prisoners with disabilities was generally worse than that of prisoners without disabilities, with considerable variation in provision for disabilities between prisons. There was insufficient staff training and opportunities to disseminate good practice through the prison system. Some prisons had failed to make any adjustments to make prisons more accessible. If officers refused to push wheelchairs on the ground that they had not received adequate training, some prisoners inevitably suffered disadvantage. Although all prisons had disabilities policies, these were often perfunctory with no monitoring processes. The Report found under-reporting of disabilities, that disabled prisoners were less likely to report being treated with respect than prisoners without disabilities, and experienced problems of access to showers and to activities, so spent more time in their cells. The complaints procedure for dealing with problems of victimization was inadequate. Prisoners with disabilities were also less likely to reach the enhanced level of the privileges scheme. There was also insufficient attention paid to the needs of disabled visitors.

However, male prisoners with disabilities were more positive about health services than prisoners without disabilities, but this did not apply to female prisoners with disabilities. Although some examples of good practice were reported, such as peer support schemes, they were not widespread. Recommendations from the Report include better identification and monitoring of disabled prisoners, regular reviews of treatment and sharing of information, disability awareness training for all staff and ensuring that diversity incident reporting forms are available for disabled prisoners to report any issues of victimization arising from diversity issues including disability, and providing alternative activities for prisoners unable to work because of a disability. A new PSI on disabled prisoners has been introduced and monitoring has improved, but as the Inspectorate concluded, prisons have a long way to go in fulfilling their equality duty in relation to this group of prisoners.

Black and minority ethnic prisoners

There has been considerable research on the differential treatment of black and white prisoners, as well as at earlier stages of the criminal justice process, and an extensive literature on the treatment of ethnic minorities in police custody. Over one-quarter of the prison population in England and Wales is made up of ethnic minorities. In 2009 black and minority ethnic groups, including foreign national prisoners made up just under 27 per cent of the prison population. This consisted of 14.4 per cent black, 7.2 per cent

Asian, 3.4 per cent Mixed and 1.7 per cent Chinese (Ministry of Justice 2010b: 47).

> Black and ethnic minority groups also made up a higher proportion of remand prisoners than those from white groups. Among young sentenced prisoners, BME prisoners were more likely to be serving longer sentences which reflected the type of offences and seriousness of offences. Black and ethnic minorities are not homogenous but include a wide range of groups who may have quite different experiences.

The number of ethnic minority prisoners has increased since 1984 when ethnic monitoring was first conducted in prisons. The disproportionate number of ethnic minorities in prison has raised questions about their treatment at each stage of the criminal justice process as black people are more likely to be stopped and searched, and arrested (Ministry of Justice 2010b). Within prison, prison authorities are under a duty to promote racial equality and to ensure that ethnic minority prisoners are not treated less favourably than others on grounds of race or ethnic origins.

Prison authorities have a duty not to discriminate under the provisions of the Race Relations (Amendment) Act and the Equality Act 2010. In addition, the Prison Rules include disciplinary offences of racially aggravated assault and racially aggravated damage and of course prisoners are subject to the ordinary criminal law which includes racially motivated offences. All prisons must conduct general equality impact assessments under the race equality duty.[5] A new PSO on Race Equality 2800 was issued in 2006 so all prisons must have race equality action teams, collect information, carry out impact assessments and deal with racist incidents. It also sets out procedures for dealing with complaints and informing the complainant of the outcome. Forms for racist incident reporting should be available on all wings and complaints dealt with promptly. A racist incident is defined in the Macpherson Report as one which is perceived as racist by the victim or any other person (Macpherson 1999). In the first instance a complaint can be made on a racist incident reporting form which should be available on all wings. The Race Equality Officer (REO) will discuss the case with the prisoner. If an ordinary complaint indicates that there may be a racial element this will also be referred to the REO. If the issue is not resolved then a full investigation will be carried out.

Promoting equality of opportunity is a key aim for the Prison Service. Although there is a strong commitment at the level of management to combating racism, there have been concerns about the treatment of prisoners in terms of access to work and training, but also over racial harassment and abuse. Ethnic minority staff as well as prisoners may be the victims of racist abuse. The Director General of the Prison Service has acknowledged the problems of dealing with racism at an individual and institutional level. As we have seen, prison life is characterized by the exercise of discretion which can arise in relation to allocation of resources, decisions to charge with disciplinary offences and reports on behaviour, which may allow scope for prejudice and racial stereotyping.

Race relations policies have operated in the prison service since the early 1980s and have been revised regularly since then and have including monitoring, staff training and complaints procedures. Since the 1980s, there has been more interest from researchers on racism in prison and a corresponding concern within the Prison Service to develop policies and strategies to challenge racism. Race relations policies have been developed since the early 1990s, focusing on monitoring and training of staff. All prisons have Race Equality Officers, formerly called Race Relations Liaison Officers. These officers may also take on the role of diversity managers as well. So within the broad area of equality, race has received the most attention and support and it has been the only area where there has been regular monitoring for a long period. These officers deal with complaints and reports of racist incidents. At the national level, the Race and Equalities Action Group has replaced the Race Equality Action Team to reflect the wider focus on a range of equalities to meet recent changes in the law. So there is a clearly a strong commitment to equality at a formal level but embedding this in practice may be more difficult. While the behaviour of staff may be controlled through training and sanctions, the behaviour of prisoners will be less easy to control. Efforts have been made to recruit more ethnic minority staff who now make up over 6 per cent of staff. The number of black and minority ethnic staff had increased to 6.3 per cent by February 2009. There are also prisoner support groups for ethnic minorities and more encouragement for outside bodies from the community to become involved in prison support.

Reports and studies on racism in prisons over the past ten years have focused principally on procedural issues, such as how complaints are processed. At the level of formal law, a framework of regulation has been put in place so the challenge is to put this into practice. A number of practical measures may be needed, including staff training, for example, to understand the value of ethnic monitoring procedures rather than seeing them as a chore, more support for ethnic minority staff and creating a culture in which prisoners feel able to report racist incidents and that they will be dealt with appropriately. Some progress has been made in these areas, but clearly changing the attitudes and behaviour of prisoners remains a formidable task. But challenging discrimination and respecting prisoners' right to equality can benefit prisons as well as prisoners in helping to maintain good order in prisons.

Prisoners have brought complaints and legal actions relating to racism with some success, although there are still relatively few cases to date and under the original Act the focus was narrower and did not extend to all the functions of the prison. One of the first major cases under the Race Relations Act 1976 was *Alexander v Home Office* [1988] 2 All ER 118 where the court found that the prisoner had been discriminated against in the allocation of work as a report on him contained racist comments which led to him being refused work in the prison kitchen.

Recent complaints have focused more closely on issues such as harassment and racist violence, but also complaints that the treatment of black prisoners' visitors are more likely to be searched. Issues may also arise if interpreters are not provided for foreign national prisoners subject to disciplinary charges. Complaints may be made within the formal complaints system discussed in Chapter 5, but also to the Equality and Human Rights Commission (formerly the CRE), to the Prisons and Probations Ombudsman, and a civil legal action case could be brought using human rights law.

The experience of race issues by different groups has been described by the Inspector of Prisons as 'parallel worlds', to refer to the fact that different subgroups within staff and prisoners may have different experiences and attitudes towards race relations within prison (HMIP 2005). White prisoners were more positive on issues such as safety and respect. However, within ethnic minorities there were variations in responses on these issues between young and adult prisoners and prisoners from different religious groups. Black prisoners felt safer than Asian prisoners. White staff were more likely than ethnic minority staff to see race relations policies working effectively.

The Report also found variations between prisons on the effectiveness of policies and the priority given to such work and recommended improved training. The majority of complaints about racism were about prisoners' racism. But there were problems in dealing with complaints, including delays, lack of staff training, and the fact that some prisoners believed it was not worth complaining, although prisoners with a BME background had more confidence in the complaints procedure. There is also the issue that prisoners may be reluctant to complain if they feel it will cause trouble or not be taken seriously. At the same time the Report found some good practice such as using mediation to deal with racist complaints.

There have also been a number of official reports and inquiries, including the Commission for Racial Equality Report in 2003, which found instances of racial discrimination at three prisons, Brixton, Parc and Feltham, following which the Prison Service devised an Action plan with the CRE to address concerns over racist abuse and incidents. The Action Plan included revised procedures for ethnic monitoring, improved treatment of complaints and enhanced race and diversity training, and more involvement of external community groups in race relation management teams, and better monitoring of race equality measures. The CRE was very critical of the Prison Service's failure to challenge and remove discrimination. Its Report focused on a wide range of issues including access to goods and services, the incentives and earned privileges scheme, complaints procedures and the use of discretion.

While most of the literature on prisoners' rights has focused of course on rights against public bodies and states, in many cases prisoners need protection from other prisoners and this is where prisoners are most vulnerable. This is highlighted by the murder of prisoners by their cellmates, the most extreme manifestation of racism. The inquiry into the death of Zahid Mubarek, a prisoner killed by his racist cellmate, Robert Stewart, at Feltham

Young Offenders Institution in 2000, has highlighted key areas of concern and made several recommendations, including improved sharing of information and the use of single cells (Keith 2006). The Mubarek Report was very critical of the failure to manage the potential risk posed by Stewart. Two key issues were highlighted, the failure to pass on information about Stewart, on his racism and previous instance of violence, to the appropriate bodies and the fact that prisoners had to share cells, both of which increased the risk of harm.

Many of the Report's proposals have been accepted by the Government and integrated into its Race Equality Action Plan. Procedures for handling information have been improved, but the problem of cell sharing remains and is likely to increase with the pressure on the prison population. Given the problems of overcrowding, the use of single cells to protect prisoners from racism and violence cannot be assumed, so improved monitoring of high-risk individuals is even more important. Prisons now have to formulate and implement a violence reduction strategy.

This five-year Action Plan was concluded by the publication of the Race Review Report in December, *Implementing Race Equality in Prisons Five Years On* (NOMS 2008). The Report said that that although considerable work on combating and monitoring racism had been undertaken BME staff and prisoners were still reporting problems. Key Performance Targets on race equality had been introduced and met. More training had been introduced for Race Equality Action Team (REAT) members. A new manual for detecting and managing racism had been introduced. There was more involvement of outside bodies with representatives on the REAT. This review found that new structures had been put place, and a detailed Race Equality Action Plan (REAP) had been created at NOMS headquarters, an externally recruited Race Advisory Group had been set up, the PSO on Race Equality (PSO 2800) had been revised, and a new monitoring tool had been introduced covering more areas of prison life. At local level the REAP is managed by the Race Equality Action Team (formerly Race Relations Management Teams) and all prisons have Race Equality Officers, now called Race and Equality Officers. The Report noted that there had been considerable progress in challenging overt racism and monitoring with new systems which had not been in place at the time of the CRE inquiry. There had been improvements in catering and prison shops to meet the needs of BME prisoners and the complaint form and handling of racist incidents had been improved. A manual for identifying and managing overt racism had also been published.

However, the review, which included a survey of 900 prisoners, showed that despite all these changes 'the experience of prisoners and staff has not been transformed' (NOMS 2008: 15). Black prisoners were more likely to be charged with disciplinary offences, to be on the basic regime of the IEPS and to be on segregation for reasons of good order and discipline, and felt that they had less access to good-quality work. These are all areas where discretion is exercised by officers and where negative stereotypes may still find expression and may be difficult to control.

The focus now is on the wider equality agenda and extending the work undertaken on race equality to other key areas, to raise awareness and improve monitoring. The most recent document from NOMS, *Promoting Equality in Prisons and Probation: the National Offender Management Service Single Equality Scheme 2009–2012*, sets out the obligations of prisons and the Probation Service in response to the equality duty and also includes an Action Plan (NOMS 2009). Reports on progress in meeting equality obligations which extend beyond race will be made regularly to NOMS and to the new Independent Equalities Advisory group. In addition, annual reports will be published which will include monitoring and updates on the progress of the Action Plan. This review focuses on race gender and disability equality but also refers to religion, sexual orientation and transgender issues. This document emphasizes the importance of handling equality issues fairly for good order in prison, but also for reducing reoffending, for example in ensuring that disabled prisoners are not excluded from programmes. Meeting the equality duty is also a key element of the decency agenda. It envisages extending the reporting of racist incidents and dealing with such complaints to all other areas of hate crime.

Recent research suggests that relations between staff and prisoners in women's prisons is better than in men's prisons and black and ethnic minority female prisoners are less negative about their treatment than black and ethnic minority male prisoners (HMCIP 2010a). Although there is limited research on black female prisoners, the level of interest has increased.[6] Black and minority ethnic women prisoners may face problems of both racial and sexual discrimination. Less race relations work is undertaken in women's prisons than men's (HMCIP 2001). We are also now more aware of the particular problems faced by female foreign national prisoners who may be drawn from a wide range of ethnic groups, including white ethnic minorities. The Report by the Inspectorate of Prisons, *Race Relations in Prison: Responding to Adult Women from Black and Minority Ethnic Backgrounds* refers to black and minority ethnic women prisoners as the forgotten minorities (HMIP 2009b). They are over-represented within the criminal justice system but their needs are overlooked with no clear diversity strategy for these women and not referred to in the Race Review. These women report greater levels of victimization and lack of respect from staff and poor access to prison resources and concerns over health care and food. Black women are more likely to be single mothers, so will have particular problems in maintaining households while in prison and also higher levels of social disadvantage compared to white female prisoners. They also have different health patterns and different patterns of drug use compared to white women prisoners. They may also be more reluctant to report health problems.

The latest Report from the Prison Inspectorate found that a 'higher proportion of black and minority ethnic, Muslim and foreign national prisoners said they had felt unsafe' (HMCIP 2010a: 19). The response from black and minority ethnic prisoners remained more negative in response to over half of the questions in the HMCIP surveys particularly in men's prisons. These prisoners reported more problems in day-to-day life in the prison and poorer relationships with staff. However, they were more likely to take part in education and training and less likely to report drug and alcohol problems. Black prisoners expressed most concerns about relationships with staff while Asian prisoners were most concerned about safety. The surveys also found negative responses from white Irish respondents.

Foreign national or non-British prisoners make up a relatively large proportion of the prison population, particularly the female prison population and a similar pattern is found in the Netherlands and throughout Europe. Within Europe as a whole the rise of foreign national prisoners is linked to issues of migration and drugs trafficking. There are disproportionate numbers of foreign nationals and ethnic minorities in prison in the Netherlands, for example, where the number of foreign national prisoners from a wide range of nationalities increased from 12 per cent of the prison population in 1981 to 26 per cent in 1992 and is now 27.4 per cent, and is higher in relation to the female prison population, where a large number are convicted of drug courier offences. There also large numbers of migrants detained under administrative detention for failing to have the appropriate residential permits and detention boats have been used to deal with the expansion, and the number of deportations has also increased in recent years (van Kalmthout 2007). Those detained within prisons will have greater access to facilities and support than those held in administrative detention. However, as the total prison population in the Netherlands in April 2010 amounted to 15,604, including those held as illegal aliens, the actual number of foreign nationals in custody is still relatively small (ICPS 2010).

In England and Wales foreign nationals now constitute 13 per cent of the overall prison population in England and Wales and 17 per cent of the female prison population and foreign nationals make up 38 per cent of the BME population in prison. Foreign nationals accounted for 21 per cent of women prisoners and 13 per cent of male prisoners in 2008 (Ministry of Justice 2009c: 171). Their percentage of the total prison population has fluctuated between 12 and 14 per cent over the last few years. In June 2009 there were 11,350 foreign national prisoners (Ministry of Justice 2010e: 106). In England and Wales, the increase in numbers in recent years reflects the rise in the number of drugs-related offences where they may be used as couriers. For female prisoners, many of the worries experienced by female prisoners regarding their families may be exacerbated because of the distance from home. Foreign national prisoners may face particular problems of isolation and communications if they do not speak English well, problems with access to offending behaviour courses and other programmes and resources. If the prisoners have limited language skills, they will find it harder to obtain access to work.

Foreign national prisoners may be concentrated in particular prisons, for example, Canterbury and Bullwood Hall, and Downview for female prisoners, to concentrate resources and to make it easier for arrangements for deportation to be effected more easily. The Prison Inspector found foreign national prisoners made up 40 per cent of the population in Holloway and Brixton, and between 10 and 20 per cent of the population in 23 other prisons (HMCIP 2010a: 41) But the Inspectorate has criticized the lack of a national strategy or policy for treatment of these prisoners and lack of training. These prisoners also responded more negatively than British nationals on nearly half of the questions in their survey, in terms of safety and staff relations, and being treated with respect, although this last issue varied considerably between prisons. There were also problems of obtaining interpreters which also made it difficult for prisoners to deal with immigration issues. Moreover, some of these prisoners who have completed their sentence may still be held in prison while awaiting deportation. Foreign national prisoners were more likely to report feeling unsafe (HMCIP 2010a: 19). Foreign national prisoners also reported problems with access to visits and phone calls. In most of the prisons visited free phone calls were available only to those who had received no visits in the last month while in others free phone calls were only available if prisoners applied in English. So focusing on the improvement of language skills would assist these prisoners considerably. All prisons are required to have a local policy for managing foreign national prisoners and if the numbers are large, it may be appropriate to set up a Foreign National Committee to supervise that policy (PSO 4630, para 1.18).

The decision to place foreign national prisoners together, however, may mean they are subjected to a higher level of security than necessary (PSO 0900 para 6.8.5). In considering allocation the prison authority will take into account the particular risk of absconding, especially as they may be deported on release from prison, in deciding whether to categorize them as Category D and send them to an open prison (PSO 4630). The UK has ratified the Additional Protocol to the Council of Europe's Convention on the Transfer of Sentenced Persons which makes it easier for prisoners to serve sentences in their own countries or third states, but so far there has been little use made of it. Prisoner transfer agreements are being pursued between the UK and Nigeria, and Jamaica which would allow prisoners to return home to serve their sentences, which would address the problems of isolation, although of course the conditions in those prison systems in some respects may be worse than in the UK.

Following public and press concern over foreign national prisoners who went missing before they could be deported in 2006, the government transferred foreign national prisoners held in open prisons en bloc to closed ones. A challenge to this failed in *R (Chindamo) v Secretary of State for the Home Department)* [2006] EWHC 3340 (Admin) despite the increasing focus on individual risk.

In considering whether foreign national prisoners sentenced to less than 12 months should be held in open conditions, the risk of escape or absconding may be increased by the likelihood of deportation, but open conditions should not be ruled out simply on the basis that the prisoner is a foreign national. The decision should be made on the basis of individual risk (PSO 4630: para 14.1). At the allocation stage, they should be considered in the same way as other prisoners and risk should be assessed on an individual basis. However, in practice, prisoners may find problems in being transferred to open conditions and the concentration of foreign national prisoners in specific prisons may improve access to resources and be more cost-effective.

What is needed are specific policies for foreign national prisoners, but with the expansion of the prison population it may be more difficult to implement such policies, especially when economies of scale are being sought because of the pressure on budgets. The treatment of foreign national prisoners is receiving increased attention internationally and highlighting their treatment. A strengthened framework of prisoners' rights would benefit this particular group of prisoners, who may be disadvantaged in a system based on privileges.

Religious minorities

The prison population includes a wide range of religious groups comprising the major religions of Christianity, Judaism, Buddhism and Islam and sects within them, as well as minor religions such as paganism. Clearly, prisoners retain their right to freedom of religion and to practise their religion under Article 9(1): 'Everyone has the right to freedom of thought, conscience and religion; this right includes freedom to change his religion or belief, and freedom, either alone or in community with others and in public or private, to manifest his religion or belief, in worship, teaching, practice and observance.' However, it is made clear under Article 9(2) that 'Freedom to manifest one's religion or beliefs shall be subject only to such limitations as are prescribed by law and are necessary in a democratic society in the interests of public safety, for the protection of public order, health or morals, or the protection of the rights and freedoms of others.'

The prison authority has an obligation under Article 9 to take account of their religious beliefs and any restrictions have to be justified under Article 9(2). Prisoners are asked their religious affiliation at the time they enter prison. If the inmate does not speak English, the prisoner is shown a card of symbols of recognized religions, including Christianity and Christian sects, Judaism, Islam, Sikhism and Buddhism.

Freedom of thought, conscience and religion is also protected by the European Prison Rules: EPR 29(1) provides that 'Prisoners' freedom of thought, conscience and religion shall be respected'. EPR 29(2) states that:

> The prison regime shall be organised so far as is practicable to allow prisoners to practise their religion and follow their beliefs, to attend

services or meetings led by approved representatives of such religion or beliefs, to receive visits in private from such representatives of their religion or beliefs and to have in their possession books or literature relating to their religion or beliefs.

However, there should be no pressure on individuals to participate in religious activities: 'Prisoners may not be compelled to practise a religion or belief, to attend religious services or meetings, to take part in religious practices or to accept a visit from a representative of any religion or belief' (EPR 29.3). The Rules also make clear that prisoners should be given meals which comply with their religious requirements (EPR 22.1).

The UK Prison Rules 13–19 set out the duties of ministers of religion, the conduct of services and the relief from work on days of religious observance. Guidance on dealing with religious needs is also set out in the Religion Manual (PSO 4550). Prisoners have the right to practise their religion which means that the Prison Service has a statutory obligation to allow them to do so and prisoners should not be discriminated against by declaring themselves a member of a religion or by belonging to no religion.

These duties include the appointment of chaplains or ministers, providing a place of worship, a multi-faith room suitable for a wide range of faiths and ancillary facilities, such as washing facilities. Prisoners should be allowed a minimum of one hour a week for corporate worship or religious observance, unless there are security issues to justify their exclusion. Pastoral care should be available to all prisoners and if a prisoner applies to see a chaplain or minister, this should normally be within 24 hours. Provision should also be made for religious education classes. Prisoners should not be required to do non-essential work on days of special observation, or work that is offensive or unsuitable for their religion, and should be provided with a suitable diet which meets the requirements of the religion. They should also be allowed to wear clothes which meet religious requirements and access to relevant artefacts of the religion. But prisoners should also be protected from pressure to change their religious affiliations, so ministers or chaplains should not visit prisoners without their consent, or seek to persuade them to change their religious affiliations.

Paganism is also recognized as a religion, and prisoners should be provided with robes, wands, runes and other paraphernalia needed and this may include tarot cards. The advice on implementing freedom of religion includes advice on veganism which, while not a religion, is based on a specific philosophical approach to the use and exploitation of animals. So vegans should be provided with a suitable diet and clothing and should not be expected to work in contexts involving the use of live or dead animals, such as prison farms or butchery.

The number of Muslim prisoners has increased sharply in recent years and they have now received more attention and their treatment has highlighted the issue of treatment of religious minorities (Spalek 2005, Spalek and

El-Hassan 2007). In 2010 there were about 10,300 Muslim prisoners who constitute just over 12 per cent of the prison population in England and Wales, compared to 8 per cent in 2004. The numbers are particularly high in high-security prisons, for example comprising about one-third of prisoners in Whitemoor and a quarter of prisoners in Long Lartin. The Race Review in 2008 said there had been considerable progress since 2003 in meeting the needs of Muslim prisoners, although many still felt unsafe. It also noted that the progress made in dealing with Muslim prisoners needed to be extended to other faiths.

The treatment of Muslim women raises particular issues, for example, in relation to full body searching of Muslim women. Female visitors or prisoners wearing veils should not be asked to uncover themselves in public in the presence of a male officer; arrangements should be made to remove them in private in the presence of female staff. Female prisoners should have access to women doctors. Other issues which may arise are contact with prison dogs or their saliva which is seen as offensive and unclean, so particular care needs to be taken in the context of cell searches or searches of Muslim visitors. If contact with dogs is made during Friday prayers, facilities must be available for prisoners to wash themselves.

In the recent survey by the Prison Inspectorate which covered access to basic amenities, safety, respect and health care, they found that religious needs of Muslims were met well and the work of imams had been strengthened (HMCIP 2010b). Special provision is made for prisoners' meals during Ramadan and time available for Friday prayers. The review was based on interviews with 168 Muslim prisoners in eight different prisons. The Muslim prisoners are more likely than non-Muslims to be foreign nationals, young, and from a black or minority ethnic group, and in prison for the first time. Muslim prisoners were more negative than non-Muslim prisoners in response to over half the questions in the HMIP survey, which covered a range of aspects of prison life. Muslim respondents were more negative about their treatment by prison staff than non-Muslims. They were more likely to report feeling unsafe, experiencing victimization and the use of force than non-Muslims and felt unfairly treated regarding the Incentives and Earned Privileges Scheme. They also felt less safe, especially in high-security dispersal prisons. Respondents who were of mixed heritage gave the most negative responses on issues such as victimization. Some prisoners also felt they were perceived as terrorists because of their religion. However, more Muslims than non-Muslims felt their religious beliefs were treated with respect.

There have been fears expressed in the press and by some officers and prisoners over the development of gangs of Muslim prisoners controlling the drugs and mobile phone trade in prison and using their religion to mask their activities. Some prisoners have reported being bullied for showing a lack of respect for Islam and some prisoners have been subject to pressure to convert to Islam. The treatment of Muslim prisoners is overlaid by the concern over terrorism discussed in Chapter 1 and fused with fears over the radicalization of prisoners inside prison. Some of these prisoners are held under the Terrorism Act which may mean that other prisoners and staff view them as spreading extremism. Some staff found it difficult to deal with such prisoners other than as 'potential extremists'. While the strategy of meeting religious needs has met with success, the 'blanket' approach to these prisoners as potential or actual extremists may reinforce negative attitudes.

A NOMS programme to address the risk of violent extremism and radicalization in prison was introduced in response to the Government's counter-terrorism strategy PREVENT. Staff have been given training to identify radicalism since 2007, but this focus on Muslim prisoners as potential extremists may have the unintended effect of alienating these prisoners and reinforce negative staff perceptions especially in prisons holding those convicted of terrorist-related offences even though less than one per cent of Muslim prisoners are in prison for terrorist-related offences (HMCIP 2010b: 4). However, the Prison Inspectorate could find no evidence to support these claims of radicalization.

Some staff expressed concern over prisoners being forced to convert and non-Muslims being intimidated in young offender institutions, but the Inspector found no clear evidence of this or of the operation of Muslim gangs. There was no monitoring of these issues in terms of religion so it is difficult to see if the perceptions of Muslim prisoners are corroborated by evidence and the Report recommended obtaining further information on conversion to Islam.

Muslim prisoners include converts and those who are Muslim by birth. For the prisoners surveyed by the Prison Inspectorate, converts' motives were mixed, for one-third the primary reason was religious as individuals found that their faith played a positive part in lives and helped them negotiate the pains of imprisonment. Others cited the feeling of protection from being in a group with a strong identity and others were motivated by material advantages, such as more time outside their cells and better food during Ramadan. The Report recommends that NOMS develops a national strategy for Muslim prisoners, giving staff better training on religious diversity to improve awareness of faith issues, the monitoring of conversions in prison, and the creation of mechanisms to engage in a dialogue with these prisoners.

In the Netherlands prisoners obviously have the same right to practice their religion and access to services as in the UK under Article 9 and under the Penitentiary Principles Act. Prisoners are permitted to attend corporate worship unless there are security issues and to receive visits from the appropriate chaplain. As in the UK, there is a range of religions practised including major and minor faiths. Special diets are provided and prisoners are allowed religious artefacts in their cells subject to permission from the prison governor. There are also special wings for prisoners convicted of terrorist offences separate from other prisoners which is intended to prevent radicalization of other prisoners, but this has meant considerable isolation.

Equality issues in the American prison system

In the United States, the right to equal protection has been advanced by prisoners from a range of different groups, including women, disabled prisoners, gay prisoners, transgender prisons and black prisoners. As the Prisoner Litigation Reform Act has meant that there are fewer cases being heard, some of these equality issues still remain undecided. The right to equality has also been advanced by women prisoners in the USA to challenge their conditions of imprisonment, using the equal protection clause of the constitution to achieve parity with male prisoners, to demand due process rights, and to challenge conditions.

While women make up a relatively small proportion (7 per cent) of the American prison population, the numbers more than doubled during the 1990s. The expansion results from the same factors which affected the expansion of the male prison population, namely changes in sentencing law and guidelines which constrained the powers of sentencers, the war on drugs, and the rise in both the public and the government's punitivism, as well as the increased involvement of women in crime. The majority of women, as in the UK, are serving time for non-violent offences and female prisoners are less likely to reoffend than male prisoners. The smaller number of offenders means fewer prisons and given the geographical size of the USA, women prisoners may be housed some way for home. Moreover, the majority of female prisoners are prime carers of young children (see Phillips and Harm 1998, Amnesty International 1999). So women prisoners have problems in maintaining contact with and access to their children. Prisoners are allowed to make reverse charge calls but this can still be very expensive for families and the costs of travelling to prisons in the USA may be substantial.

Women prisoners have also been described as the 'forgotten prisoners' in the sense that they have often had the worst facilities and conditions which in part reflected the fact that women were less likely to respond aggressively to their treatment and the majority of prison litigation has been pursued by men and focused on issues which concerned them. To defend the differential treatment of female prisoners, the prison administration must show objective justification but this may be not be difficult. For example, if there are fewer female prisoners, it may be easy to justify differences on grounds of expense and administrative efficiency. However, in US penal policy there is now more interest in and awareness of the need for gender-specific policies which recognize women's needs, but problems still remain.

There were some successful challenges on prison conditions, provision of educational and vocational programmes, and on issues such as privacy in the late 1970s and early 1980s (see Leonard 1983). The impact of the women's movement outside prison has raised the expectations of women prisoners and in some cases women have united with men to challenge their conditions of imprisonment and this has had an impact on change in women's prison conditions (Lown and Snow 1980). Some women prisoners have brought actions regarding discrimination in access to programmes in prison because of the differential access to facilities (Resnik 1982).

For example, women prisoners brought a class action in the federal court under 42 USC s 1983, in *Glover v Johnson* 478 F. Supp. 1075 (1979) which focused on the issue of parity for women prisoners and highlighted double standards in the treatment of women in the Michigan prison system in the 1970s. This case established that prison authorities must provide women with facilities substantially equivalent to men including a range of recreational and educational programme, even if they are dealing with smaller numbers of women and that disparities are unconstitutional. The case challenged disparate treatment as unconstitutional, as the prisoners argued that differences in the provision of facilities, including law libraries, violated the equal protection clause of the Fourteenth Amendment and also raised First Amendment issues, in relation to correspondence.

However, if prisoners succeed in bringing equality claims, prisons may respond by cutting back provision for both to accommodate the extra costs. Women's prisons still provide, in many cases, fewer recreational, educational or vocational programmes than men's prisons, some do not provide services specifically defined for women, and some focus on women's traditional roles thereby reinforcing their dependency on men. As in England and Wales, the profile of women prisoners is marked by high levels of social exclusion, poor health, housing, work issues and drug dependence, so access to good work, educational and therapeutic programmes is crucial.

The courts' treatment of discrimination claims brought by female offenders has been variable. In some cases the courts have been reluctant to intervene, but in others the courts have found breaches of the equal protection clause, for example in relation to access to work and education in *Women Prisoners in the District of Columbia Department of Corrections v District of Columbia* 877 F. Supp. 634 (DDC 1994). In this case the Court also ruled that the shackling of women in labour and the sexual abuse of women by officers breached the Eighth Amendment. While as we saw earlier, the failure to provide appropriate health care in women's prisons was ruled unconstitutional in *Todaro v Ward* 565 F. 2d 48 (2d Cir. 1977), there are still problems in accessing appropriate health care.

The drive for equal opportunities has been a double-edged sword in the USA. In the past women prisoners were mostly supervised by female officers but there were equal opportunity claims brought by men on this issue. Title VII of the Civil Rights Act has allowed male officers to work in female prisons and vice versa which has raised concerns over the potential for sexual assault and sexual exploitation of women prisoners by officers. While women's prisons have a much lower incidence of violence, especially sexual violence, than men's prisons and the issue of sexual abuse in women's prisons has received less attention, the problem has been documented by researchers, for example the work of Girshick and the Report by Amnesty International on this problem (Girshick 2003, Amnesty International 1999).

There has also been litigation on the issue of sexual abuse within prison. *Women prisoners in the District of Columbia Department of Corrections v District of Columbia* 877 F. Supp. 634 (DDC 1994) recognized sexual abuse of women prisoners as a violation of the Eight Amendment. One of the most notorious examples was a case in California, *Lucas v White* 63 F. Supp. 2d 1046 (N.D.Cal 1999), where officers were found to have given male prisoners sexual access to female prisoners for money. The case was settled out of court. Following this case, there have been stricter controls on abuse. However, there are still reported instances of women abused by male officers and a culture of sexual harassment.

Now male officers can work in women's prisons and female officers in male prisons, this has also raised the problem of privacy. The courts have recognized the right for privacy for women prisoners searched by male officers. Given that large numbers of women have experienced sexual and physical abuse before entering prison, living in close proximity to male officers and being searched by them may be particularly stressful. In *Jordan v Gardner* 986 F. 2d. 1521 (9th Cir. 1993) the Court of Appeals held that subjecting women to strip-searches by a male officer could amount to a cruel and unusual punishment given that the female prison population includes high numbers of abused women. However, in an earlier decision, *Grummet v Rushen* 779 F. 2d 491 (1985), the same court ruled that when male prisoners were strip-searched by female officers and observed by them using shower and toilet facilities, this did not breach their constitutional rights.

The Amnesty International Report was critical of the treatment of pregnant women, the poor medical help and the loss of contact with children. The majority of women who enter prison are parents and mostly parents of younger children. When women are incarcerated, the fact that they are in prison will be used against them in parental rights proceedings. Women have no right to stay with their children when they give birth in US prisons. There are very few mother-baby units which are found in very few states, namely, Ohio, California New York, Nebraska and Washington. So if a relative cannot care for the child, then the child will enter the care system.

Cases have also been brought in relation to the rights of gay and transgender prisoners. In *Johnson v Johnson* 5th Circ. Court of Appeals No. 03–10455 (2005) the Court of Appeal affirmed the right of a gay man to bring a case for discrimination on grounds of sexual orientation against prison officials. The treatment of transgender prisoners also been considered in the USA. One research study reported that 59 per cent of California's transgender prisoners said they had been sexually assaulted compared with 4 per cent of the general prison population (Sexton, Jenness and Sumner 2009). They are also marginalized in a number of areas and have also been described as the forgotten group of prisoners. In the case of *Giraldo v California Department of Corrections* Case No. A119046 (November 14, 2008) the offender, born male but now living as a woman and now on parole, sued the state prison authority and prison officers. Giraldo was placed in a cell with a male prisoner and repeatedly raped before being transferred into protective custody. The prison policy was to allocate prisoners to a men's or women's prison, depending on whether they had completed a sex change operation. The Court said that the inmate in custody was in a vulnerable position and his jailors had a duty to protect a prisoner in this situation from assault.

In *US v Georgia; Goodman v Georgia* 546 US 151 (2006) the Supreme Court ruled that the Americans with Disabilities Act 1990 protects disabled prisoners held in state prisons from discrimination by prison officials. Here a paraplegic prisoner had been held in a cell which was too small, so he was unable to move his wheelchair and he did not have access to disabled toilets, washing facilities or proper medical care.

Race is also crucial in understanding the impact of imprisonment in the USA. The emergence of a black urban underclass and its presence in penal custody in the USA has been well charted by Wacquant, Clear and others (Wacquant 2001, 2007, Clear 2007). But this has also particularly affected women from these communities who have been adversely affected by the war on drugs and harsher sentences, as women who act as drug couriers will receive heavy sentences and swell the prison population. Women committed for drugs-related crimes make up a large number of female offenders in prison.

The issue of race is clearly significant in understanding the composition of the prison population in the USA as African-American males have disproportionately high incarceration rates, relative to their numbers in the wider population. As Clear notes. 'Black men are seven times more likely to go to prison than are white men; black women are eight times more likely to go than are white women' (Clear 2007: 63).

African Americans and Latinos make up the majority of prisoners sentenced for drugs offences. The numbers have increased substantially in the past twenty years owing to changes in sentence length, increased punitiveness, the war on drugs and the Three Strikes laws. The disparity reflects to some extent the differential involvement in crimes which attract custodial sentences. Black males will also be disproportionately affected by Three Strikes laws because they are more likely to have prior criminal convictions. The war on drugs focused on inner city drug crime and crack cocaine use rather than on the use of powder cocaine, favoured by the middle class. These different drug enforcement policies for crack and powder cocaine reflected the devastating effects of crack cocaine on poor urban neighbourhoods, but it has meant that African Americans, both male and female, are more likely to end up in prison and to be serving longer sentences then white drugs offenders. However, the Fair Sentencing Act 2010 reforms sentencing for crack cocaine related offences and addresses this problem to some extent. It has been passed by Congress and the sentencing guidelines have been amended.

In wealthier middle-class communities there may be more resources for alternatives to imprisonment, such as therapeutic and detoxification programmes. While white and black males may be involved in crime during adolescence, white males have access to more legitimate opportunities for status in work and education. This over-representation of black males in prison has led to arguments for better drug treatment programmes outside prison and more support for deprived urban communities to combat these problems and for a review of the drug enforcement policies and the use of drug courts. It also has implications for the disenfranchisement of black voters which will be considered in Chapter 8.

A considerable body of research has been conducted assessing the significance of racism in leading to entry into prison, and examining police and prosecutorial decision-making, the use of guilty pleas and jury selection. There has also been considerable research on the question of whether the death penalty has been imposed by means of a procedure which allows room for racial bias, issues raised in the key cases of *Furman v Georgia* 405 US 238 (1972) and *Gregg v Georgia* 428 US 153 (1976) and discussed by Mauer and Tonry, but there has been less research on the differential treatment of ethnic groups within prison (Mauer 1999, Tonry 1995).

However, the landmark case of *Lee v Washington* 390 US 333 (1968) established the right of prisoners to be free from racial discrimination in prison. This case ruled that the segregation of black and white prisoners in Alabama's prisons was unconstitutional and violated the Fourteenth Amendment. It extended the prohibition on segregation from school to other public institutions and ruled that prisoners had standing to bring a class action. The question of racial disparity in relation to felon disenfranchisement has also been raised in several constitutional challenges as we shall see in Chapter 8.

Challenges have been brought in relation to religious discrimination in the USA. Many of the earlier religious rights cases were brought by black Muslims active in the civil rights movement in the 1960s and 1970s and these often succeeded. A key case in the recognition of prisoners' religious rights in 1960s was *Cooper v Pate* 378 US 546 (1964) where the Supreme Court upheld the right of black Muslim prisoners to challenge religious discrimination under s 1983 of the Civil Rights Act 1871. The outcome often depended on whether concessions entailed additional expenditure for prisons. For example, in *Walker v Blackwell*, 411 F. 2 d 23 (1969) the court ruled that the prison was not obliged to serve meals at special times for prisoners during Ramadan. The court stressed the need to take account of the needs of administering a large prison population. Since *Cooper v Pate* the courts have usually deferred to the need for good order and security in the prison.

Recent cases have focused on whether new religious sects, such as the Holy Mizanic faith, also have religious rights, as in the case of *Theriault v A Religious Office in the Structure of the Government requiring a Religious Test as a Qualification and the Religious Agents Thereof at Otisville, New York, and elsewhere* 895 F. 2 d. 104 (1990). In *Cruz v Beto* 405 US 319 (1972) the Federal District Court ruled that a Buddhist could not be denied the right to practise his religion. The courts will consider the implications for security, as well as financial and administrative burdens, whether the prison can show a legitimate state interest, and whether the measure bears a rational or reasonable relationship to that governmental interest. If the right to freedom of religious expression clashes with the equality right of homosexuals not to be subjected to discrimination, this may also create problems for institutions, issues discussed by the Supreme Court in the recent case relating to a university law school in *Christian Legal Society v Martinez* No. 08–1371 (28 June 2010) where the Court ruled that the equality right trumped the right to religious belief.

A new provision, the Religious Freedom Restoration Act 1990, stipulates that if states infringe on the person's ability to practise his religion, then the state must be in pursuit of a compelling governmental interest and use the least restrictive means to achieve that interest. However, issues such as prison security will very likely continue to be seen as a compelling state interest. There are also now more foreign national Muslim prisoners held in the USA for terrorist offences and as we saw earlier, the treatment of foreign national prisoners held under anti-terror provisions has been subjected to several constitutional challenges.

Conclusions

As we have seen, a number of equality issues are raised in the context of imprisonment. The prison population is not a homogeneous bloc, but a collection of groups, many of whom have special requirements and needs. However, meeting all these claims may be burdensome for prison regimes and there may be problems when the rights of different groups bring them into conflict with each other. While the grounds of discrimination, race, gender and religion, have received considerable attention, there has been less attention given to the issues of age, disability and sexual orientation, although the strategy is now to extend the progress made in these established areas to other areas of discrimination.

8 The prisoner as citizen

The right to vote

Introduction

This chapter considers the issue of prisoners' right to vote with reference to recent developments in law and policy in the UK and the United States. The implications of the judgment of the European Court of Human Rights in *Hirst v UK (No. 2)* Application No. 74025/01 (6 October 2005) will be considered. Attention will also be given to campaigns in the USA to restore the vote to serving and released prisoners.[1]

The denial of voting rights to prisoners in both jurisdictions has led to considerable criticism and it will be argued that voting rights should be restored to convicted prisoners on the grounds of both principle and policy. The UK Government's justification for the ban and the arguments in favour of disenfranchisement will be critically reviewed and the proposals for change in response to *Hirst* will be assessed. It will be argued that prisoner enfranchisement would have both individual and public benefits and that withholding the vote cannot be justified on any of the established justifications of punishment. Re-enfranchisement should be pursued on grounds of both principle and policy as the right to vote has both symbolic and practical importance. The right to vote might seem insignificant compared to the other rights lost or diminished on imprisonment. Loss of the right may be less damaging to the individual than, say, poor health care, or segregation. Nonetheless it is significant both symbolically, as a recognition of the prisoner's citizen status and practically, as part of the process of rehabilitation.

In the UK convicted prisoners, with few exceptions, are denied the right to vote in national or local elections while they are incarcerated. The provisions disenfranchising offenders are in s 3 of the Representation of the People Act 1969, as amended in 1983 and 2000, which states that 'A convicted prisoner during the time that he is detained in a penal institution in pursuance of his sentence … is legally incapable of voting in any parliamentary or local election'. Remand prisoners retain their right to vote while incarcerated. Sentenced prisoners imprisoned for contempt of court and for non-payment of fines are also allowed to vote under ss 3(2)(a) and 3(2)(c) respectively. Nonetheless this still means that a substantial number of prisoners are disenfranchised. It was estimated at the time of the *Hirst* judgment that about 48,000 prisoners were disenfranchised through the voting ban and as the prison population has now risen since then, the number may now be higher.

The European Court of Human Rights judgment in *Hirst v UK*

Hirst v UK successfully challenged the validity of the prohibition on voting for convicted prisoners in the European Court of Human Rights. The decision in *Hirst* was the culmination of a long debate in penal policy and raises fundamental questions including the nature of the social contract and the meaning and extent of citizenship. It also raises questions regarding the role of public opinion in sentencing, as a central element of the UK government's voting ban was that allowing the vote to prisoners would cause offence to the public.

Hirst had already completed the punitive part of his discretionary life sentence but was not allowed to vote during the remainder of his sentence, when he was being detained on the ground of public protection because of a perceived risk to the public, having pleaded guilty to manslaughter on the ground of diminished responsibility. Hirst initially failed in the Divisional Court in an application for a declaration of incompatibility in relation to the provision in s 3 of the Representation of the People Act 1983, but succeeded in Strasbourg. Hirst argued that the denial of his democratic right to vote violated Article 3 of Protocol No. 1 of the Convention, which imposes an obligation on states to hold free elections under conditions which will ensure the free expression of the people in the choice of the legislature, because the ban did not meet its purported aims and there was no link between disenfranchisement and the prevention of crime or respect for the rule of law. If it was a punishment, it was disproportionate as it did not relate to the seriousness of the offence and was arbitrary as its impact depended on the timing of an election during the period of incarceration. On the contrary, it undermined respect for the law by alienating prisoners and denied them a voice in the penal process or an opportunity to influence penal policy. The effective result of the ban was the 'elected choosing the electorate' (*Hirst v UK*, para 46). The ban was also inconsistent as prisoners had been allowed to vote while in intermittent custody.[2]

The European Court of Human Rights recognized that states who had adopted the Convention varied in their practice, some allowed all prisoners to vote, some allowed prisoners in certain categories to vote, while others did not permit it at all. But the Court held that the right should not be casually removed as this would undermine the democratic process. The UK's ban excluded thousands of people from voting and was disproportionate as it applied to large numbers of people regardless of the gravity of the offence. While accepting that states had a wide margin of appreciation to determine whether restrictions were justified or should be limited to particular offences, the Court ruled that a blanket voting ban on all convicted prisoners fell outside the margin of appreciation.

At the Government's request, the case was referred to the Grand Chamber who upheld the Chamber's decision. The majority decided that a blanket ban on convicted prisoners violated Article 3 of Protocol No. 1. Although Article 3 refers to 'the free expression of the people in the choice of the legislature', past Convention jurisprudence makes clear that it does include the right to vote, as well as the right to stand for election. While the Court acknowledged that the right to vote is a right and not a privilege, Article 3 of Protocol No. 1 is not absolute, there is room for implied limitations, and states must be given a margin of appreciation, a blanket restriction which applies regardless of the gravity of offence, or individual circumstances falls outside the margin of appreciation (para 82). Any restrictions imposed must be in support of a legitimate aim and the means used should be proportionate to the aim, and must maintain the integrity of the electoral procedure. So minimal age limits are permitted, for example, and if people engage in 'uncitizenlike conduct', such as gross abuse of a public office, this may result in a justifiable deprival of the right to stand for public office in future (para 65). But the Court said that there is certainly no place for an automatic disqualification and the fact that public opinion might be offended if the ban were rescinded was an insufficient ground to limit the right (para 70). The Court did accept that the Government's stated aims of the prisoner disqualification – to prevent crime, to sanction the conduct of prisoners, to enhance civic responsibility, to mete out an additional punishment, and to give an incentive to citizen-like conduct – were legitimate aims. But, they argued, the measures used by the UK were not rationally linked to that aim as they were automatic, and arbitrary in their effect. They applied to the prisoner even when he had completed the minimum punitive part of his sentence, which is intended to meet the aims of retribution and deterrence, and was being further detained on the grounds of public protection. So it was difficult to find a link to the aims of punishment during the latter part of the sentence. Moreover, whether the punishment took effect depended on the timing of elections which introduced an element of arbitrariness. The ban excluded a large number of prisoners and a wide range of offences. There was no evidence that Parliament ever sought to weigh competing arguments, or to assess the proportionality of the general ban, although a Working Party on Electoral Procedures which reported in 1999, had examined the issue in relation to remand prisoners. Hirst also argued that the ban breached Articles 10 and 14 but as the Grand Chamber decided the issue under Article 3 of Protocol No. 1, it did not consider that separate issues arose under Articles 10 and 14.

The Court noted that any restrictions should be prescribed by law, should not be a blanket ban, and should be restricted to major crimes (para 7). This now seems to be the most likely route to be taken by the UK. The Second Consultation Paper on this question suggested that the furthest the Labour government would go would be to allow prisoners serving less than four years to retain the vote (Ministry of Justice 2009e). The Strasbourg Court will look very closely at the rationale for infringements.

The response to *Hirst*

Because of the ruling in *Hirst v UK* the legislation will have to be amended and the Government has engaged in a lengthy public consultation process and a feasibility study of possible options has been undertaken before new legislation is enacted. When the Court delivered its judgment, the UK Government initially said it did not mean the UK's ban was wrong, but only that it had not made clear the legal basis of the restriction. The Strasbourg Court had been critical of the fact that the limit on voting had not been based on a reasoned consideration of the issues, but by the time of the 2010 election, five years had elapsed since the Grand Chamber's decision and two Consultation Papers had been published. The Government published its first Consultation Paper in December 2006 to elicit responses on matters of principle (DCA 2006). The Government accepted that retaining the existing law was not an option, but was strongly opposed to full re-enfranchisement of convicted prisoners. At best it seems likely that the vote will be restored to some categories of prisoners. A Second Consultation Paper was published in 2009 and the Government's response had not been published by the time of the 2010 election. The Government could have introduced an amendment to the Electoral Administration Act in 2006, but favoured deferring change pending further consultation. It could also have included the changes in the Constitutional Reform and Governance Act 2010 or could have issued a Remedial Order under s 10 of the Human Rights Act to amend the relevant legislation. This lengthy process has yet to result in any concrete proposals or Parliamentary bills. The Parliamentary Joint Committee on Human Rights expressed its concern over the delay and warned that it could render the election illegal if a chunk of the population is unlawfully disenfranchised. The Committee of Ministers of the Council Europe issued an interim resolution expressing its concern over the delay in December 2009 (M/ResDH 2009). In March 2010 it advised the UK to adopt measures to allow prisoners to vote in the May election, in part anticipating a rush of applications to the Court if it failed to do so. The Government has said that it is still considering responses and intends to use primary legislation to allow for a full parliamentary debate. At its meeting on 3 June 2010 the Committee of Ministers expressed its 'profound regret' that despite its repeated calls the election was held in May with the blanket restriction still in place and 'expressed confidence that the new United Kingdom government will adopt general measures to implement the judgment ahead of elections scheduled for 2011 in Scotland, Wales and Northern Ireland, and thereby also prevent further, repetitive applications to the European Court' (Decision No. 18: para 4). The issue will be considered in September and a draft interim resolution will be prepared if necessary.

The Government has framed possible changes within very limited para-meters, not least because it anticipated that the public mood will be hostile to re-enfranchisement. The leadership of the Conservative Party has also opposed giving the vote to prisoners. During the 2010 election a Labour candidate in Birmingham published a leaflet suggesting the Liberal Democrats would give murderers and paedophiles the vote, with a picture of a convicted paedophile on the leaflet. Although the leaflet had not been approved or supported by the Labour Party head office and was withdrawn after complaints, it highlights the assumption that the parties fear the public may be hostile to change. The Liberal Democrats responded by saying that they were critical of delays and did not favour restoring the vote to existing convicted prisoners, but favoured a discretionary system in which judges would decide when sentencing whether prisoners were allowed to vote, taking account of the length of sentence and type of crime and when the system is established, other prisoners would be able to submit an appeal for restoration.

The judgment in *Hirst* and the approach of the court was welcomed by prison reform groups and advocates of prison rights. It reaffirmed the pro-tection of the Convention while prisoners are incarcerated and demanded that prisoners be recognized as citizens and downgraded the role of public opinion in penal policy. The claim that removing the ban would be offensive to the majority of the public was given short shrift by the Court. As Judge Caflisch noted, even if this were to offend the public, 'decisions taken by the court are not made to please ... members of public but to uphold human rights prin-ciples' (para 4). The perception of the importance of public opinion, and the fear of alienating the public have contributed to the punitiveness of successive Governments, but the Court rightly concluded that these should be given a lower weighting where rights issues are concerned (para 71).

Cases were brought in Scotland and Northern Ireland challenging the legality of the May 2007 elections on the grounds of incompatibility with the European Convention and the Scottish National Party has also been campaigning on this issue. In *Smith v Scott* [2007] CSHI9 XA33/04 a con-victed prisoner denied registration brought a claim against the Electoral Registration Officer. The Scottish Court of Session said that the legislation in the Representation of the People Act cannot be read down as Convention compliant and that it intended to make a formal declaration of incompat-ibility. Lord Abernathy was critical of the length of time the Government has spent responding to *Hirst*. In *DB* [2007] CSOH 73, Lord Malcolm refused to free a prisoner who wanted to vote in the May Scottish parliamentary elec-tions. DB had been released on licence, so he would have been allowed to vote if he was in the community, but his licence was revoked. A challenge to stop those elections proceeding was rejected by the Court of Session in *Traynor and Fisher* [2007] CSOH 78. A similar case brought in Northern Ireland by prisoners who were unable to vote in the March Northern Ireland Assembly elections also failed in *Toner and Walsh* [2007] NIQB 18. Even if the envi-saged changes are introduced, it is possible that these applicants would still be denied the vote in future under the proposed changes, if they are serving longer sentences. In *R (Chester) v Secretary of State for Justice and another* [2009] WLR (D) 316 the Court indicated that it would not issue a further declaration of incompatibility and said that it was offensive to constitutional principles to put pressure the government to speed up the process given that it was already engaged in a process of preparing a bill for consideration by Parliament. A prisoner, Leon Punchard, has also filed an application to the Strasbourg Court for compensation for the failure to allow him to vote in the May 2010 general election, which could pave the way for numerous other claims.

Proposals for change

A number of options have been considered by the Government, as set out in its First Consultation Paper, which invited comments on the general principle of prisoner enfranchisement and possible avenues, including making a relaxation of the ban dependent on sentence length, giving discretion to sentencers, and removing the vote for those convicted of electoral offences. Partial bans based on the length of sentence and therefore on the gravity of the offence, are found in Belgium, but there the ban applies to those sentenced to over four months, in Austria it is for those serving over one year and Italy over five years. In Greece there is a permanent loss of the right to vote for those sentenced to life imprisonment while in Romania, the ban is dependent on the type and seriousness of offences. Although this is less arbitrary than a blanket ban, the problem remains of where to draw the threshold for disenfranchisement. Comments on this were invited by the second Consultation Paper (Ministry of Justice 2009e). A complex system of qualifications and disqualifications may also lead to problems in administering schemes which has happened in the United States.

Giving discretion to sentencers to impose a disqualification or to restore the vote, in the light of their knowledge of the crime, and its impact on victims, is also problematic. This has been used in Italy, for example, where the disqualification from voting is discretionary for these sentenced up to five years, but automatic for those sentenced to five years or more. But it is difficult to see what criteria might be used by the sentencer when reviewing the merits of individual cases, as most offences will not be voting-related. It raises issues unrelated to the original offending behaviour in most cases and increases the burdens on sentencers who are already hard pressed. It is difficult to see how they could justify taking a vote away from one offender, but not from another serving a similar term, for an offence of similar gravity. If would also add to the length of the trial. Divergent decisions between offenders convicted of offences of similar gravity would need to be justified, but it is hard to see how coherent non-arbitrary decisions could be made here, although presumably the Sentencing Council would be instructed to draft appropriate guidelines.

A further option being considered is whether offenders convicted of electoral offences should lose their right to vote. Here a ban might be justified and Convention compliant if there is a risk of future offending, and of damaging the democratic process and in the recent case of *Frodl v Austria* Application No. 20201/04 (8 April 2010) the Strasbourg Court indicated that there needs to be a connection between the offence committed and the deprivation of the vote for this sanction to be justified. This is found in some European states so Germany imposes a ban on voting rights for those who attack the integrity of the state and the democratic order, and for political insurgents. The Government also invited comments on whether voting rights should be given to all those detained in mental hospitals on the same basis as ordinary prisoners but these issues are now being addressed in a separate consultation process.[3]

Responses to the first Consultation Paper were mixed, although a greater number of respondents (47 per cent) favoured enfranchisement of all prisoners compared to 25 per cent who favoured continued disenfranchisement. There were also mixed views on where to draw the line if full enfranchisement is not pursued. Some respondents thought that if sentencers are involved in the decision this will keep the issue of prisoners' voting rights in public view, while others thought this would be an unnecessary burden on sentencers. There was also some support for retaining disenfranchisement for electoral offences. The Electoral Commission favoured prisoners convicted of electoral offences being banned from registering, voting or standing for election (Ministry of Justice 2009e: 18). Respondents also discussed practical ways of implementing change. The second Consultation Paper, published in 2009, made clear that the government is contemplating granting the vote only to selected prisoners, depending on sentence length so the ban will most likely continue for those serving longer sentences (Ministry of Justice 2009e). It invited comments on the appropriate threshold and the procedures for registration and voting, but also revisited some of the earlier questions. It asked for comments on the role of judicial discretion in determining a prisoner's right to vote and how it would work, whether individuals convicted of electoral fraud should be permitted to vote in any circumstances and whether voting rights should be granted to post-tariff prisoners or prisoners serving indeterminate sentences. Comments are sought on the practical issues relating to voting and problems which might arise for institutions. The government recognizes that relying on judicial discretion to restore the vote would increase burdens on the sentencing court and that ultimately this should be a matter for parliament rather than the courts. So linking to sentence length, in its view, would be both proportionate and administratively easier to implement.

Comments are invited on four different options: allowing prisoners to vote automatically if they have been sentenced to less than one year's imprisonment, less than two years, or less than four years, subject to certain exceptions based on the type of offence for which they have been convicted. The fourth option is to allow prisoners sentenced for less than two years to automatically retain the right to vote but prisoners who have received more than two years but less than four years, would have to apply for entitlement to vote, subject to a judge's permission in the specific case. It sees the loss of the vote as an 'additional element of punishment' (Ministry of Justice 2009e: 23), but one which highlights the nature of the offender's relationship with civil society. But it does now accept 'the re-instatement of the right marks his re-entry into society and is aimed at enhancing his sense of civic responsibility and respect for the rule of law' (ibid: 23).

The document makes clear that re-enfranchisement is not contemplated for prisoners serving more than four years in any circumstances, including prisoners serving life or indeterminate sentences, and including cases where prisoners are post-tariff but remain in prison because the Parole Board does not consider them safe enough to be released. The Labour Government's view was that it would not be appropriate to restore the vote while in prison because of both the seriousness of the offence and the dangerousness of the offender. It also does not plan to restore the vote to prisoners convicted for electoral offences regardless of sentence length, an issue which received more support in responses to the First Consultation Paper. However, in *Frodl v Austria* Application No. 20201/04 (8 April 2010) the Strasbourg Court stressed that a decision to deprive an offender of the vote should be made by a judge and where there is a connection between the offence and the sanction, so an automatic ban on longer-serving prisoners may well be rejected by the Court.

The estimated impact of the possible changes, based on the number of total sentenced prisoners in February 2009 of 63,600 is that a vote given to those serving under four years would affect approximately 28,800 prisoners, which is 45 per cent of the total, less than one year would be 11 per cent, and two years, 22 per cent of the total. Of the options being considered clearly the 4 year one is preferable as it would maximize the number of eligible prisoners and will most likely satisfy the European Court of Human Rights, although they may well be concerned about the exclusion of post-tariff prisoners, as this was precisely the issue which arose in *Hirst*. The alternative of allowing applications to the court for those serving between two and four years, is more problematic as it would add to the burdens on the courts and make sentencing more complex. Guidelines are envisaged, but it is not clear how they would be drafted to distinguish appropriately between different offenders and there are likely to be further arguments about their interpretation and application.

Registration options being considered are prisoners registering at their home address where they could be included in the application form of their original household, or through a declaration of local connection, or in the area where the prison is located although their prison address would not be included on the electoral roll. As they could not attend voting stations, voting would have to be by post or proxy but a postal vote is the safer route.

The proposed changes, which link voting rights to the seriousness of the offence, demonstrate some commitment to proportionality, and are clearly an improvement on the current law. But it is still difficult to justify the continued exclusion of large numbers of offenders on the established principles of punishment, including public protection, rehabilitation and desert. There seems to be little appetite for more radical change among any of the major parties. If it is accepted that voting can encourage a sense of civic responsibility, then it is hard to see why this should be denied those guilty of serious crimes as this is where the question of reintegration is most important and most challenging.

The practical suggestions for procedures are less contentious. Rolling registration is preferable to an annual deadline given prisoners' transient status and would make the system more workable. Using the prisoner's previous address or a making a declaration of local connection, instead of using the prison address for registration, would deal with the problem of bloc voting. In most cases prisoners' only connection with the area where the prison is located will be the fact of imprisonment. Clear procedures for registration and voting would avoid the problems in the USA where eligible voters do not register because of confusion over the rules. Manifestos could be circulated and the mechanics of voting is not difficult. There is an established procedure allowing remand prisoners to vote by post or proxy, set out in PSO 4650 which could be extended to sentenced prisoners. The Electoral Commission in its response to the Second Consultation Paper has set out simple procedures to deal with prisoners voting, using postal or proxy votes (Electoral Commission 2009).

These changes would need to be carefully presented to the public to overcome their hostility. It should be made clear that the change would not undermine prison order or the security of the public and that prison voting is permitted in other states such as the Republic of Ireland, without problems and that there may be long-term benefits.

Justifications of felon disenfranchisement

Successive UK governments have taken the view that those who commit offences can justifiably be disenfranchised, and that this is a reasonable restriction with a legitimate aim of discouraging crime and promoting civic responsibility. Underpinning this is the view that prisoners do not deserve the right to vote and that the ban is proportionate because it is imposed in pursuance of legitimate aims, to promote respect for the law and as a justifiable element of punishment. By committing crimes and breaching social rules, it is argued the prisoner loses the right to participate in how the country is governed for the duration of his sentence. The right to vote is not absolute, the UK Government has stressed, and there is a wide margin of appreciation to decide under what conditions the right should be exercised, and it has claimed that its denial fell clearly within the margin. Disqualification is intended to prevent crime, to punish offences, enhance civic responsibility and promote respect for the law. The Government claimed that the ban pursued these legitimate aims, and that the measure was proportionate to these aims (*Hirst v UK (No. 2)*: para 47). Prisoners who had breached the social contract by their criminal acts 'could be regarded as temporarily forfeiting the right to take part in the government of the country' (ibid: para 50). The measure is proportionate as there are appropriate exceptions and it affects only those convicted of sufficiently serious crimes which warrant an immediate custodial sentence. Moreover, all prisoners on their return to the community are able to exercise their right to vote. These arguments will be considered in more detail, although both are problematic.

The undeservingness of prisoners

The case for disenfranchisement reflects the view that prisoners are undeserving of rights because of their disrespect for the law. By breaching the social contract, it is argued, prisoners have forfeited their key citizenship rights. Citizenship may include the right to vote as an essential element but is not limited to this. The right to vote has thus been construed by governments here and the USA as a revocable privilege rather than a fundamental right, despite nearly a century of universal suffrage. The denial of the right to vote to prisoners is often justified on the ground that prisoners lack the moral standing or 'virtue' expected of citizens and therefore do not deserve that right while incarcerated. Prisoners forfeit the right to take part in the political process because of their misdeeds. This is backed up by the less eligibility principle which reinforces the gulf between the deserving and undeserving.

In its submission to the court in *Hirst*, the UK Government argued that those who had breached the basic rules of society should be deprived of the right to participate in the government of the country (ibid: para 50). The Labour Government has also subsequently made it clear that it thinks it is morally right in principle to deny prisoners the right to vote and that it believes that the majority of the public feel the same way (DCA 2006, paras 56, 57). Indeed it specifically invited comments in support of retention of the *status quo* (DCA 2006, para 58).

Although no formal or large-scale studies of public attitudes to re-enfranchisement have been undertaken in the UK, when *Hirst* was decided in October 2005, a poll conducted in Manchester by the *Manchester Evening News* found that 74 per cent were opposed to giving prisoners the right to vote and 26 per cent were in favour. But there is also some support for change here and the USA among prison reformers and civil libertarians and the general public. A review of the survey evidence on this issue in the United States found that 31 per cent of those interviewed favoured re-enfranchisement for serving prisoners (Manza, Brooks and Uggen 2004). A Harris Interactive Poll in 2002 of adult Americans found that 80 per cent of the respondents favoured voting rights for ex-offenders.

Historically, the voting ban represents the notion that prisoners are in a state of 'civil death'. The disqualification of prisoners is well established in English law and in feudal England, offenders were forced to surrender their property rights to the Crown and lost their family rights, as an additional punishment as well as serving their sentence. The view that that it is morally right and politically efficacious to disenfranchise convicted prisoners is also found earlier in the law of Ancient Greece and Rome (Drapkin 1989 and Sellin 1976).

Felon disenfranchisement today can be seen as the last vestige of the notion of 'civil death' in relation to prisoners. Forfeiture of assets as an additional penalty for crime or treason was not abolished until the 1870 Forfeiture Act, but that Act retained the disqualification from voting, which was perpetuated by subsequent Representation of the People Acts. Moreover, in the UK there has been a tendency in recent years for the number of civil disqualifications to increase, to extend, for example, to employment bans and driving bans for convicted felons. This expansion has been criticized by von Hirsch and Wasik, as ill-conceived and hard to justify, as civil disqualifications are potentially more damaging in their impact than formal penal sanctions (von Hirsch and Wasik 1997). In recent years the number has increased further with a raft of measures designed to deal with sex offenders living in the community and sex tourists.[4]

Linked to this notion of moral corruption of the prisoner is the belief that denying the offender the right to vote will 'preserve the purity of the ballot box' (*Washington v State* 75 Ala 582 (1884) at 585). Disenfranchisement protects the purity and integrity of the voting process. The argument that offenders will sully the purity of the ballot box by irresponsible or incompetent voting, or by electing those unfit to hold office, has also been a key influence in the jurisprudence on felon disenfranchisement in the United States, for example, in *Shepherd v Trevino*, 575 F. 2d. 1110 (5th Cir. 1978) and *Bailey v Baronian*, 120 R.I. 394, A.2d 1338 (1978). One fear is that felons will elect criminals to positions of power, leading to the corruption of public life, a point expressed by the Latvian government in its third party submission in *Hirst* (at para 55).

But the denial of the right to vote to those who lack 'moral virtue' was rejected by the Court in *Hirst* who emphasized that the right to vote was a right and not a privilege. While prisoners lost their right to liberty, their rights under the Convention were not lost by the mere fact of imprisonment. The Court thought that voting was an essential element of the democratic process which should not be casually removed and that there 'is no room in the Convention for the old idea of "civic death" that lies behind the ban on convicted prisoners' voting' (*Hirst v UK*: 33). Similarly, the Canadian Supreme Court in *Sauvé v Canada (No. 2)* [2002] 3 SCR 519, in considering a Charter challenge to a provision denying prisoners the right to vote, argued that seeing prisoners as morally unworthy to vote 'runs counter to our constitutional commitment to the worth and dignity of every citizen' which is essential to the legitimacy of the democratic process (McLachlin, CJ at para 35). A blanket ban denying the vote to federal prisoners serving over two years in s 51(e) of the Canada Elections Act 1985, which originated in a civil death statute, the 1791 Constitutional Act, was unconstitutional and a regressive and obsolete law which could not be justified in a modern democracy.

To deny the right to vote to the non-virtuous also misunderstands the meaning of rights. The UK Government's case is weak because rights do not rest on deservingness, but apply to all, even to those whom we might see as unworthy individuals. Fundamental civil and political rights, such as the right to vote, are universal and do not depend on the moral character of the right-holder. The defining feature of a right is that it should not be infringed simply because others might think that the person is morally unworthy and this concept of a right is fundamental to western liberal thought, exemplified by Dworkin's work (1977, 1986). It is the mark of a civilized society to accord due process rights at the pre-trial and trial stages, to everyone regardless of the crimes of which they are accused, and this respect for rights should also extend to the sentencing and punishment stages. Furthermore, as the right to vote arguably has a special status, it should command greater protection than other rights. To use moral worth as a precondition would be moving on to a potentially politically dangerous slippery slope.

The argument that prisoners do not deserve the benefits of citizenship because of their lack of moral worth is also problematic, as prisoners are expected to fulfil other civic obligations imposed by the state, such as paying taxes, while in prison. If a sentenced prisoner were able to earn sufficient to reach the tax threshold, then the prisoner would be liable to pay tax and national insurance contributions, or a prisoner who inherited property while in prison, could still face a tax demand. In the USA where the ban may extend after prison, ex-offenders may be serving in Iraq and Afghanistan. So if the government imposes the burden, arguably the prisoner should have some of the benefits of citizenship provided that the rights of others are not adversely affected, and in the case of voting, it will be argued no harm or risk to the public have yet been conclusively established sufficient to justify a blanket ban. Moreover, due process rights are not denied to prisoners because of their lack of virtue as we saw in Chapter 5, and it would therefore seem inconsistent to deny prisoners other crucial civic rights. If virtue were the criterion then arguably the vote should be denied to those engaging in anti-social behaviour or morally reprehensible behaviour which might mean the pool of eligible voters would be very narrow. It is clearly neither practicable nor desirable to deny voting rights to 'asocial' individuals. Even if it is a risk because of their flawed character, because it is a fundamental right, it is worth taking that risk and protecting this right, while considering ways in which the risk may be reduced.

Furthermore, as noted earlier, citizenship in Ancient Greece was seen as promoting virtue, in imposing duties and obligations on citizens and directing their attention away from private interests, and was not limited to the virtuous (see Chapter 1 above). Persons who were not fully virtuous could retain citizenship provided that they performed their public duties properly (Aristotle 1992). Participation in political life was itself seen as a means of *improving* moral behaviour as it ensured that citizens looked towards the good of the polis rather than their own narrow concerns. This argument that participation promotes a sense of civic responsibility is also found in Mill's work on representative government (Mill 1861). Similarly, one could argue that allowing voting rights will encourage prisoners to reflect on their obligations to other members of society.

Disenfranchisement as a legitimate and proportionate punishment

A further element of the defence of disenfranchisement found here and the USA is that it is a legitimate and proportionate punishment. Denying prisoners the right to vote, it is argued, has a legitimate aim, namely to punish offenders as well as enhancing civic responsibility and respect for the law. Loss of the right to vote is justifiable and reasonable, as it is intended to discourage crime, and is an appropriate element of punishment. In *Hirst* the UK Government argued that this restriction on voting is not excessive given that prisoners do have the right to vote restored when they return to the community, in contrast to some states in the USA where felons are disenfranchised for life. It emphasized the fact that many other states, including Russia and America, withdraw voting rights from prisoners and pointed to the wide variations in state practice within Europe and around the world. Several Eastern European States, including Romania, Bulgaria and Hungary, imposed a blanket ban. In the USA felon disenfranchisement is well established and in some states, applied to a wide range of offences, including relatively minor offences, and to probationers and parolees as well as serving prisoners. This has a substantial impact on the number of prisoners disenfranchised with a disparate impact on African Americans. However, in Western Europe, South Africa and many democratic states around the world a ban is not imposed.

It is difficult to defend prisoner disenfranchisement on retributivist or utilitarian grounds, whether deterrence or public protection and risk-management. In *Hirst* the Court accepted that the government's aims to encourage civic responsibility and to impose punishments were legitimate and compatible with Article 3 of Protocol 1, but concluded that the ban was not rationally linked to those aims and was therefore disproportionate and arbitrary. The Court was influenced by the Canadian Supreme Court's ruling in *Sauvé v Canada (No.2)* [2002] 3 S.C.R. 519 that felon disenfranchisement was unconstitutional because it was an arbitrary and additional punishment and conflicted with s 3 of the Charter. The Canadian Court thought that the measure was hard to justify on retributivist grounds because it was not linked directly to the blameworthiness of, or harm caused by the offender (para 51). It was too broad and also had a negative impact on the Aboriginal community, who were disproportionately represented in prison (para 60).

As a retributivist measure, felon disenfranchisement is not clearly linked with desert, to the degree of harm caused, the seriousness of the offence, or the culpability of the offender, but applies to all offenders and offences. It is a blanket restriction, which is why the majority of the Strasbourg Court in *Hirst* also found it unacceptable. The provisions in the 1983 Act strip the right from prisoners indiscriminately regardless of the seriousness or type of offence. It does not satisfy the retributivist demand for ordinal proportionality, as it is not linked to the gravity of the offence committed as it applies to most prisoners, with few exceptions, or to the type of offence. It is not, for example, limited to those convicted of electoral crimes. Even if defended as an expression of moral censure, there is sufficient censure in the punishment of the original offence without additional sanctions. Felon disenfranchisement is also an arbitrary and variable punishment, since its impact will depend on the timing of an election, which itself depends on the vagaries and contingencies of political life which are outside the prisoner's control and unrelated to the original offence. One could also argue that it is a particularly degrading punishment in so far as it reduces the prisoner to a state of social or civil death. Even if were accepted as a legitimate punishment, then this could not justify the UK ban, as in Hirst's own case, the ban lasted for the duration of the sentence but he was serving a discretionary life sentence, and had already served the part of the sentence intended to punish, and was now serving the extended part of the sentence deemed necessary to protect the public. So the ban went beyond what was necessary for retributive purposes. It certainly could not justify the situation where felons are disenfranchised on their return to the community as found in some states of the USA.

Justifying the ban on the utilitarian grounds of deterrence, rehabilitation and public protection is also difficult. It is hard to imagine that a prospective offender would be deterred from criminal behaviour by the prospect of losing voting rights compared to the threat of incarceration itself. Prospective offenders may well be unaware of the provision in the UK Act, although the issue has now received more publicity because of *Hirst* and subsequent cases. But even if there were greater awareness of the loss of voting rights, the deterrent effect of losing the right to vote while incarcerated may be marginal compared to the many other disadvantages of incarceration. A justification on the ground of rehabilitation is also problematic. By excluding the offender from participation in the political process, the ban further weakens social bonds which may have implications for reoffending and rehabilitation. The UK Government has argued that denial of voting rights enhances civic responsibility but disenfranchisement perpetuates isolation and social exclusion. Conversely, restoring the vote and participation in the political process would assist in rehabilitation by reminding prisoners of the obligations and duties of citizenship and encourage a sense of responsibility. This was also the view of the Canadian Supreme Court in *Sauvé v Canada* who found no evidence the voting ban would rehabilitate or deter, or that it enhanced respect for the law or democracy. Instead the Court stressed the connection between having a voice in the making of law and the obligation to obey the law. The Canadian Supreme Court thought the stated aim of the disenfranchising statute, of promoting civic responsibility, was vague and there was no rational connection between the denial of the right to vote and that objective. Instead of promoting civic responsibility, it undermined respect for the law and democracy, given that the law's legitimacy is ultimately derived from the right of every citizen to vote. It went against the principles of inclusiveness, equality and citizen participation which are essential to a democracy.

It is also difficult to justify prisoner disenfranchisement on public protection grounds. If an offender has been convicted of voting offences, there might be concerns of future interference with the electoral process, but the ban is much more general and applies to all offenders. To justify the loss of the vote would need an extra element of risk, and of a substantial risk to override such a fundamental right, which would seem to be lacking in most cases. A voting ban for offenders convicted of voting offences, particularly where there is a risk of reoffending and committing further voting offences, would be justifiable, but this would apply to relatively few sentenced prisoners. The concern over the purity of the ballot box is a key element of the felon disenfranchisement in the United States but this has not been supported by evidence that former felons are more likely to commit electoral offences, or that probationers or parolees have a greater propensity for voting offences.

But imposing a civil disqualification on the majority of sentenced prisoners is harder to justify. The distinction between civil disqualifications and penal sanctions in UK penal practice has not been clear-cut or well-thought-out, which means we may end up with measures which are difficult to justify according to both the traditional justifications of punishment or the alternative grounds of risk. The use of civil disqualifications has been used increasingly in recent years to avoid Convention challenges. As von Hirsch and Wasik argue civil disqualifications generally are ill-suited as penal sanctions; as they are not linked to censure, or to the gravity of the offence, their impact is variable, for example the impact of a driving ban will depend on where the offender lives and the availability of public transport, and they may run the risk of increasing recidivism by making normal life more difficult for offenders (von Hirsch and Wasik 1997). Instead, they argue, the appropriate justification for civil disqualifications should be risk-based rather than punitive, so they should be used only in cases where, for example, an occupation is sensitive to abuse and the defendant's criminal conduct indicates that there is a risk of potential harm to those who are vulnerable. If there is a perceived risk, then there should be a proper risk assessment with safeguards to challenge a ban on the ground that the risk requirement had not been met in that case. But fundamental rights such as the right to liberty should not be subject to civil disqualifications even if there is a risk. Applying these criteria, they argue, would reduce the numbers of civil disqualifications considerably, although any risk-based model is still open to criticism because of the problems of over-prediction and denial of the actor's human agency.

Most of the existing civil disqualifications including driving bans and bans on working with children for sex offenders are risk-based and linked to specific risk of future harm to others, but it is difficult to see what future harms will accrue from prisoners voting given that in the vast majority of cases the offenders' previous offending behaviour is unrelated to electoral offences. There is no obvious vulnerable group at risk of harm from the act of voting. The only area where risk might be construed is in relation to those convicted of voting offences. The Strasbourg court has accepted that removal of the right to vote is justified by the offender's behaviour, for example on the grounds of abuse of a political position and misconduct in a public office, for example, in *Glimmerveen and Hagenbeek v the Netherlands*, Application Nos. 8348/78, 8406/78 (11 October 1979). In *MDU v Italy* Application No. 584500/ 00 (23 January 2003), a ban of two years on voting and holding public office was upheld. In *Hirst v UK*, the Court said a ban would be justified, in cases of gross abuse of a public position where the individual undermined the rule of law and the democratic foundations of society.

But if there are concerns over the potential future risk of electoral fraud by allowing prisoners to vote by postal vote, this could be managed by proper supervision of the voting process which would be easier in prison where access to opportunities for electoral crime is reduced because of the constant checks on identity and officers could ensure that declarations of identity are properly and honestly completed and these procedures are already used for remand prisoners. However, this is not to deny that voting fraud has been a concern in recent UK elections, for example, in the Birmingham local elections in 2004, where Mr Justice Mawrey said that the evidence of fraud would have 'disgraced a banana republic' (Mawrey 2005, Stewart 2006). There were also concerns of electoral fraud in the May 2007 local elections, including Nottingham and Slough. A former Conservative councillor in Slough, Eshaq Khan and five others were convicted of electoral fraud offences relating to bogus postal votes or 'ghost voters' in the May 2007 elections in Slough Central Ward.[5] Police investigations have been conducted following concerns over postal fraud in Bow and other areas of London in the 2010 general election. But it is much easier to check on a prisoner's identity than checking on an unknown postal voter in the community.

There are also new measures to deal with voting fraud and to increase confidence in the integrity of the electoral system, in the new Electoral Administration Act 2006, based on the recommendations of the Electoral Commission (2003). This Act strengthens registration procedures by requiring more information for postal votes, including dates of birth and records of signatures. It creates a new offence of providing false information for the purposes of registration when applying for a postal or proxy vote. These measures reduce the risk of personation, that is, assuming someone else's identity when voting, although postal voting is still seen as the major risk to electoral integrity in UK elections in a recent report by the Council of Europe Parliamentary Assembly (Council of Europe Parliamentary Assembly 2007).

There may also be concerns about bloc voting which might possibly affect the outcome of an election. An example often given is of the Isle of Wight constituency where the Isle of Wight prison, created by the amalgamation of three substantial prisons, Parkhurst, Albany and Camp Hill, with an operational capacity of 1,658, is sited within the constituency in which the successful candidate won by a majority of 2,826 in the 2001 election, so with a narrower majority the result might have been skewed by the prison vote. Although in the 2005 election the successful candidate won by a larger majority, this might be a potential problem, particularly if the candidate had a particular interest in prison conditions or is a former prisoner. Behan and O'Donnell give an example from the Republic of Ireland, where there was a very close result in Limerick West in 2002 and one of the candidates was a former prisoner who lost by only 19 votes (Behan and O'Donnell 2008). But in many constituencies the margins may be greater so the numbers of prisoners voting may be less of a problem. However, any concerns regarding bloc voting could be met by using the prisoner's former home address for registration which will diffuse the impact of the prison vote and this is the procedure favoured by the UK government (Ministry of Justice, 2009e). But concerns regarding electoral fraud are not the main rationale of the government's denial of the vote to prisoners.

In the recent case *Frodl v Austria* Application No. 20201/04 (8 April 2010) the Strasbourg Court found a breach of Article 3 of Protocol No. 1 when a prisoner serving a life sentence for murder was deprived of the vote. The Court accepted that the domestic law which applied to prisoners serving more than one year and convicted of crimes with intent, was in pursuit of at legitimate aim and was not a blanket provision of the kind considered in *Hirst*. However, it ruled that the decision should have been taken by a judge and there should be a connection between the offence committed and specific issues relating to elections: 'it is an essential element that the decision on disenfranchisement should be taken by a judge, taking into account the particular circumstances, and that there must be a link between the offence committed and issues relating to elections and democratic institutions' (ibid: para 34).

In the absence of either penal or risk-based grounds, this leaves one further potential 'justification', namely to reduce offenders to second-class citizens. But this is short-sighted as there are sound policy reasons for allowing the right to vote, namely that it encourages commitment to civil society, a sense of responsibility, and promotes social inclusion. The UK Government argued that prisoners have violated the social contract, but serving a sentence is a reparative compensatory measure, which cancels out or annuls their crime, and is the price of re-entry into society. The social contract may be threatened, but is not negated by, the prisoners' anti-social acts and in accepting and undergoing punishment, prisoners affirm their commitment to the social contract of which voting is the most tangible manifestation.

The case for re-enfranchisement

The loss of the right to vote is difficult to justify on penological principles, unless we are dealing specifically with electoral fraud. The disenfranchisement of prisoners increases their social exclusion and marginalization, denying them the opportunity to put pressure on their MP. But re-enfranchisement would arguably have the opposite effect, strengthening their citizen status, giving them a voice and would also affirm the democratic values of equality and inclusion. Moreover, it would also further their rehabilitation by promoting the reintegration of offenders, and thereby enhance the protection of the public. It is reasonable to assume that voting rights would have an indirect positive effect on crime rates, as they encourage participation in public life, increase a sense of being a stakeholder in society and may encourage law-abiding behaviour. So enfranchisement may promote social inclusion and benefit society.

There have been no large-scale research studies of the link between voting and offending, but using available statistical data, from a longitudinal study of a cohort of Minnesota public school students, Uggen and Manza found that there were 'consistent differences between voters and non-voters in rates of subsequent arrest, incarceration and self-reported criminal behaviour' (Uggen and Manza 2004: 213). Clearly they are not arguing that voting is the key factor in law-abiding behaviour, but this association is worth investigating, and would be consistent with the argument advanced above that participation in political life can promote a sense of citizenship.

There have been vigorous campaigns to restore the vote to serving prisoners in the UK and to former felons in the United States. Restoration of the vote has been supported by a wide range of groups and political perspectives. In the UK support for change has also come from prison reform groups including the Prison Reform Trust and UNLOCK, the National Association for Ex-Offenders. Some Conservative backbenchers and the former Conservative minister Douglas Hurd and the Scottish National Party would support re-enfranchisement while the leadership has been strongly opposed to it. In the 2005 election the Liberal Democrats had supported allowing convicted prisoners to vote and this was fiercely opposed by the Conservatives. However, as we saw earlier, by the time of the 2010 election they were much more cautious.

The Chief Inspector of Prisons and some prison governors are also in favour of re-enfranchisement of sentenced prisoners. In the United State interest groups supporting voting rights for all released felons, include the National Association for the Advancement of Colored People (NAACP) and the American Civil Liberties Union, the National Black Police Association, the American Probation and Parole Association, the American Bar Association and the Association of Paroling Authorities. The consensus seems to be that voting is essential for participation in the civitas and promotes reintegration of ex-offenders into the community and denying the vote has the opposite effect.

The act of voting is a reaffirmation of citizenship. It is an important element of social participation which reinforces awareness of one's civic duties and obligations. Restoring the vote affirms that individuals are entitled to equal concern and respect, regardless of their past deeds, that they have worth despite their criminal history. Even if the public do not always fully value their own voting rights, insofar as they often will not turn out to vote, this does not detract from the symbolic importance of suffrage.

In the past, citizenship rights, including the right to vote, have been secured through struggle as weak groups have fought to improve their conditions. In England in the nineteenth century, as E. P. Thompson in his seminal work, *The Making of the English Working Class* has shown, the demand for suffrage was a crucial element of the realignment of classes in the 1830s (Thompson 1968). There was intense agitation in 1831–32 over the Reform Bill which symbolized the prospect of social change. Thompson depicts the crisis of 1831–32, through which English society was passing, as one in which revolution was possible. The constitutional and political crisis reflected the sharp social and economic inequalities of the time and class conflicts crystallized around the Reform Bill. The Bill's rejection by the House of Lords in October 1831 stimulated widespread demonstrations and unrest. If it had not ultimately been enacted, there could have been a revolution. Reflecting on the public mood of the 1830s, Thompson says:

> The vote, for the workers of this and the next decade, was a symbol whose importance it is difficult for us to appreciate, our eyes dimmed by more than a century of the smog of 'two-party parliamentary politics'. It implied, first, *egalité*: equality of citizenship, personal dignity, worth'.
>
> (Thompson 1968: 910)

Even then the vote was limited by property qualifications and restricted to men. In the 1832 Act, only one in seven males was eligible to vote. Since then the extension of the franchise has been a result of continued political struggles. The franchise was extended further in 1884, but still only 60 per cent of male voters were eligible. Eventually, the 1918 Representation of the People Act abolished property qualifications and allowed all men over 21 and women over 30 to vote. The denial of the vote to soldiers returning from the war, who had been fighting to defend English democracy, but were excluded from its benefits, was clearly an embarrassment for the government. Women over 21 finally got the vote in 1928 after their own protracted struggle.

The fact that the demand for universal suffrage has led to imprisonment, deaths, and hunger strikes, with women being force-fed, attests to both its symbolic and practical significance, notwithstanding the apathy and complacency of many modern voters, who have elected voluntary disenfranchisement, forfeiting their right to participate in the process of government. The vote is not something to be surrendered lightly, even if there is dissatisfaction with the choice of candidates in a particular election. Voting rights may be prized by some prisoners even if the turnout is low. However, in the Republic of Ireland where the vote was restored in 2006 and the first opportunity to exercise the vote was in the 2007 election, turnout was not low and

71.4 per cent of registered prisoners voted which was higher than the percentage of the registered national population who voted (Behan and O'Donnell 2008: 328). However, as Behan and O'Donnell point out, not all eligible prisoners were registered, and registration levels vary between prisons. Prisoners serving shorter sentences did not register. There was also a requirement that if prisoners were released before election day, they would have to vote at a police station which for many prisoners may not be an attractive prospect. Not surprisingly registration of prisoners was higher in prisons holding those serving longer sentences.

Of course, in other circumstances, refraining from voting may be a political protest reflecting on the lack of integrity of the electoral process, as in the case of the Belarus elections in 2000 and the second round of the Zimbabwean elections in 2008, reflecting the awareness that the democratic process had been violated and the reluctance to legitimize a corrupt and repressive regime.

Enfranchisement has a real value as it would give prisoners some influence in the political process. MPs may be more likely to take notice of their views, especially if the seat is a marginal one. So it may strengthen prisoners' position in terms of influencing policies which may affect them while in prison, and when they return to the community. If prisoners are without a vote, without a citizen status, they are effectively non-persons, which legitimates the view the prisoners should be forgotten and marginalizes them in the minds of governments and the public. Even if some prisoners may be indifferent to their voting rights, this does not undermine the importance of giving prisoners a voice in public debates and affording them some representation. If this led to improvements in penal regimes, this would benefit all prisoners, albeit indirectly, including the increasing numbers of foreign national prisoners held in the UK, who would not be entitled to vote.

For the offender, voting is, in some respects, even more important than for the ordinary citizen, because it is reminds them of their duties under the social contract. But denial of voting rights, as the Court stressed in *Sauvé*, undermines civic respect and respect for the rule of law and therefore erodes the process of prisoner rehabilitation, which should be concerned with promoting an understanding of the obligations and burdens of citizenship.

Restoring the right to vote can be seen as a key element of rehabilitation in giving people another chance to build a better life. Reintegration into normal society depends on range of issues including work, and housing but also involvement in community and voting. Civic reintegration is arguably a key step towards citizenship away from law breaking (Visher and Travis 2003). The right to vote would not solve all the problems of social exclusion or guarantee substantive rights, any more than giving women the vote ensured their equal treatment, but it is a positive step. Social inclusion may be seen as an important element of citizenship as Marshall has emphasized (Marshall 1950).

The voting ban also raises potential disparate impact issues, given the disproportionate numbers of black and ethnic minority prisoners in the UK.

In the United States, black and Latino males are disproportionately incarcerated relative to their numbers in the population which means that large numbers of African Americans are excluded from the democratic process (see Wacquant 2001). Similarly in Australia, a voting ban has a disparate impact on aboriginal communities as the Court acknowledged in *Roach v Electoral Commissioner* [2007] HCA 43.

Prisoner disenfranchisement in the United States

In the United States today the majority of states (48) ban sentenced prisoners from voting, and some states disenfranchise ex-offenders as well. Constitutional challenges to this disenfranchisement have so far failed, and, given the exceptionally high incarceration rate of the United States, this means that large numbers of citizens are disenfranchised. In the USA 5.3 million people are now disenfranchised because of criminal convictions, four million of whom are living in the community, and as members of the community they may of course be contributing to the community through taxes and work, or serving in the armed forces in war zones. Yet in other parts of world, there is a move towards enfranchisement and in some countries prisoners are allowed to vote while inside prison and the argument is over *which groups* of prisoners should be denied the right to vote, rather than disenfranchisement per se. Nearly half of those in the world who are disenfranchised because of criminal convictions live in the USA (Manza and Uggen 2006).

Thirteen per cent of African-American males have lost their votes which is seven times the national average.[6] It is estimated that one in seven African Americans cannot vote because of a felony conviction. The disparate impact is particularly high in Virginia as African Americans make up about 20 per cent of the population of Virginia, but over half of the disenfranchised population, and Virginia has one of the strictest felon disenfranchisement regimes. As Mauer and King observe 'there are now nine times as many African Americans in prison or jail as on the day of the *Brown* decision' (Mauer and Scott King 2004). They point out that on the basis of the current rates, one in three black males born now is likely to receive a custodial sentence. The possible reasons for this relatively high incarceration rate of African Americans were discussed in Chapter 7. There is also a disparate impact in terms of class and wealth, as in several states there are requirements to meet all outstanding court fines, fees and restitution, before being allowed restoration of voting rights, requirements which have been described by Wood and Trivedi and the ACLU as a modern day poll tax which arbitrarily links voting to income (Wood and Trivedi 2007). This means that the restoration of the vote may depend on the individual's means which gives an unfair advantage to white-collar criminals and means disenfranchisement is effectively determined on class grounds. A challenge by the ACLU to strike down the fee provision in the Alabama felon disenfranchisement laws in part on this ground that it discriminates on grounds of wealth and there is no compelling governmental interest in retaining a voting restoration system based on wealth, failed in *Baker v Chapman* No. 03-CV-2008-900749.00 (2008) although this campaign is ongoing.

From disqualification to restoration

There is a wide variation in state voting provisions for offenders, from automatic disqualification, which may be permanent, to automatic restoration on release and states where the restoration is dependent on judicial discretion and the governor's approval and decided on an individual basis.[7] Only two states, Maine and Vermont, allow prisoners, parolees and probationers to vote from prison. Thirteen states allow parolees and probationers but not prisoners to vote. Rhode Island allowed probationers and parolees to vote in 2007, so prisoners can now vote there on release, as well as in Massachusetts and New Hampshire. Twenty states have restored the vote to those who have completed sentences, but each state has different processes and limits on eligibility. Eight states have reinstated probationers' voting rights. In some states restoration depends upon the seriousness of the offence. Some of the schemes are very complex, and there has been considerable litigation, for example, on whether the term of imprisonment can include time on parole for the purposes of the rules.

Florida's law, for examples, divides applications for restoration of felon voting rights into three classes, based on the seriousness of the crime. Those convicted of non-serious offences do not need to apply for restoration of voting rights but must re-register as voters. Violent criminals who are not murderers or rapists must apply to the Clemency Board, who may then either restore those rights or investigate on a case-by-case basis. Most violent criminals are subject to investigation and have to attend a hearing of the Clemency Board before their rights are reinstated. In Alabama serving prisoners can vote from prison if they are convicted of lesser offences. Kentucky and Virginia impose permanent disenfranchisement unless the vote is restored by the Governor's clemency. In Virginia offenders convicted of voting fraud, violence or a drug trafficking offence are excluded. Non-violent offenders can apply for restoration if they have not reoffended for three years after their release, violent offenders and drug offenders have to be free of reoffending for five years. If applications succeed, then the right to sit on a jury and hold public office will also be restored. Applicants in Virginia must also demonstrate civic responsibility through community service. In Georgia those convicted of crimes involving 'moral turpitude' lose their right while in prison, as do those in Alabama, although clearly this may raise problems of interpretation.

Recently the Governor of Virginia, Robert F. McDonnell, proposed that ex-offenders should, in addition to existing requirements for restoration of the vote, be required to write a letter describing what they have contributed to society since their release and set out why they believe their vote should be restored. The proposal met with intense criticism as it was seen as asking felons to write an essay and made the outcome arbitrary, if the result rested on literacy skills. It was also compared unfavourably to the literacy tests outlawed by the Voting Rights Act especially in view of the fact that the rules disparately impact on African Americans.[8]

To make the voting process more complicated, some states changed their rules in the period leading up to the 2008 election. In the 2008 legislative year there were 75 bills relating to felon disenfranchisement in 22 states, some of which were progressive while others were regressive and made the process of registration harder (ACLU 2008). Very few of the bills promoting enfranchisement succeeded as politicians are wary of being associated with measures they think they will be unpopular with the public. Florida restored the vote to over 100,000 offenders convicted of non-violent offences in 2007, but less than three-quarters of felon voters registered to vote despite the changes. Some letters were sent to the wrong address, because of poor records and prisoners' high geographical mobility. There was also a large backlog of voters who might be eligible but first who had to be reviewed and needed a certificate to vote but there were not enough staff to deal with them. Florida, Maryland and Rhode Island broadened the range of felons who can vote in 2007 and voters in RI voted for automatic restoration on release in 2006.

Constitutional challenges to felon disenfranchisement have been raised since the 1950s in the USA under the equal protection and due process clauses of the Fourteenth Amendment, and under the Fifteenth Amendment, which prohibits abridgement of the right to vote on race and other grounds, and using s 2 of the Voting Rights Act 1965 (see Handelsman 2005). This Act has been used to strike down some voting restrictions which have a racially disparate impact, but attempts to use it to challenge felon disenfranchisement laws have repeatedly failed, as for example in *Richardson v Ramirez* 418 US 24 (1974). The applicant has to show discriminatory intent which is a formidable obstacle as the Court made clear in *Hunter v Underwood* 471 US 222 (1985). However, a challenge in Washington State succeeded in 2010 in *Farrakhan v Gregoire* No. 06-35669 (5th January 2010), which was the first case to acknowledge that felon disenfranchisement laws have a disparate impact on black Americans. In this case the Ninth Circuit Court of Appeals held that racial bias in the criminal justice system is a relevant social and historical factor which the courts may consider in determining whether disenfranchisement laws discriminate on account of race. The court decided that the law in Washington State denying the vote to those with felony convictions was racially discriminatory and violated section 2 of the Voting Rights Act. The Court found that African Americans, Native Americans and Latinos are more likely than white citizens to be searched, arrested, prosecuted and detained. As disproportionate numbers of these groups are incarcerated relative to their numbers in the wider population, this means that the felon disqualification rules have a disparate impact on them and are tainted by racial bias at earlier stages of the criminal process.

The Court struck down the felon disqualification scheme but an appeal against this decision is expected.

Campaigns to assist offenders in applying for restoration have been conducted by the Brennan Center for Justice based at New York University, the Sentencing Project and the ACLU. During the 2008 election the Sentencing Project and local activists briefed also the Obama campaign in key states such as Virginia and Florida. Prisoner advocacy groups, including, All of Us or None in San Francisco, have campaigned to restore voting rights in California. A group in Colorado did succeed in persuading the Denver county jail system to register felons on release. A voter outreach campaign was also conducted in Florida. A campaign drive was also launched within prisons in Alabama, but halted by the governor because of concerns about electoral fraud.

The ACLU takes the view that felon disenfranchisement undermines the integrity of the election system if large numbers are excluded and that it discourages individuals from civic responsibility. Its campaign for voting rights has been an important part of its Racial Justice Programme. It also prepared a Felon Enfranchisement Law Kit for campaigners and activists with practical information and advice and a 'Breaking Barriers to the Ballot Box' toolkit. Civil rights lawyers have also been assisting at a practical level providing prisoners and ex-offenders with information on voting rights and registration.

Voting rights in practice

The wide variation in rules and procedures between states has caused problems and limited the registration of voters. Where there is a range of qualifying or disqualifying offences, this has led to criticisms of arbitrariness in interpreting which felonies qualify for inclusion and raised the question of whether officials are interpreting the law correctly unlawfully broadening the list in practice. Prisoners may be unsure whether they are eligible, for example, if they have committed only a minor crime or misdemeanour. Some prisoners may think they are permanently disenfranchised and not realize that they may vote again if they are given incorrect advice on eligibility. If they are unsure, they will not register if they think they will be committing a crime, and of course they will be acting illegally if they wrongly register.

Given these complex and confusing rules and procedures, there is a lack of awareness by felons that they may be able to vote. In states which do not restore the vote automatically, ex-offenders have to go through a lengthy application process. Registering to vote may be low on a released offender's list of priorities on release, there may also be issues such as a revealing a current address to an electoral official or details of past crimes, which may be a sensitive matter. Some felons prefer not to register because they do not want to fill in more forms. Others may be embarrassed to admit that they are felons. With different rules in different states, it is difficult for an outside observer to get to grips with this system, so it must be very difficult for an offender with language or literacy problems to register. Moreover, offenders are often geographically mobile, so it may difficult for election officials to contact them. There may also be the requirement to pay court-imposed fines before restoration which in effect disenfranchises the poor.

Electoral officials may themselves be uncertain of the precise rules for registration for former offenders and may misinform felons on their eligibility or wrongly ask for documentation, or single out black voters to ask if they have a felony offence. It is a difficult area as, if they register someone who is not eligible, they are unwittingly participating in voting fraud. Of course, it may be the case that even if ex-offenders are correctly advised on their eligibility, they prefer not to vote, as with any other member of the electorate, but the issue here is whether they have that right not whether they choose to exercise it.

There have been cases, for example, in Florida where eligible voters have been wrongly excluded and this may be significant when the result is close. There have also been cases where individuals have been prosecuted and in some cases imprisoned for voting illegally. For example, Kimberley Prude, a felon on state supervision for a forgery offence, was given a custodial sentence in Wisconsin for voter fraud in 2007. Actions were also brought against former felons in several states in 2009, where the voters mistakenly thought they were allowed to vote.

The ACLU and the Brennan Center conducted a series of interviews with election officials between 2003 and 2008 across 23 states and found misunderstandings by officals of the relevant law. The results are discussed in the report *De Facto Disenfranchisement* where the authors report a lack of understanding of the rules or the registration procedures for those with felony convictions (Wood and Bloom 2008). They also found problems of communicating with election officials. The ACLU found that officials were actually using the wrong forms, the forms were often misleading and with incomplete explanations of eligibility, applicants were referred to other statutes of which they were unlikely to be aware, and were given misleading information on how voting rights are restored, the effects of which is that applicants will be nervous about ticking boxes (ACLU 2008). In some states, there was no guidance on registering for voters with criminal records.

Given the confusion on the part of officials, this has meant a de facto disenfranchisement of people who would otherwise be eligible. If individuals are (wrongly) told they are not allowed to vote, they are unlikely to try again and may even tell others in the community so this could have a wider deterrent effect, discouraging others from voting. In fact states with strong felon disenfranchisement laws do have a lower voter turnout than states with less restrictive laws (McLeod *et al.* 2003). The outcome of the confusion and misunderstanding is that both eligible and ineligible ex-felons may register, so clearly a more comprehensible form and simpler procedures are needed. The ACLU Report makes a number of recommendations to this effect and also offers guidelines for amending the forms, which could be extended to all states. The Report also advocates expanding the categories available to vote which would be beneficial for the democratic process but also increase public safety as it argues, those who vote are less likely to be re-arrested. There would also be practical public protection benefits in having up-to-date addresses and information, making it easier to trace people and harder for ex-offenders to go underground.

The Right to Vote Project is a campaign led by the Brennan Center for Justice at New York University to restore voting rights to those with criminal convictions. As well as providing information, the Project has also initiated litigation challenging disenfranchisement, drafted relevant legislation and conducted public education and outreach initiatives to encourage ex-offenders to register and campaigned for appropriate training and education of state officials. The Center favours automatic restoration of voting rights on release from prison without any requirements to pay fees or fines first. While ex-offenders could still be liable for such debts, they would not be prevented from voting. It recommends that offenders should be informed before conviction and sentence of the loss of voting rights and then told on release that they are now eligible. The Department of Corrections should take responsibility for helping with voter registrations and ensure that all officers follow the same procedures. Offenders' names should be marked as inactive on a database when they go to prison and then marked as active on release and this information should be shared between criminal justice agencies.

The Brennan Center has campaigned for new legislation to restore the vote on leaving prison, highlighting the advantages of such change and was involved in the Democracy Restoration Act. This was a federal bill introduced in 2009 in the House of Representatives. If the bill is passed it would restore voting rights to offenders to vote in federal elections on their release from prison. The House Committee on the Judiciary held a hearing on the Act in March 2010. The Center also filed amicus briefs in the recent landmark case of *Farrakhan v Gregoire* and has supported legal actions to compel registration in Alabama. In Washington State in 2009 a Voting Rights Restoration Act was passed which removed requirements that all fees, fines and restitution as well as surcharges and interest be passed before becoming eligible to vote. The Center has also filed briefs challenging similar fee requirements in Tennessee and Arizona.

The Brennan Centre recommends automatic post-incarceration restoration of voting rights in all the states which still take the vote from those who are back in the community, so they would become eligible automatically and able to register like any other person, without any additional procedures or forms, and without any requirement to pay fees, fines or other financial demands (Wood 2009). Better sharing of information should make it possible to reactivate voting on return to the community. The chief election official in each state should be responsible for ensuring that the public and other government agencies are aware of the new law and its implications. Automatic restoration would have practical advantages in addressing the above problems and make administration easier for officials as well as offenders.

Of course there are political implications if the state is seen to be making great efforts to include prisoners, as politicians may fear this will not be popular with the public although there is some evidence that the public is becoming more favourable to change. Yet the public may well support such moves despite politicans' fears of political unpopularity. Manza, Brooks and Uggen found that over 60 per cent of the respondents in their survey supported allowing those on probation or parole to vote (Manza, Brooks and Uggen 2004). Sixty per cent of respondents in a poll in 2006 by the National Council on Crime and Delinquency believed that voting is a key element in the offender's reintegration into society. While most of the American campaigns focus on post-incarceration restoration, which is clearly the most urgent change required, arguably change should be further extended to restore the vote to convicted felons inside prison but politically this may be harder to achieve at the present time.

While campaigners see felon enfranchisement as a civil rights matter, it also raises political questions. If the results of the elections are close and highly contested as in Florida in 2004, the presence or absence of a segment of the electorate may be crucial. The registering of ex-felons to vote was a significant feature of the 2008 American election as civil rights activists and campaigners sought to assist ex-offenders with registration. There was a perception that the disenfranchised felons were the right demographic group, namely black and low income, who were most likely to be potential supporters of the Obama campaign, although it was politically contentious to become actively involved, and a party presenting itself as the party for felons may run the risk of alienating other voters. It was estimated that about 70 per cent of ex-offenders were likely to be Democrat voters, because of their social profile especially in an election where many black voters voted for first time because they felt there was now a candidate who reflected their interests. The Obama campaign aimed to mobilize black voters who had not bothered to vote in the past which proved to be a very successful strategy and ex-felons were part of this group, so it included them as part of a general drive to register voters. Within the Republican campaign, the personal view of McCain was that ex-felons who committed serious crimes should lose the right to vote and for other crimes the right to vote should be restored on a case-by-case basis as happens in Virginia. His political view was that it should be a matter for states to decide. But in some states, efforts to restore felon votes received support from both parties. Virginia was certainly seen as a key state for Obama and prisoners in Virginia made up a large chunk of unregistered voters. Republicans there were critical of efforts to register felons in time for the election as this was seen as directly helping the Obama campaign. Since taking office the Obama Administration has said that it supports full restoration of voting rights for ex-offenders.[9]

Conclusions

Although radical change has yet to be implemented in the USA or the UK, there are some favourable developments which may improve the prospects for change. It is clear from both *Hirst* and *Sauvé* that international rights standards are a much stronger influence on penal conditions than in the past and may trump the principle of less eligibility on this issue. The right to vote is also protected by Article 25 of the International Covenant on Civil and Political Rights which states that 'All citizens have the right to vote and to be elected'. Amending the law would also satisfy European Prison Rule 24:11 which stipulates that 'Prison authorities shall ensure that prisoners are able to participate in elections, referenda and in other aspects of public life, in so far as their right to do so is not restricted by national law.' The UN Human Rights Committee has also said that disenfranchisement post-imprisonment in the USA violates the International Covenant on Civil and Political Rights (Wood 2009: 6).

While there are variations in state practice, it is also true to say that the general trend worldwide and within Europe, has been towards re-enfranchisement. Most European countries now allow some, if not all, prisoners to vote. It is likely that the *Hirst* judgement may also impact on other European countries and pave the way for the re-enfranchisement of prisoners across Europe. For example, there have been recent changes in the Irish Republic. Prisoners did have the right to vote under the 1992 Electoral Act. They could be registered in their home communities but had no right to be given a postal vote or attend a voting station, although they could vote if they happened to be in the community, either on parole or temporary release during an election. So in practice most were unable to vote. The new Electoral (Amendment) Act 2006, introduced by the Irish Government to ensure Convention compliance following *Hirst*, modernizes the law and gives prisoners a right to vote by post. Given the much smaller size of the prison population re-enfranchising prisoners was a less significant political issue for the government.

In South Africa, prisoners have been allowed to vote since 1999, following the Constitutional Court's decision in *August and another v Electoral Commission and others* (1999) (3) SA 1 (CC), without impairing the integrity of the ballot box, and suffrage was viewed by the Court as crucially important in showing that everyone counts. In Australia in *Roach v Electoral Commissioner* (2007) HCA 43, the High Court quashed provisions introduced in 2006 disenfranchising all convicted prisoners. The Court found that the wording of the Australian Constitution prevented Parliament from introducing a blanket ban on the ground that there was no rational connection between the disqualification and conduct incompatible with participation in the electoral process. However, it upheld the pre-2006 law which restricted disenfranchisement to those serving more than three years. Other states closer to home which allow voting include Spain and also the Netherlands, where prisoners have had the right to vote since 1986. In Israel the Supreme Court refused to deny voting rights to the person convicted of assassinating the Prime Minister Yitzhak Rabin.[10] In Kenya in June 2010 prisoners were given the right to vote in a referendum on the new constitution which may pave the way for a further expansion of voting rights in elections.

As in the UK, the debate in other jurisdictions has centred on whether prisoners being allowed to vote would have adverse effects, or whether the enfranchisement actually promotes social cohesion and inclusion, and reinforces the core values of democracy. It is clear that the European Court of Human Rights sees rights extending beyond the prison door, and that any restrictions need to be properly justified but, in the case of a voting ban it is difficult to justify restrictions. Moreover, compared to some of the other rights we have considered in previous chapters, this is a 'safe' right to grant as it should not involve substantial costs or undermine good order or disrupt daily life in the prison.

9 Conclusion

Making room for prisoners' rights

Introduction

The recognition of prisoners' rights, including social, political and civil rights, is a crucial step in redefining prisoners as citizens. Citizenship and the social contract itself is affirmed by the serving of punishment which acknowledges the harm to the social fabric resulting from the crime and seeks to redress that harm. Recognizing prisoners as citizens, for example, by allowing them to vote, as we saw earlier, may also have implications for reoffending as correlations have been found, for example, between voting and reduced recidivism (see Uggen and Manza 2004). By focusing on prisoners as citizens we recognize them as moral agents capable of reflection and reform.

The offender remains a citizen, that is, a member of society possessing rights to participate in the political processes of a democratic state, and the rights to have basic needs met while incarcerated. So citizenship means the right to vote, the right to work, the right to welfare support, the right to rehabilitation, the right to be treated with respect, and the right not to be subject to discrimination. So prisoners' rights should encompass a right to a minimum standard of living within prison, including rights to work, education and training, a right to rehabilitation, a right to a reasonable standard of medical care, the right to vote, right to association, and a right to maximum autonomy compatible with the rights and freedoms of others and with the fact of imprisonment. Degrading and stigmatizing punishments should be prohibited. Essentially, citizenship means the social inclusion of the prisoner both while incarcerated, and on his return to the community, through resettlement and rehabilitation programmes. If rights are infringed, then this infringement must be objectively justified and should be limited no more than is necessary to safeguard the security of others, including staff, other prisoners and the public. On modern concepts of prisoners' rights, rights inhibit the use of prison to impose a further means of inflicting punishment beyond the loss of liberty. So rights may be the most effective means of change within the prison system. In addition, imprisonment may generate rights specific to imprisonment, for example, the right to be informed of the reasons for transfer or segregation and due process rights in the context of prison disciplinary hearings. So rights should trump weak or speculative policy considerations (Dworkin 1977). If these rights are infringed they should not be for arbitrary reasons or weak policy grounds, but must be linked to clear aims and the least restrictive means should be used.

The approach to rights advocated here is one which goes beyond civil and political rights to encompass social rights. There is evidence of a shift towards the recognition of social rights in some recent judicial decisions relating to imprisonment and the wider context (Burca and de Witte 2005, O'Cinneide 2005 and Fredman 2008). As O'Cinneide has argued, there has been a move towards some recognition of socio-economic rights in the domestic courts in recent years with the recognition of a common law right to freedom from destitution, for example in the case of asylum seekers challenging the denial of welfare. He also points to evidence of a growing recognition that human rights enshrined in the Convention are meaningless without a minimal standard of living.

Within the context of imprisonment, the acceptance of social rights would focus attention on prison conditions but also include special rights for prisoners such as the right to rehabilitation. Rotman argues that prisoners should have the right to rehabilitation, to services and activities which enable them to address problems, which might lead them to reoffend, although any involvement in rehabilitative programmes should be non-coercive (Rotman 1990). In return for future compliance, the state gives the offender the opportunity to avoid reoffending. Such programmes open up the possibility of reintegration into society. The state has a positive duty to provide offenders with an environment which facilitates their rehabilitation. So while the earlier debates on punishment in the 1960s and 1970s focused on the conflict between due process rights and treatment, because of the coerciveness of treatment programmes, modern conceptions of rehabilitation see rights as compatible with and integral to the process of rehabilitation. Moreover, if rehabilitation were elevated to a right, this would protect it from infringement to satisfy a punitive public or from financial pressures. Prison reformers have emphasized the positive duties of the state to provide a range of services, medical, educational and rehabilitative. So in considering the treatment of prisoners, this will mean providing appropriate medical or other care to protect the individual from inhuman or degrading treatment. Prisoners' rights provide a counter to the principle of less eligibility which has been an essential element of imprisonment in the UK and elsewhere, and to the subsumption of the prisoner into the apparatus of risk management.

The paradox of the prisoner is that inside the modern prison or panopticon he or she is subjected to high levels of surveillance and observation, but outside achieves a high level of invisibility. Prisoners are isolated, cut off from society, physically and socially excluded and marginalized, and on the fringes of the polity to the extent that politicians perceive concessions to prisoners as politically damaging. So rights are crucial in giving prisoners a voice and rescuing the prisoner from social death and a key right to bring them back into the public domain is the right to vote. If prisoners were involved in the political process, they could raise issues of concern over treatment in prisons with their MPs and as voters rather than mere constituents, they would have a stronger voice.

Prisoners' rights offer more than the fruits of new managerialism, for example, Key Performance Targets and Indicators, in protecting prisoners. Managerialism offers at best a form of paternalism, but one circumscribed by cost-effectiveness, without any recognition of the prisoner as a person, or citizen. The problem now is finding room for nurturing respect for prisoners' rights within the new cultural climate of late modernity, with its emphasis on crime control, risk management and cost-effectiveness.

Rights also provide a counterweight to populist punitiveness, so rights are better able to withstand surges of public hostility than less stringent measures. Rights are valuable, because prisoners are a low-status group in terms of their claims on society, and economically weak. The prison population may well include some of the most reviled members of the community, including sex offenders and those committed for crimes against children and for terrorist offences, who may be most at risk of harm from other prisoners. Similarly, in modern conflicts, the respectful treatment of prisoners is essential for legitimacy, and international rights standards are seen as key guarantees of good treatment. Moreover, the essential feature of rights is precisely that they are available to all, even those who through their actions may appear to be less deserving than others. They should also not be limited on the ground that public opinion might be offended which has also been emphasized in recent decisions in the European Court of Human Rights, such as *Hirst v UK (No. 2)* Application No. 74025/01 (6 October, 2005).

However, as we have seen, the recognition of prisoners' rights is largely dependent on the political climate, and progress can be impeded in a punitive political climate. The enactment of the Prison Litigation Reform Act in the USA testifies to the fear that too much latitude had been given to prisoners and that retrenchment was needed. But there are some indications of a greater willingness by the courts to recognize social rights. The political importance of promoting social inclusion in order to reduce crime is now well established. It is also possible that in Europe there may be a move towards European constitutional protection of prisoners' rights. The revival of social rights, combined with a focus on social exclusion, may mean that prisoners' rights claims are more likely to succeed.

It is true that prisoners' rights have expanded in the last 10 years and some decisions of the courts would have been surprising or unlikely 10 or 15 years ago. Prisoners' demands for rights were a catalyst in the development of judicial review in the 1980s and a prisoners' rights movement emerged in both the UK and the USA, although this litigation was mainly confined to issues of procedural fairness, access to the courts and to lawyers, within the limits of what could be achieved by judicial review at that time.

It is now clear that the view of the prisoner as citizen is well established in Strasbourg jurisprudence. We have also seen an interlocking of the different sources of prison law through the European Convention, the CPT and the European Prison Rules. The CPT has influenced Convention jurisprudence which is significant as in the past the Strasbourg Court sometimes lagged behind the CPT in its view of acceptable treatment and awareness of the psychological impact of imprisonment. The Convention jurisprudence has in turn become more embedded in domestic law.

In a line of cases stretching back to the 1970s it is clear that prisoners retain their rights under the Convention while in custody, including their right of access to the courts, their right not to be subjected to inhuman and degrading treatment, and more recently their right to vote. The Strasbourg Court is also less receptive to government's appeals to public opinion or the impact on budgets in defending breaches. In addition, we have seen the evolution of procedural justice in relation to parole decisions and disciplinary hearings, using and expanding the scope of Articles 5 and 6. Indeed, more areas of prison life are coming under the scrutiny of the courts in Strasbourg and in the domestic courts, who are more willing to scrutinize the exercise of discretion on the part of the Secretary of State. So the Convention compliance of prison conditions and procedures is regularly reviewed in the domestic courts.

More constraints have been imposed on prison officers' discretion and there has been a move away from discretion towards rights bringing the prisoner closer to a full citizen. In the United States constitutional challenges have continued and it is hoped that with the changes in the composition of the Court, that this progress will continue despite attempts to limit prisoners' claims.

In the UK despite attacks on the rights culture, it seems the Human Rights Act will survive recent political changes. However, the pursuit of rights does raise the question of whether the demand for rights in the context of prison reform essentially legitimates the prison system rather than challenges it and undermines abolitionist and reductionist campaigns which have been waged by activists and penal theorists since the late 1960s (Mathieson 2000, Ruggiero 2010).

The question might be raised of whether it is better to pursue an abolitionist approach than to seek to improve or reform prisons through a focus on rights and whether the pursuit of reformist measures undermines the case for abolition. However, the sharp distinction between reform and abolition may be problematic. In the current political crime the abolitionist approach is unlikely to obtain public or political support, although we may well see a reductionist approach, because of the costs implications of the pressures on the prison population. Moreover, even if the courts uphold prisoners' rights within prison, they have limited powers in restraining the expansion of prisons as they operate within sentencing parameters. It is not practicable to abandon reform in the quixotic hope of an abolitionist programme, especially in the current punitive political climate. However, there may be more options now than in the 1970s when the abolitionist movement was at its height. There are now alternatives such as mediation, restorative justice and a wide range of community sentences and programmes available to deal with less serious offenders. But prison may still be necessary for some offenders. The issue should not be construed as reform versus abolition, but rather pursuing measures which are empowering rather than disempowering and which assist rehabilitation and inclusion and promote civic responsibility. Some also question how much impact rights can have on a coercive rigid organization like the prison system. Of course the increased respect for prisoners' rights may increase the legitimacy of the prison system and strengthen its role. Rights themselves may become the territory in which radical and conservative claims are fought out. The emphasis on rights has been criticized by the Right for tipping the balance in favour of the offender which, if construed as a zero-sum relationship, undermines the victim and the public interest, and by the Left for ignoring the social context of offending and the way in which prison serves the interests of capital in asserting work discipline, as well as providing cheap labour and potential profit for private companies.

Similar questions have been raised over the role of feminists working in the area of prison reform as it is questionable how far radical theories of women's empowerment can flourish within what is essentially a coercive environment, and whether feminists working within such an environment legitimize them. But focusing on what happens inside prison can make a substantial difference to individuals' lives and have wider ramifications. The origins of prisoners' rights in the USA lay in the civil rights movement and that connexion is still significant and should guide modern approaches to prisoners' rights.

Given that prison abolition is not likely, it is important to focus on conditions within prison. Most advocates of reductionism would accept that there should be secure confinement for serious or dangerous offenders. Some individuals may not be deterred or reformed, but will need to be incarcerated to protect society. Others may benefit from opportunities offered in prison to develop skills and change attitudes and the removal of the offender from the community may offer a way of doing this in a way which cannot be achieved within community programmes. Recognition of the damage caused by imprisonment, especially to vulnerable individuals, is important, but a rights culture provides one way of addressing and limiting this damage.

Nor does this focus on rights in prison preclude investments in 'community justice', in building up deprived or lawless communities. But even in societies with well-established and advanced systems of social welfare and social justice such as Sweden, prison may still serve an important role in dealing with more serious offenders. Prison reform and a rights-based strategy can humanize the prison even if its basic structure or purpose is unchallenged. In the USA, as we have seen, the prisoners' rights movement there in the 1970s did achieve some crucial victories and in Europe the jurisprudence of the Strasbourg Court has advanced the treatment of prisoners.

The recent report of the Commission on English Prisons Today has stressed the need for investment in local communities to reduce crime, to change what is happening outside prison as well as within. It advocates a reduction in prison numbers and a closure of some prisons, as well as greater use of community responses and local partnerships involving representatives from the criminal justice, health and education sectors (Commission on English Prisons Today 2009).

When the Human Rights Act was passed, prison reformers were optimistic that there would be a sea change in the way in which prisoners were treated and that a new culture of rights would become embedded in prison practices. This raises the question of whether the drive towards a rights-based approach has been squeezed out by prison expansion and populist punitiveness, and whether the increased respect for rights has itself increased hostility towards prisoners.

Progressive developments

Strasbourg jurisprudence on the treatment of prisoners has increasingly focused on the individualization of prisoners, when considering issues such as allocation and transfer. Risks should be assessed on an individual basis. It has been very critical of 'blanket' policies applied to whole groups of prisoners and this criticism is influencing the domestic courts' approach as well. Secondly, the Court is more willing to criticise arrangements in state penal systems and to raise its expectations of appropriate treatment compared to its reluctance to do so in earlier cases, on issues such as isolation and segregation, and the treatment of prisoners who are ill or infirm. With the removal of the barrier of the European Commission more cases have been heard and the Court was generally seen as less conservative than the Commission. The Strasbourg Court has firmly challenged the notion that prisoners should be reduced to a state of civil death as inappropriate in modern society. The court will look carefully at the state's case for a particular policy or regime to see if breaches are justifiable and the principle of proportionality is applied robustly. The Court is less willing to see issues concerning the treatment of prisoners as falling within the margin of appreciation, especially where key substantive rights are concerned. Moreover, in recent years the scope of rights claims has broadened considerably with advances in relation to the issues of voting rights and artificial insemination, following the cases of *Hirst v UK (No. 2)* Application No. 74025/01 (6 October 2005) and *Dickson v UK* Application No. 44362/04 (4 December 2007). It is likely that many prisoners serving shorter sentences will have their voting rights restored and access to AI may be easier. There have been improvements in procedures following deaths in custody, and the cases of *Edwards v UK* (2002) 35 EHRR 19 and *Keenan v UK* (2001) 33 EHRR 38 and the recognition of the rights of prisoners' relatives and visitors on prison visits following *Wainwright v UK* (2007) 44 EHRR 40. Prison procedures have also been amended in anticipation of litigation and out-of-court settlements have been reached to avoid protracted litigation in some cases.

Furthermore, in recent cases such as *Hirst* and *Dickson*, the Court has been critical of governments appeals to what will offend the public, or the public's opinion on likely developments in penal policy, as a key criterion in deciding on concessions to prisoners and access to their rights under the Convention. Public opinion is one factor governments may consider among others but it should not be determinative of the issue. The courts have also been more reluctant to accept lack of resources as an adequate justification for rights infringement. In *Gusev v Russia* Application No. 67542/01 (15 May 2008), for example, where a detainee was held in very poor physical conditions where prisoners did not even have their own sleeping places, the Court found a breach of Article 3 and said that 'Irrespective of the reasons for the overcrowding, the Court reiterates that it is incumbent on the respondent Government to organise its penitentiary system in such a way as to ensure respect for the dignity of detainees, regardless of financial or logistical difficulties' (para 58). The court will look carefully at the state's case for a particular policy or regime, but if there are no cost implications or safety issues, then the court is unlikely to see a breach of Convention rights as justifiable.

The impact of this has filtered down to day-to-day prison life, as the Prison Service Orders and Instructions been revised to ensure Convention compliance. So we can see a number of positive trends and developments, the effect of which is a restraint on the full expression of the principle of less eligibility. However, we can also find counter-developments both in the domestic courts and outside the courtroom in the wider political context which, in some respects, is becoming more hostile to the development of prisoners' rights.

The attack on human rights

As we have seen, moves towards stronger rights protection have been resisted by states because of the resource implications and the fear of the floodgates of litigation opening. While there have been many positive developments in the growth of prisoners' rights, these advances are overlaid by increasing hostility to human rights jurisprudence and specifically to the Human Rights Act. At the same time the expansion of prison numbers has continued unabated and anxieties over crime have not been reduced by falls in the crime rate. Cuts in public spending may also impede advances as resources for the prison regime will be affected. We have identified a number of areas where improvements are needed, but prison expansion, lack of resources and the impact of public opinion may slow progress. Moreover, because prisoners themselves are much more aware of their rights, and more likely to frame claims in rights terms, this has provided more opportunities for the press to criticize more frivolous cases, such as Nilsen's demand for access to pornography in prison (see Chapter 6). The popular press has also reported critically on cases such as the prisoners who have received settlements for the failure to give them methadone, or a convicted drug trafficker's application for artificial insemination for his girlfriend.

There is still considerable lack of sympathy among the public for offenders and there are some indications that public attitudes are more hostile now than twenty years ago. The view that prisoners are undeserving of rights discussed in Chapters 1 and 8 seems to persist in the academy, among students, and in the general public, many of whom seem unsympathetic to the notion that prisoners should have rights beyond the most basic subsistence level. It may be that media reporting on high-profile cases of atrocious crimes and the concessions given to prisoners have contributed to the lack of public support for prisoners' rights. So the claims of governments that the public are opposed to enhanced rights such as the right to vote for prisoners may bear some relation to the truth. But public attitudes are complex as the public may also be sceptical whether prison works in the rehabilitation of prisoners rather than as a training ground for offenders, but still may be reluctant to consider alternatives and it has been found that when the public conduct mock sentencing exercises they often give a less severe sentence than sentencers (Roberts and Hough 2002, Piper and Easton 2006/07, Hutton 2005).

However, a Norwegian study of attitudes towards prisoners of students, prison officers and prisoners, using the Attitude towards Prisoners scale of Melvin *et al.* (1985), found that students had negative attitudes towards prisoners similar to those of prison officers and business students were more negative than student nurses (Kjelsberg *et al.* 2007). The students interviewed also thought sentences were too short. A correlation was found between negative attitudes towards prisoners and punitiveness and pessimism about their rehabilitation. This research study found that older prison officers had more positive attitudes to prisoners than their younger colleagues. Perhaps not surprisingly the respondents with the most positive attitude towards prisoners were the prisoners themselves. The only comparable British study of attitude to prisoners was undertaken in 2000 and this found attitudes which were more negative than in the Norwegian study (Murphy and Brown 2000). Reports of prisoners receiving funding for Open University courses may also alienate students and their parents struggling to meet their fees, but while prisoners may apply to the prison for support with fees, funding may also be supplied from the prisoner's own private funds, contributions from relatives, charities or from third parties (PSO 4201 9.1).

While significant changes to the UK prison system were made in response to the Woolf Report, we have seen in recent years, increasingly a focus on penal austerity rather than penal improvements. In the early 1990s, it was not so difficult for the public to accept the need for improved physical conditions and to abolish slopping out and to reduce overcrowding. But they seem less receptive to benefits such as the provision of televisions and methadone for inmates, even though TVs are linked to good behaviour and the supply of methadone may be necessary to prevent Article 3 challenges.

There is also the concern that with the expansion of the Council of Europe to include states with limited resources for upgrading prison regimes that the drive towards increasing prison standards will be slowed down. Notwithstanding the Strasbourg Court's comments on cost, it is clear that some states such as Belarus do not have the resources to upgrade their prison regimes in the short term and the political and cultural context and public attitudes towards prisoners may also inhibit change. Even in more affluent economies such as the UK, the current economic climate and public spending cuts, may make it harder for states to justify spending on prisons and particularly on issues such as education. As we saw earlier there were insufficient Offending Behaviour Courses before the recession, so it may be difficult to provide more now to deal with the IPP prisoners who are waiting. While short tariff IPP prisoners may be given priority, this may mean those serving longer sentences may be obliged to wait longer for access to these courses.

Furthermore, the last few years have seen a backlash against the Human Rights Act and rights culture in general so there is a danger that prisoners 'rights will be caught up in this. The Act has been portrayed or caricatured by the media and some politicians as a charter for crooks, career criminals and terrorists and some have questioned whether a strong commitment to human rights can survive (Gearty 2006). The view that we should exchange the Human Rights Act for a British Bill of Rights has been expressed by politicians from all parties. The former Justice Secretary Jack Straw argued for a new British Charter of Rights and Responsibilities. The Coalition Government has said that it may establish a Commission to investigate the creation of a British Bill of Rights, although if it includes Convention rights supplemented by additional rights as has been indicated, it is unclear what it would achieve.

Moreover senior judges in the domestic courts have become more critical of the Strasbourg Court's jurisprudence and whether it is appropriate to the UK adversarial system. Some members of the judiciary, have argued that the Strasbourg Court has gone too far in applying approaches inappropriate to an adversarial system and have questioned its authority. In *R v Horncastle and another R v Marquis and another, R v Carter* [2009] EWCA Crim 964, for example, the Court of Appeal said the court is not bound by the judgments of the Strasbourg Court as a matter of precedent and while this was a case on hearsay and criminal procedure, it illustrates the current mood. We also find a gap between Strasbourg and the domestic courts in the willingness to find breaches of Article 3 as we saw earlier, in the cases of *Broom v Secretary of State for the Home Department* (2002) EWHC 2401 and *R (on the application of BP) v Secretary of State for the Home Department* (2003) EWHC 1963 (Admin).

Although what is emerging from Strasbourg jurisprudence is positive, there is of course lots of scope within the Convention rights' qualifications for justification of infringements in terms of security and good order. The courts will always try to balance prisoners' rights claims with institutional needs for efficiency and cost-cutting and this is built into the Convention as well. Any scope for discretion may mean the courts will give weight to the needs of the prison regime. Even if a breach is proved, financial compensation is not always very high and in some cases a declaration, rather than financial compensation, has been seen as a sufficient remedy.

Respect for rights will not solve all the problems facing modern prisons or prisoners, and even when rights are acknowledged by the courts and by prison administrators, prisoners may lack the means and resources to ensure their observance. For individual prisoners, there are deterrents to bringing rights claims as litigation may involve costs of time, money and efforts and demand a high level of skills and literacy. Given the time it takes to bring a claim it may mean that only prisoners serving longer sentences find it worthwhile to bring claims. It is therefore not surprising that some of the recent cases have been brought by lifers and IPP prisoners. Changes in legal aid funding for prisoners' claims with revised fees and fixed fees were introduced in July 2010. The outgoing government wanted support for judicial review limited to public interest cases. So it may be necessary for campaign groups to take up issues on behalf of prisoners and to focus on class actions for prisoners.

So any prisoners' rights instrument needs an effective enforcement mechanism and full cooperation of the courts who, as we have seen, have in the past often been reluctant to intervene to meet prisoners' demands and to place considerable weight on the smooth running of the prison. There may be a gap, as we have seen, between formal rights and practice. So, when prisoners in the USA succeeded with their claims in the 1970s, they still faced the problem of non-compliance on the part of the prison, and bringing a claim was a very lengthy process. It took until 2000 for the Attica prisoners to finally win a settlement in the courts. Similarly in the UK, Hirst had already been released from a life sentence by the time his case was heard in Strasbourg. In the earlier landmark case of *Campbell and Fell v UK* (1984) 7 EHRR 165, it took the applicants about 16 years to get to Strasbourg. Although these delays will have been reduced by the Human Rights Act, it still remains the case that for prisoners' serving shorter sentences, it may not be worth proceeding, or they may feel that they will create more problems for themselves by bringing a claim. So it is not simply a case of possessing the rights, but prisoners have to be able to exercise them. Once granted, rights may be depoliticized or neutralized by poor enforcement, lack of assistance in bringing claims, or inadequate remedies.

The concern with public protection still dominates penal policy and practice and the new managerialist approach remains the key principle for the organization and running of prisons. The high numbers in prison continue to impact on the day-to-day life in custody as prisons try to cope with the large influx of prisoners. However, while there is a danger that this will undermine progress towards acceptance of the prisoner as citizen, in the context of overcrowding and cost-cutting, the existing rights become even more important.

Conclusions

Despite threats to abolish the Act, it seems unlikely to be jettisoned in the near future and, of course, even without the Human Rights Act, the European Convention would still have a role to play within domestic law just as it did before 1998 and the Convention is also a guiding principle of EU law. The demand that all groups should be treated with respect and should be fully included within social and political life underpinned the case for prisoners' rights in the 1970s, as we saw in Chapter 2, as the focus of the civil rights movement was on including Black Americans, women, and the gay rights movement, as well as prisoners. This emphasis on social inclusion has persisted today: some prisoners' groups, for example, the Australian Prisoners' Union, have emphasized the common cause of all prisoners worldwide, wherever they are incarcerated. In recent years international attention has shifted from prison conditions in general, to confinement of specific groups of prisoners, particularly on the treatment of those held on suspicion of terrorist offences.

The move towards including prisoners is found worldwide in a number of jurisdictions, reflecting the increasing importance of international rights standards, so the time may now be ripe for the recognition of prisoners' rights. Defining prisoners as citizens with rights and duties may have broader benefits, as fair treatment is likely to reduce prisoners' sense of injustice and thereby contribute to good order in the prison. Bringing a rights-based claim can itself promote respect for the law on the part of the prisoner and strengthen the prisoner's status, reaffirming his or her citizenship. In doing so, it promotes social inclusion, rather than exclusion, affirms the proximity of the prisoner to the ordinary person and reduces the social distance between them. The focus on rights has also opened up the way for recognizing the impact of imprisonment on the families of prisoners which in turn has an impact on communities. As we have seen this problem is particularly acute in the United States but there has also been increasing interest in the issue in the UK.

But politicians need to become aware of the advantages of respect for rights; apart from the inherent benefits for prisoners, it may enhance the legitimacy of the criminal justice system, reduce tensions in prison, so prisoners are less likely to riot, or resort to violence. A strong commitment to rights may lead to enhanced stability in prisons by reducing prisoners' sense of grievance. While not removing completely the potential for disorder in prison, it is a step towards it. Treating prisoners as citizens may also promote their rehabilitation and reintegration into society. Respect for prisoners' rights may also satisfy states' obligations under international law and improve their standing in the international community. These positive elements should be deployed to promote more constructive attitudes towards prisoners and imprisonment.

As we have seen a key problem is reconciling the growth of prisoners' rights with the principle of less eligibility. A limit to further consolidation of prisoners' rights is the public's attitude towards penal austerity so it is crucial to consider ways in which the public could be better informed of the benefits of a rights-based approach. The public need to be convinced that there is no inherent conflict between the public interest and prisoners' rights and that respect for rights is beneficial to society. Focusing on the relationship between rights and responsibilities may be an important element of this strategy.

Although prison conditions in England and Wales have improved dramatically since the 1980s and early 1990s, more still needs to be done. One possibility is a rights framework directed specifically at prisoners, such as a European Prisoners' Rights Charter. This might be more effective in improving conditions, perhaps offer a speedier way of dealing with prisoners' rights' claims and give specific statutory rights for key areas of prison life. While under the Prison Rules, there are statutory rights to visits, there are no rights not to be subject to overcrowding, or to a reasonable time outside cells. A Charter could include a right to a fair hearing in disciplinary matters, the right to certain standards of living and basic necessities including health care.

Alternatively a Protocol on Prisoners' Rights could be added to the Convention but this has been considered and rejected. A European Prisons Charter was proposed by the European Parliament and by the Council of Europe's Parliamentary Assembly but in the end the Committee of Ministers rejected the proposal for a binding Charter of Prisoners' Rights in favour of using the European Prison Rules. One of the problems, as we saw in Chapter 3, is that as the Council of Europe has expanded to encompass a diverse range of prison regimes and standards, it may be harder to get agreement on minimal standards. Although the Council of Europe has published recommendations on different aspects of prison life including conditional release, they are not binding on states. It has also been suggested that a kite mark be used for prison standards and a move towards this could be seen in the Prison Performance Tables which give an indication of conditions in individual prisons.

The view that prisoners do not deserve rights, that prisoners, are second-class citizens and that civic rights may be earned through good behaviour and forfeited through wrongful acts, remains very strong. As we have seen it underpinned the Labour Government's reluctance to restore voting rights to sentenced prisoners and this is unlikely to change with the recent change of Government in the UK. It is not surprising that prisoners' rights did not figure in the election campaigns of the major parties or their party manifestos as there seem to be few or no political advantages in promoting prisoners' rights. The Labour Party was committed to more prison building, to house persistent serious and violent offenders but reducing the numbers of women and mentally ill prisoners, and to the transfer of EU prisoners. The Conservative Party focused on the abolition of early release, expanding prisons but with a stronger focus on rehabilitation and early deportation of foreign national prisoners, with one organization responsible for preventing reoffending. The Liberal Democrats were critical of prison expansion and the failure of prisons to address reoffending, and argued for the removal of mentally ill offenders from prison into secure accommodation, more involvement of communities in dealing with anti-social behaviour through Neighbourhood Justice Panels and the expansion of restorative justice programmes and for prisoners to undertake paid work to compensate victims. So it will be interesting to see how these policies are negotiated in the Coalition Government. There are signs of a shift in policy on imprisonment. The new Justice Secretary, Ken Clarke, in a speech to judges at the Mansion House in July 2010, made it clear that he did not accept that there was a link between the expansion of the prison population and falling crime rates (Clarke 2010). He has also indicated that he wants more focus on rehabilitation and community sentences with greater use of the private sector and voluntary organizations, and to base payments on results in terms of cutting reoffending. Clarke has criticized the use of prison as a costly and ineffective way of dealing with many offenders and argued that a cut in prison numbers is necessary.

In her recent valedictory lecture the departing Chief Inspector of Prisons has pointed to the progress made during her term in office on issues such as health, education and resettlement, and the decline in suicides but has also pointed to the persistent problems of self-harming, the high numbers of individuals with mental health problems being held in prison and the issues surrounding IPP prisoners (Owers 2010). While the aim of reducing prison numbers is desirable, then the resources saved from prison places need to be available for investment in measures outside prison.

It remains to be seen what precise direction prison policy will take under the new Coalition Government or its effect, but it is hoped that the protection of prisoners' rights will continue and that the current prison crisis will provide an opportunity for change.

Notes

1 Prisoners' rights: from social death to citizenship

1 Some of the ideas in this chapter were first published in the following article S. Easton. (2008) 'Constructing citizenship: making room for prisoners' rights', *Journal of Social Welfare and Family Law*, 30: 2, pp. 127–46.
2 Discussion of a range of penal system and their implications for the treatment of prisoners in other societies may be found in Cavadino and Dignan (2006), Lazarus (2004) and Piacentini (2004).
3 See Brown and Wilkie (eds) 2002.
4 Anonymous (September 2009) 'Prison law funding under attack', *Legal Action* 3.
5 The public's fear of crime should not be underestimated as the experience of Nazi Germany shows how fears about crime can be exploited to capture support for repressive regimes and policies (Gellately 2001).
6 See report www.Dutchnews.nl (21/4/09).
7 Partij voor de Vrijheid.
8 See the manual designed to assist applicants in preparing for the exam, Home Office (2007) *Life in the United Kingdom: A Journey to Citizenship*, London, Stationery Office.
9 See Cabinet Office, Policy Review document (May 2007) *Building on Progress: the Role of the State*, London, Cabinet Office, paras. 5.1, 5.8.
10 For example Bentham's critique of the Universal Declaration of the Rights of Man in 'Anarchical Fallacies', reprinted in J. Waldron (ed.) (1987) *Nonsense upon Stilts: Bentham, Burke and Marx on the Rights of Man*, London, Methuen, pp. 46–76.
11 The Fabian Society (2007), *A Common Place*, London, Fabian Society. The links between citizenship and voluntary work has also been present in discussions of the anti-social behaviour of young people and the 'respect' agenda. See Home Office (2003) *Respect and Responsibility: Taking a Stand against Anti-Social Behaviour*, Cm 5778, London, Stationery Office; Russell Commission (2005) *A National Framework for Youth Action and Engagement*, London, Stationery Office; see also J. Williams and A. Invernizzi (2007) (eds) *Children and Citizenship*, London, Sage.
12 However, African Americans were segregated in the military until 1949.

2 The historical development of prisoners' rights: rights versus discretion

1 See *R v Secretary of State for the Home Office ex p McAvoy* [1984] 1 WLR 1408.
2 Cited by Senator Robert Dole when introducing the bill. See 141 Cong Rec S14,413 (daily ed. Sept 27 1995).
3 See Franke (2007).
4 See Law Commission (10 October 2006) *Remedies against Public Bodies: A Scoping Report*, London, Law Commission.

3 The increasing importance of international human rights law and standards

1 Resolutions 663 C (XXIV) of 31 July 1957 and 2076 (LXII) of 13 May 1977.
2 See *Report of the Human Rights Committee* (2008) Volume 1, 91st session 15 October–2 November 2007; 92nd Session 17 March–4 April 2008; 93rd session 7–25 July 2008, New York, United Nations.
3 See: https://wcd.coe.int/ViewDoc.jsp?id=955747.
4 These standards may be accessed on: http://www.cpt.coe.int/en/docsstandards.htm.
5 Morgan and Evans (eds) (1999) review the work of the CPT in the period 1989–97 and a discussion of recent developments may be found in van Zyl Smit and Snacken (2009).
6 Although in *Ireland v UK* (1978) 2 EHRR 25 the Commission was more willing to rule interrogation practices as torture than the Court.
7 See for example in relation to Article 2 in the case of *Edwards v UK* (2002) 35 EHRR 19, in relation to Article 3, *Price v UK* Application No. 33394/96 (10 July 2001) and *Keenan v UK* Application No. 27229/95 (3 April 2001) on Article 6, *Ezeh and Connors v UK* Application Nos. 39665/98 and 40086/98 (15 July 2002).
8 For example in *Hirst v UK (No. 2)* Application No. 74025/01 (6 October 2005).
9 This is the test in *Osman v UK* (1998) 29 EHRR 245.
10 On Article 9 see *Poltoratsky v Ukraine*, No. 38812/97 (29 April 2003) and on Article 10 see *R v Secretary of State for the Home Department, ex parte Simms and O'Brien* [2000] 2 AC 115.
11 See *Hamer v UK* Application No. 7114/75 (13 December 1979), *Dickson v UK* Application No. 44362/04, (4 December 2007).
12 See *Gusev v Russia* Application No. 67542/01 (15 May 2008).

4 Prison conditions

1 See for example, *R (Vary and others) v Secretary of State for the Home Department* [2004] EWHC 2251 (Admin).
2 See *Napier v Scottish Ministers* (2005) 1 SC 229.
3 Ministry of Justice/NOMS (July 2009) *Annual Report and Accounts 0809*, London, Stationery Office.
4 See http://www.justice.gov.uk/publications/docs/prison-ratings-q3-09-10.pdf.
5 See *R v DPP ex parte Manning* (2001) QB 330 where the refusal to prosecute the officers concerned and to give reasons for that failure to proceed was challenged.
6 See *Denmark, Norway, Sweden and the Netherlands v Greece* (Greek case) Application Nos. 3321/67; 3322/67; 3323/67; 3344/67 Report of the European Commission of Human Rights (5 November 1969,Yearbook 12).
7 The appropriate treatment of dirty protests is now in PS0 1770 as this is most likely to happen in the context of segregation.
8 See *Price v UK* (2002) 34 EHRR 53.
9 Security conditions in Peterhead Prison in the early 1990s were criticized by the CPT because of the intense security as well as poor physical conditions (Council of Europe 1996).
10 See *Rohde v Denmark* Application No. 69332/01 (21 July 2005) para 93.
11 See *Ramirez Sanchez v France* Application No. 59450/00 (4 July 2006).
12 *X and Y v State of Western Australia* [1996] HREOCA 32, HIV-positive prisoners complained to the Human Rights and Equal Opportunity Commission about the very restrictive regime under which they were held with limited facilities and their complaint was upheld by the Commission.
13 See the Code for Crown Prosecutors, February 2010, available at htpp://www.cps. gov.uk.
14 Ministry of Justice, the Netherlands, press release 7 March 2007.

15 Ministry of Justice Press Release 24 November 2006.
16 Ministry of Justice (2003) *Psychische Conditie van Gedetineerden in de Extra Beveiligde Inrichtingen en de Afdeling voor Beperkt Gemeenschapsgeschikte Gedetineerden in PI Nieuw Vosseveld in Vught.*
17 *Response of the Authorities of the Kingdom of the Netherlands to the report of the European Committee for the Prevention of Torture and Inhuman or Degrading Treatment or Punishment (CPT) on its visits to the Kingdom in Europe, Aruba, and the Netherlands Antilles, in July 2007,* CPT/Inf (2009) 7, Strasbourg, Council of Europe.
18 US Department of Justice, Bureau of Justice Statistics.
19 For example, its endorsement of Tamms Supermax Prison in Southern Illinois has been criticized for failing to take account of prolonged solitary confinement used in the prison and absence of regular reviews (see Kurki and Morris 2001).
20 For further discussion of these problems see Pollock (2003).
21 See respectively, *Baze v Rees* 553 US 35 (2008), *Roper v Simmons* 543 US 551 (2005) and *Atkins v Virginia* 536 US 304 (2002).
22 See, for example, in the Pelican Bay case, *Madrid v Gomez* 190 F.3d. 990 (9th Cir. 1999).
23 Hansard 11 January 2010, 795W.

5 Procedural justice

1 See *Secretary of State for Justice v Walker, Secretary of State for Justice v James* [2008] EWCA Civ 30), *Secretary of State for Justice v James (formerly Walker and another)* [2009] UKHL 22.
2 See, for example, *Ezeh and Connors v UK* [2002] 35 EHRR 28.
3 These provisions were replaced by s 109 of the Powers of Criminal Courts (Sentencing) Act 2000. However the Criminal Justice Act 2003 repealed these provisions for offences committed after 4 April 2005 and instead introduced the new sentence of Imprisonment for Public Protection (IPP).
4 For further discussion see N. Padfield (2002) *Beyond the Tariff: Human Rights and the Release of Life Sentence Prisoners,* Cullompton, Willan Press.
5 It was conjoined with the similar case of *R (Lee and Wells) v Secretary of State for Justice* [2008] EWHC 2326 (Admin) where the Administrative Court had also found a breach of Article 5(1).
6 Under the Mental Health Act 1983 as amended by the Mental Heath Act 2007.
7 These have now been replaced by the IPP for offences committed on or after April 2005.
8 At that time court martials were not Convention compliant but their procedures have been revised following legal challenges and the view of the Strasbourg Court is that they are now compliant.
9 Report of the Committee on the Prison Disciplinary System (Prior Report) London, HMSO 1985, Cmnd 9641
10 See *The Prison Discipline Manual: Adjudications,* PSO 2000, 30/12/2005.
11 See *Associated Provincial Picture Houses Ltd v Wednesbury Corporation* (1948) 1 KB 233.

6 Contact with the outside world

1 See *Messina v Italy (No. 2)* Application No. 25498/94 (28 September 2000). However in this case the prisoner was involved in organized crime and some limits on his letters and visits were found to be proportionate.
2 *Szuluk v Secretary of State for the Home Department* [2004] EWCA (Civ) 1426.
3 See *Kopp v Switzerland* (1998) 27 EHRR 91.

4 *Associated Provincial Picture Houses Ltd v Wednesbury Corporation* (1948) 1 KB 233.
5 Netherlands Ministry of Justice, Press Release: 10.12.09.
6 *X v UK* [1974] 46 CD 112.
7 See also *Loving v Virginia* 338 US 1 (1967) which establishes that the right to marry is of fundamental importance.
8 See for example *Evans v UK* Application No. 6339/05 (10 April 2007).
9 Reported in *Der Spiegel* 13 April 2010.
10 Reported in *Los Angeles Times* 21 June 2008.

7 The right to equality

1 See the Macpherson Report for discussion of this concept in relation to policing (Macpherson 1999).
2 See http://www.justice.gov.uk/publications/docs/women-criminal-justice-system-2008-09.pdf and http://www.justice.gov.uk/stats-race-and-the-criminal-justice-system-2008-09c1.pdf.
3 PSO 4800 (28/04/08).
4 See Equality and Human Rights Commission website for further details.
5 PSI 40/2007.
6 See Chigwada (1989), Chigwada-Bailey (2003), Fawcett Society (2006).

8 The prisoner as citizen: the right to vote

1 Some of the ideas in this chapter were first published in the following articles: Susan Easton (2006) 'Electing the electorate: the problem of prisoner disenfranchisement', *Modern Law Review* 69(3) 443–52, published by John Wiley and Susan Easton (2009) 'The prisoner's right to vote and civic responsibility', *Probation Journal* 56(6) 224–37, by SAGE Publications Ltd, All rights reserved ©: http://online.sagepub.com. This article in the *Probation Journal* was the final definitive version of this paper.
2 In the 2005 General Election, the UK government did allow prisoners held on intermittent custody to vote if they were outside the prison on that day as a concession, but the numbers involved, only 40 prisoners, were negligible and intermittent custody has now been shelved.
3 Patients detained in mental hospitals can vote, but not if they are offenders detained under criminal powers. This is governed by sections 2 and 4 of the RPA 2000, and s 35 of the Electoral Administration Act. The Government is considering relaxing the rules so that some offenders detained in mental hospitals may vote, but not those subject to restriction orders under s 41 of the Mental Health Act, where an Order is imposed to protect the public from serious harm, from those defined as dangerous. But it could be argued that all patients detained in mental hospitals should still be treated as citizens and to disenfranchise them is inappropriate in modern conditions, with more enlightened attitudes towards mental illness and this would be the view of mental health campaigners. Similar issues of social inclusion apply to this group as to ordinary prisoners and both should be given access to the electoral process. The implications of voting for the social inclusion of individuals with mental health problems are considered further by Nash (Nash 2002).
4 For example, new civil preventative orders, namely, Sexual Offences Prevention Orders, Foreign Travel Orders and Risk of Sexual Harm Orders, respectively, in sections 104, 114 and 123 of the Sexual Offences Act 2003.
5 *Lydia Simmons v Eshaq Khan* M/326/07, High Court; the six men received custodial sentences following their conviction in May 2009 at Reading Crown Court. See also discussion in White (2010).

6 Figures from Brennan Center for Justice, New York.

7 A map giving a state by state analysis of the regulations may be found on the website of the Brennan Center: http://www.brennancenter.org/page/-/d/download_file_48642.pdf.

8 See Editorial, 'Virginia's disgraceful move to discourage restoration of ex-cons' voting rights', *Washington Post*, 13 April, 2010.

9 White House VT 5 February 2010.

10 HCJ 2757/96 *Alrai* [1996] 1srSC 50(2) 18, at 7.

Bibliography

ACLU (2008) *Voting Rates for People with Criminal Records: 2008 State Legislative and Policy Changes*, New York, ACLU.

Allen, C. and Abril, J. C. (1997) 'The new chain gang: corrections in the next century', *American Journal of Criminal Justice*, 22(1), 1–12.

American Friends Service Committee (1971) *Struggle for Justice: A Report on Crime and Punishment in America* New York, Hill and Wang.

Amnesty International (1999) '*Not Part of Her Sentence: Violations of the Human Rights of Women in Custody*', New York, Amnesty International.

Anonymous (September 2009) 'Prison law funding under attack', *Legal Action*, 3.

Aristotle (1992) *Politics*, London, Penguin.

Bagaric, M. (2001) *Punishment and Sentencing: A Rational Approach*, London, Cavendish.

Bain, D. (2007) *Report of the Chief Electoral Officer for Northern Ireland 2006–07*, Belfast.

Bales, W. D. and Mears, D. P. (2008). 'Inmate social ties and the transition to society: does visitation reduce recidivism?', *Journal of Research in Crime and Delinquency*, 45(3), 287–321.

Banbury, S. (2004) 'Coercive Sexual Behaviour in British Prisons as Reported by Adult Ex-Prisoners, *Howard Journal of Criminal Justice*, 43(2), 113–30.

Baynes, K. (August 2000) 'Rights as critique and the critique of rights: Karl Marx, Wendy Brown and the social function of rights', *Political Theory*, 28(4), 451–68.

Beckett, K and Western, B. (2001) 'Governing social marginality: welfare, incarceration and the transformation of state policy, *Punishment and Society*, 3(1), 43–59.

Behan, C. and O'Donnell, I. (2008) 'Prisoners, politics and the polls', *British Journal of Criminology*, 48(3), 319–36.

Belbot, B. (September 2004) 'Report of the Prison Litigation Reform Act: what have the courts decided so far?', *The Prison Journal*, 84(3), 290–316.

Bellamy, R. and Greenaway, J. (1995) 'The new right conception of citizenship and the Citizen's Charter', *Government and Opposition*, 30(4), 469–91.

Bentham, J. (1789) *Introduction to the Principles of Morals and Legislation*, ed. J. L. Burns and H. L. A. Hart (1996) Oxford, Clarendon Press.

—— (1843) 'Anarchical fallacies' reprinted in J. Waldron (ed.) (1987) *Nonsense upon Stilts: Bentham, Burke and Marx on the Rights of Man*, London, Methuen, pp 46–76.

Bernstein, N. (2005) *All Alone in the World: Children of the Incarcerated*, New York, New York Press.

Bloch, E. (1967) 'Man and citizen according to Marx', in E. Fromm (ed.) *Socialist Humanism*, London, Allen Lane.

Boone, M. (2007) 'Selective rehabilitation', in Boone, M. and Moerings, M. (eds) (2007) *Dutch Prisons*, The Hague, BJu Legal Publishers, 231–48.

Boone, M. and Moerings, M. (eds) (2007) *Dutch Prisons*, The Hague, BJu Legal Publishers.

Boutellier, H. (2004) *The Safety Utopia: Contemporary Discontent and Desire as to Crime and Punishment*, Dordrecht, Kluwer.

Bradley, Lord (2009) *Lord Bradley's Review of People with Mental Health Problems or Learning Disabilities in the Criminal Justice System*, London, Department of Health.

Bronstein, A. J. (1980) 'Prisoners' rights: a history', in G. P. Alpert (ed.) *Legal Rights of Prisoners*, 19–45, Beverly Hills, Sage.

Brown, D and Wilkie, M. (eds) (2002) *Prisoners as Citizens*, Annandale, New South Wales, Federation Press.

Burca, G. and de Witte, B. (2005) (eds) *Social Rights in Europe*, Oxford, Oxford University Press.

Butting, B. and Jorg, N. (1983) 'Criminal justice in the Netherlands 1970–80', *Contemporary Crises*, 7, 135–54.

Cabinet Office (1991) *The Citizen's Charter: Raising the Standard*, Cm 1599, London, The Stationery Office.

—— (May 2007) *Building on Progress: The Role of the State*, Policy Review Document, London, Cabinet Office.

Caddle, D. (1998) *Age Limits for Babies in Prison: Some Lessons from Abroad*, Home Office Research Findings 80, London, Home Office.

Carens, J. H. (2000) *Culture, Citizenship and Community*, Oxford, Oxford University Press.

Carlen, P. (ed.) (2003) *Women and Punishment: The Struggle for Justice*, Cullompton, Willan.

Carlson, B. and Cervera, N. (1991) 'Inmates and their families: conjugal visits, family contact, and family functioning', *Criminal Justice and Behavior*, 18(3), 318–31.

Cavadino, M. and Dignan, J. (2006) *Penal Systems: A Comparative Approach*, London, Sage.

Chigwada, R. (1989) 'The criminalization and imprisonment of black women', *Probation Journal*, 37, 100–5.

Chigwada-Bailey, R. (2003) *Black Women's Experience of Criminal Justice, A Discourse on Disadvantage*, 2nd edn, Winchester, Waterside.

Clare, E., Bottomley, K. *et al.* (2001) *Evaluation of Close Supervision Centres*, Home Office Research Study 219, London, Home Office.

Clarke, K. (13 July 2010) *Speech at the Dinner for the Judges Mansion House*, London, Ministry of Justice.

Clear, T. (2007) *Imprisoning Communities*, New York, Oxford University Press.

Clemmer, D. (1940) *The Prison Community*, New York, Holt, Rhinehart and Winston.

Codd, H. (2007) 'The slippery slope to sperm smuggling: prisoners, artificial insemination and human rights', *Medical Law Review*, 15(2), 220–35.

—— (2008) *In the Shadow of Prison: Families, Imprisonment and Criminal Justice*, Cullompton, Willan.

Code for Crown Prosecutors (2010) available at www.cps.gov.uk.

Colvin, M. (1992) *The Penitentiary in Crisis: From Accommodation to Riot in New Mexico*, New York, SUNY Press.

Commission on English Prisons Today (2009) *Do Better Do Less: The Report of the Commission on English Prisons Today*, London, Howard League.

Committee against Torture (CAT) (2003) *Conclusions and Recommendations of the Committee against Torture. Turkey: 27/05/2003. CAT/C/CR/30/5 (Concluding Observations/Comments)*, Geneva, United Nations.

—— (2006) *Conclusions and Recommendations of the Committee against Torture. United States of America. 25/07/2006. CAT/C/USA/C0.2. (Concluding Observations/Comments)*, Geneva, United Nations.

Coote, A. and Grant, L. (1972) *Civil Liberties: The NCCL Guide*, Harmondsworth, Penguin.

Corston, J. (2007) *The Corston Report: A Report by Baroness Jean Corston of a Review of Women with Particular Vulnerabilities in the Criminal Justice System*, London, Home Office.

Council of Europe (2000) *10th General Report on the CPT's Activities Covering the period 1 January–31 December 1999*, CT/Inf 2000 [13 EN].

Council for the Administration of Criminal Justice and Youth Protection (CAJ) (2005) *Annual Report*, The Hague.

—— (2010) *Annual Report*, The Hague.

Council of Europe (1991) *Report to the United Kingdom Government on the Visit to the United Kingdom Carried out by the European Committee for the Prevention of Torture and Inhuman or Degrading Treatment or Punishment from 29 July 1990 to 10 August 1990*, CPT/Inf (91) 15 [EN], Strasbourg Council of Europe.

——(1993) *Report to the Dutch Government on the Visit to the Netherlands Carried out by the European Committee for the Prevention of Torture and Inhuman or Degrading Treatment or Punishment (CPT) from 30 August to 8 September 1992*, CPT/ Inf 93, 15 [EN] Strasbourg, Council of Europe.

——(1996) *Report to the Authorities of the Kingdom of the Netherlands on the Visit to the Netherlands Antilles Carried out by the European Committee for the Prevention of Torture and Inhuman or Degrading Treatment or Punishment (CPT) from 26 to 30 June 1994*, CPT/Inf (96) 1 EN, Strasbourg, Council of Europe.

——(1996) *Report to the Authorities of the Kingdom of the Netherlands on the Visit to Aruba Carried out by the European Committee for the Prevention of Torture and Inhuman or Degrading Treatment or Punishment (CPT) from 30 June to 2 July 1994*, CPT/Inf (96) 27 [EN] Strasbourg, Council of Europe.

——(1996) *Report to the United Kingdom Government on the Visit to the United Kingdom Carried out by the European Committee for the Prevention of Torture and Inhuman or Degrading Treatment or Punishment (CPT) from 15 to 31 May 1994*, CPT/Inf (96) 11 [EN], Strasbourg, Council of Europe.

——(1998) *Report to the Netherlands Government on the Visit to the Netherlands Carried out by the European Committee for the Prevention of Torture and Inhuman or Degrading Treatment or Punishment (CPT) from 1 to 27 November 1997*, CPT/ Inf 98, 15[EN] Strasbourg, Council of Europe.

——(2002) *Report to the Authorities of the Kingdom of the Netherlands on the Visits Carried out to the Kingdom in Europe and to the Netherlands Antilles by the European Committee for the Prevention of Torture and Inhuman or Degrading Treatment or Punishment (CPT) in February 2002*, CPT/Inf, 30, Strabourg, Council of Europe.

——(2008) *Report to the Authorities of the Kingdom of the Netherlands on the Visits Carried out to the Kingdom in Europe, Aruba and the Netherlands Antilles by the European Committee for the Prevention of Torture and Inhuman or Degrading*

Treatment or Punishment (CPT) in June 2007, CPT/Inf (2008) 2, Strasbourg, Council of Europe.

——(2009a) Committee for the Prevention of Torture (2009) *Response of the Authorities of the Kingdom of the Netherlands to the Report of the European Committee for the Prevention of Torture and Inhuman or Degrading Treatment or Punishment (CPT) on Its Visits to the Kingdom in Europe, Aruba, and the Netherlands Antilles, in July 2007*, CPT/Inf (2009) 7, Strasbourg, Council of Europe.

——(2009b) *Report to the Government of the United Kingdom on the Visit to the United Kingdom Carried out by the European Committee for the Prevention of Torture and Inhuman or Degrading Treatment or Punishment (CPT) from 18 November to 1 December 2008*, CPT/Inf 30, Strasbourg, Council of Europe.

Council of Europe Parliamentary Assembly (2007), *Application to Initiate a Monitoring Procedure to Investigate Electoral Fraud in the United Kingdom*, AS/Mon (2007) 38.

Davis, A.Y. (2003) *Are Prisons Obsolete?*, New York, Seven Sisters Press.

——*et al.* (1971) *If They Come in the Morning*, London, Orbach and Chambers.

Davis, D. B. (2006) *Inhuman Bondage: The Rise and Fall of Slavery in the New World*, New York: Oxford University Press.

Dawes, J. (2002 'Institutional perspectives and constaints', in Brown, D. and Wilkie, M. (eds) *Prisoners as Citizens: Human Rights in Australian Prisons*, New South Wales, Federation Press, 115–30.

de Jonge, G. (2007) 'European detention standards', in M. Boone and M. Moerings (eds) *Dutch Prisons*, The Hague, BJu Legal Publishers, 281–96.

de Vos, M. (2007) *Beyond Formal Equality*, Brussels, European Commission.

Department of Constitutional Affairs, (2006) Consultation Paper, *Voting Rights of Convicted Prisoners Detained in the UK*, London, DCA.

Ditchfield J. (1994) *Family Ties and Recidivism: The Main Findings of the Literature*, Home Office Research Bulletin 36, London, Home Office.

Diver, A. (2008) 'The earned privilege of family contact in Northern Ireland: judicial justification of prisoners' loss of family life', *Howard Journal of Criminal Justice*, 47(5), 486–500.

Downes, D. (1988) *Contrasts in Tolerance: Post-War Penal Policy in England and Wales*, Oxford, Oxford University Press.

——(1998) 'The buckling of the shields: Dutch penal policy 1985–95', in R. P. Weiss and N. South (eds) *Comparing Prison Systems: Towards a Comparative and International Penology*, Amsterdam, Gordon and Breach, 143–74.

Drapkin, I. (1989) *Crime and Punishment in the Ancient World*, Lexington, Mass., Lexington Books.

Duker, W. F. (1980) *A Constitutional History of Habeas Corpus*, Westport, Conn., Greenwood Press.

Dworkin, R. (1977) *Taking Rights Seriously*, London, Duckworth.

——(1986) *A Matter of Principle*, Oxford University Press.

Easton, S. (2006) 'Electing the electorate: the problem of prisoner disenfranchisement', *Modern Law Review*, 69(3), 443–52.

——(2008a) 'Dangerous waters: taking account of impact in sentencing', *Criminal Law Review*, 2, 105–20.

——(2008b) 'Constructing citizenship: making room for prisoners' rights', *Journal of Social Welfare and Family Law*, 30: 127–46.

—— (2009) 'The prisoner's right to vote and civic responsibility', *Probation Journal*, 56(6), 224–37.

Easton, S. and Piper, C. (2008) *Sentencing and Punishment: The Quest for Justice*, Oxford, Oxford University Press, 2nd edn.

Edgar, K. and Rickford, D. (2009) 'Neglecting the mental health of prisoners', *International Journal of Prisoner Health*, 5(3), 166–70.

Electoral Commission (2003) *Voting for Change*, London, Electoral Commission.

——(2009) *Electoral Commission Response to the Ministry of Justice Consultation Voting Rights of Convicted Prisoners Detained within the United Kingdom, Second Stage.*

Etzioni, A. (1993) *The Spirit of Community: Rights, Responsibilities and the Communitarian Agenda*, New York, Crown Publishers.

Evans, M. D. and Morgan, R. (1999) 'The CPT: an introduction', in R. Morgan and M. D. Evans (eds) *Protecting Prisoners:The Standards of the European Committee for the Prevention of Torture in Context*, Oxford, Oxford University Press, 3–30.

Fabian Society (2007) *A Common Place*, London, Fabian Socety.

Fallon, P. *et al.* (1999) *Report of the Committee of Inquiry into the Personality Disorder Unit Ashworth Special Hospital*, Cm 4194, London, HMSO.

Fawcett Society (2006) *Good Practice in Meeting the Needs of Black and Minority Ethnic Women at Risk of Offending and Offenders*, London Fawcett Society.

Feeley, M. and Simon, J. (1992) 'The new penology: notes on the emerging strategy of corrections and its implications', *Criminology*, 30(4), 449–74.

Franke, H. (2007) 'Two centuries of imprisonment: socio-historical explanation' in M. Boone and M. Moerings (eds) *Dutch Prisons*, The Hague, BJu Legal Publishers, 6–50.

Fredman, S. (2006) 'Human rights transformed: positive duties and positive rights', *Public Law*, (Autumn) 498–520.

——(2008) *Human Rights Transformed: Positive Rights and Positive Duties*, Oxford, Oxford University Press.

Garland, D. (2001) *The Culture of Control*, Oxford, Oxford University Press.

——(2005) 'Capital punishment and American culture', *Punishment and Society*, 7(4), 347–76.

Gearty, C. (2006) *Can Human Rights Survive?*, Cambridge, Cambridge University Press.

Gellately, R. (2001) *Backing Hitler: Consent and Coercion in Nazi Germany*, Oxford, Oxford University Press.

Gibbons, J. J. and Katzenbach, N. de B. (2006) *Confronting Confinement: A Report of the Commission on Safety and Abusein America's Prisons*, New York, Vera Institute.

Girshick, L. B. (2003) 'Abused women and incarceration', in B. Zaitzow and J. Thomas (eds) *Women in Prison: Gender and Social Control*, Boulder, Colorado, Lynne Rienner Publishers, 95–117.

Goffman, E. (1961) *Asylums: Essays on the Social Situation of Mental Patients and Other Inmates*, New York, Doubleday Anchor.

Graham, F. P. (1970) *The Due Process Revolution: The Warren Court's Impact on Criminal Law*, New York, Hayden.

Greer, S. (2006) *The European Convention on Human Rights: Achievements, Problems and Prospects*, Cambridge, Cambridge University Press.

Handelsman, L. (2005) 'Giving the barking dog a bite: challenging felon disenfranchisement under the voting Rights Act of 1965', *Fordham Law Review*, 73, 1875–1940.

Harrington, J. A. (2005) 'Citizenship and the biopolitics of post-nationalist Ireland', *Journal of Law and Society*, 32(3), 424–49.

Hensley, C. Rutland, S. and Gray-Ray, P. (2000) 'Inmate attitudes towards the conjugal visitation program in Mississippi Prisons: an exploratory study', *American Journal of Criminal Justice*, 25(1), 137–45.

Herivel, T. J. and Wright, P. (eds) (2008) *Prison Profiteers: Who Makes Money From Mass Incarceration*, New York, New Press.

HM Chief Inspector of Prisons (HMCIP) (1997) *Women in Prison: A Thematic Review*, London, HMIP.

——(2001) *Follow up to Women in Prison: A Thematic Review*, London, HMIP.

——(2008) *Older Prisoners in England and Wales: A Follow Up to the 2004 Thematic Review*, London, HMIP.

——(2010a) *Annual Report 2008–09*, London HMIP.

——(2010b) *Muslim Prisoners' Experiences: A Thematic Review*, London, HMIP.

HM Inspectorate of Prisons (HMIP) (2005) *Parallel Worlds: A Thematic Review of Race Relations in Prison*, London, HMIP.

——(2009a) *Disabled Prisoners: A Short Thematic Review on the Care and Support of Prisoners with a Disability*, London, HMIP.

——(2009b) *Race Relations in Prison: Responding to Adult Women from Black and Minority Ethnic Backgrounds*, London, HMIP.

——(2010) *Women in Prison: A Short Thematic Review*, London, HMIP.

HM Prison Service (2008): *HMP Whitemoor Review and Report 26–28 February 2008*, London HM Prison Service.

Hobbes, T. (1651) *Leviathan*, Oxford, Oxford University Press (1998).

Home Office (2003) *Respect and Responsibility: Taking a Stand against Anti-Social Behaviour*, Cm 5778, London, The Stationery Office.

——(2007) *Life in the United Kingdom: A Journey to Citizenship*, London, The Stationery Office.

Howse, K. (2003) *Growing Old in Prison: A Scoping Study of Older Prisoners*, London, Prison Reform Trust.

Human Rights Watch (2001) *No Escape: Male Rape in US Prisons*, New York, HRW.

Hutton, N. (2005) 'Beyond popular punitiveness', *Punishment and Society*, 7(3), 243–58.

Independent Monitoring Board (IMB) (2007) *Annual Report, Covering the Period 1 April 2006–31 March 2007*, London, IMB.

International Centre for Prison Studies (ICPS)(2010) *World Prison Brief*, London, King's College.

Jackson, E. (2007) 'Prisoners, their partners and the right to family life', *Child and Family Law Quarterly*, 19(2), 239–46.

Jackson, G. (1971) *Soledad Brother*, Harmondsworth, Penguin.

——(1972) *Blood in My Eye*, New York, Random House.

Jacobson, J. and Hough, M. (2010) *Unjust Deserts: Imprisonment for Public Protection*, London, PRT.

Jansen, T., Chioncel, N. and Dekkers, H. (2006) 'Social cohesion and integration: learning active citizenship', *British Journal of Sociology and Education*, 27(2), 189–205.

Joppke, C. (1999) 'How immigration is changing citizenship: a comparative view', *Ethnic and Racial Studies*, 22(4), 629–52.

Keith, B. (2006) *Report of the Zahid Mubarek Inquiry*, HC 102, London, The Stationery Office.

Kelk, C. (2007) 'Medical care', in Boone, M. and Moerings, M. (eds) (2007) *Dutch Prisons*, The Hague, BJu Legal Publishers, 249–77.

Kensey, A. and Tournier, P. (1999) 'Prison population inflation, overcrowding and recidivism, the situation in France', *European Journal on Criminal Policy and Research*, 7(1), 97–119.

King, R. and Elliot, K. (1977) *Albany: Birth of a Prison – End of an Era*, London, Routledge and Kegan Paul.

King, R. D. (1999) 'The rise and rise of supermax: an American solution in search of a problem?', *Punishment and Society*, 1(2), 163–83.

King, R. D. and Resodihardjo, S. L. (2010) 'To max or not to max: dealing with high risk prisoners in the Netherlands and England and Wales', *Punishment and Society*, 12(1), 65–84.

Kiviston, P. and Faist, T. (2007) *Citizenship: Discourse, Theory and Transnational Prospects*, Oxford, Basil Blackwell.

Kjelsberg, E., Skoglund, T. H. and Rustad, A.-B. (2007) 'Attitudes towards prisoners, as reported by prison inmates, prison employees and college students', *BMC Public Health*, 7(71), 1–9.

Kurki, L. and Morris, N. (2001) 'The purposes, practices and problems of supermax prisons', *Crime and Justice: A Review of Research* 28, Chicago, University of Chicago Press.

Law Commission (10 October 2006) *Remedies against Public Bodies: A Scoping Report*, London, Law Commission.

Lazarus, L. (2004) *Contrasting Prisoners' Rights: A Comparative Examination of Germany and England*, Oxford, Oxford University Press.

Leeke, W. D. (1980) 'The negotiated settlement: prisoners' rights in action', in G. P. Alpert (ed.) *Legal Rights of Prisoners*, Beverly Hills, Sage.

Legal Services Commission (July 2009) *Prison Law Funding: A Consultation Response*, LSC.

Leonard, E. B. (1983) 'Judicial decisions and the impact of litigation on women prisoners', *Social Problems*, 31(1), 45–58.

Letsas, G. (2006) 'Two concepts of the margin of appreciation', *Oxford Journal of Legal Studies*, 26(4), 705–32.

Lippke, R. L. (2007) *Rethinking Imprisoment*, Oxford, Oxford University Press.

Locke, J. (1689) *Two Treatises of Government*, Cambridge University Press (1988).

Long, A. A. (2007) 'Stoic communitarianism and normative citizenship', *Social Philosophy and Policy*, 24, 241–61.

Loucks, N. (2007) *No One Knows: The Prevalence and Associated Needs of Offenders with Learning Difficulties*, London, PRT.

Lown, R. D. and Snow, C. (1980) 'Women, the forgotten prisoners: *Glover v. Johnson*', in G. P. Alpert (ed.) *Legal Rights of Prisoners*, Beverly Hills, Sage.

Lynd, S. (2004) *Lucasville: The Untold Story of a Prison Uprising*, Philadelphia, Temple University Press, 2004.

Macpherson, W. (1999) *The Stephen Lawrence Inquiry, Report of an Inquiry by Sir William Macpherson*, Cm 4262-1, London, Stationery Office.

Manza, J., Brooks, C. and Uggen, C. (2004) 'Public attitudes towards felon disenfranchisement in the US', *Public Opinion Quarterly*, 68, 276–87.

Manza, J, and Uggen, C. (2006) *Locked Out: Felon Disenfranchisement and American Democracy*, New York, Oxford University Press.

Marshall, T. H. (1950) *Citizenship and Social Rights*, Cambridge, Cambridge University Press.

Martinson, R. (1974) 'What works? Questions and answers about prison reform?', *The Public Interest*, 35, 22–54.

Mathieson, T. (2000) *Prison on Trial*, 2nd edn, Winchester, Waterside Press.

Mauer, M. (1999) *The Race to Incarcerate*, Washington, D.C., The Sentencing Project.

Mauer, M and Scott King, R. (2004) *Schools and Prisons: Fifty Years after Brown v Board of Education*, Washington D.C., The Sentencing Project.

Mawrey, J. (2005) *In the Matter of a Local Government Election for the Bordesley Green Ward of the Birmingham City Council held on 10th June 2004; In the Matter of a Local Government Election in the Aston Ward of the Birmingham City Council Held on 10th June 2004, Judgment*, London, HM Courts Service.

McGowen, R. (1995) 'The well-ordered prison: England 1780–1865', in N. Morris and D. J. Rothman, *The Oxford History of the Prison*, Oxford, Oxford University Press, 79–109.

McGuire, J. (ed.) (1995) *What Works? Reducing Reoffending*, Chichester, John Wiley.

McLeod, A., Gavin, A. and White, I. (2003) 'The locked ballot box: the impact of state disenfranchisement laws on African American voting behavior and implications for reform', *Virginia Journal of Social Policy and the Law*, 11(1), 66–88.

Melvin, K. B., Gramling, L. K. and Gardner, N. M. (1985) 'A scale to measure attitudes towards prisoners', *Criminal Justice and Behaviour*, 12, 241–53.

Mill, J. S. (1861) *Considerations on Representative Government*, London, Parker, Son and Bourn.

Ministry of Justice (2009a) *NOMS Strategic and Business Plans 2009–10 to 2010–11*, London, Ministry of Justice.

——(28 August 2009b) *Prison Population Projections 2009–2015*, Ministry of Justice Statistics Bulletin, London, Ministry of Justice.

——(2009c) *Offender Management Caseload Statistics 2008: Ministry of Justice Statistics Bulletin*, London, Ministry of Justice.

——/NOMS (July 2009d) *Annual Report and Accounts 0809*, London, Stationery Office.

——(2009e) *Voting Rights of Convicted Prisoners Detained within the United Kingdom, Second Stage Consultation*, London, Ministry of Justice.

——(2010a) *Statistics on Women and the Criminal Justice System*, London, Ministry of Justice.

——(2010b) *Statistics on Race and the Criminal Justice System 2008/09*, London, Ministry of Justice.

——/NOMS (2010c) *Annual Report and Accounts 0910*, London, Stationery Office.

——(2010d) *Prison Population Projections 2010–2016*, Ministry of Justice Statistics Bulletin, London, Ministry of Justice.

——(2010e) *Offender Management Caseload Statistics 2009*, Ministry of Justice Statistics Bulletin, London, Ministry of Justice.

Mitford, J. (1973) *Kind and Usual Punishment: The Prison Business*, New York, Random House.

Moreham, N. A. (2008) 'The right to respect for private life in the European Convention on Human Rights: a re-examination', *EHRLR*, 1, 44–79.

Morgan, R. and Evans, M. D. (eds) (1999) *Protecting Prisoners: The Standards of the European Committee for the Prevention of Torture in Context*, Oxford, Oxford University Press, 221–34.

Mullally, S. (2005) 'Citizenship and family life in Ireland: "who belongs?"', *Legal Studies*, 25(4), 578–600.

Murphy, E. and Brown, J. (2000) 'Exploring gender role identity, value orientation of occupation and sex of respondent in influencing attitudes towards male and female offenders', *Legal and Criminological Psychology*, 5, 285–90.

Murray, J. and Farrington, D. P. (2005) 'Parental imprisonment: effects on boys' anti-social behaviour and delinquency through the life-course', *Journal of Child Psychology and Psychiatry*, 46(12), 1269–78.

Nagle, J. F. (1978) *Report of the Royal Commission into New South Wales Prisons*, New South Wales, Government Printer.

Nash, M. (2002) 'Voting as a means of social inclusion for people with a mental illness', *Journal of Psychiatric and Mental Health Nursing* 9(6), 697–703.

National Audit Office (NAO) (10 March 2010) *Managing Offenders on Short Custodial Sentences*, London, The Stationery Office.

National Prison Rape Elimination Commission (2009) *Final Report*, Washington Department of Justice.

Neal, D. (1991) *The rule of Law in a Penal Colony: Law and Power in Early New South Wales*, Cambridge, Cambridge University Press.

Netherlands, The, Ministry of Justice (2003) *Psychische Conditie van Gedetineerden in de Extra Beveiligde Inrichtingen en de Afdeling voor Beperkt Gemeenschapsgeschikte Gedetineerden in PI Nieuw Vosseveld in Vught*.

Neumann, P. and Rogers, B. (2008) *Recruitment and Mobilisation for the Islamic Militant Movement in Europe*, London King's College, ICSR.

NOMS (National Offender Management Service) (2008) *Implementing Race Equality in Prisons Five Years On*, London, NOMS.

——(2009) *Promoting Equality in Prisons and Probation: the National Offender Management Service Single Equality Scheme 2009 – 2012*, London, NOMS.

O'Cinneide, C. (2005) 'Socio-economic entitlements and the UK Rights Framework', Irish Human Rights Commission Conference on Economic and Social Rights: models of enforcement, Dublin.

O'Connell, R. (2009) 'Cinderella comes to the ball: Art 14 and the right to non-discrimination in the ECHR', *Legal Studies*, 29(2), 211–29.

O'Donnell, I. (2004 'Prison rape in context', *British Journal of Criminology*, 44(2) 241–55.

Oshinsky, D. S. (1997) *Worse than Slavery: Parchman Farm and the Ordeal of Jim Crow Justice*, New York, Free Press.

Owers, A. (2010) *Valedictory Lecture*, Westminster Central Hall, 13 July.

Padfield, N. (2002) *Beyond the Tariff: Human Rights and the Release of Life Sentence Prisoners*, Cullompton, Willan Press.

Page, J. (2004) 'Eliminating the enemy: the import of denying prisoners access to higher education in Clinton's America', *Punishment and Society*, 6(4), 357–78.

Pakes, F. (2007) 'An international comparative perspective', in M. Boone and M. Moerings (eds) *Dutch Prisons*, The Hague, BJu Legal Publishers, 297–314.

Patterson, O. (1982) *Slavery and Social Death*, Cambridge, Mass., Harvard University Press.

Phillips, S. D. and Harm, N. J. (1998) 'Women prisoners: a contextual framework', *Women and Therapy*, 20(4), 1–9.

Piacentini, L. (2004) *Surviving Russia's Prisons: Punishment, Economy and Politics in Transition*, Cullompton, Willan.

Pinkerton, S. D., Galletly, C. L. and Seal, D.W. (2007) 'Model-based estimates of HIV acquisition due to prison rape', *Prison Journal*, 87(3), 295–310.

Piper, C. (2007) 'Should impact constitute mitigation? Structured discretion versus mercy', *Criminal Law Review*, 1, 141–55.

Piper, C. and Easton, S. (2006/07) 'What's sentencing got to do with it? Understanding the penal crisis', *Contemporary Issues in Law*, 8(4), 356–76.

Pollock, J. M. (2003) *Prisons and Prison Life: Costs and Consequences*, New York, Oxford University Press.

Prior, P. J. (1985) *Report of the Committee on the Prison Disciplinary System* (Prior Report) London, HMSO 1985, Cm 9641.

Prison Reform Trust (PRT) (2000) *Justice for Women, the Need for Reform: Report of the Committee on Women's Imprisonment, Chaired by Professor Dorothy Wedderburn*, London, PRT.

——(2003) *Troubled Inside: Responding to the Mental Health Needs of Women in Prison*, London, PRT.

——(2004) *Barred from Voting: The Right to Vote for Sentenced Prisoners*, London, Prison Reform Trust.

——(February 2007) *Response of the Prison Reform Trust to the Prisoners Detained within the UK, Consultation Paper*, London, PRT.

——(July 2010) *Bromley Prison Briefings*, London, PRT.

Prisons and Probations Ombudsman for England and Wales (2009) *Annual Report 2008–2009*, London, OPSI, Cm 7661.

Resnik, J. (1982) '"Women's prisons" and "men's prisons": should prisoners be classified by sex?', *Review of Policy Research*, 2(2), 246–52.

Roberts, J. V. and Hough, M. (eds,) (2002) *Changing Attitudes towards Punishment: Public Opinion, Crime and Justice*, Cullompton, Willan.

Rogers, A. and Tillie, J. (eds) (2001) *Multicutural Policies and Modes of Citizenship in European Cities*, Aldershot, Ashgate.

Ross, J. I. (2007) 'Supermax prisons', *Society*, 44(3), 60–64.

Rothman, D. J. (1995) 'Perfecting the prison: United States, 1789–1865', in N. Morris and D. J. Rotman (eds) *The Oxford History of the Prison*, Oxford, Oxford University Press, 111–29.

Rotman, E. (1990) *Beyond Punishment: A New View of the Rehabilitation of Offenders*, Connecticut, Greenwood Press.

—— (1995) 'The failure of reform: United States, 1865–1965', in N. Morris and D. J. Rotman (eds) *The Oxford History of the Prison*, Oxford, Oxford University Press, 169–97.

Rousseau, J-J. (1762) *The Social Contract*, Harmondsworth, Penguin (1968).

Ruggiero, V. (2010) *Penal Abolitionism*, Oxford, Oxford University Press.

Russell Commission (2005) *A National Framework for Youth Action and Engagement*, London, The Stationery Office.

Sandel, M. (1982) *Liberalism and the Limits of Justice*, Cambridge, Cambridge University Press.

Sellin, T. (1976) *Slavery and the Penal System*, New York, Elsevier.

Serrarens, J. (2007) 'Complaints procedures', in M. Boone and M. Moerings (eds) *Dutch Prisons*, The Hague, BJu Legal Publishers, 209–30.

Sexton, L., Jenness, V. and Sumner, J. (November 2009) 'Where the margins meet: a demographic assessment of transgender inmates in men's prisons, *Irvine Justice Quarterly*, 1–32.

Shaw, S. (1999) 'The CPT's visits to the United Kingdom' in R. Morgan and M. D. Evans (eds) *Protecting Prisoners:The Standards of the European Committee for the Prevention of Torture in Context*, Oxford, Oxford University Press, 265–72.

Singer, R. (1980) 'The *Wolfish* case: has the *Bell* tolled for prisoner litigation in the federal courts?' in G. P. Alpert, (ed.) *Legal Rights of Prisoners*, Beverly Hills, Sage, 67–112.

Social Exclusion Unit (2002) *Reducing Re-Offending by Ex-Prisoners*, London, Social Exclusion Unit.

Spalek, B. (2005) 'Muslims in British jails', *Prison Service Journal*, September, 1–9.

Spalek, B. and El-Hassan, S. (2007) 'Muslim converts in prison', *Howard Journal of Criminal Justice*, 46(2), 99–114.

Steurer, S., Smith, L. and Tracy A. (1999) *Three State Recidivism Study*, Lanham, MD, Office of Correctional Education.

Stewart, J. (2006) 'A banana republic?' The investigation into electoral fraud by the Birmingham Electoral Court', *Parliamentary Affairs*, 59(4), 654–67.

Struckman-Johnson, C. and Struckman-Johnson, D (2000). 'Sexual coercion rates in seven Midwestern prisons for men', *The Prison Journal*, 80(4), 379–90.

Sutherland, E. (2003) 'Procreative freedom and convicted criminals in the United States and the United Kingdom: is child welfare becoming the new eugenics?', *Oregon Law Review*, 1033–65.

Sykes, G. (1958) *A Society of Captives: A Study of a Maximum-Security Prison*, Princeton, New Jersey, Princeton University Press.

Sylla, M. (2008) 'Prisoner access to condoms in the United States – the challenge of introducing harm reduction into a law and order environment', New York, Stony Point Center.

Tak, P. J. P. (2003) *The Dutch Criminal Justice System: Organisation and Operation*, The Hague, BJu Legal Publishers.

——(2008a) 'Prison policy, prison regime and prisoners' rights in the Netherlands under the 1998 Penitentiary Principles Act', in P. Tak and M. Jendy (eds) *Prison Policy and Rights and Prisoners' Rights: Proceedings of the Colloquium of the International Penal and Penitentiary Federation*, Nijmegen, Wolf Publishing, 457–92.

——(2008b) *The Dutch Criminal Justice System*, 3rd edn, Nijmegen, Wolf Publishing.

The Sentencing Project (2010) *Felony Disenfranchisement Laws in the United States*, Washington D.C., The Sentencing Project.

Thompson, E. P. (1968) *The Making of the English Working Class*, Harmondsworth, Penguin.

Titmuss, R. (1968) *Commitment to Welfare*, London, Allen & Unwin.

Tonry, M. (1995) *Malign Neglect: Race,Crime and Punishment in America*, New York, Oxford University Press.

Uggen, C. and Manza, J. (2004) 'Voting and subsequent crime and arrest: evidence from a community sample', *Columbia Human Rights Law Review*, 36(1), 193–216.

uit Beijerse, J. and van Swaaningen, R. (2007) 'Non-custodial sanctions', in M. Boone and M. Moerings (eds) *Dutch Prisons*, The Hague, BJu Legal Publishers, 77–98.

UNGA Human Rights Council (HRC) (2009), *Report of the Special Rapporteur on the Right to Education: The Right to Education of Persons in Detention*, A/HRC/11/8 (2 Apri).

UNODC, WHO and UNAIDS (2006) *HIV/AIDS Prevention, Care, Treatment and Support in Prison Settings: A Framework for an Effective National Response*, Vienna and New York UNODC/WHO/UNAIDS.

Valette, D. (2002) 'AIDS behind bars: prisoners' rights guillotined', *Howard Journal of Criminal Justice*, 41(2), 107–22.

van Kalmthout, A. (2007) 'Foreign prisoners', in M. Boone and M. Moerings (eds) *Dutch Prisons*, The Hague, BJu Legal Publishers, 101–26.

van Langendonck, G. (3 June 2009) 'Less is more in debate about prison population', NRC, Nederland.

van Reenan, P. (1999) 'Inspection and quality control: the CPT in the Netherlands', in van Zyl Smit, D. and Snacken, S. (2009) *Principles of European Prison Law and Policy: Penology and Human Rights*, Oxford, Oxford University Press.

Visher, C. A. and Travis, J. (2003) 'Transition from prison to community, understanding individual pathways', *Annual Review of Sociology*, 29, 89–113.

von Hirsch, A. (1976) *Doing Justice: The Choice of Punishments*, New York, Hill and Wang.

——(1993) *Censure and Sanctions*, Oxford, Clarendon Press.

Wacquant, L. (2001) 'Deadly symbiosis: when ghetto and prison meet and mesh', *Punishment and Society*, 3(1), 95–134.

von Hirsch, A. and Wasik M. (1997) 'Civil disqualifications attending conviction: a suggested conceptual framework', *Cambridge Law Journal*, 56(3), 599–626.

Wacquant, L. (2007) *Urban Outcasts: A Comparative Study of Advanced Marginality*, Cambridge, Polity Press.

White, I. (2010) *Postal Voting and Electoral Fraud*, London, House of Commons.

Whitman, J. Q. (2003) *Harsh Justice: Criminal Punishment and the Widening Gap between America and Europe*, New York, Oxford University Press.

——(2005) 'Response to Garland', *Punishment and Society*, 7(4), 389–96.

Williams, J. (2002) 'Have the courts got it right? – the queen on the application of *Mellor v Secretary of State for the Home Department*', *Child and Family Law Quarterly*, 14, 218–28.

Williams, J. and Invernizzi, A. (2007) (eds) *Children and Citizenship*, London, Sage.

Wood, E. (2009) *Restoring the Right to Vote*, 2nd edn, New York, Brennan Center for Justice.

Wood, E. and Bloom, R. (2008) *De Facto Disenfranchisement*, New York, ACLU/ Brennan Center.

Wood, E., Budnitz, L. and Malhotra, G (2009) *Jim Crow in New York*, New York, Brennan Center.

Wood, E. and Trivedi, N. (2007) 'The modern-day poll tax: how economic sanctions block access to the polls', *Clearinghouse Review Journal of Poverty Law and Policy*, 30–45.

Woolf, H. and Tumim, S. (1991) *Prison Disturbances April 1990, Report of an Enquiry*, Cm 1456, London, HMSO.

Wyatt, R. (2006) 'Male rape in U.S. prisons: are conjugal visits the answer?' *Case Western Reserve Journal of International Law*, 37(2/3), 579–614.

X, Malcolm (1987) *The Autobiography of Malcolm X*, New York, Ballantine Books.

Zedner, L. (1995) 'Wayward sisters: the prison for women', in N. Morris and D. J. Rotman (eds) *The Oxford History of the Prison*, Oxford, Oxford University Press, 329–61.

Zimring, F. E.(2003) *The Contradictions of American Capital Punishment*, New York, Oxford University Press.

Prison Service Orders

Index